Myrtle O'Brien
L.C.M. 1926

FROM THE LIBRARY OF
Nellie Priest Dietzman

THE OPERA BOOK

© Aimé Dupont

GERALDINE FARRAR
AS CHO-CHO-SAN, IN "MADAME BUTTERFLY"

THE OPERA BOOK

REVISED AND ENLARGED

By

EDITH B. ORDWAY

NEW YORK
GEORGE SULLY AND COMPANY

Copyright, 1915, 1917. By
SULLY AND KLEINTEICH

All rights reserved

PRINTED IN U. S. A.

PREFACE TO THE SECOND EDITION

THE second edition of The Opera Book contains six additional operas that have been given presentation during the last two years (except "The Children of Don," the première of which was in 1912), whose inclusion adds materially to the completeness of the book. Three are novelties which are significant in many ways, although not yet have they achieved notable success. They are: "The Children of Don," by Josef Holbrooke; "Goyescas," by Enrique Granados; and "The Canterbury Pilgrims," by Reginald De Koven. Of revivals, the three chosen are: "Andrea Chénier," by Umberto Giordano; "Die Entführung aus dem Serail," by Mozart; and "Grisélidis," by Jules Massenet. The stories of these additional operas appear at the end of the text, and not in alphabetical order in the body of the book. These operas also have a separate index.

In the narration of opera plots, the historical present tense has been used because it affords the most vivid method of depicting events which the audience as well as the actors are supposed to be living. Were the interest any less intense, to aim at an effect of immediate action might seem overstrained; but opera, in common with drama, knows no event save that of the present moment.

The author acknowledges with gratitude the kindly reception given the first edition, and hopes that this edition may even more fully meet the needs of the large and increasing public of opera lovers.

August, 1917   E. B. O.

PREFACE

AMONG the hundred and ten operas the stories of which are told in this book are all the grand operas that have been put upon the stage during the last five seasons in the four opera centers of the eastern United States—New York, Chicago, Philadelphia, and Boston—and also half a dozen others whose *première* or first American production or American revival is announced for the coming season by one or another of the leading companies. Therefore, the book contains the larger number of the grand operas that remain in repertory throughout this country and Canada, as well as on the English and European stages. It includes the favorites among the older operas and several significant new ones, some of American composition.

As they are the operas chosen by popular interest, the collection has a wide range in character, varying from lyric comedy to epic tragedy, from simple settings of allegorical or fairy tales to elaborate presentations of heroic music-drama. Their musical rank is that of *grand* opera, that is, opera in which every word is sung and the recitative is generally accompanied by the orchestra. They are characterized as comic, tragic, fairy, allegorical, sentimental, or heroic, according to the prevailing interest, which is revealed as much by the music as by the plot. They are given in alphabetical order for convenient reference, except that the members of Wagner's tetralogy are given under the title, "The Ring of the Nibelung."

The story of an opera, difficult as it is clearly and worthily to relate, is that central dramatic situation which furnished the composer with his major inspiration, and moved the librettist to impassioned recital. It, therefore, makes the chief appeal to the hearer. Without a knowledge of it on his part, the most realistic of opera music fails of its full effect. With such a knowledge, the music is vivified and the actual force of the tragedy or comedy felt.

With each opera are given interesting and carefully verified data. The name of the composer and the date of the first production serve to place the opera in the line of artistic succession. The name of the writer of the book, or libretto, is often of great musical or literary significance. The full list of the characters, together with their singing parts, is included in order that the musical nature of the work and the dramatic force of each scene may be realized.

The difficulty in pronouncing foreign names for which no English equivalent is in common use has been met by simple suggestions under each foreign title, and by an Index in which the pronunciation of the more important names is given.

E. B. O.

Medford, Mass., September, 1915.

CONTENTS

OPERA	COMPOSER	PAGE
Aïda	Verdi	1
Amore dei Tre Re, L'	Montemezzi	5
(The Love of Three Kings)		
Amore Medico, L'	Wolf-Ferrari	8
(Doctor Cupid)		
Andrea Chénier	Giordano	553
Aphrodite	Erlanger	12
Ariane et Barbe-Bleue	Dukas	19
(Ariadne and Bluebeard)		
Armide	Gluck	22
Barber of Seville, The	Rossini	25
(Il Barbiere di Siviglia)		
Bartered Bride, The	Smetana	28
(Die Verkaufte Braut)		
Bohème, La (The Bohemians)	Puccini	31
Bohemian Girl, The	Balfe	34
Boris Godounov	Moussorgsky	38
Canterbury Pilgrims, The	De Koven	561
Carmen	Bizet	41
Cavalleria Rusticana	Mascagni	45
(Rustic Chivalry)		
Cendrillon	Massenet	48
Children of Don, The	Holbrooke	569
Chimes of Normandy, The	Planquette	52
(Les Cloches de Corneville)		
Cid, Le (The Cid)	Massenet	55
Conchita	Zandonai	61
Cricket on the Hearth, The	Goldmark	66
Crispino e la Comare	Ricci	68
(The Cobbler and the Fairy)		
Cyrano	Damrosch	71

CONTENTS

OPERA	COMPOSER	PAGE
Déjanire	Saint-Saëns	78
Djamileh	Bizet	84
Don Giovanni	Mozart	86
Don Pasquale	Donizetti	90
Don Quichotte	Massenet	94
Donne Curiose, Le (Inquisitive Women)	Wolf-Ferrari	98
Elektra	Strauss	103
Entführung aus dem Serail, Die	Mozart	578
Ernani	Verdi	106
Euryanthe	Weber	110
Evangelimann, Der	Kienzl	116
Fairyland	Parker	120
Falstaff	Verdi	128
Faust	Gounod	131
Favorita, La	Donizetti	137
Fidelio	Beethoven	141
Flying Dutchman, The (Der Fliegender Holländer)	Wagner	147
Forêt Bleue, La (The Blue Forest)	Aubert	151
Fra Diavolo	Auber	155
Francesca da Rimini	Zandonai	158
Freischütz, Der (The Free Shot)	Weber	165
Gioconda, La	Ponchielli	168
Girl of the Golden West, The (La Fanciulla del West)	Puccini	172
Götterdämmerung (The Twilight of the Gods)	Wagner	457
Goyescas	Granados	583
Grisélidis	Massenet	588
Gwendoline	Chabrier	176
Habanera, La	Laparra	180
Hamlet	Thomas	183
Hänsel und Gretel (Hansel and Gretel)	Humperdinck	186
Hérodiade (Herodias)	Massenet	189

CONTENTS

OPERA	COMPOSER	PAGE
Huguenots, The (Les Huguenots)	Meyerbeer	193
Iris	Mascagni	198
Jewels of the Madonna, The (I Giojelli della Madonna)	Wolf-Ferrari	202
Juggler of Notre-Dame, The (Le Jongleur de Nôtre-Dame)	Massenet	204
Julien	Charpentier	206
Königskinder (Kingly Children)	Humperdinck	212
Kuhreigen, Der (Le Ranz des Vaches)	Kienzl	217
Lakmé	Delibes	220
Lobentanz	Thuille	225
Lohengrin	Wagner	229
Louise	Charpentier	237
Lovers' Quarrel, A (I Dispettosi Amanti)	Parelli	243
Lucia di Lammermoor	Donizetti	247
Madame Butterfly	Puccini	252
Madame Sans-Gêne	Giordano	258
Madeleine	Herbert	266
Magic Flute, The (Die Zauberflöte)	Mozart	270
Manon	Massenet	275
Manon Lescaut	Puccini	283
Marriage of Figaro, The (Le Nozze di Figaro)	Mozart	289
Martha	Flotow	297
Masked Ball, The (Un Ballo in Maschera)	Verdi	303
Mefistofele (Mephistopheles)	Boito	309
Meistersinger von Nürnberg, Die (The Master-singers of Nuremburg)	Wagner	316
Mignon	Thomas	325
Mona	Parker	331
Monna Vanna	Février	335
Natoma	Herbert	339
Noël	Erlanger	346

CONTENTS

OPERA	COMPOSER	PAGE
NORMA	Bellini	349
ORACOLO, L' (The Sage)	Leoni	355
ORFEO ED EURIDICE	Gluck	361
(Orpheus and Eurydice)		
OTELLO (Othello)	Verdi	366
PAGLIACCI (Players)	Leoncavallo	374
PARSIFAL	Wagner	379
PÊCHEURS DE PERLES, LES	Bizet	390
(The Pearl Fishers)		
PELLÉAS ET MÉLISANDE	Debussy	395
PIPE OF DESIRE, THE	Converse	404
PRINCE IGOR	Borodin	408
QUO VADIS?	Nouguès	415
RHEINGOLD, DAS (The Rhine-Gold)	Wagner	438
RIENZI	Wagner	424
RIGOLETTO	Verdi	431
RING DES NIBELUNGEN, DER	Wagner	438
(The Ring of the Nibelung)		
ROMEO AND JULIET	Gounod	464
ROSENCAVALIER, DER	Strauss	469
(The Cavalier of the Rose)		
SACRIFICE, THE	Converse	473
SALOME	Strauss	476
SAMSON AND DELILAH	Saint-Saëns	479
SEGRETO DI SUSANNA, IL	Wolf-Ferrari	484
(Susanna's Secret)		
SIEGFRIED	Wagner	452
TALES OF HOFFMANN, THE	Offenbach	487
(Les Contes d'Hoffmann)		
TAMING OF THE SHREW, THE	Goetz	495
TANNHÄUSER	Wagner	501
THAÏS	Massenet	508
TOSCA	Puccini	514
TRAVIATA, LA	Verdi	520
TRISTAN UND ISOLDE	Wagner	525
(Tristan and Isolda)		
TROVATORE, IL (The Troubadour)	Verdi	533
VERSIEGELT (Sealed)	Blech	539

OPERA	COMPOSER	PAGE
WALKÜRE, DIE (The Valkyrie)	*Wagner*	446
WERTHER	*Massenet*	542
WILLIAM TELL (Guglielmo Tell)	*Rossini*	548

LIST OF COMPOSERS 553

KEY TO PRONUNCIATION 556

INDEX 557

THE OPERA BOOK

AÏDA
(Ah-ē'-dah)

ITALIAN* tragic grand opera. Music by Giuseppe Verdi. Plot by Mariette Bey; French prose version by Camille du Locle; Italian verse form by Antonio Ghislanzoni. Composed for the Khedive of Egypt. First production, Cairo, 1871. The scene is laid in Memphis and Thebes at the time of the Pharaohs.

CHARACTERS

PHARAOH, King of Egypt..........................*Bass*
RADAMÈS, Captain of the Egyptian guards............*Tenor*
RAMFIS, High Priest of Egypt........................*Bass*
AMONASRO, King of Ethiopia and father of Aïda....*Baritone*
AMNERIS, daughter of Pharaoh............*Mezzo-Soprano*
AÏDA, an Ethiopian slave........................*Soprano*

A messenger, priests, priestesses, ministers, captains, soldiers, functionaries, slaves, Ethiopian prisoners, and the Egyptian populace.

ACT I. In the hall of the Egyptian king's palace at Memphis stand Ramfis, the high priest, and Radamès, the young captain. Ramfis announces that an invading army of Ethiopians has appeared before Thebes and that the goddess Isis has designated who shall be commander-in-chief of the Egyptian forces; he then hastens to the king. Radamès reveals his ambition by imagining himself a victorious war-

*This refers to the language in which the opera was originally written, not to the nationality of the composer nor to the setting of the plot, except where the composer is an American.

rior returning to crown his love, Aïda, and he bursts into a song upon her beauty. Amneris, who also loves Radamès, surprises him in his ecstasy, and her jealousy is aroused by his greeting of Aïda as she enters. Amneris feigns friendship for Aïda, and tells her that she shall be no longer slave, but companion. The king and high priest enter, with a retinue of soldiers and priests, and confer upon Radamès the leadership of the army. All go out but Aïda, who bewails her love for the man that is to head the forces against her father. Meanwhile, within the temple of Vulcan, prayer for victory is offered and Radamès is invested with the consecrated armor.

Act II. In the apartments of Princess Amneris, Moorish slaves dance before her. Aïda, in mourning for the defeat of her people, enters, and Amneris, by telling her falsely that Radamès has been slain, causes her to betray her love. The jealous princess then tells her of the trick and of her own love for him, and spurns Aïda as a slave.

Before Thebes the Egyptian king sits on his throne to receive the returning conqueror. Amneris sits beside him, while Aïda crouches by the throne as a slave. Radamès and his retinue of soldiers and captives enter in a triumphal procession. The king crowns him with the wreath of victory and bestows upon him the hand of Amneris as his reward. Amonasro, the father of Aïda, is among the captives. They recognize each other and he begs her not to disclose his real rank. The king pledges to grant any boon that the victorious Radamès may ask; so when he requests the lives and liberty of the captives, the king reluctantly grants them.

Act III. A night scene on the banks of the Nile. Amneris, accompanied by Ramfis, is at her devotions in the

© Mishkin

EMMY DESTINN
AS "AÏDA"

temple of Isis on the eve of her wedding. Aïda comes to meet Radamès for the last time; but Amonasro surprises her, and asks her to learn from her lover the path by which the Egyptians are to march against the still hostile Ethiopians. He pleads with her to find it out for the love of her country and her people, and threatens to disown her if she fails. He hides when Radamès comes. The lover declares that he will not marry Amneris, but plans again to conquer the Ethiopians and upon his return to declare his love for Aïda and ask her of the king as a boon. Aïda tells him that Amneris will never permit it, and begs him to flee with her. He consents, and she asks by which path; then he unwittingly discloses the plan of the army. Amonasro rushes from his hiding-place, exultant and announcing his rank, and Radamès realizes that he has betrayed his country. The three are about to flee together when Amneris and the high priest come from the temple. Amonasro starts to stab Amneris, but Radamès interposes, and the priest raises the alarm. His guards seize Radamès, but Aïda and her father escape.

Act IV. In the hall of the king's palace, from which opens a large portal leading to the subterranean hall of justice, sits Amneris, torn with jealousy and with sorrow that Radamès is in danger of death, having been charged with treason by the priests. She has him brought before her. When he accuses her of having separated him from Aïda and hints that she may have killed her, she tells him that Amonasro is dead, but that Aïda escaped and has vanished. Then she offers to try and save his life if he will marry her, but he refuses and vows to be true to Aïda. He is led away for sentence and Amneris hears the words "Burial alive!"

In the temple of Vulcan all is light. Below in the dimness of the subterranean chamber, Radamès still stands on the steps of the staircase by which he has descended, while above in the temple two priests seal the stone of his tomb. He gropes about, and calls upon Aïda. From the shadows she appears before him. She has stolen in to share his doom. He is heartbroken at the thought of her fate, and makes frantic efforts to find some way of escape. Slowly they both are overcome by the deadly air of the tomb, and after calm farewells to earth lose consciousness. Above, Amneris enters the temple and, repentant now, kneels in prayer on the stone that closes the tomb, and prays for him whom she still loves.

L' AMORE DEI TRE RE
(*Lah-mō'-rā dā'-ē Trā Rā*)
(THE LOVE OF THREE KINGS)

ITALIAN tragic grand opera. Music by Italo Montemezzi. Book by Sem Benelli. First production, Milan, 1913. The scene is laid in a remote castle in the mountain country of Italy, and the period is about the tenth century.

CHARACTERS

ARCHIBALDO, King of Altura..........................Bass
MANFREDO, the young King of Altura, son of Archibaldo,
                                                 Baritone
AVITO, a prince of Altura............................Tenor
FLAMINIO, a servant..................................Tenor
FIORA, wife of Manfredo............................Soprano

A young man, a young boy (voice within), young and old women, and other people of Altura.

Forty years before the drama opens King Archibaldo, one of the northern barbarians, had conquered Altura, and has since ruled the land. He is now old and quite blind, but seems to know intuitively what goes on around him. His love for his son, Manfredo, whom he has carefully trained in a virtuous life, and the honor of his name are now the great passions of his heart. Manfredo is away to the wars much of the time; but with Archibaldo in the castle, besides his guardsmen, are two of the royal line of the conquered people —Fiora, whom Manfredo has married, and Avito.

ACT I. One night King Archibaldo cannot sleep, so with his trusted servant, Flaminio, he walks upon the battlements of the castle. There a torch is kept constantly burning for Manfredo, who may return at any time. Archibaldo, with strange foreboding, talks of Manfredo, and says that he thinks he will that day return. Restless he goes back to his chamber. Suddenly Fiora and Avito, who had been betrothed before her marriage, come out upon the battlements. As day breaks Avito goes away, but Archibaldo returns and, though Fiora is silent, feels her presence and asks her why she is there when all others are asleep. She evades answering. His suspicions are aroused, and he fears she has received a lover there; but, for Manfredo's sake and pride of his line, he keeps it secret. Manfredo's men are seen approaching, and soon the young king joins his father upon the tower. He has returned because of longing for Fiora. When she appears she is cold and distant, but Manfredo pours out his love for her. As they go to their chamber the old father, greatly troubled, thanks God he is blind.

Act II. Manfredo lingers several days, wooing his wife gravely and nobly. Then upon the battlements of the castle he bids her good-bye, and begs of her some token of her affection for him. She agrees to stand upon the terrace, which for a long time is in the line of vision of her husband and his men as they march away, and wave her white scarf till they have gone out of sight. As he departs Avito comes up the stairs disguised as Flaminio. When he discloses himself to Fiora she begs him to leave her and bids him farewell. He refuses to go. Fiora takes her white scarf and begins to wave it. Torn between her sense of duty to Manfredo and her love for Avito, she waves it wearily, while Avito pleads with her, kneeling at her feet and kissing the hem of her robe. At last Fiora ceases to wave the scarf and abandons herself to her lover.

While they are still there together old Archibaldo steals upon them. He fails to discover Avito, who escapes, but he has heard Fiora's voice. Fiora acknowledges that she has a lover, but she will not name him. Then Archibaldo, angered by her shameful avowal, seizes her by the throat in an effort to make her speak the lover's name. When she does not, he chokes her to death.

Her body lies upon the great stone seat and King Archibaldo is standing before it to conceal it, when Manfredo enters. He returned when he saw that Fiora had ceased to wave her scarf. The old king tells his son what Fiora has done, and Manfredo is heartbroken that, with such a power of love, she could not have so loved him. He demands the name of her lover, but Archibaldo cannot tell him. When his son shrinks from him as a murderer, the old man takes up the dead body and bears it away.

ACT III. In the crypt of the castle the body of Fiora lies in state. The young men and old women of the castle are lamenting, and are whispering that Fiora has been slain in vengeance. Suddenly Avito comes among them, dispersing them, and kneels at the bier, praying that he may die with her. He kisses her passionately, and finds her lips smeared with a hot poison, which the crafty old king has spread upon them. As he falls down stricken, Manfredo also comes. He recognizes Avito, knows that he must be the lover, and would kill him, but sees that he is already dying. Manfredo starts to kiss the lips of the dead, but Avito tries to restrain him, and asks how he could desecrate her sacred lips. Avito dies, and Manfredo, kissing her lips, receives the poison and, dying, calls upon Fiora. King Archibaldo enters and seizes him, thinking him to be the lover; but Manfredo's dying words cause him to recognize his son and to know that he has killed him also.

L' AMORE MEDICO
(*Lah-mṓ-rā Mā́-dĭ-kō*)
(DOCTOR CUPID)

ITALIAN comic grand opera, founded on Molière's "L'Amour Médecin." Music by Ermanno Wolf-Ferrari. Book by Enrico Golisciano. First production, Dresden, 1913. The scene is the vicinity of Paris in the reign of Louis XIV, about 1665.

CHARACTERS

ARNOLFO, a rich, elderly landowner.
CLITANDRO, a young cavalier.
TOMES
DESFONANDRES
MACROTON } doctors.
BAHIS
LUCINDA, a daughter of Arnolfo.
LISETTA, Lucinda's maid.

A notary, servants and dependents, peasants and peasant girls, musicians, friends and acquaintances, gardeners, pages, dancing girls, and apothecaries.

In his garden Signor Arnolfo sits sobbing with his face in his hands. Old friends, servants, and dependents are about him with rather comical expressions of grief upon their faces. They lament the indisposition of their pretty little mistress, Arnolfo's daughter, who for two months now has been pining away. He asks them to leave him alone with his grief, so they go off. Arnolfo wonders what is the cause of the illness—if by any chance she might be in love. That is impossible, he thinks, because of their seclusion. He intends to keep her to himself, as the solace of his old age.

Lucinda, dressed in white like a child, comes into the garden. As she gathers flowers, keeping an eye meanwhile upon her father, she talks to them, telling them of the mysterious fever that rages within her in mingled torment and joy. She fervently embraces a statue of Hebe. Arnolfo, watching, groans that her visions will surely cause her death, and when she begs the clouds to bear her away because of her loneliness, he calls her. With forced cheerfulness she responds. He takes her in his arms and rocks her like a baby. At his order pages bring her boxes of gowns, ribbons, jewelry, and a large lifelike doll. Still she is listless and shows no interest. When he asks what she would like, Lisetta, her maid, who has come up unobserved, breaks in with the answer that she desires a husband. Lucinda confesses that it is true. Arnolfo is very angry. He discharges Lisetta from his service, finally driving her from his presence. When he has himself gone off she returns. Suddenly a man's voice is heard singing. Lucinda is alert. It is Clitandro. Her joy in his coming is changed to despair, however, when he goes off without a word of welcome and without a sign that she heard or cared.

Lisetta thinks of a plan to outwit the doting Arnolfo, and goes off with her charge. Arnolfo returns to plan about taking Lucinda away to an inaccessible mountain top, or to a desert island, that she may never love any one but him. Then he happens to think that waiting will solve the difficulty, for in time she will be content to settle down with him. Relieved, he falls asleep, but is soon awakened by Lisetta, who comes rushing toward him screaming. She tells him that Lucinda, frightened by his scolding and desperate because her hopes were shattered, locked herself into her chamber, opened the window that overlooks the lake and—then closed it slowly and fell into violent weeping, which has left her so exhausted that Lisetta fears she will not live until evening.

Arnolfo, greatly alarmed, sends his servants for all sorts of remedies and many physicians. As he rushes about, wild with impatience, he falls and hurts his hand. The apothecaries have arrived and Lisetta insists that it be bound. He tears himself away from their officious services as four doctors come. Lisetta hastens off to call a doctor she knows, while the servants stand by weeping.

The doctors are ushered respectfully into a spacious salon, where they take snuff and consult with one another. They disagree among themselves, each one having and keeping to his own opinion, until finally they are shouting and brandishing their canes at one another. Lisetta enters silencing the uproar, and tells them that this is no case for medicine, but for a handsome man. They begin to preen themselves and each tries to impress her with his merits, but she flouts them and goes off. They start after her, but Arnolfo collides with them at the door. They resume their dignified airs, each in turn gives in Latin his diagnosis and holds out his hand to Arnolfo for his fee, then disappears.

Arnolfo becomes suspicious and runs out after the last doctor as Lisetta and Clitandro enter, the latter with a doctor's gown over his cavalier's dress. She hides him when Arnolfo returns annoyed and out of breath. She tells the father that Lucinda will get well now for they have found the king of doctors for her—Doctor Codignac. Clitandro comes forth with two baskets in his hand. The two men salute each other solemnly. Clitandro tells Arnolfo that he has an exclusive method of cure, and his title is doctor of hearts in pain. He says that the baskets contain flowers to charm spells and win the heart. Lucinda is brought in on a couch, dressed wholly in white and weakly sighing. She and the young doctor exchange furtive glances as her father introduces them to each other. Lisetta draws Arnolfo away to play chess with her while Clitandro and Lucinda exchange tender words and he scatters the flowers over her.

At last Arnolfo, noticing that Lucinda shows some animation, takes Clitandro aside and asks his opinion. The young doctor says it is a case of pure hallucination, that she longs for marriage. He suggests that she be allowed to think that he desires to marry her. So before the startled Lucinda Clitandro tells Arnolfo that he comes not as a doctor, but as one who desires to marry her, if she is willing. Lucinda is overjoyed and quickly consents. In order that the farce may be complete a contract must be signed, and the resourceful Clitandro sends for a notary, while Lisetta assists Lucinda to robe herself in gay attire. Arnolfo himself dictates the terms of the marriage contract, giving his daughter a half of his property. Clitandro gives Lucinda the marriage ring, and they both sign the paper.

Arnolfo takes delight in carrying out the farce and in its speedy and favorable effect upon Lucinda. As musicians and dancers enter to make merry, he embraces his new son. Lucinda feels compunction when she sees how thoroughly her father is deluded, but Lisetta reassures her, saying that he will forgive her. As Clitandro and Lucinda dance together they go out unobserved. After some time Arnolfo looks for her and fails to find her, but hears their voices in the distance, rejoicing in their love. Then he understands. The dancers crowd around the astonished father, and Lisetta enters with the large doll that he had given Lucinda and throws it into his arms.

APHRODITE
(Ăf-rō-dĭ´-tā)

FRENCH tragic grand opera, founded on a romance of the same name by Pierre Louÿs. Music by Camille Erlanger. Book by Louis de Gramont. First production, Paris, 1906. The scene is Alexandria, Egypt, in the reign of Berenice about 50 B. C.

CHARACTERS

DEMETRIUS	Tenor
TIMON	Baritone
PHILODEMUS	Tenor
THE HIGH PRIEST	Bass
CALLIDÈS	Bass
THE JAILER	Bass
CHRYSIS	Soprano
BACCHIS	Mezzo-Soprano
MYRTO	Soprano
RHODIS	Mezzo-Soprano
CHIMAIRIS	Mezzo-Soprano
SESO	Soprano

Mousarion, Tryphera, Philotis, Corinna, Selene, Heliope, Hermione, Crobyle, Diomede, Joessa, all soprano; Theano, sister of Rhodis, a dancer; courtesans, philosophers, guardians of the temple, sailors, merchants, dancers, and young men.

ACT I. Upon the pier at Alexandria the people are gathered—gay courtesans, philosophers, sailors, beggars, and vendors. Rhodis and Myrto play their flutes, while Theano dances. The courtesans talk of a banquet to be given by the rich Bacchis, at which she is to liberate her favorite slave, Corinna. Theano and the flute players go out as Demetrius, the handsome sculptor, whose beautiful statue of the goddess Aphrodite stands in their temple, comes upon the pier. The people make way for him as he slowly and haughtily advances. Philotis, Tryphera, and Seso try to attract his attention, but he shuns them, and Mousarion laughs at them, saying that the proud sculptor will have none of them, now that Queen Berenice is in love with him and through her favor he is master of Egypt.

Chimairis, the sorceress, enters. She refuses to tell the fortunes of the courtesans, saying that their futures are all alike. Approaching Demetrius as he stands apart, she tells him that he had great happiness, but it is in the past; that the future is dark with blood—that of two women and, a little later, of himself. He scorns her predictions and she leaves him. The crowd has dispersed when a courtesan passes near him. He notes her exquisite beauty and accosts her. She is Chrysis, and taunts him with being a slave to beauty, while she vaunts her own. He tells her that he is tired of love. When he offers her gold, she says that she is tired of gold, that all she wants is a mirror, a comb, and a necklace. He swears by Aphrodite that he will get them for her. She promises him herself if he will fulfill his vow. Then she tells him that the mirror is a silver one from Rhodope, in which the beautiful Sappho is said to have gazed and which Bacchis now has; the comb is the ivory one that the wife of the High Priest wears in her hair; the necklace is the seven rows of pearls that hang upon the neck of his statue of the goddess within the temple. To procure these he must commit theft, murder, and sacrilege, yet she holds him to his vow if he would see her again.

ACT II. Within the temple of Aphrodite stands Demetrius. He has committed two crimes and has now come to commit the third and greatest. Three guardians of the temple enter, and he hides until they pass on. He contemplates with devout emotions the statue, feels anew the thrill of its beauty, and fancies that it glows with life. For no queen nor courtesan will he despoil the goddess and incur her just wrath.

He is about to leave empty-handed when the High Priest enters, followed by courtesans who have come to offer their sacrifices. Again he hides. He sees them one by one bring their offerings. Suddenly Chrysis appears on the threshold, and although all the courtesans except Rhodis and Myrto protest against her entering, because she is part Greek and part Jew, the High Priest silences them and welcomes her. With due ceremony she offers first a mirror, next a comb, and finally a necklace, and the hidden sculptor sees her lay a necklace of emeralds before the statue whose necklace of pearls she so desperately covets. The High Priest assures her that her offerings are accepted by the goddess, and with the others she goes out. But her presence has so wrought upon the man that he determines to keep his vow to her at all costs.

ACT III. At the house of Bacchis all is revelry. Beside the hostess on her throne is her favorite slave, Corinna. At one of the tables sits Chrysis with Timon by her side, but to-night she is silent and gives small response to words or caresses. Bacchis says that Callidès has paid a large sum of money for Corinna. At this Corinna's six sisters, all slaves, whisper together, for they hate her. Refreshments are brought in, and Theano dances. All are greatly pleased, and as she throws herself down on a couch exhausted they give her wine to drink. Soon she rises up, disheveled, dazed, and her garments half off of her. They laugh at her appearance, and Bacchis orders the mirror of Rhodope brought that she may see herself. Selene hastens to obey.

At the word "mirror" the languid Chrysis is alert. Unconsciously she rises and remains standing with her eyes fixed on the door by which Selene went out. She wonders if Demetrius has not kept his word, and is breathless with suspense, for her fate hangs in the balance—if he is forsworn she will see him no more. The banqueters continue their revelry, but she stands tense and silent. At length Selene appears in the doorway empty-handed, exclaiming that the mirror has been stolen.

Bacchis, infuriated, seizes the slave and shakes her violently. The frightened Selene accuses her sister, Corinna, of having taken it, and the other sisters take up the charge. They rush upon Corinna and cast her, terrified and speechless, at the feet of her mistress. They instigate her punishment, and draw aside a curtain which conceals a cross in an adjoining room. Bacchis, beside herself with fury, calls for hammer and nails. Timon tries to interfere, but Bacchis will not listen, saying that the slave belongs to her. Callidès claims the slave, but Bacchis tells him that he is no longer the master. Terrified at her ferocity, he covers his face with his mantle and hastens from the house. Ruthlessly Corinna is laid upon the cross, and with maledictions Bacchis drives the nails amid cries of pain from the victim and murmurs of protest among the guests. Chrysis, jubilant that Demetrius has kept his vow, has eyes and ears for nothing. She is absorbed in the rising tide of her passion for this lover, and with her face turned from the cross and its quivering burden, she gloats over the submission to her of "the master of Egypt."

At length Bacchis reseats herself at the table and begins to drink, and the guests follow her. Only Timon turns toward the crucified one, stands by her as she breathes her last, kisses her brow, and closes her eyes. Then with one long look he drops the concealing drapery before the cross and goes away as morning dawns.

Act IV. Within his studio Demetrius stands before a roughhewn statue, trying to work. But he sees only the features of Chrysis, thinks only of her. Without are sounds of uproar to which at first he pays little attention, but soon he listens intently. He catches cries of "sacrilege" and "vengeance." He realizes that he has covered himself with shame at the order of a courtesan. Suddenly from behind a tapestry Chrysis appears. He tells her that he has obeyed her wishes. She replies that she has come to give him the prize for his obedience. She slips off her cloak and Demetrius gazes in admiration upon her beauty. He brings from a coffer the three gifts she desired, and she puts the comb in her hair, the necklace about her neck, and looks at herself in the mirror. He seizes her in his arms and embraces her long. As they repeat vows of love the shouts of the people recall him to himself, and he looks at her coldly. Remorse overwhelms him, and he tells her that they must part. She says that she would rather die than leave him, that she will do for him all and more than he has done for her. He bids her swear it, not by Aphrodite, in whom she does not believe, but by the God of Israel. And she, forced by his taunts, tremblingly swears. Then he commands her to go show herself, decked in the jewels and with the mirror in her hand, that day to the people, and promises her that to-morrow he will visit her—in prison. With a long look at him she draws her cloak about her and goes silently out.

Act V. From the pier to the island of Pharos surges a tumultuous crowd, horrified by the sacrilege and fearful of the vengeance of the gods. Their murmurs are changed to wails of despair when the news is brought by Timon that the wife of the High Priest has been found murdered in the consecrated grove. Chrysis appears among the courtesans and, taking Myrto and Rhodis aside, tells them that they are about to see a sight never seen since the goddesses descended upon Mount Ida. While they stand amazed, she moves toward the door of the tower of Pharos, pushes it open, and disappears within.

The frantic people are clamoring for the punishment of the criminal, and falling on their knees, with clasped hands and eyes turned toward heaven, are praying that the anger of the gods may be appeased. Chrysis suddenly appears upon the first landing of the spiral staircase that ascends the outside of the tower. She is clad only in a tunic, but in her streaming hair is fixed the ivory comb, about her neck are the pearls of Aphrodite, and in her hand the mirror of Rhodope. Suddenly a flash of lightning from the gathering clouds lights up the almost naked woman mounting the tower. The people catch sight of her and cry that a miracle has been performed, that Aphrodite herself has appeared to them. The clouds settle down and she is lost to view. When they dissipate Chrysis is still ascending. The people believe themselves pardoned, and they rejoice. As she reaches the top she calls down to them that she is the immortal Aphrodite, and sings a song of triumph. But some have recognized her. A rush is made for the staircase by a mob furious at the deception and fanatic in the cause of the insulted goddess. They ascend, while Chrysis stands motionless at the top.

The next morning Chrysis lies in prison awaiting eagerly the coming of Demetrius. She laments her fate, that she must leave life and love while youth is hers; but she will bow to her destiny if she may see Demetrius once more. The jailer enters and places a cup in her hand, bidding her drink it at the order of the Queen. It is the deadly hemlock, and she begs for respite, at least until Demetrius comes; but the jailer cannot grant it, and reminds her that she is permitted a sweet instead of a cruel death. She drinks the poison, hoping that he will arrive before it shall take effect. She hears the voices of Rhodis and Myrto as, outside the prison walls, they sing their farewell to her. Drowsiness steals over her limbs and she lies down. She is dying, murmuring the love vows she and Demetrius repeated together, when he and the jailer hasten in. Remorseful and disconsolate he remembers the prophecy—how that two women should die and *after a little* he also. Distraught he sees a vision of the goddess Aphrodite with the fateful jewelry upon her. He charges her with rendering them fools by the fatal intoxication of her beauty and, crying out that she has destroyed him, recoils suddenly as the vision makes a gesture as if to smite him.

In a garden consecrated to the god Hermanubis the two girlhood friends of Chrysis, Rhodis and Myrto, bury by moonlight her still beautiful body, thinking kindly of her and lamenting her untimely death.

ARIANE ET BARBE-BLEUE
(*Ahr-ē-ăn ā Barb-Blur*)
(ARIADNE AND BLUEBEARD)

FRENCH allegorical grand opera, founded upon the story of Bluebeard and his seven wives, by Charles Perrault. Music by Paul Dukas. Book by Maurice Maeterlinck. First production, Paris, 1907. The scene is a castle near a village in France during the Middle Ages.

CHARACTERS
BARBE-BLEUE (Bluebeard) .... *Bass*
ARIANE (Ariadne) .... *Mezzo-Soprano*
THE NURSE .... *Contralto*
SÉLYSETTE .... *Mezzo-Soprano*
YGRAINE .... *Soprano*
MÉLISANDE .... *Soprano*
BELLANGÈRE .... *Soprano*
ALLADINE .... *Rôle mimé*
  Peasants and a mob.

ACT I. From a semi-circular apartment in the castle of Bluebeard lead one large and six smaller doors, now closed and locked. Above them are open windows, through which come the cries of an excited and indignant crowd. From these cries it appears that a beautiful young woman has just been brought in a coach to the castle, and the crowd is for warning her that five women before her have gone in there and have never come out. Twenty suitors have followed her and are lamenting that she enters such a trap, for she is too lovely to die. Some think that she knows all, and that she is daring her fate.

The windows close upon the noise of the crowd as Ariadne and her nurse enter the apartment. The nurse is much alarmed, but Ariadne reassures her by showing her the keys of the bridal treasure, which her husband has given her. There are six silver keys that she may use, but one golden one for the lock of the large door she is not to try. That one alone she cares to use, but the nurse is interested in all, and, taking the silver keys, opens a door. A shower of amethysts, set in every possible device, rains upon her. She revels in them, but Ariadne is for opening the other doors. The nurse tries a second, and sapphires in abundance fall upon them. Upon opening the third door pearls are released; upon opening the fourth, emeralds; while from the opened fifth door falls a cascade of rubies. The sixth door releases a torrent of diamonds. Then Ariadne tries the golden key within the lock of the seventh door. The nurse protests, but she turns the key and the door opens. From darkness comes the weird sound of the wailing of women.

Bluebeard enters. She asks him how long the women have been there. He answers that some of them have been there long, the last a year. He tells her that she has lost her happiness unless she will give up knowing. She refuses. He seizes her arm and involuntarily she cries out. A stone is thrown through a window, and immediately the people rush into the house; but when Ariadne says that he has done her no ill and dismisses them, they go away disconcerted.

Act II. Ariadne and her nurse are descending a subterranean stairway and plunge into the darkness. They come upon the forms of five women, who are so motionless that Ariadne believes them dead. They are the five daughters of Orlamonde, who have been long wandering through endless halls in search of light. They have knocked upon the closed door, but have not dared to open it. At her voice they tremble, so she goes to them and strives to arouse them with kisses and caresses. At last they respond and ask her if she too has disobeyed. She replies that she has obeyed, but other laws than those of Bluebeard's. She asks them what they

© Mishkin

LEON ROTHIER
AS BARBE-BLEUE, IN "ARIANE ET BARBE-BLEUE"

do in their prison, and they tell her that they can only pray and sing and weep and watch. She rebukes them for their passivity, and asks them if they do not know that there is sunlight and the splendor of springtime outside. Just then the one lamp is extinguished, and she gropes her way to the far end of the vault where there is a faint light, and drags them with her. She climbs up high rocks and gropes along until she comes to bars and locks. They want her not to try farther, and she taunts them with loving the darkness. At last she succeeds in opening a door and noonday light breaks in. The five wives are blinded, but when they can look they exclaim with delight at the trees and flowers and fields. She guides them to a stairway, and all together they climb laboriously out into the light.

Act III. Within the castle the five wives are decking themselves with the treasure, to which Ariadne has led them. She insists on their making themselves as beautiful as possible, because they are going to be free. The nurse enters in fright, saying that Bluebeard is coming under guard, and that the villagers are assembled to take him. The wives watch the monster descend from his coach, and see the peasants attack and capture him. When he is wounded the women cry out that he should not be killed. He is brought into the room bound, and laid at the feet of Ariadne. The peasants offer to aid her, but she disperses them. The wives serve Bluebeard, Ariadne herself dressing his wounds. One of them furtively kisses him. Ariadne looses his bonds. He rises and, looking from one to another of his wives, he turns at length to Ariadne. She starts to go, though he wishes to detain her, and at the door she asks each of the wives to go with her. But they each in turn bid her farewell and will not leave him.

ARMIDE
(*Ahr-mēēd*)
(ARMIDA)

FRENCH tragic grand opera, founded upon Tasso's "Jerusalem Delivered," and considered the composer's masterpiece. Music by Christopher Wilibald Gluck. Book by Philippe Quinault. First production, Paris, 1777. The scene is partly in Damascus and partly in a land of enchantment, at the time of the First Crusade, 1098.

CHARACTERS

ROLAND, a Knight of the Cross, most renowned of the army of Godfrey of Bouillon	*Tenor*
ARTEMIDOR, a captive Christian knight, delivered by Roland,	*Tenor*
THE KNIGHT OF DENMARK } Crusaders	*Tenor*
UBALD, A KNIGHT }	*Bass*
ARONTES, commander-in-chief of the Saracens	*Bass*
HIDRAOT, King of Damascus	*Bass*
ARMIDA, magician, niece of Hidraot	*Soprano*
PHŒNICIA } her attendants	*Soprano*
SIDONIA }	*Soprano*
HATE, a Fury	*Soprano*
LUCINDA } apparitions	*Soprano*
MELISSA }	*Soprano*

A NAIAD AND A LOVE, both apparitions.

People of Damascus, apparitions, and furies.

ACT I. In her palace Armida, the beautiful Saracen princess, sits thinking of Roland, the heroic Crusader. Although his victories mean the defeat of her people, yet he has won her heart. Nevertheless, because Hidraot the King, her uncle, is desirous that she should wed, she is pledged to marry the man who defeats the Crusaders. News comes that Arontes, commander-in-chief of the Saracens, has been victorious and will return with many captives. The report, so full of import to Armida, proves false, as Roland has routed the Saracens and released the captives; so the exultation of the people is changed into vows of vengeance.

ACT II. Armida, whose love for Roland is fanned by his heroism and is mingled with hate because of the Saracen losses, conjures up an enchanted garden about him as he wanders alone in the desert. While he lies sleeping in a bower of roses, Armida goes to him with a drawn dagger in her hand. He is now completely in her power and she can avenge her country's wrongs. His presence, however, kindles her love into flame, and she passionately clasps him in her arms.

ACT III. In her palace Armida realizes what she has done, and her heart is torn with remorse and with both love and hate of Roland. She summons the Fury of Hate before her, and the Fury tells her that through her dalliance Roland will now surely escape. Instead of infuriating her, this restores her love for him, and she dismisses the sprite.

ACT IV. Roland and Armida are again together in the enchanted garden, when Ubald and a Danish knight, who have been sent by the Crusaders to search for their absent general, enter. Armida tries by her wiles to bar their way to Roland, but she is forced to fall back by the consecrated scepter which Ubald lifts on high. The apparitions she conjures up are also made powerless by it.

ACT V. Armida spirits Roland away to her palace, where by luxurious living she causes him to forget his responsibilities and all his past life. She is successful in keeping him so long as she is with him, but when she leaves him Ubald and the Danish knight gain access to him. By the scepter and a shield in whose polished surface he beholds the man he once was, they recall him to himself. Aroused, he grasps his sword. Armida returns and tries by every art to deter him from leaving her. He departs, and she, desperate with grief and passion, sets fire to her palace and perishes in the ruins.

THE BARBER OF SEVILLE
(IL BARBIERE DI SIVIGLIA)

ITALIAN comic grand opera, founded upon Beaumarchais' comedy, "Le Barbier de Seville." Music by Gioacchino Antonio Rossini. Book by Cesare Sterbini. First production, Rome, 1816. The scene is Seville, Spain, in the seventeenth century.

CHARACTERS

COUNT ALMAVIVA	Tenor
DOCTOR BARTOLO	Bass
BASILIO, a singing master	Bass
FIGARO, a barber	Baritone
FIORELLO, servant to the count	Bass
AMBROZIO, servant to the doctor	Bass
ROSINA, ward of the doctor	Soprano
BERTHA (or Marcellina), Rosina's governess	Soprano

A notary, constable, musicians, and soldiers.

ACT I. Before the house of Doctor Bartolo, in the early dawn, Count Almaviva, disguised as an humble youth by name Lindoro, with Fiorello and some musicians is serenading the wealthy and beautiful Rosina. She is jealously watched by her guardian, who is planning to marry her himself. The count dismisses Fiorello and the musicians, but Rosina does not appear and he is about to give up in despair when Figaro, the barber and general factotum of the city, comes along. The count confides in him and, although Figaro is a trusted servant of Bartolo, he consents to help along the count's acquaintance with Rosina. The lady appears followed closely by Bartolo, and she has to feign accident in order to drop a note to her admirer, Lindoro. Bartolo is suspicious and commands her to go into the house, while he hastens away to finish preparations for marrying her. The count succeeds in declaring his love to Rosina in a song to which she responds, but he does not disclose his name or rank. Figaro and the count now decide that the latter shall pose as a soldier billeted to the doctor's house, as a company of soldiers have that day arrived in the city.

In the library of Doctor Bartolo's house Rosina is sitting, singing happily of her love for Lindoro and of her determination to marry no one but him. Figaro enters, but has no chance to tell Rosina of the count's intention before Bartolo and Basilio come in. Rosina and Figaro go out, and Basilio tells Bartolo that Rosina's unknown lover is no other than Count Almaviva, and suggests that they circulate false stories to discredit the count. Bartolo is more than ever anxious to marry Rosina at once, and they go to prepare the documents. Figaro and Rosina return, and he tells her that he will arrange an interview with her lover if she will send him a line. She gives him a note, which she has already written. Figaro departs, and Bartolo entering finds evidence in Rosina's ink-stained hands and the missing letter paper that she is deceiving him, and vows that she shall be more closely watched. A drunken soldier, imperiously demanding admittance, now comes in, and during the doctor's indignant inquiries and his distress at having a soldier billeted upon him when he was supposed to be exempt, the lovers exchange notes. The uproar has called out an officer, who starts to arrest the count but stops, much to the surprise of Bartolo, when the count quietly tells the officer who he is.

Act II. To the library of Bartolo the count is again admitted, this time as a teacher of singing, sent, he says, by Basilio, who is ill. Bartolo is suspicious, and the count shows him the letter from Rosina to Lindoro, which he says came

© Aimé Dupont

GUISEPPE CAMPANARI
AS FIGARO, IN "THE BARBER OF SEVILLE"

into his hands from Count Almaviva through a lady at the inn where he was stopping, proving how lightly the count holds Rosina's favor. Rosina is summoned and the lesson begins. Meanwhile Figaro comes to shave the doctor, who, although he wishes to watch this new music-master, is obliged to submit to Figaro's ministrations. But Basilio appears. The count and Figaro, by means of a convincing purse, persuade him to go away. When the count has arranged with Rosina to elope and Figaro has stolen the key to the window lattice, all go out.

Shortly after, Bartolo is alone with Rosina and shows her the letter she wrote to Lindoro, thus arousing her jealousy and anger. She then confesses the planned elopement and, in order to escape her lover's treachery, promises to marry Bartolo. He hastens away to summon a notary for the marriage and to order the count arrested when he shall come to get Rosina. The girl is therefore alone when the count and Figaro enter. Rosina upbraids the faithless Lindoro, who reveals himself as Count Almaviva and tells how he himself gave the letter to Bartolo in order to see her. His explanation is satisfactory, and, the notary arriving, they are married. Bartolo and the officers then arrive. The surrender of Rosina's dowry to the doctor appeases his wrath and he gives the lovers his blessing.

THE BARTERED BRIDE
(DIE VERKAUFTE BRAUT)   (PRODANA NEVESTA)

BOHEMIAN comic grand opera. Music by Friedrich Smetana. Book by Karla Sabina. German text by Max Kalbeck. First production, Prague, 1866. The scene is a large Bohemian village in the last century.

CHARACTERS

KRUSCHINA, a peasant	*Baritone*
KATHINKA, his wife	*Soprano*
MARIE, their daughter	*Soprano*
MICHA, a landowner	*Bass*
AGNES, his wife	*Mezzo-Soprano*
WENZEL, their son	*Tenor*
HANS, Micha's son by a first marriage	*Tenor*
KEZAL, a marriage-broker	*Bass*

The director of a troop of minstrels, a dancer, a comedian, villagers, and horseback performers.

Micha has two sons, Hans, a likely fellow, by his first wife, and Wenzel, a half-witted, stuttering fellow. Agnes, the second wife, drives Hans away from home, but Wenzel is coddled.

ACT I. In a public square before an inn Marie and Hans, her lover, sit talking anxiously; for Marie's parents wish her to marry Wenzel. Hans assures the girl that they will not force her to marry a man whom she does not love. At the sound of footsteps he goes away, and Marie hides as the marriage-broker and her parents enter. They discuss the coming marriage, and though Kruschina is for making the arrangements without consulting Marie, Kathinka asks that they hear what she will say to it. Marie enters, and although the broker sings loudly the praise of Wenzel, she will not listen, but declares that she loves Hans. Nevertheless, Kruschina writes out a promise to Micha that Marie shall marry his son. The broker sends her father to talk the matter over with Micha and goes to consult with Hans.

ACT II. Within the inn Hans and Kezal are seated at either end of a table, drinking and talking. Hans is rhapsodizing on the joys of love, but Kezal tells him that love is nothing unless a man has money. Wenzel, who has been dancing with the young people before the inn, comes in quite the worse for drink. Marie also enters and, approaching Wenzel, tells him not to marry the girl that his father has promised him, because she is in love with another man, and says she knows a very pretty girl who loves him. Wenzel, touched by her interest, promises her.

Meanwhile Kezal makes Hans an offer to pay him a certain sum of money if he will give up Marie. Hans protests at first, then agrees, but stipulates that Marie shall marry no one but the son of Micha. The contract is signed and they return to Marie's parents, who are overjoyed to hear that everything is arranged so easily, while Hans is secretly rejoiced at his own clever scheme.

ACT III. A company of traveling players come to the town, and the still drunken Wenzel is much attracted by a tight-rope dancer, Esmeralda. When the man who was to have played the part of a bear fails to appear, the manager succeeds in persuading Wenzel to get into the hide of the bear and go through its tricks.

Wenzel's mother comes to take him to Marie, but he refuses to go because his dull mind has gathered from the girl's warning that if he marries Marie she will torture him to death. At last he is persuaded, and with his father and the marriage-broker they go to the house of Marie's parents. Then the broker announces to Marie that Hans has relinquished his claim upon her for a sum of money. She will not believe it, but he shows her the contract and receipt for the money. She asks them to leave her and they go out. Soon Hans comes and tries to explain it to her, but she refuses to listen. The others enter, glad that he is no longer in her favor, though they despise him because of his treatment of her. Hans makes an effort to show her that she will fulfill the stipulation he has made anyway, but she still thinks that Micha's son must mean only Wenzel. Micha and his wife enter and at once recognize Hans. Kezal, the broker, is much chagrined, but Marie, seeing what Hans has done, declares that she still loves him. Wenzel enters, dressed in the bear skin, and Micha gives his consent to the marriage of his eldest son and Marie, who begin their married life richer by the sum of money paid for the bride.

LA BOHÊME
(*Lah Bō-ĕhm*)
(THE BOHEMIANS)

ITALIAN tragic grand opera, founded on Henry Murger's "La Vie de Bohême." Music by Giacomo Puccini. Book by Giuseppe Giacosa and Luigi Illica. First production, Turin, 1896. The scene is Paris in 1830.

CHARACTERS

RUDOLPH, a poet .... *Tenor*
MARCEL, a painter .... *Baritone*
COLLINE, a philosopher .... *Bass*
SCHAUNARD, a musician .... *Baritone*
BENOIT, an importunate landlord .... *Bass*
ALCINDORO, a state councilor and follower of Musetta.. *Bass*
PARPIGNOL .... *Tenor*
MUSETTA, a grisette .... *Soprano*
MIMI, a maker of embroidery .... *Soprano*

Students, workgirls, citizens, shopkeepers, street vendors, soldiers, restaurant waiters, boys, girls, etc.

ACT I. In an attic-studio in the Latin Quarter of Paris Rudolph and Marcel sit working. Marcel is painting what he considers his masterpiece. It is too cold to work, however, their money and fuel are gone, and Marcel is about to burn a chair when Rudolph, discouraged by the rejection of his drama, kindles a blaze with his manuscript. Colline enters, downcast because he cannot pawn his books; but Schaunard has had better luck. He comes, bringing fuel and provisions, and they prepare a feast. The landlord enters and demands the rent, but they give him wine and forcibly but jollily turn him out. At length the rest go out, leaving Rudolph alone to write.

Mimi, a beautiful but frail girl, who lives on the same

floor and supports herself by making embroidery, knocks and asks Rudolph for a light for her candle. She falls in a faint at the door and Rudolph, giving her wine, restores her to consciousness. She tells him that she has consumption, but he is very much stirred by her beauty and clear coloring, and by her small white hands. Upon leaving she discovers that she has lost her key. While they are looking for it, both candles are extinguished. As they grope about the floor, Rudolph finds it and puts it in his pocket. Still groping, their hands meet, and Rudolph holds hers to warm them, and tells her about himself and his life. Then Mimi tells him of her struggles, and soon they declare their love for each other.

Act II. To the Café Momus, where these talented young men are wont to dine, the three repair upon leaving Rudolph. It is Christmas Eve and every one is celebrating. Hawkers are vaunting their wares in the streets and the shops are all open. Rudolph and Mimi, arm in arm, enter a milliner's, where Rudolph is to buy her a bonnet. Colline, Schaunard, and Marcel have a table set for them before the café, and to them Rudolph brings Mimi and introduces her. Musetta, with whom Marcel was once in love but has now quarrelled, enters with Alcindoro. Marcel is deeply stirred at seeing her, and Musetta sends Alcindoro off on an errand for her, and she and Marcel become reconciled. The party find that they have not money enough among them to pay for their suppers, so carry Musetta off with them, leaving the bills for Alcindoro to pay upon his return.

Act III. Several months have elapsed. Rudolph and Mimi have been very happy together and also very miserable, for Rudolph is passionately in love with her and exceedingly jealous. From a tavern within a city gate of Paris—the

© Mishkin

BELLA ALTEN
AS MUSETTA, IN "LA BOHÊME"

signboard of which is Marcel's treasured canvas—comes the painter one snowy winter's day just as Mimi, exhausted and coughing, appears. She asks help of Marcel, telling him of Rudolph's love and jealousy, and that she believes they must part. Rudolph also enters and, not seeing Mimi, tells of the torment of their life together, and that he loves her but believes her dying. Mimi's cough betrays her, and though she says farewell to Rudolph, they find they cannot part, and determine to wait until spring. Meanwhile Musetta and Marcel, who are living at the tavern together, have a violent quarrel.

ACT IV. Some time later Marcel and Rudolph are again living in their attic-studio, having parted from Musetta and Mimi. Both are making a pretense of working, while each secretly cherishes a memento of the woman he loves. Schaunard and Colline enter with rolls and herring for a frugal meal. They have a jolly and boisterous time, and are dancing and singing when Musetta enters. She tells them that Mimi is outside, but is weak and ill and can come no farther. They prepare the bed for her and bring her in. She embraces Rudolph affectionately, and begs him not to leave her. Mimi tries to reconcile Marcel and Musetta. The latter tells the others that Mimi is dying, and, much distressed, offers her earrings and begs them to sell them and get a doctor.

All go out, leaving Rudolph and Mimi alone. While they recall their love for each other, she is seized with a fit of coughing, and falls back fainting. Just then Musetta and the rest reënter with medicine. Mimi speaks again to Rudolph, telling him of her love for him, and falls asleep. Amid the prayers of Musetta, the frantic sobs and cries of Rudolph, and the grief of all, she dies.

THE BOHEMIAN GIRL

ENGLISH sentimental grand opera, founded on the ballet by St. Georges and Mazzilier, "The Gypsy," with the scene changed from Scotland to Hungary. Music by Michael William Balfe. Book by Alfred Bunn. First production, London, 1843. The scene is Pressburg, Hungary, and its vicinity, in the eighteenth century.

CHARACTERS

COUNT ARNHEIM, Governor of Pressburg	*Baritone*
THADDEUS, an exiled Polish nobleman and fugitive from Austrian troops	*Tenor*
FLORESTEIN, nephew of the count	*Tenor*
DEVILSHOOF, leader of a gypsy band	*Bass*
CAPTAIN OF THE GUARD	*Bass*
ARLINE, daughter of the count	*Soprano*
BUDA, her governess	*Soprano*
QUEEN OF THE GYPSIES	*Soprano*

Nobles, soldiers, gypsies, retainers, and peasants.

ACT I. Before the castle of Count Arnheim, Governor of Pressburg, nobles and retainers are gathered for the chase, and on the bank of the Danube near by the Austrian flag is being raised over a statue of the emperor. Count Arnheim and Florestein enter, and as Arline and her governess come out of the castle, the count greets his daughter affectionately. When he goes into the castle and the hunters and nobles are departing, Arline asks that she may go also, and the governess consents. All have left when Thaddeus rushes in, sees the statue of the emperor, and realizes that he is still among enemies and must resort to disguise in order to escape. Devilshoof with his gypsies comes along and Thaddeus accosts him. He tells the gypsy chief his danger, and Devilshoof gives him gypsy garb and conceals him, throwing the pursuing soldiers off his track. He also invites him to join his band.

An outcry is made that the hunters' quarry has attacked Arline and her nurse, and that the child is probably killed. Thaddeus seizes the gun of Florestein, who has fled from the scene of the attack, and goes to the rescue. While all is suspense, and the count is asking the cause of the tumult, Thaddeus comes back with Arline, having rescued her uninjured but for a flesh wound in the arm. The count expresses deep gratitude to Thaddeus, and invites him to a feast they are about to hold. The nobles second the invitation, and Thaddeus accepts.

Count Arnheim proposes a toast to the emperor, which all but Thaddeus drink. The count challenges him to do likewise, but he takes the glass and hurls it at the statue in contempt. Count Arnheim and the nobles spring up indignantly, and are about to seize Thaddeus when the count, remembering that to him he owes the life of his child, interposes and asks that they let him go free. He flings him a purse of gold, which Thaddeus haughtily flings back. Devilshoof rushes in and defies any one who would lay hands upon Thaddeus. Devilshoof is seized and taken into the castle, while Thaddeus is allowed to depart, and the feast continues. Shortly after a cry is raised that Arline, left alone in her room for a few moments, is gone, and Devilshoof is seen climbing the mountain with Arline in his arms. Over a chasm a single tree is the only bridge, and Devilshoof, having passed, knocks the tree trunk away and so prevents pursuit.

ACT II. Twelve years later in a camp near Pressburg Arline lies sleeping in the tent of the gypsy queen, while Thaddeus keeps watch and the gypsies are out on their nightly raid. Florestein, whose uncle, the count, has never found a trace of his daughter and so mourns her as dead, is robbed by the gypsies as he returns intoxicated from a revel. The Queen of the Gypsies appears and restores to Florestein his possessions, except a diamond-set medallion, which Devilshoof has made away with.

Arline, aroused by the commotion, awakens, and Thaddeus avows his love for her. Arline tells him that she loves him, and he then tells her the story of the scar upon her arm—how he saved her from a stag when she was a child; but he does not disclose her real rank. The queen enters, and though angry, for she herself loves Thaddeus, is obliged to approve their betrothal.

In the city streets in fair time, Count Arnheim and Florestein are watching a group of gypsies. Florestein is attracted by Arline's beauty, and attempts to kiss her, but she resents the liberty. The queen praises Arline for her spirit in repulsing Florestein, and puts about the girl's neck the stolen medallion, which she has made Devilshoof surrender to her. The angry Florestein, spying it, has the girl and Thaddeus, who interposes, arrested. The count is in his room in the hall of justice, musing before the portrait of his lost daughter, when the gypsy girl is brought before him for judgment. Seeing that the evidence is all against her and realizing the perfidy of the queen, Arline is so frightened and distressed that she attempts to stab herself. Arnheim catches her hand and sees the scar that proves she is his daughter. Thaddeus, rushing in to defend Arline, confirms her story and then goes away with Devilshoof during the general rejoicing.

ACT III. As Arline waits in the large hall of her father's castle for the coming of the guests to whom the count wishes to introduce his daughter, her father and Florestein enter.

The latter makes advances for her hand, but she repulses him, although her father commends his suit, for in her heart she remembers Thaddeus. She is left alone for a moment, and takes her gypsy dress from a cupboard and looks at it longingly, for that is her only reminder of the happy days with Thaddeus. Devilshoof and Thaddeus surprise her by entering at the window. They beg her to come away and live with the gypsies. Guests are heard approaching, and Devilshooff makes his escape, but Thaddeus delays so long that he is obliged to hide.

The gypsy queen, still jealous and revengeful, has tracked Thaddeus to the castle, and now enters and announces to the count that his daughter is concealing a man within the room. The count, angry and amazed, accuses his daughter, and Thaddeus comes forth. The count orders him to leave, but when Arline resolves to go with him, her father relents. Thaddeus tells of his own noble blood and produces his commission, and the count consents to their marriage. The Queen of the Gypsies orders one of her attendants to shoot Thaddeus, but Devilshoof turns the gun so that the queen herself is killed.

BORIS GODOUNOV
(*Bŏ'-rĭs Gŏ'-dōō-nŏff*)

RUSSIAN tragic grand opera, founded on Poushkin and Karamzin's historical drama, "Boris Godounov." Both music and book by Modeste Petrovich Moussorgsky. First production, St. Petersburg, 1874. The scene is partly in the palace of the Kremlin, Moscow, and partly on the borders of Poland. The time is from 1598 to 1605.

CHARACTERS

BORIS GODOUNOV, Czar of Russia.................*Baritone*
FEODOR } his children................. { *Mezzo-Soprano*
XENIA   { *Soprano*
PRINCE SHOUÏSKY.................................*Tenor*
PIMEN, monk and chronicler......................*Bass*
THE PRETENDER DMITRI, called Gregory.............*Tenor*
RANGONI, a Jesuit priest........................*Bass*
MARINA MNICHEK, beloved of Gregory........*Mezzo-Soprano*

A nurse, the clerk of the Duma, an innkeeper, an idiot, a constable, Jesuit priests, pilgrims, vagabonds, courtiers, nobles, peasants, Polish lords and ladies, women, young girls, and children.

PROLOGUE. Boris Godounov, the regent guardian of the children of Ivan the Terrible, has, upon the death of the elder prince, murdered the younger, Dmitri, that he himself may obtain the throne. In the courtyard of a monastery near Moscow the people are assembled, and he is acclaimed as king, although there is some dissension and misgiving. Soon in the Kremlin his coronation takes place amid the plaudits of the people. There is no evidence that his crime is known.

ACT I. It is night in a lonely cell in the Monastery of the Miracle. Pimen is writing by the light of a lamp a history of Russia, with the high ideal of telling the truth so that

God can look upon it unashamed. Gregory, a lad of much spirit and of the age and appearance of the murdered Prince Dmitri, lies asleep in the cell. Suddenly Gregory awakes from a dream of power, and Pimen tells him that the present king is a regicide and that the boy who should be czar was about Gregory's age. Gregory, impressed with the story, exclaims that, though no man dare accuse the king, yet the obscure monk has recorded the tale and God will judge.

Some years later when Gregory, disguised and attended by two monks as valets, is passing an inn on the Lithuanian border, he is accosted by the police, who are watching for a certain Gregory, who has escaped from a monastery. The Czar has ordered that he be arrested and hanged as a thief and a heretic. Gregory barely escapes across the border.

ACT II. In the apartments of the Czar at the Kremlin, Xenia is weeping over the portrait of her lover, who has died, while her brother, Feodor, sits reading. Boris enters, and dismissing Xenia with comforting words, commends his son's learning. Soon he dismisses him and sits alone, brooding remorsefully and anxiously over his misfortunes. The nobles are plotting against him, and a revolt of the Poles is brewing. Prince Shouïsky, who was responsible for the carrying out of the murder of Prince Dmitri, comes seeking audience with the king. Admitted by Boris, who is repelled and made greatly suspicious by his friendly greeting, he tells of the rise of a pretender to the throne, coming out of Poland, whom the nobles and the Pope acclaim. Boris, greatly alarmed for fear the pretender is indeed the lawful heir to the throne, asks Shouïsky if he really did carry out his commands and have the child murdered. Shouïsky then relates in horrible detail the death of the prince. Boris, overcome with remorse and fear, dismisses the noble,

Act III. In the apartment of Marina Mnichek at Sandomir a Jesuit priest succeeds by dire threats in converting her to the Romish church, in order that she may use her influence with Gregory in its behalf. Later, in the garden of her father's castle by moonlight, the false Dmitri is met by the priest, who strives to kindle his passion for Marina. They both hide as Marina and a party of nobles come out, so Dmitri overhears the plots for the overthrow of Boris. Later when he and Marina are together, she spurs him on, kindling his ambition, to hasten at once to Moscow and claim the throne.

Act IV. Near Krom there is an uprising of the peasants against the nobles and the Czar. The crime of Boris is the talk of all the people, and his death is plotted. The false Dmitri appears with his troops and they acclaim him king. But an idiot watching the crowd prophesies woe to the Russian people.

In the palace of the Kremlin the duma of the nobles is holding a special session. They are plotting the downfall of the pretender and the crushing of his rebellion. Shouïsky enters and brings sad news of the Czar, who seems to be haunted by a specter. While he is yet speaking Boris enters, babbling in delirium, "What voice said, 'Thou murderer'? No murderer I!" and is accusing Shouïsky. Boris comes to himself and takes his seat. An old monk begs audience with the Czar, and is admitted. Pimen enters and tells the story of a miracle in which the spirit of Prince Dmitri appeared to an old shepherd and told him that he would cure him of his blindness, which was done immediately the man had made a pilgrimage to the tomb of the prince. As the story ends Boris falls unconscious, but, recovering, gives farewell advice to his son, the heir apparent, and dies.

CARMEN

FRENCH tragic grand opera, founded upon Prosper Mérimée's novel of the same name. Music by Georges Bizet. Book by Henri Meilhac and Ludovic Halévy. First production, Paris, 1875. The scene is Seville, Spain, about 1820.

CHARACTERS

Don José, a corporal of dragoons	Tenor
Escamillo, a toreador	Baritone
Zuniga, a captain of dragoons	Bass
Moralès, an officer	Baritone
Lillas Pastia, an innkeeper	Bass
El Dancaïre } smugglers	Tenor
El Remendado }	Tenor
Carmen, a gypsy girl	Soprano
Micaëla, a village maiden	Soprano
Frasquita } gypsy girls, companions of Carmen	Soprano
Mercédès }	Soprano

A guide, officers, dragoons, lads, cigar-girls, gypsies, smugglers, peddlers, toreadors, an alcalde, an alguacil, and the populace.

Act I. In a square of Seville Moralès and his soldiers are grouped before the guardhouse when Micaëla comes in search of Don José. Not finding him, she goes away. The relief guard under Zuniga comes, and José is told of the young woman's asking for him. Zuniga and José remain outside the guardhouse, José mending his sword-chain and Zuniga questioning him about the girls in the cigar factory opposite. José says there never were girls bolder. When Zuniga banters him on his not knowing whether or not they are pretty, and on thinking only of Micaëla, José acknowledges his love for her.

Soldiers and workmen gather as the factory girls, smoking cigarettes, come out at noon. Among them is Carmen, a handsome, bewitching, but fickle young woman, to whom all the men except José make love. She sings gaily of the caprices of love, and, as the girls reënter the factory, flings at the oblivious José the cassia-flowers she had in her bodice. José picks them up and remembers the challenging look she gave him. Micaëla, returning, gives him a letter, some money, and a kiss from his mother, with the message that she forgives him. José is touched, and replies that he repents.

There is a disturbance within the factory, and the girls rush out, saying that Manuelita and Carmen quarreled, and that Manuelita is wounded. Zuniga orders José to find out what is the matter, and the latter soon returns, leading Carmen, whom he has arrested. Carmen will not confess. Her hands are tied and she is left in José's charge. She casts coquettish glances at him, and so fascinates him by her beauty, and by avowing that she loves him and will meet him at an inn on the ramparts of the city, that he agrees to let her escape. As José and two dragoons are taking her away, she pushes the soldiers down and runs off.

Act II. At the inn of Lillas Pastia, Carmen, Frasquita, and Mercédès are entertaining Zuniga, Moralès, and other officers, and gypsies are dancing to the sound of the guitar and the tambourine. Zuniga tells Carmen that José is now released after two months in prison for letting her escape. Carmen seems glad; but when Escamillo comes, is welcomed by all, then turns to her, she flirts with him. As he goes, he says he will wait and hope. Zuniga and the other officers have left when two smugglers, El Dancaïre and El Remendado, are admitted, and ask the girls to help them evade the customs officers. Carmen declines to go, as she awaits José. The smugglers and girls go off, telling Carmen to persuade him to join them.

© Aimé Dupont

EMMA CALVÉ
AS "CARMEN"

José is rejoiced to find Carmen, and tells her of his love for her. She sings and dances for him until suddenly the bugles sound the retreat, and José knows that he must return to camp. Carmen is angry that he attends to the bugles rather than to her, and in a passionate outburst bids him go. He tries to prove his love for her, and shows her the flowers she threw at him that first day, yet she scorns a love that will not follow her to the mountains. He begs her not to ask him to desert his flag, and she declares she hates him. He is sadly bidding her good-bye when voices are heard without. Zuniga forces an entrance, and orders José to be off, but he refuses to go. They are about to fight when Carmen interferes. The smugglers and gypsies appear and disarm Zuniga, keeping him prisoner. José realizes that his army career is now over, and consents to go away with them.

Act III. At a wild spot in the mountains, where is the camp of the smugglers and the gypsies, José is sitting looking out over the valley. To Carmen's question he replies that he is thinking of his good, loving old mother, who believes him to be a man of honor. Carmen tells him he had better leave a life for which he is not fitted. When he realizes that she means him to leave her behind, he is so angry that she declares he wishes to kill her, and indifferently says that to live or to die is the award of Fate. She joins Frasquita and Mercédès, who are telling their fortunes with cards, and tries her own. Over and over again she reads that she is soon to die, and her lover also.

When the smugglers go on, José remains to guard the goods left behind. Micaëla comes, but before she is seen, José lifts his gun and shoots, and she disappears behind the rocks. The ball just misses Escamillo, who says he comes in search of his lady love, the gypsy girl, Carmen, who has had a lover, a deserter, but that affair is past. José, wild with jealousy, threatens him, and they are fighting with knives, José having just gained the advantage, when Carmen rushes in and stays José's arm. Escamillo promises to meet José again, invites them all to the bullfight that week in Seville, and goes away. Micaëla is discovered, and pleads with José to go to his mother, who is dying. In spite of his passion for Carmen he goes with Micaëla, though vowing that he will return soon.

Act IV. Before the amphitheater in Seville the people are gathering for the bullfight. The procession forms and enters the theater,— the alguacil, torredors, banderilleros, and picadors, while in the place of honor is the Espada, Escamillo, and with him Carmen, magnificently dressed. Before they part, they pledge each other their love. The alcalde comes, and soon everybody has entered the amphitheater except Carmen, whom Frasquita and Mercédès beg not to wait there, for José is hiding in the crowd. She is defiant, however. José comes and implores her to go away with him. She scorns him, fearless of his anger, and taunts him, though he pleads passionately with her. At length, flinging away his ring, she says she loves him no more. When applause for Escamillo rings out, she starts to enter the theater, but José steps in front of her. She declares her love for the toreador, and José, realizing how fickle is the affection for which he has sacrificed his honor, is seized with fury and, as Carmen again starts to go, stabs her. She dies at his feet. Overwhelmed with grief, he falls on his knees beside her, and as the crowd returns, acknowledges that it was he who struck her down, and tells them to do with him what they will, now that Carmen is dead.

CAVALLERIA RUSTICANA
(*Cah-vahl-lā-rē'-ah Rōōs-tē-kah'-nah*)
(RUSTIC CHIVALRY)

ITALIAN tragic grand opera, founded on a story by Giovanni Verga, the Sicilian novelist. Music by Pietro Mascagni. Book by Giovanni Targioni-Tozzetti and G. Menasci. First production, Rome, 1890. The scene is a Sicilian village of the present time on Easter Day.

CHARACTERS

TURIDDU, a young soldier............................*Tenor*
ALFIO, the village carter..........................*Baritone*
LOLA, wife of Alfio.........................*Mezzo-Soprano*
LUCIA, mother of Turiddu.......................*Contralto*
SANTUZZA, a village girl, betrothed to Turiddu......*Soprano*

Villagers, peasants, and boys.

Turiddu, a young soldier just returned from the wars, was pledged to marry Lola, but during his absence she has married Alfio.

Santuzza enters the open square before the church and the tavern just as Lucia comes out of her house. She asks the mother where her son Turiddu is. Lucia is surprised and angry, and will not tell, and when Santuzza persists in trying to find out, she says that she does not know. Santuzza then passionately begs her to take pity on her and tell her. Lucia then says that he has gone to Francofonte to buy wine. But when Santuzza declares that he has not as he was last night seen in the village, Lucia suggests that he may have returned and asks Santuzza to come in and see. Santuzza exclaims that she cannot enter the house because she is excommunicated. Lucia asks what interest then her son has in her, but Santuzza does not answer.

Just then with loud cracking of his whip Alfio enters accompanied by villagers. He is singing the praises of his faithful and loving wife Lola. Lucia accosts him and he asks her if she has some of her old wine. She says that Turiddu has gone to Francofonte for it. Alfio denies it, saying that he saw him near his house. Santuzza motions Lucia to check her surprise, and after Alfio and the people with him have entered the church Santuzza tells her how Turiddu loved Lola before he went away and how, coming back and finding her married, he made love to Santuzza herself, and that she returned his love. But Lola, not content, stirred up the old flame of passion in Turiddu, and now he is hanging round Lola and has deserted Santuzza. Lucia is sorely burdened, and, at Santuzza's suggestion, goes into the church to pray for them both.

Turiddu enters the square, and finding Santuzza alone asks if she also is not going into the church. She says that she wishes to speak with him, and asks him where he has been. He says to Francofonte, but she denies it and says that he has been seen at the entrance of Lola's house. He accuses her of spying upon him, and she tells him that Alfio told her. He is alarmed and asks her to leave him, denying that he still loves Lola. When she reproaches him he spurns her. Lola enters and asks Turiddu if Alfio has passed. When he answers that he does not know, she spies Santuzza and asks her if she is coming to mass. But Santuzza replies that only those who have not sinned can enter the church. Lola feigns humility, and when Turiddu would follow her, bids him remain where he is, and enters the church alone.

Turiddu is very angry with Santuzza and is deaf to her pleadings, casting her upon the ground when she would detain him. After he goes into the church, Santuzza curses him in her wrath. Just then Alfio enters and to him Santuzza tells her story and of his wife's perfidy. Alfio is finally convinced, and though he restrains his anger vows such summary vengeance that Santuzza is alarmed and regrets that she has spoken. They both leave the square, but in different directions. The people come out of the church and Lucia enters her house. Turiddu takes the opportunity to speak to Lola, and asks her if she were going to pass him without speaking. In a reckless mood he invites the people to drink with him. They gather about the tables before the tavern and take up their glasses. Lola and Turiddu secretly drink to their own love and good luck.

Alfio enters and Turiddu offers him a full glass. He refuses it, saying that it might be poison. Lola is overcome at this quarrel and goes out, accompanied by the women. Turiddu then challenges Alfio by biting his ear, according to the Sicilian custom. Having arranged to meet in the garden, Alfio goes out followed by the villagers. Turiddu calls his mother, and asks her blessing, bidding her, should anything happen to him, be a mother to Santuzza, whom he has promised to marry. He bids her farewell, half-disclosing, half-concealing the fact that danger threatens him. Lucia, Santuzza, and other women are gathered in the square when the cry is raised that Turiddu has been killed.

CENDRILLON
(*Săn-drēl-yŏn*)
(CINDERELLA)

FRENCH fairy opera, after the story of Cinderella by Charles Perrault. Music by Jules Massenet. Book by Henri Cain. First production, Paris, 1899. The scene is the French fairyland.

CHARACTERS

PANDOLFE ....*Baritone*
THE KING...*Baritone*
PRINCE CHARMING...............................*Soprano*
MADAME DE LA HALTIÈRE....................*Mezzo-Soprano*
CINDERELLA, daughter of Pandolfe.................*Soprano*
THE FAIRY.......................................*Soprano*
NAOMI } daughters of Madame de la Haltière { *Soprano*
DOROTHY }   { *Mezzo-Soprano*

The dean of the faculty, the superintendent of players, the prime minister, a herald, servants, courtesans, doctors, ministers, lords and ladies, and six spirits.

ACT I. In a large room in his home, by the side of the fireplace, Pandolfe sits lamenting the incessant tumult in which his second wife and his two step-daughters keep his home, and deploring his own state, and that of his daughter Cinderella. Madame his wife and her two daughters, who are nearly past the marriageable age and are anxious to obtain husbands, enter and soon with Pandolfe start for the ball. Cinderella comes in and sits down by the hearth. She laments the drudgery she has to do, and wearily falls asleep. She dreams by the fire of the scenes she would like to shine in. Then fairies appear, marshaled by the Fairy Godmother, and all together they make her a fine dress out of moonbeams, and then awaken her. They start her off for the great ball dressed in her shiny robe, in a coach with attendants, and tell her that promptly upon the stroke of twelve o'clock she is to return.

ACT II. The prince sits upon his throne, silent and disconsolate because he has no sweetheart. His court enters and dancers come, and all seek to divert him, but he pays no heed. The king is distressed over the indisposition of his son. Even the arrival of the guests for the ball, among whom are Madame de la Haltière and her two daughters, fails to cheer or even impress him. Suddenly, to the sound of fairy music, Cinderella enters. She and the prince stand agaze at each other. They talk together and prove to be great companions. Finally they tell each other their love. Suddenly, upon the stroke of midnight, she runs off, and the prince has nothing left but her glass slipper to tell him that she is real.

ACT III. Cinderella is home again and laments that she has lost her slipper. She goes into her room as the rest of the family of Pandolfe come in. They are excitedly discussing a strange young woman who appeared at the ball and talked with the prince. Cinderella enters and to her questions they relate the event with increasing indignation against the unknown one, who has spoiled their plans of impressing the prince. Cinderella is quite overcome by their hatred of this intruder and their anger, which they vent upon her father. He takes her in his arms and tells them to stop their noise. The three women go to their rooms in hysterical indignation at him, as he drives them out. He thinks that he has done a great wrong to Cinderella in obeying his ambitious wife and coming to the court, and promises her to take her back again to their quiet country place, where they will live in peace together away from the others. After her father goes out,

Cinderella is still distressed, and determines to go away alone that her father may not be burdened by her misery. She grieves because she will never see the prince again, and because she must leave her home for her father's sake. She goes around the room saying good-bye to the different pieces of furniture. Then, although it is thundering and lightening, she goes out into the night.

Under an oak over which the fairies preside, in a land full of flowers, Cinderella and the Prince Charming come, each without seeing the other, and address their prayers to the Fairy. Cinderella asks for pardon that she has caused her father such pain, and the prince begs the Fairy to relieve his pain because his happiness in an instant vanished. Cinderella hears his prayer and thinks his misery greater than her own, so she prays for him. At last they recognize each other's voices and then the Fairy gives them power to see each other. As they are rejoicing in being together again, a magic sleep falls upon them, into which they are lulled by the voices of spirits.

Act IV. On a spring morning Pandolfe comes upon Cinderella sleeping. As she awakens she asks if it is all a dream, and he tells her that she has been talking in her sleep of Prince Charming, whom she has never seen. A chorus of young girls' voices is heard greeting Cinderella as Pandolfe brings her back to her home. They are in the garden when Madame de la Haltière enters, saying that she and her two daughters are summoned by the king. The herald is heard proclaiming that the prince will receive all princesses in order to find out to whom belongs a glass slipper. Cinderella is jubilant to find her dream indeed true.

At the palace the prince beholds the assembled princesses and announces that he does not see the one he desires among them. Then the Fairy interposes, and Cinderella stands before him. They greet each other rapturously, and the assembled people rejoice to see their prince restored to joy. At this point Pandolfe, Madame de la Haltière, and her two daughters enter, and all greet Cinderella tenderly, especially Madame de la Haltière.

THE CHIMES OF NORMANDY
(LES CLOCHES DE CORNEVILLE)
(SOMETIMES TRANSLATED, THE BELLS OF CORNEVILLE)

FRENCH sentimental grand opera. Music by Robert Planquette. Book by Louis François Nicolaie ("Clairville") and Charles Gabet. First production, Paris, 1877. The scene is Corneville, an old village in Normandy, France, during the reign of Louis XV, in the seventeenth century.

CHARACTERS

HENRY DE VILLEROI, Marquis of Corneville..........*Baritone*
GASPARD, a miser...................................*Bass*
JEAN GRENICHEUX, a young fisherman................*Tenor*
THE SHERIFF.......................................*Bass*
GERMAINE, the ward of Gaspard, daughter of the proscribed nobleman, Count de Lucenay....*Mezzo-Soprano*
SERPOLETTE, a vain, madcap girl..................*Soprano*

Four young women, the village registrar, an assessor, a notary, villagers, and attendants of the marquis.

Henry, who by the exile of his father has been absent from his ancestral home since childhood, returns while a fair is in progress in the village near his castle.

ACT I. A large company of peasants, both men and women, are gathered in the great square of the village of Corneville. The news is passed around that Gaspard has pledged Germaine in marriage to the old and pompous sheriff, and that Germaine had given her word, because he claims to have saved her from drowning, to the young fisherman, Jean Grenicheux, although he had previously been keeping company with Serpolette. The latter enters, and, catching her name, taunts each of the gossipers in turn until she has enraged them, then goes out. The people go off to the dance. After the registrar, assessor, notary, and other village functionaries come and make announcements concerning the fair, Gaspard and the sheriff enter. There is some friction between them because the marriage with Germaine does not come off promptly, and the sheriff accuses Gaspard of having mismanaged the estate of the absent marquis. Gaspard repudiates the charge and promises to hasten the marriage.

Germaine and Jean Grenicheux come upon the scene as the two old men leave, and Germaine, although she declares she feels no affection for the fisherman, promises to be true to the pledge she made when she first found that she owed her life to him, and marry him. They go off to join the others at the dance. Soon the marquis, dressed in the costume of a Mexican, enters with a crowd of villagers, and announces that he wishes to hire servants to help him open his castle. Germaine, being struck by his appearance, as he with hers, conceives the idea of hiring herself out into service for six months, that she may escape the hated marriage with the sheriff or with Jean, and Gaspard's harshness as well. Jean follows suit, that he may be near Germaine, as does Serpolette, that she may be near Jean.

ACT II. To the castle the marquis has come with his servants to take possession. He is first of all intent on discovering the reason why the castle has been reputed to be haunted for many years. So, although the servants, except Germaine, are very fearful, especially Jean, he explores the halls of the castle and comes here and there upon traces of the intruders, which he is not inclined to consider ghostly. Some one is heard approaching, so he retires with the others to an adjoining hall, leaving Jean, encased in a suit of armor, to watch and face the ghost. Gaspard, who seems not to be aware of the return of the marquis, now stealthily enters. He makes use of a sheet to simulate a ghost, draws the armored Jean upon a wheeled pedestal before a lighted window, that any villager who happens to be looking may be frightened away from the castle, and eventually comes to his pile of gold, which he has stored there. The marquis and his attendants enter, the armored fisherman moves, and Gaspard, taking them for the ghosts he has pretended to evoke, is wild with terror. Just at the height of his frenzy the bells of the castle ring out—bells that were never to ring again until the marquis should return—and in his terror he becomes insane.

Act III. In the banquet hall of the castle a grande fête is being given in honor of the return of the marquis. All the villagers are invited. Serpolette arrives, dressed as a marchioness and with a retinue, some papers having been found in the castle which indicate that a marchioness, daughter of the Count de Lucenay, was lost, and she having claimed the title and given apparent proofs of her right. She is, therefore, the heiress of all Gaspard's long-hoarded wealth. During the festivities the old man, who has been demented ever since the return of the marquis, suddenly recovers his reason, and when he learns that Serpolette's claim is based upon the date on which he found her, a babe, in the fields, he denies that she is anything but a peasant, and proves that Germaine is the true marchioness. The marquis, who has been all along wooing Germaine, and to whom she would not listen because she would not let him marry a servant, is now rejoiced that her sole cause of opposition is removed; and the bells of the castle ring out the happy news of their betrothal, bringing to Gaspard no longer fear but great satisfaction.

LE CID
(*Ler Sĭd*)
(THE CID)

FRENCH sentimental grand opera, founded equally upon the Spanish drama of Guillen de Castro and the French tragedy of Corneille, both of the same title as the opera. Music by Jules Massenet. Book by Adolphe d'Ennery, Louis Gallet, and Edouard Blau. First production, Paris, 1885. The scene is Burgos, Spain, and the time is the eleventh century.

CHARACTERS

RODRIGO, the Cid, the national hero of Spain..........*Tenor*
DON DIEGO, father of Rodrigo........................*Bass*
THE KING..*Baritone*
COUNT DE GORMAS..................................*Bass*
ST. JAMES DE COMPOSTELLA.......................*Baritone*
CHIMÈNE, daughter of Count de Gormas...........*Soprano*
THE INFANTA....................................*Soprano*

A Moorish envoy, knights and ladies of the court, bishops, priests, monks, captains, soldiers, and the populace.

ACT I. In the castle of Count de Gormas the count and a few knights, his political friends, are assembled, when they hear the trumpet summoning them into the presence of the king. That day the young Don Rodrigo is to be knighted, not for his yet untried prowess, but for the distinguished services of his father, Don Diego. The friends of Count de Gormas say that he also should receive some reward for his services to the Crown, and suggest that probably the position of preceptor to the prince will be given him. They go out and the count, left alone, is found by his daughter, Chimène, who confesses to him that she loves Rodrigo. De Gormas is pleased with his daughter's choice, and leaves to join the knights. Chimène is rejoicing in her father's approval when the infanta is announced. She enters and comments upon Chimène's happy face, confiding that she herself is far from happy because she loves one beneath her rank, whom she can never marry. The fact is soon disclosed that they both love Rodrigo, but the infanta generously reassures Chimène by saying that, as she cannot marry him herself, she will do all she can to hasten Chimène's marriage.

In the cloister leading from the royal palace to one of the entrances of the cathedral the king, the nobles, and the people, jubilant because of a victory over the Moors, are assembled. The king announces the honor to be conferred upon Rodrigo because of the services to the Crown of his father. When Don Diego starts to kneel before his sovereign the latter bids him take a place at his side. Rodrigo, who has been keeping his knightly vigil within the church, is summoned and in the presence of the court and the people is knighted. He pledges allegiance to his God, his king, and the church, and, receiving the accolade, is invested with the order of the patron saint of Spain, St. James of Compostella. The people join in prayers that he may be faithful to his vow, and follow him as he goes into the church to pray.

The king, alone with the nobles, tells Don Diego that he has only repaid in part his services, and appoints him preceptor to his son. The friends of Count de Gormas protest, but the king will brook no criticism and reënters his palace. Don Diego offers to shake hands with the count, and though the latter refuses, he further shows his friendliness by begging of him the hand of his daughter to bestow it upon the young knight. Still the count wrathfully refuses, and in spite of Don Diego's tolerance, the quarrel grows until Count de Gormas has answered Don Diego with a blow. Don Diego, thus forced to fight, challenges the count. The latter speedily disarms the aged knight, and he and his friends tauntingly leave the old man in shame and disgrace. As he lingers he hears Rodrigo's voice taking the oath in the church, and remembers that he has one young and strong who will avenge him. As Rodrigo comes from the cathedral Don Diego meets him, and tells him the insult he has suffered and at whose hands. Rodrigo is horrified to realize that he must avenge his father at the sacrifice of his love, and as Chimène comes from the church and goes away, he is torn with love and sorrow. But Rodrigo assures his father that he shall not long stay disgraced, and solemnly swears to avenge him.

ACT II. Along a street of Burgos, upon which opens the principal door of the palace of Count de Gormas, comes Rodrigo, weighed down with sorrow that he must kill the father of the girl he loves. He first plans suicide, but remembers his debt to his father and nerves himself to fight. The count himself appears at the door and Rodrigo asks a few words with him. He is haughty and insolent, even when Rodrigo tells him who he is and why he challenges him to fight, but at length draws his sword. He soon finds that his adversary is in earnest and is an able opponent. Finally Rodrigo gains the advantage, and runs his sword through the body of the count. As the latter falls, Rodrigo is overwhelmed with despair. People rush to the scene, and Don Diego, happening along with some friends, points with pride to what his son has done. The body has been borne into the house when Chimène rushes out, seeking the murderer and vowing that she herself will strike him dead. She tells how her father had told her that very morning that she could best please him by loving Rodrigo. Rodrigo, lingering, numb with despair, hears her words, and as she goes from one to another of the bystanders, asking each if he was the one who killed her father, she has only to look at the horror in his face to read her answer.

In the square before the royal palace the people are gathered for a festival, at which the king and the infanta are present, when Chimène rushes in and, throwing herself at the feet of the king, beseeches him to do justice to her father's murderer. The king replies that it was not to be expected that Rodrigo would let the insult to his father pass unavenged. Then Chimène entreats the king, and Don Diego overhears her. He approaches leaning heavily upon his son, and as the people make way they are divided into two factions, those who sympathize with Rodrigo and those who sympathize with Chimène. Don Diego addresses the king, acknowledging that he is the murderer because, had he not been so old and weak, he would himself have taken the count's life in answer to the count's insult. So he begs to be punished in his son's stead, for the latter is young and may yet do great services for the Crown.

Suddenly a herald from the Moorish king, Boabdil, is announced, and he bears a challenge and says that the Moors are advancing to reconquer Andalusia. The king sends the envoy back with a message of contempt, and the people shout their defiance as the Moor goes away. The king in this new emergency reproaches Rodrigo for having killed his best general, but Don Diego offers the services of Rodrigo as leader of the army. The people acclaim him, and when Rodrigo begs to be allowed to serve his country before he dies, the king consents.

Act III. In her chamber Chimène sits alone, lamenting the death of her father and the loss of her lover, when Rodrigo enters, having come to bid her a last farewell. Their hearts are heavy and yet they realize that each has only done his duty. Rodrigo tells Chimène that he intends never to return from battle, and she begs him to come back, but with such laurels that no one will ever remember the past. Overjoyed that she still loves him, Rodrigo goes forth, vowing that he will conquer.

In the camp the soldiers are singing and drinking when Rodrigo enters and rebukes them for their frivolity when they are to go into battle on the morrow. They become alarmed and some advise a retreat, but a handful determine to stand by their leader. Rodrigo tells the fearful ones to go back to the city, returns to his tent, and is bravely contemplating the almost certain disaster of the morrow when St. James appears to him and tells him that the Spanish army will conquer. At daybreak Rodrigo calls upon his men, makes a stirring speech to them, tells them of the vision and the prediction, and leads them into the fight.

ACT IV. In a hall of the royal palace in Granada Don Diego is listening to the story brought back by the men who fled. They report that Rodrigo was killed in the first impetuous rush upon the enemy. Don Diego tells them that such a death is glorious, and when he sees their craven spirits and realizes that they deserted the night before the battle, he drives them from his presence with words of shame.

The infanta and Chimène have overheard the report of Rodrigo's death, and now enter to mingle their tears with those of his father, Chimène confessing that she still loves him. A joyous blare of trumpets interrupts their sorrow and the king enters, telling of a great victory. Don Diego and Chimène rush to the window and see Rodrigo, unwounded, borne home in triumph.

In the courtyard of the palace all the people are gathered to receive the troops. They acclaim Rodrigo as the Cid, or conqueror, and the triumphal procession marches before the king. Rodrigo surrenders his sword to the king and gives God the glory of the victory. The king asks him to name any boon he desires and it shall be granted him. Rodrigo answers that the boon he desires is not within the king's power, so the king turns to Chimène and demands that she decide what shall be the fate of the conqueror. The people await her decree, and hesitatingly she says that while all are indebted to him for his services to the country, it should not be hers to award her father's murderer. Rodrigo steps forward and, drawing his dagger, says that he loves her utterly and devotedly, and will save her the necessity of avenging her father's death by slaying himself. Chimène springs to him and snatches the dagger from his hand, praying her father to forgive her, but acknowledging that she loves Rodrigo and cannot condemn him to death. The king and Don Diego give their approval of the marriage, and the people acclaim their Cid and his love.

CONCHITA
(*Kōn-kēēt'-ah*)

ITALIAN sentimental grand opera, founded upon Pierre Louÿs' "La Femme et le Pantin" ("The Woman and the Puppet"). Music by Riccardo Zandonai. Book by Maurizio Vaucaire and Carlo Zangarini. First production, Milan, 1911. The scene is Seville, Spain, at the present time.

CHARACTERS

DON MATEO DE DIAZ, a wealthy Spanish nobleman	Tenor
CONCHITA PEREZ	Soprano
THE MOTHER OF CONCHITA	Mezzo-Soprano
ANNA, housekeeper to Don Mateo	Soprano

An inspector, an overseer, visitors, cigar-girls, a mother and child, a fruit-seller, a flower-girl, a restaurant waiter, the proprietor of a dance hall, a bull-fighter, two Englishmen, a guide, a lady, a young man, girls, the watch, Enrichetta, Morenito, Gallega, Sipario, a dancer, a sailor, a guitar-player, citizens, and distant voices.

ACT I. Within a cigar factory on a hot August day the women workers are talking about their lovers and teasing each other. Conchita tells of three men who followed her yesterday, exclaiming at her beauty, and says that one of them she loves. Some visitors to the factory then enter the room, and she recognizes one as Don Mateo, the man of whom she had been speaking. He accosts her and says that he will return. After the visitors have gone out the cigar-girls question Conchita, and she tells them that this man saved her from the unpleasant attentions of a soldier in a restaurant some months before. Mateo comes back and asks her when she can see him again. She tells him, when the factory closes. He gives her a gold coin and goes away. Conchita says that with so much money she will no longer work, and bids good-bye for a month to her envious fellow-workers. They watch her from the window and see Mateo join her. Mateo questions her about her life and finds out that she goes daily to the cigar factory to support herself and her mother, who is a very devout woman. She says that they live a simple life together, and invites him home with her. He goes, telling of his great pleasure in meeting her again, and buying some fruit for her mother on the way.

Conchita's mother sits in her armchair in their humble home fingering her rosary as Conchita enters. The girl explains her early return, gives her mother the fruit, and shows her the gold piece, saying that the man who protected her from the soldier gave it to her and is waiting outside. The mother tells her to invite him in, and Mateo enters and introduces himself to her. The mother bids him be seated, and they eat the fruit. In the course of their talk the mother shows a very avaricious spirit, and expresses her desires so plainly that Mateo gives her also a gold coin. When she leaves the room Mateo makes love to Conchita. Later Mateo gives the mother some bank notes and tells her that he loves Conchita. After he has gone Conchita discovers that her mother has taken money from him, and is very angry. She vows that she will go away and never see him again. Her mother asks her how she will live and she replies that she will sing and dance. She goes out, excrating Mateo because he has given money for her love.

ACT II. Conchita is dancing upon the stage of a dance hall and restaurant. Mateo, who has been searching for her for months, enters and seats himself at a table. Conchita spies him and stops dancing, though there is great applause. She goes from table to table and remarks complimentary to her are heard on all sides. Finally she seats herself at the table where Mateo is. He tells her that he has searched everywhere for her, but that he is disgusted to find her among such people. She pretends that it is in her blood to be vulgar, and gives him no satisfaction. When she leaves him Mateo is in despair, but as she starts to go home, he insists on speaking with her. She refuses to listen to him, and seeks to evade him.

By bribing the porter Mateo gains a vantage point outside a window, where he can watch Conchita as she takes part with Morenito in a private dance before the proprietor of the dance hall and a few guests. At last he breaks into the hall, and when the proprietor goes threateningly toward him, Conchita acknowledges that he is known to her and has come to speak with her. The others go out, and Mateo expresses his shame and sorrow at seeing her in such company. He reveals both his love and his jealousy. She reminds him of the day she met him at the factory and how he gave her mother money. He asks her why she was so long silent, and she says it was because she wished to love as others love, to be happy her whole life long, and he had tried to buy her love. Mateo replies that he loves her and will do whatever she wishes. Conchita tells him of her dream of a little house, her very own, where they two could live quietly and happily. Mateo says that he has a quiet little house near a certain wood, to which he never goes. He gives her the key of it and tells her to go there and take possession. Conchita accepts joyously, and playfully plans to be there and when he comes at midnight to open her lattice as to a mysterious lover. He humors her in her fancy and they go out together, pledging themselves to meet the next night.

Act III. In a moonlit street of Seville, near the house that Mateo has given Conchita, two loving couples are fondly bidding each other good-night as Mateo enters. When they leave he goes expectantly to the lattice of his house and calls Conchita. She comes, but is slow to admit him, and puts him off, teasing and provoking him. He grows impatient of listening to her jibes and taunts. At last she hints that she already has a lover, and he is violently jealous. He begs her that she will not deceive him, but she grows more and more distant, and at length actually speaks to "Morenito" within, a name he recalls as that of the man she was dancing with the night before. Frantic now and quite beside himself with rage, he tears his hair, shakes the door, and tries to enter the house, but all in vain. She tauntingly bids him good-bye and responds no more to his cries and imprecations. At last, in a furious passion of despair, he staggers away.

Act IV. The next morning Mateo awakens upon a couch within his own house, where he had flung himself on his return after leaving Conchita. He does not bestir himself, as now he has no desire to live longer. His faithful housekeeper, Anna, tries to arouse him, and when she sets his breakfast before him, he tells her to be gone. He notices in the mirror his worn and haggard face, and the gray hair which has come to him overnight. He cares for nothing, and is in a state of stupor when Anna tells him that there is some one to see him. When Anna goes out Conchita enters unbidden. Mateo's anger stirs at the sight of her, and, without giving any time for apology or explanation beyond her saying that it was all a farce, that neither Morenito nor any one else was with her, and she did it only to test his love, he angrily strikes at her. In passionate remembrance of his suffering he beats and kicks her. Even her curiosity as to the strength of his passion for her is satisfied when at last he stops, and she raises her bruised head from the floor and tells him that she loves him and him only, that she has never loved but him, and will now be his obedient and loving wife. From the wreck of his anger his love for her springs quite restored, and they pledge mutual fidelity.

THE CRICKET ON THE HEARTH
(DAS HEIMCHEN AM HERD)

GERMAN fairy grand opera, founded upon Charles Dickens' story of the same name. Music by Carl Goldmark. Book by A. M. Willner. First production, Vienna, 1896. The scene is a village in England at about the beginning of the nineteenth century.

CHARACTERS

JOHN PEERYBINGLE, postilion	Baritone
EDWARD PLUMMER	Tenor
TACKLETON, toy-manufacturer	Bass
DOT PEERYBINGLE, wife of John	Soprano
MAY FIELDING, worker on toys	Soprano
THE CRICKET, an insect elf	Soprano

Villagers and elves.

ACT I. In the home of John Peerybingle, his wife is sitting before the hearth when a fairy chorus comes in, and the Cricket, the tutelary spirit of the Peerybingle hearth, appears. Dot and the Cricket confer about the expected advent of an heir to the house, but the Cricket and fairies vanish as May Fielding comes in. May laments because her lover, Edward Plummer, has not been heard from for seven years, and says that now she has decided to marry the rich toy-manufacturer, Tackleton, who has promised to provide for her blind foster-father, Caleb. A great flourish of horns is heard and John the postilion enters and fondly greets his wife. There is with him a traveler, who is Edward Plummer disguised as a sailor. Soon John gets the mailbags open and the villagers crowd in while he distributes the mail, Edward being an interested observer of the scene.

ACT II. The happy and very devoted couple, John and Dot, are at supper in the garden of their home, with Edward as their guest. May comes in with Tackleton, as this is the eve of their wedding. Edward displays the curios he has gathered in his travels. As he handles the gifts something he unguardedly says causes the quick-witted Dot to suspect that he is really May's long-lost lover, but she cleverly conceals her knowledge, betraying it only by the look of understanding that passes between her and Edward. Tackleton observes this look and reads into it his own meaning. He takes John aside and tells him that he has observed that the stranger and Dot have a secret understanding. In spite of his effort to arouse John's jealousy, John ridicules the idea, but when he returns later, after Edward and Dot have been left alone together, just in time to see Dot in Edward's arms in her warm welcome of the absent one, his suspicions are thoroughly aroused. Nevertheless, he says nothing to Dot, and it is only when he sits alone before his hearth that he gives way to his jealousy and grief. The Cricket with fairies enters, and they try to console him; and, by the vision of a river from which arises an infant postilion whose resemblance to himself proclaims his sonship, they reveal to him that he is to have an heir.

ACT III. The next day Tackleton appears before John's house, attired for his wedding. Villagers come along and Tackleton, in his vanity and too gay spirits, is made the butt of their jokes. While the bridegroom is thus furnishing entertainment without, May in her bridal finery is within the house with Dot. John and Edward enter, and Edward's identity is disclosed. May finds that she still loves him and the minister performs the marriage ceremony for them, and they depart in the unwitting Tackleton's carriage. John's jealousy dies suddenly, and he and Dot are reunited as she tells him her secret, while the Cricket and the fairies pronounce a songful benediction upon the home.

CRISPINO E LA COMARE
(*Krĭs-pē'-nō ā lah Kō-mah'-rā*)
(THE COBBLER AND THE FAIRY)

ITALIAN comic fairy opera. Music by Luigi and Frederico Ricci. Book by Francesco Maria Piave. First production, Venice, 1850. The scene is laid in Venice in the seventeenth century.

CHARACTERS

CRISPINO TACCHETTO, cobbler........................*Bass*
FABRIZIO, a doctor................................*Baritone*
MIRABOLANO, an apothecary.........................*Bass*
CONTINO DEL FIORE, lover of Lisetta.................*Tenor*
DON ASDRUBALE DI CAPAROTTA, rich Sicilian miser......*Bass*
BORTOLO, mason....................................*Bass*
ANNETTA, wife of Crispino........................*Soprano*
LISETTA, niece and ward of Don Asdrubale..........*Soprano*
THE FAIRY..*Soprano*

Doctors, scholars, and citizens.

ACT I. Crispino, the cobbler, is very poor and his work is not much in demand. His wife, Annetta, sings ballads on the street in order to help support their large family. But there is little money coming in, and the rent is overdue. The unscrupulous landlord, Don Asdrubale, comes demanding that they pay him, and when he has left they are in despair.

Don Asdrubale's ward, Lisetta, has some property, and though she is loved by the young Contino del Fiore, Asdrubale opposes the young man's suit because he does not wish to surrender her dowry.

Again Asdrubale comes to the house of Crispino and demands the rent of the cobbler and his wife. When it is not forthcoming he suggests that if Annetta favor his suit, he will let the rent go. Crispino is driven to desperation by this and, running out frantically, is about to drown himself in a well, when as he looks down into it, he sees a fairy rising from its depths, who commands him to do nothing rash. She bids him relate his difficulties, and when he has finished she hands him a bag of gold, and says that she will make him a renowned doctor and thus end his troubles. She tells him that when a patient comes to him for treatment he must be very sure that she is not present, although only he can see her,—otherwise the patient will die. Perplexed, for he cannot read and thinks himself quite incompetent to be a doctor, Crispino runs home to tell his wife, and to show her the bag of gold and the doctor's sign and gown, which the fairy has given him.

Act II. Before the house of Crispino the people are laughing in derision at the sign the cobbler has hung out and at the thought of Crispino's setting up as a doctor. The other doctors ridicule his pretensions to learning because of his poor Latin. Bortolo, a mason, has had a bad fall, and he is brought to the cobbler-doctor's house for treatment. Crispino first looks everywhere for his good fairy and, not seeing her, then undertakes to do the best he knows how for the unfortunate man. He prescribes a bottle of wine, which he himself then drinks. The treatment is successful and the mason recovers very promptly. The people who before scoffed at him are now convinced, and, placing him upon his cobbler's bench, they lift it to their shoulders and carry him through the streets in triumph, much to the chagrin of the regular doctors.

Act III. Contino persuades Fabrizio, who is in attendance upon Asdrubale, to carry a note to Lisetta for him. As they talk Mirabolano enters. He has had the conventional education for his work, and is highly indignant at the success of

Crispino's quackery. He declares that he will not put up Crispino's prescriptions, but Fabrizio persuades him to refrain from persecuting Crispino as all efforts against him come to naught. Crispino himself enters, and the three argue hotly. Asdrubale is worse and they are summoned to his presence. While the other doctors prescribe, Crispino looks for the fairy and, seeing her, says that Asdrubale is dying. Soon the rich man dies, confirming Crispino's opinion and solving the problem for the lovers.

Crispino has now built a large and beautiful palace on the site of his old shop. Prosperity has changed him. He is harsh and niggardly with Annetta and the children. While he is away Annetta invites some friends to the house and entertains them lavishly. Crispino unexpectedly returns, drives the guests from the house, and is about to break into the room in which Annetta has taken refuge when the fairy appears before him. He is haughty and arrogant even to her. Immediately she sinks into the earth, taking him with her. Down in her abode he comes face to face with two stern personages, Truth and Judgment. He is very much frightened, especially when the fairy shows him numerous vases in which flames are burning and tells him that they are the flames of life. A feebly burning one, almost quite gone out, is his own. Another burning high and bright is that of his wife. The fairy tells him that his time to die has almost come, and she suddenly changes into a specter of death. He is commanded to make his will. Then he begs for one last hour with his family, and as in a mirror sees them gathered together praying for his safety. The vision fades and Crispino falls, senseless with fright at the thought that he is dying. Thereupon he wakes up and finds that he has been asleep in his armchair and that it was all a bad dream. He announces, however, that he is a changed man.

CYRANO
(*Seer′-ah-nō*)

AMERICAN tragic grand opera, after the drama "Cyrano de Bergerac," by Edmond Rostand. Music by Walter Damrosch. Book by W. J. Henderson. First production, New York, 1913. The scene is in France and the time is 1640.

CHARACTERS

Cyrano de Bergerac	*Baritone*
Christian, a lover of Roxane	*Tenor*
Ragueneau, a pastry cook	*Tenor*
DeGuiche, a lover of Roxane	*Bass*
LeBret, a friend of Cyrano	*Bass*
Montfleury, an actor	*Tenor*
Roxane	*Soprano*
Her Duenna	*Alto*
Lise, wife of Ragueneau	*Soprano*

Précieuses, actors, nuns, Gascony cadets, marquises, cavaliers, a musketeer, a flower-girl, apprentices to the pastry-cook, poets, and the people.

Act I. In a large hall of the Hotel de Bourgoyne there is to be a theatrical performance, and the audience is arriving. Cavaliers, marquises, a musketeer, a flower-girl, and pages enter and take places as spectators. Christian and LeBret enter, and the former inquires who is the lady that usually sits in a certain box, and confesses that he has fallen in love with her. LeBret replies that it is Roxane, a cousin of the brave Cyrano de Bergerac, and a lady of notable wit and spirit. Ragueneau enters and, catching the name of Cyrano, tells of his prowess both with wit and sword, and also mentions the unusual size of his nose. Others enter and soon Roxane appears and is surrounded by suitors. To them all she is deaf, but as DeGuiche comes forward, she accepts his escort to her box. The play begins.

Montfleury, who has been forbidden by Cyrano to play for a month because of his lack of skill and also some presumption in regard to Roxane, is declaiming when Cyrano enters and commands him to stop. DeGuiche attempts to withstand Cyrano and insults him by reference to his nose. Cyrano challenges him, and as they fight he makes a ballad and touches his opponent as he ends the refrain. DeGuiche is wounded and goes out. The audience leaves, and Cyrano and LeBret only remain when Roxane with her duenna comes down from her box. She greets the victor and goes out. Cyrano reveals to LeBret that he fought but to win a look from her, and then declares his love, at the same time mentioning the shame he feels at the thought of his own large nose. A message from Roxane is brought, asking for an interview with her cousin, and it is set for the next day at Ragueneau's cook-shop. LeBret goes out but returns immediately, saying that DeGuiche with a hundred men is seeking Cyrano with intent to fight him. Meantime actors and actresses have entered to rehearse upon the stage, and Cyrano invites them all out to see the contest.

Act II. At Ragueneau's pastry shop, which is known as the poets' eating-house, Cyrano, while waiting for Roxane, writes her a letter, telling her of his love for her. When he sees her duenna approaching, he drives the people—mostly hangers-on and apprentices—out of the shop, and orders food for the duenna, which she must eat in the street while he speaks with Roxane. Roxane thanks him for his punishment of DeGuiche and, asking him if he is still the same friendly, elder brother to her that he used to be when they played together as children, starts to tell him her request when she sees that he is wounded. He explains that he has had a fight with some five-score fools. Then she tells him that she

loves a man who has not yet declared his love for her, that he is a Gascony cadet and in Cyrano's company, and, telling him how handsome the man is, asks that he keep him safe from harm. Cyrano finds out that the man is Christian, and makes the promise that he will not let him fight in duels, but will shield him for Roxane's sake. Thus pledged, he sorrowfully destroys his letter.

Roxane has scarcely gone out when the Gascony cadets enter, LeBret and Christian among them, and congratulate Cyrano on his victory. Immediately DeGuiche with attendants comes to announce that, as the chances of war ordain that they shall battle side by side, he will forget the past. When he has gone out, the cadets demand of Cyrano the story of his fight with the hundred men. At one side a cadet informs Christian, in answer to his inquiry, that no one ever dares to mention his nose to Cyrano for every one is aware that there would then be a fight on hand. As Cyrano is tersely relating the incident, Christian proves his bravado by insolently interrupting the story with a reference to Cyrano's nose, and Cyrano learns for the first time that the fine-looking fellow is the man whom Roxane loves. For that reason he passes over the insult, but Christian twice repeats it, and Cyrano orders that the room be cleared. The cadets go out, expecting a serious fight. Cyrano, however, makes advances to Christian, who is amazed to learn from Cyrano that the lady whom he loves is favorably disposed toward him and is expecting a letter from him. Christian confesses that he is a fool, unskilled in speech, and cannot write. Cyrano wishes that he himself had but half the man's beauty, but unselfishly offers to be wit for him and to assist him in winning her. Christian agrees to the compact. The cadets reënter amazed to see Christian and Cyrano unwounded and friendly.

Act III. In the square before Roxane's house music is heard and soon she and her duenna come from the house opposite. Roxane lingers alone at the fountain. DeGuiche comes to say farewell before going to the war, and tells her that the Gascony cadets, including her cousin Cyrano, are in his command. She speaks kindly to him because she fears for Christian, and he, taking advantage of it, tries to embrace her. She sees his spirit of revenge toward Cyrano and how she can protect Christian, so she tells DeGuiche it will be happy news to Cyrano that he is ordered to the war, and that, if the commander really wishes to take revenge upon him, he will keep Cyrano here at home in inaction while he himself goes. DeGuiche is delighted that she is helping him, and he plans to pretend to start out, but to leave the Gascony cadets behind and to be in a monastery near by and meet Roxane again in a short time. Roxane goes into her house as he departs, feeling that she has done right in making an appointment with DeGuiche if thereby she may keep Christian safely at home.

Meanwhile Cyrano and Christian enter the square, the former desiring Christian to make sure of the speeches he is to make to Roxane. But Christian is tired of being coached in love-making. Cyrano sees Roxane approaching and goes away. Roxane, expecting to meet DeGuiche, is surprised and delighted to find Christian, who tries to make love to her. He is so stupid in his talk that she becomes impatient and goes into her house. Christian, quite desperate, throws himself on Cyrano's mercy as the latter returns, and Cyrano, relenting, promises to prompt him in a serenade to Roxane. They stand under her window and at Christian's call she appears. So successful is Cyrano's wit, that the quarrel is made up and she suggests that she come out again, but as that would be disastrous, Christian is obliged to urge her not to. When she invites him to ascend to her balcony, Cyrano tells Christian to go take his kiss.

Cyrano, vigilant though sorrowful, hears some one coming and calls Roxane. As she and Christian enter the square a monk approaches with a letter for her. It is from DeGuiche, saying that he will meet her there alone within an hour. Roxane, finding that the priest does not know the contents of the letter, says that it is a command from DeGuiche for her to be married to Christian immediately. She reënters the house with Christian and the monk, leaving Cyrano to meet and detain DeGuiche. As the latter approaches Cyrano falls in front of him as from a great height, and being accosted, gives a most fantastic explanation, which detains DeGuiche the necessary time. Then Cyrano discloses his identity. Roxane and Christian, followed by the monk and the duenna, appear at the door of the house, and Cyrano tells DeGuiche that they are man and wife. DeGuiche angrily commands Christian to say farewell to his wife and go to the war. He hands Christian the order, so there is nothing for the lovers to do but part. Cyrano is secretly delighted, and when Roxane entrusts Christian to his care, he promises that a letter shall be sent her daily.

ACT IV. In the camp of the Gascony cadets at sunrise all are asleep but LeBret, who is on guard, and Cyrano, who enters. LeBret rebukes him for risking his life to send off a letter for another man, but Cyrano tells of his promise, and goes into his tent to write another letter. Christian comes to him there, wishing that he had time to write a last letter before they go into battle. Cyrano hands him one already written and asks him if that will do. Christian discovers a tear upon it, which Cyrano explains by saying that he made himself believe that he was in earnest. He also tells Christian that because Roxane was so eager for letters, he has sent off more than Christian knew about, two a day sometimes. Christian realizes the danger he must have risked to send them, and is looking at him in astonishment, just as a coach, in the service of the king, comes up.

In the presence of DeGuiche and the cadets, drawn up in salute, Roxane, attended by Ragueneau, appears. She has come to see the man she loves, and turns to Christian. Cyrano protests that she must not stay, and DeGuiche announces that within an hour the battle will be where they now stand. Roxane dismisses him and Cyrano goes into his tent. Then Roxane tells Christian that his wonderful letters have revealed to her his spirit and that she loves him doubly now. He protests, but can only break away by asking her to go speak with his comrades, who are about to take the chances of battle. As she goes Cyrano enters, and Christian tells him that it is he whom Roxane loves and not himself. Cyrano replies that then Christian must tell her of their compact and let her choose between them, but Christian rushes off. Roxane enters searching for him, and as she is speaking to Cyrano a shot is heard and Christian's body is brought in. Roxane in her grief flings herself upon it, and draws from his pocket his last passionate letter to her. Cyrano realizes that now more than ever she will love the man she supposes her husband to have been, and that because of his death it is impossible for the real writer of the letters to be declared. Roxane is borne off and Cyrano fights valiantly in the battle, at last falling seriously wounded.

In the garden of a convent several miles distant from the battle-field nuns are gathered praying when Roxane, pale and disheveled, enters with Ragueneau, seeking shelter. The mother superior welcomes her and tells her that already two fugitives are within. As they all go into the convent, Cyrano, sorely wounded, wanders into the garden and seats himself upon a stone bench. Roxane comes out of the convent and, recognizing him, pities his wounded condition, but he speaks of Christian, and she draws forth the last letter of his. Cyrano takes it and at her request begins to read it aloud. Meanwhile night is falling, and though he still keeps on reading Roxane knows that he cannot see the pages. The tones of his voice, his words, stir the remembrance of her past affection for him and his for her. She tells him that she knows he is repeating not reading the letter, and that it must be his. Then she realizes what he has done, and that she has been loving his rival for his wit and virtues. He has strength, however, to deny everything, even that he loves her. He becomes delirious with pain and weakly babbles of past battles, then regains his senses, speaks of his coming death, and rejoices that when his soul enters heaven his soldier's honor will be unstained. So rejoicing and with Roxane's kisses upon his lips he dies.

DÉJANIRE
(*Dā-zhahn-ēēr*)
(DEJANI'-RA)

FRENCH tragic grand opera. Music by Charles Camille Saint-Saëns. Book by Louis Gallet and the composer. First production, Monte Carlo, 1911. The scene is ancient Greece in mythological times.

CHARACTERS
HERCULES .... *Tenor*
PHILOCTETES .... *Baritone*
DEJANIRA .... *Soprano*
IOLE .... *Soprano*
PHENICE .... *Contralto*

Lichas, chief of the Heraclidæ; the Heraclidæ, companions of Hercules; the Œchalians, companions of Iole; the Ætolians, companions of Dejanira.

ACT I. Upon the esplanade of the palace of Hercules, which commands a distant view of the Acropolis, the Heraclidæ are recounting the prowess of their prince, Hercules, son of Jupiter and the mortal Alcmene. They tell how he has conquered the tyrant Eurytos and brought back captive his beautiful daughter, Iole. A group of Œchalian women cross the esplanade to the women's quarters, followed by their princess, Iole, who is lamenting bitterly the fate of her father and her country, and the lot of herself and her women. Hercules and Philoctetes enter. The hero is telling Philoctetes of the hatred that Juno has for him because of jealousy of his mother, and that now she has inspired in his heart a criminal love for Iole, against which it is hopeless for him to fight. He charges Philoctetes to be the minister of his love to Iole, and also to avert the just anger of his outraged and loyal wife, Dejanira, who awaits his return in Calydon.

Phenice, the aged prophetess, enters with a message from Dejanira. The queen has come to meet her husband and awaits his welcome at the foot of the Acropolis. Hercules bids Phenice to tell Dejanira that a jealous destiny separates them, in spite of his will, and that she must return to Calydon. Phenice asks what monster has arisen to conquer the unconquerable Hercules, and calls upon the avenging gods. In her prophetic vision horrible images rise in frightful darkness, then she hears cries of despair and sees bright and mounting flame. She rushes away in terror.

Hercules and his companions enter the palace, and Philoctetes is left alone. He cries out against his fate,—that he must woo for another the woman he loves. Iole appears at the door of the women's apartments and begs him to save her from her conqueror. But Philoctetes can only say that Hercules is his master, and advise her to submit. She recoils in horror from the thought of her father's murderer, and desires Philoctetes to tell the prince to forget her. As she bids Philoctetes good-bye, she avows her love for him, and they sorrowfully part bemoaning their fate.

Some of the Heraclidæ enter in agitation and gaze off toward the Acropolis. They say that Dejanira, raging like a mænad in delirium, comes shrieking and weeping to the palace. Close upon their words she enters, her hair and clothes in disorder, followed by Phenice and some Ætolian women. Phenice tries to calm Dejanira's cries to Juno, the protector of the home, for vengeance against her faithless husband, by saying that it is Juno who has torn the heart of Hercules with these warring passions. Dejanira relates the wonderful exploits that Hercules has done for her sake, and tells how he mortally wounded the Centaur Nessus when the latter was carrying her off. With words of hate Dejanira disappears within the palace.

ACT II. In an inner court Iole is sitting with her women when Dejanira appears before her. They gaze searchingly at each other, and Iole recognizes the noble wife of Hercules. Dejanira sees that her rival is a woman as worthy as herself, and, liking the fierce pride which Iole shows in her looks and bearing, she tells the maiden that she will take her to Calydon chained to her chariot. As Iole replies that she is not the author of her misfortunes, Hercules enters, terrible in his wrath. He approaches Dejanira silently, and she recoils before him as if frozen with fear and respect. Iole and her attendants go out. Hercules exacts of Dejanira obedience to his command that she return to Calydon, telling her that his destiny is not yet fulfilled and is not that of other men. She says that she will go but that she will take with her the royal captive. He swears she shall not, and bids her fear his wrath. She denounces him and goes angrily away.

Hercules sends for Philoctetes, and demanding Iole's message, orders him to learn what Dejanira intends to do. He summons Iole, and tries to reassure her, saying that his love will destroy all her sorrowful memories. When she replies that love no one can command, he fears he has a rival and seeks to learn his name, but she is silent. Philoctetes enters, and her involuntary greeting arouses the hero's suspicions, and he accuses Philoctetes of perfidy The unhappy man confesses that he loves Iole. She also avows her love for him, and they pledge fidelity to each other. Hercules commands Lichas to cast Philoctetes into prison, and calls upon the gods to help him and upon Juno to have mercy upon him. As he goes out furious the Œchalian women take up his prayer.

ACT III. As Dejanira and Phenice enter the courtyard

the queen is telling her companion how the Centaur Nessus staunched the blood flowing from his wound with a very beautiful robe, and then gave it to her, saying that if ever Hercules' affection should waver from her and she gave him this robe to wear, as soon as the rays of the setting sun struck it his soul would again flame with the fires of love. Iole comes and flings herself at the feet of Dejanira, begging her to save her. She tells her that she and Philoctetes love each other and that he has now been imprisoned. Dejanira promises to take her by hidden roads to Calydon, and all go out to make ready for the journey.

Hercules enters, pale and troubled and not knowing what he should do. Dejanira approaches him, and speaking very gently, bids him farewell as she is going away to leave him to triumph in peace. He is softened by her gentleness, but when she has gone out he remembers the joy in her eyes and suspects her of treachery. Iole, closely veiled and with two maids, crosses the court and he accosts her. She says that she goes to the temple, but he knows that she is taking flight, and says that only Dejanira can leave the city. He tells her that he intends to make her his own, and threatens that unless she submits Philoctetes shall die. She appeals to him in the name of his mother, but he will not listen. Then she consents to be his if he will free Philoctetes. He makes her solemnly swear it, then he goes away triumphant and praising the gods.

Iole still remains prostrate where she has fallen when Dejanira steals in. Iole tells the queen that she cannot go because she has vowed to remain in order that Philoctetes may not die. Philoctetes himself comes in, surprised at his freedom, and when he learns how it was obtained, reproaches her for her weakness, saying that she should have let him die rather than be untrue to their love. Dejanira tells them of the robe of Nessus, which she bids Phenice bring. She gives it to Iole for her to present to Hercules as a wedding gift, as it is a talisman of love. Phenice warns them that the charm may also contain death and that the omens she has read presage it. As they all go out the Œchalian and the Ætolian women unite in calling upon the god of love to fire the soul of Hercules.

Act IV. Before the temple of Jupiter an altar has been erected. The people come in dancing, and Hercules bids them offer many sacrifices that his father Jupiter may bless his marriage. He plays the lyre and sings his homage to Iole. Entering with her companions, she herself bears in her arms a coffer which she presents to Hercules, bidding him to accept her gift and to wear the tunic as a nuptial robe. He takes it and enters the temple, while she remains seated among her women. Dejanira accompanied by Philoctetes and Phenice is among the crowd, rejoicing that her plan is being accomplished.

As the people join in the hymeneal chorus Hercules appears clothed in the enchanted garment, and there is solemn silence as he and Iole approach each other. He leads her to a throne in the midst of the Heraclidæ, then gives the signal for the sacrifices to be offered, and himself throws the incense into the tripod, calling upon Jupiter and praying him to descend in the rays of the setting sun and light the sacrifice upon the altar. The people take up the prayer.

Suddenly as Hercules is pouring the libation, the cup falls and he, placing his hands upon his breast, groans in pain, crying out, "What fire burns my flesh?" He bids his startled companions tear the robe from him or cast him into the sea. Dejanira, seeing the terrible result of her scheming, groans that instead of his being restored to her she has lost him forever. Failing to get any relief from the burning, Hercules mounts upon the altar and calls on Jupiter to deliver him. A bolt of lightning comes from the sky and fires the wood upon the altar. A thick smoke obscures the scene, and when it has dissipated Hercules is seen seated among the gods upon Olympus, purged of the mortal part of his nature.

DJAMILEH
(*Zhăhm-ē-lĕ*)
(OR, THE SLAVE IN LOVE)

FRENCH sentimental light opera. Music by Georges Bizet. Book by Louis Gallet. First production, Paris, 1872. The scene is Cairo, and the setting medieval.

CHARACTERS
DJAMILEH, a beautiful slave................*Mezzo-Soprano*
PRINCE HAROUN, a Turkish nobleman................*Tenor*
SPLENDIANO, secretary to Prince Haroun.............*Tenor*
A SLAVE-DEALER.

In the palace of Haroun at Cairo the Turk and his secretary are conferring. The prince tells his secretary to procure a new slave girl for him as he is about to dismiss his present slave, Djamileh. The secretary asks permission of his master to win her himself, as he has fallen in love with her. Haroun consents, and the secretary goes out. When Djamileh enters Haroun perceives that she is sad, and being questioned she reveals that she loves him. He offers to free her, but even liberty has little attraction for her. He goes out for other amusements, and Splendiano enters. Moved by her sorrow he offers her his hand. She refuses him, and he then tells her that Haroun is about to dismiss her. She is much grieved at this, and at length persuades Splendiano to let her disguise herself as a new slave and be brought to Haroun. She promises to marry the secretary if she fails to make the master love her.

Haroun is receiving the slave-dealer, who has new slave girls for his purchase. The secretary is about to select one, at Haroun's orders, when the slave-dealer asks one to dance.

After a fantastic dance, she is chosen. But Splendiano privately offers to pay the dealer well, and persuades him to let Djamileh exchange clothes with the slave. When Djamileh reveals herself to Haroun and tells him that she loves him more than liberty, and begs him to keep her as his slave, he hesitates, but finally responds to her love and takes her to his heart.

DON GIOVANNI
(*Dohn Jō-vahn'-nē*)
(DON JUAN, OR, THE MARBLE GUEST)

ITALIAN sentimental grand opera, the greatest and most popular of the operas founded on the Spanish drama, "El Burlador de Sevilla y Convirada de Piedra," by Tirso de Molina. Music by Johann Wolfgang Amadeus Mozart, whose masterpiece it is. Book by Lorenzo da Ponte. First production, Prague, 1787. The scene is Seville in the middle of the seventeenth century.

CHARACTERS

DON GIOVANNI, a licentious young nobleman........*Baritone*
DON OCTAVIO, betrothed to Donna Anna............*Tenor*
DON PEDRO, the commandant......................*Bass*
LEPORELLO, servant of Don Giovanni.................*Bass*
MASETTO, a peasant...............................*Bass*
DONNA ANNA, daughter of Don Pedro.............*Soprano*
DONNA ELVIRA, a lady of Burgos, deserted by Don Giovanni,
    Soprano
ZERLINA, betrothed to Masetto....................*Soprano*

Peasants, musicians, guests, servants, dancers, and demons.

ACT I. From the courtyard of the commandant's palace at Seville, by night, the wicked Don Giovanni attempts to enter the apartments of the beautiful Donna Anna. Surprised, she cries for help, and Don Giovanni tries to escape, but the girl pursues him in order to penetrate his disguise. Her father comes to her aid and is fatally wounded by Don Giovanni, who with his servant, Leporello, escapes. Donna Anna, overwhelmed with grief at the death of her father, begs Don Octavio to avenge him.

Don Giovanni and Leporello are at an inn on a lonely road outside the city when a lady comes in a carriage. Don

VICTOR MAUREL
AS "DON GIOVANNI"

Giovanni, ever attentive to a beautiful woman, approaches her deferentially and is confronted by Donna Elvira, whom he has recently deceived and deserted. She denounces him and he is glad to make his escape, leaving Leporello to cover his retreat. Leporello, as shameless as his master is base, taunts the angry woman by reading from a diary a list of Don Giovanni's social conquests. The disclosures he makes horrify Donna Elvira, who departs vowing that she will have vengeance upon the profligate.

Near the palace of Don Giovanni in the suburbs of Seville a rustic wedding party is making merry. Masetto and Zerlina are about to be married. Don Giovanni appears and, laying eyes upon the fascinating Zerlina, plots to win her. He has Leporello take the entire party to the castle for entertainment, but he himself manages to detain Zerlina, offering to fight Masetto when he protests. Flattered by his compliments and attentions, the girl is almost yielding and they are about to go off together when Donna Elvira, who has been watching, surprises the pair and takes Zerlina off with her, leaving Don Giovanni chagrined and confounded. Donna Anna and Don Octavio enter, having come to enlist Don Giovanni's aid in apprehending the murderer of Don Pedro. While he is pledging them his help, Donna Anna recognizes him as her night assailant and her father's murderer by his voice. She says nothing, however, until the gay knight has left them, then she tells Don Octavio. When they have hastened away, Don Giovanni and Leporello enter, and the latter relates how Donna Elvira, taking Zerlina to her friends, attempted to tell them what sort of man Don Giovanni was, but that he succeeded in getting her outside of the gate and in locking it. Their sport over the affair is great and Don Giovanni orders a feast for that very night.

Within the garden of the palace Zerlina, restored to Masetto, is trying to appease his anger, and at length she succeeds. As they leave the garden to go to the dance within the house, Donna Elvira, Donna Anna, and Don Octavio enter, masked and disguised, and pledge themselves to work together for the downfall of the wicked nobleman. Within the ball-room Don Giovanni is still trying to win Zerlina, and his wiles are so successful that at last she goes out with him. Soon her cries for assistance are heard and Masetto and the masked trio rush to her aid, and denounce Don Giovanni for their various grievances, while he with drawn sword defies them and escapes.

Act II. On a moonlit night Don Giovanni and Leporello enter the square before the house of Donna Elvira. The don is eager to make love to a pretty servant maid whom Donna Elvira employs, and is planning how to get the mistress out of the way. As she is sitting at her window he speaks to her, feigning repentance and grief. He and Leporello exchange cloaks and hats, so when she comes down to talk with him, the don makes Leporello meet her. He then raises an outcry that some one is approaching, and the two are frightened into running away. Thereupon Don Giovanni serenades the servant. But Masetto and a group of armed villagers enter, seeking the don, whom they intend to punish for his crimes. He then pretends to be Leporello, and helps them find and seize the supposed don, contriving to escape while they discover that their prisoner is the servant, not the master.

In the cathedral square, where stands the statue of the murdered commandant, Leporello and his master meet and relate to each other their experiences. As they talk the statue speaks to Don Giovanni. Though Leporello is greatly terrified the bravado of the don does not leave him, and he boldly invites the spirit that speaks to dine with him at his castle. Later, in the banquet hall the merrymaking is at its height when a loud knocking is heard. Terror-stricken, the guests witness strange retribution fall upon their debonair host. The commandant appears and strides toward Don Giovanni, who is still fearless and defiant. The spirit takes him by the hand, and together they sink through the opening earth, amid flames, into the arms of demons.

DON PASQUALE
(*Dohn Pahs-quah'-lā*)

ITALIAN comic grand opera. Music by Gaetano Donizetti. Book by Salvatore Cammarano, adapted from his older opera, "Ser Marc' Antonio." First production, Paris, 1843. The scene is Rome at the beginning of the nineteenth century.

CHARACTERS

Don Pasquale, an old bachelor.....................Bass
Doctor Malatesta, his friend...................Baritone
Ernesto, a nephew of Don Pasquale.................Tenor
A Notary...Baritone
Norina, beloved of Ernesto.....................Soprano

Valets, chambermaids, majordomo, dressmaker, and hairdresser.

Act I. Doctor Malatesta has promised to obtain a young and beautiful bride for his bachelor friend, and Don Pasquale is now awaiting his coming. The doctor enters and tells him that he has found just the right lady—his own sister—and Pasquale is so overjoyed that he insists upon seeing her at once. The doctor leaves to get her, and the bachelor muses on how the very thought of love gives him new youth, and how chagrined his nephew will be, whose foolish escapades have made him consider this method of cutting him off from his expected inheritance. Ernesto enters, and again his uncle orders him to cease his attentions to Norina, a young widow of whom the uncle disapproves. As Ernesto refuses, the uncle tells him of his coming marriage, and the nephew, finding himself cut off from his inheritance, vows that he will give up Norina rather than ask her to marry a poor man. Although despairing,

Ernesto makes one last effort to move his uncle by asking him to consult Doctor Malatesta, whom he believes to be his own friend as well, and is dumbfounded to learn that, so far from opposing the move, Malatesta proposed it, and that it is his own sister who is to be the bride.

Norina sits within her home reading a romance when a letter from Ernesto is brought her, in which he tells her that he is disinherited and that therefore he is leaving Rome, and now bids her farewell. As she reads Doctor Malatesta enters, and announces that he has a plan by which they can thwart Don Pasquale and force him to consent to Ernesto's marriage with Norina. She tells him that it is too late, as Ernesto has broken with her and is leaving the city. Doctor Malatesta, however, lays his plan before her and tells her that he will detain Ernesto. He then explains his suggestion to Don Pasquale that he marry, and asks Norina to go through a mock marriage. Norina is delighted with the scheme, and agrees to assume the part of a young and simple girl who is much flattered by the attentions of the don.

ACT II. In a stately hall of his house Don Pasquale, dressed in youthful wedding garments, is walking up and down awaiting the coming of Malatesta and the bride. As they enter the girl, who is closely veiled, appears frightened at the projected marriage and very reluctant. Reassured by the doctor she goes through the mock ceremony with the pretended notary and the unsuspecting Don Pasquale. The bridegroom is somewhat rash in his generosity, and unprotestingly signs over to her half his property and makes her absolute mistress of his house. Norina (for it is she) is signing the marriage papers as Ernesto enters to bid his uncle farewell. He is amazed to find her posing as the doctor's sister and wedding his uncle, but his protest is silenced by the doctor. Pasquale turns to his bride and, attempting to embrace her, is repulsed. Ernesto incurs his anger by laughing and is ordered from the room. But Norina, now mistress, says that Don Pasquale is too old to dance attendance upon a young wife, so she must have a cavalier, and chooses Ernesto for the post. The bewildered Don Pasquale attempts a protest, but Norina threatens to beat him if he does not keep his place, and he, taken aback and apprehensive, is in a daze of amazement. Malatesta offers him slight consolation, and the erstwhile bachelor stands helplessly by while Norina, in the presence of the servants, discharges whom she will and orders new carriages and new furnishings involving great expense. Ernesto, comprehending Norina's game, is quite reconciled to her, and they embrace behind Don Pasquale's back as Malatesta suggests that he go to bed to recover from his daze.

Act III. In a room in his house, now littered with dresses, furs, and bandboxes, Don Pasquale stands with a large package of bills in his hand. At last he throws them down in despair, and when Norina comes in, dressed to go out and hastening to her carriage, he stops her, forbidding her to go. She boxes his ears, and the poor old man murmurs to himself that there is nothing left for him but to drown himself. When she again starts to go, he tells her not to return, and when she says she will see him in the morning, he murmurs that she will find only a closed door. She drops a note as she goes, which he reads. It is from a lover, making an appointment at the garden gate for that evening. Don Pasquale is about to dash off to find his trusted friend, Malatesta, when the doctor and Ernesto enter. They are discussing the plot and Ernesto goes out, having been charged to be at the rendezvous at the appointed hour. Don Pasquale confides in his brother-in-law that he is sorely unhappy, and tells him his grievances. They decide that they will surprise the guilty lovers, and the injured husband gloats over the expected triumph.

That evening in the garden Ernesto is serenading Norina, who soon joins him. Pasquale and the doctor creep upon them with dark lanterns, but when Pasquale, wild with anger, rushes out he finds only Norina, who says she is out taking the air. Pasquale is in a fury of rage, so Malatesta ends the farce by revealing the plot, saying that Norina is not his sister and proposing that, as the first marriage was not real, Pasquale marry her to Ernesto. The old man is so relieved to find that he is not married to such a wife that he forgives the intriguers, consents to the marriage, and settles an income upon the lovers.

DON QUICHOTTE
(*Dohn Kē-shōt*)

FRENCH serio-comic grand opera, founded on the Spanish romance, "Don Quixote de la Mancha," by Cervantes, as transformed into a French drama by Jacques Le Lorrain. Music by Jules Massenet. Book by Henri Cain. First production, Monte Carlo, 1910. The scene is Spain in the Middle Ages.

CHARACTERS

Don Quichotte	*Bass*
Sancho	*Baritone*
Rodriguez	*Tenor*
Juan	*Tenor*
Pedro (a burlesque)	*Soprano*
Garcias (a burlesque)	*Soprano*
Dulcinea	*Contralto*

Valets, bandits, lords, friends of Dulcinea, ladies, and the people.

Act I. On a festival holiday before the house of Dulcinea in a Spanish town a crowd of people are dancing, drinking, and toasting the fair courtesan. Four lovers approach beneath her balcony and serenade her. As she appears the crowd stops dancing and the lovers greet her. After brief parley with them she reënters the house. Rodriguez and Juan, her two most favored suitors, avow to each other the pains of their love for her. The crowd bursts out in shouts of laughter as Don Quichotte and his squire, Sancho, come riding up.

Don Quichotte, the knight of the rueful countenance, lank in body and limb, grave and kindly in spirit, is clad in a suit of nondescript armor and rides his sorry-looking, lean, and bony Rosinante, while the portly Sancho comes astride his donkey. Don Quichotte modestly wonders how the people know him, and directs Sancho to distribute money to the crowd. They dismount, and when Don Quichotte joins the group of lovers they make fun of him. His gentle manners agree well with his mission to befriend the unfortunate and champion the widow and the orphan. When his exaltedly respectful words show that Dulcinea is to him a model of virtue and the lady of his dreams, they call him a fool, and declare that she herself laughs at him.

As twilight comes on the people go away, still both applauding and laughing at him. He thinks only of Dulcinea, throws a kiss at her window, and calling her name lingers by the balcony. Soon he takes his mandolin and begins to sing and play. Juan approaches unknown to the knight and breaks in upon his song with impertinent questions. They begin to dispute, and, drawing their swords, are about to fight when Don Quichotte picks up his mandolin and says that he has some verses he must sing before he kills his opponent. Dulcinea appears upon her balcony and responds to his song, though she can see neither him nor Juan. When she reënters the house he casts aside his mandolin, picks up his sword, and the fight begins.

Dulcinea enters and separates the combatants. She smilingly asks Don Quichotte if it was he who played and sung so charmingly. She trifles with the two lovers and then at her word Juan goes off. Gravely Don Quichotte woos the lady, revealing to her his love, and asking her hand in marriage. She is interested and amused, and then mockingly tells him that if he would prove his love he must obtain from the bandit Tenebrun a necklace he stole from her.

ACT II. Promptly the next morning Don Quichotte and Sancho start out to seek the robber band. As they ride along

Don Quichotte makes rhymes to his Dulcinea, while Sancho discourses ironically of the discomforts of their common life, and complainingly taunts the knight for his sentimental weakness, warning him of the deceitfulness of women. As they pass through the countryside suddenly there looms up before them in the morning mist a huge revolving windmill. Don Quichotte thinks it is a giant disputing their right to continue on their way, and he charges it. He is knocked from Rosinante and flung down by the whirling planes, but when Sancho goes to his rescue he finds him not seriously injured.

ACT III. As evening draws on the two travelers come upon the robbers in their mountain lair. Sancho hangs back in terror, but Don Quichotte, undaunted, charges into their midst valorously. He is seized and his lance taken from him. They bind him and condemn him to death. When they rail at him he replies in exaltation of soul, and tells them of his work in the world, that of helping the unfortunate. The robbers regard him with wonder and so impressed are they by his nobility of heart and his fortitude that Tenebrun, their chief, is moved to tears. When Don Quichotte tells them his reason for interfering with them,— that he was desirous of restoring to Dulcinea her lost necklace,—the robbers have been so touched by his words that they not only let him depart, but also give him the necklace. They ask his benediction as he goes off.

ACT IV. At the house of Dulcinea all is still gay and festive. She is weary of the empty compliments of her admirers, and somewhat melancholy, though forcing herself to an appearance of gaiety. Unannounced and unexpected enter Don Quichotte and his faithful Sancho. Quichotte presents her with the necklace and so pleased is she to recover it that she seizes and embraces him. Quichotte claims then her pledge, and immediately asks her to marry him, and go away with him to a remote chateau. She, instead of continuing her deception, gently disillusions him. He spares her reproaches, thanks her for telling him the truth, and on his knees again declares his undying love. He is broken-hearted and weeps. The guests deride him, while Sancho, although he cannot think well of this foolish affection for one unworthy, yet extols and faithfully if futilely excuses his master.

Act V. In the depths of a mountain forest, leaning against a tree Don Quichotte lies dying in the moonlight. In his delirium he is dreaming of Dulcinea, sees her face and hears her voice. He awakens to unfulfilled dreams and to the presence of Sancho, gentle and affectionate, and seeking to soothe with honest appreciation his master's wounded spirit. Don Quichotte reminds Sancho that he promised him an island, and says that now he will give him as his bequest the "Island of Dreams." His lance falls from the knight's hand, and his gaunt figure, still in its suit of old armor, stiffens.

LE DONNE CURIOSE
(*Lā Dŏhn′-nā Cōō-rē-ō′-sā*)
(INQUISITIVE WOMEN)

ITALIAN comic grand opera, after a story by Carlo Goldoni. Music by Ermanna Wolf-Ferrari. Book by Luigi Sugana. First production, Munich, 1903. The scene is in Venice, Italy, about the middle of the eighteenth century.

CHARACTERS

OCTAVIO, a rich Venetian	Bass
FLORINDO	Tenor
PANTALONE, a Venetian merchant	Baritone
LELIO } friends of Pantalone	Baritono
LEANDRO }	Tenor
ARLECCHINO, servant to Pantalone	Bass
BEATRICE, wife of Octavio	Mezzo-Soprano
ROSAURA, daughter of Octavio, betrothed to Florindo	Soprano
ELEANORA, wife of Lelio	Soprano
COLOMBINA, Rosaura's maid	Soprano

Members of the club, servants, gondoliers, and the populace.

ACT I. At the Friendship Club, founded by Pantalone, a rich bachelor, several members are gathered, playing chess and checkers, reading the papers, or discussing public questions. They tell of the intense curiosity that their wives or sweethearts have in regard to their doings at the club, because over the door is the sign "No Women Admitted." They plan to dine that evening together to celebrate the approaching marriage of Florindo. As the others go out Pantalone calls Arlecchino and bids him to prepare the feast. He also warns Arlecchino never to smuggle a woman into the clubhouse, and the servant, pretending to be afraid of the sex, swears he will not.

In Octavio's home his wife, Beatrice, and daughter, Rosaura, are expressing their fears as to what goes on at the clubhouse. Beatrice thinks that the men gamble there; Rosaura, being very much in love with Florindo and jealous, thinks that there are women there. Eleanora, the wife of Lelio, who is a chemist, enters and states her opinion that they carry on secret experiments in the transmutation of gold. Colombina, the maid, with whom Arlecchino is in love, enters and tells how a boy who watched the place told her that in a cellar they called up evil spirits by magic rites. Arlecchino runs in to see Colombina a moment, but, seeing Octavio coming home to dinner, he is afraid that the ladies will betray his visits to Colombina. They promise not to on the condition that he tell them what the men do at the club. His non-committal answer arouses their anger, but he makes his escape.

Eleanora goes home, and Colombina and Rosaura leave the room as Octavio enters, having invited Florindo home with him. He complains to his wife that dinner is late, and spends the intervening time in making up his accounts, which Beatrice insists on thinking are gambling accounts. When they have left the room Rosaura, very jealous and suspicious, enters, followed by Florindo. According to tactics in which she has been previously coached by Colombina, she quarrels with Florindo because he will not tell her what goes on at the clubhouse, and when he refuses to let her go there to find out, she pretends to faint. Colombina comes to his assistance when he calls, and manages to increase his distress over Rosaura's condition. After he has left the room Rosaura rapidly recovers from her faint, and they plan the next move in their game.

ACT II. In the house of Lelio his wife, Eleanora, is going through his clothes for evidence and finds only his keys to the club, which she appropriates. He ridicules her suspicion that they are transmuting gold there, and at her questions and her threats that she will find out what is done at the club, he becomes very angry and starts out for the dinner lest he should do her violence.

Octavio is made to spill his cup of coffee, which he and Florindo are having with the family before leaving for the club dinner, and the women assist him to change his coat and thereby purloin his club keys. Rosaura so keeps up her quarrel with Florindo that when he has gone out with Octavio and she is alone, he returns to make his peace with her. To gain it he is obliged to promise not to go to the club that night or ever again, and to give up his keys to her.

Act III. In a Venetian street by the side of the Grand Canal and before the door of the club Pantalone and Arlecchino meet, the latter so weighed down with packages that he cannot open the door himself. Pantalone lets the servant in, and after admiring the view of the beautiful city, goes off. Eleanora comes in a gondola and disembarks. Arlecchino surprises her and she runs away, leaving in the door her husband's key, which she has started to use. As he goes out Colombina, dressed as a man, enters and Beatrice lingers in a side street. They have caught sight of a woman leaving the doorstep and are more than ever determined to penetrate the mystery of the club. Pantalone enters and accosts Colombina, whom he suspects of being a woman in spite of her garb, the keys, and the giving of the password. She says she awaits Octavio. Pantalone snatches her keys and she runs away. Then he, much disgusted with the members of the club who have surrendered their keys, goes in.

Lelio and Octavio enter together, Lelio complaining that he has lost his keys and asking Octavio to let him in. Octavio is very willing, though he chaffs him some. Florindo comes along, asking Octavio to make excuses for him, but he has promised Rosaura that he would not go to the club that night. Meanwhile Octavio finds that he has not the right keys, and asks Florindo for his, but they too are missing. Octavio and Lelio knock at the door and Pantalone appears in bad temper. He shows them the keys that he has gathered up, and each of the men recognizes his own.

Florindo is going moodily off when he hears some one approaching. It proves to be Rosaura with a servant, whom she commands to open the door of the clubhouse. Arlecchino is behind her observing. Florindo discloses himself and snatches the keys from the servant, who runs away. Florindo angrily enters the clubhouse in spite of her protests. As she is about to faint, Arlecchino rushes forward to save her from falling into the canal. He calls for assistance and Eleanora and Beatrice hear and come. Colombina enters just as Beatrice, recognizing Rosaura, also faints. As they revive and recognize each other, Colombina and the three other women try to bribe Arlecchino with kisses, love, money, and a dinner to smuggle them into the clubhouse. When he refuses they attack him, and when they demand his keys he is obliged to give them up.

Within the clubhouse, in an anteroom to the dining-hall, the members are gathered about Pantalone and are drinking his health. As dinner is announced they all go into the large dining-hall, and the women enter the anteroom, whispering together that their confidence in their husbands is restored. They are so eager to peek into the large dining-room that they cause Arlecchino great anxiety. The food seems so good to the men, judging by the zest with which it is eaten, that the women seize some tarts that Arlecchino is about to serve, and eat them all up. While they are taking one last peek apiece to see the wonderful dessert that is being served, they press too hard upon the glass door and it gives way. The men rise from the table in astonishment, and after they have recovered from their surprise at the shower of women, some one strikes up music and a dance takes place in which the women pair off with their husbands and sweethearts, and a general reconciliation is celebrated, even Pantalone not being hard to appease.

ELEKTRA
(*E-lĕk'-trah*)

GERMAN tragic grand opera. Music by Richard Strauss. Book by Hugo von Hofmannstahl. First production, Dresden, 1909. The scene is laid at Mycenæ in the Greece of antiquity.

CHARACTERS

ÆGISTHUS, husband of Clytemnestra	Tenor
ORESTES, brother of Electra and Chrysothemis	Baritone
CLYTEMNESTRA	Mezzo-Soprano
ELECTRA } daughters of Clytemnestra and	Soprano
CHRYSOTHEMIS } the murdered King Agamemnon	Soprano

The preceptor of Orestes, a confidant, a train-bearer, an overseer of servants, five serving women, other servants, both men and women, old and young.

In an inner courtyard of the palace of the late King Agamemnon servants are gathered talking about the way in which Electra lies sighing and groaning over the death of her father and fostering hatred of his murderers. Electra, clad in mourning, passes through the courtyard at one side. At last the discussion of the servants becomes so noisy that the overseer drives them with his whip into their quarters.

Electra reënters. In her loneliness and despair she calls for her father's shade to appear to her, and she dwells with sinister gloating upon the thought that many victims shall be sacrificed at his tomb. Her ecstasy of hate and revenge increases as she imagines the high-piled corpses over which she will step at his death-dance. Her sister, Chrysothemis, enters and tells Electra that their mother, Clytemnestra, and her craven husband, Ægisthus, have decided to imprison

Electra. Then the grief-wild daughter begs her sister to join her in the scheme for revenge. But revenge is far from the spirit of Chrysothemis. She longs for a woman's joys, the happiness of wifehood and motherhood. She begs her sister to refrain from plotting, but Electra, not relenting in her purpose, denounces her sister's softness and renews her vows of vengeance. They are interrupted by the approach of their mother.

Clytemnestra speaks with her confidant and her train-bearer regarding Electra, whom they watch from a window of the palace before entering the courtyard. They would detain the queen, but she, suspicious of them as well as of Electra, comes to speak with her daughter. She says that her nights are horrid with evil dreams and asks Electra if she knows no remedy for such. While she relates her dreams at length and then in her terror says she will sacrifice anything to appease the gods, Electra patiently listens and finally draws from the queen the virtual admission that she murdered her husband, King Agamemnon. Thereupon Electra adds immeasurably to the queen's horror by depicting the vengeance of the gods of which she herself exults to be the instrument.

While Electra's fury against her mother is at its height, the confidant rushes in and whispers to the queen that her plot to kill her son, Orestes, has succeeded. The queen, exceedingly joyful at having the menace of his presence removed, leaves Electra stupefied at the change in her. Then Chrysothemis enters and tells Electra of their brother's death. She cannot at first believe the news, but when she is convinced she again pleads with her sister to join her in killing their mother and her lover. But Chrysothemis, although Electra promises her anything in payment, cannot bring herself to countenance the deed. Then Electra curses her, and in a rage of hate claws at the earth of the courtyard in an effort to dig up with her hands the murderous axe.

A stranger enters and she pauses in her work. Cautiously he discloses his identity to her, for it is none other than Orestes, who has caused the rumor of his death to be circulated in order to throw his mother off her guard. Then Electra tells him of their mother's admissions, and Orestes, nerved to redoubled fury by the account, hastens into the palace. Electra is now beside herself, and rushes to and fro before the door. A shriek is heard within and the serving women run to discover the cause. Ægisthus, also aroused, passes through the courtyard on his way in, and Electra mockingly treats him with deference as the new king. Orestes meets him just beyond the door. They struggle together and the false-hearted king falls, killed by the matricide.

Chrysothemis is heard calling Electra to come to her, as she has discovered that the slayer is Orestes. Electra is in a daze. Her mind, burdened with grief and fired by filial fury for vengeance, can now bear the horror no longer. She starts a triumphant death-dance and calls on all the people to join her. When it reaches its height of fury, she falls lifeless.

ERNANI

(*Ayr-nah'-nē*)

(HERNANI)

ITALIAN tragic grand opera, founded upon Victor Hugo's drama, "Hernani." Music by Giuseppe Verdi. Book by Francesco Maria Piave. First production, Venice, 1844. The scene is Aragon, Aix-la-Chapelle, and Saragossa, about 1519.

CHARACTERS

Don Carlos, King of Spain	*Baritone*
Don Ruy Gomez de Silva, a grandee of Spain	*Bass*
Ernani, a bandit chief	*Tenor*
Don Ricardo, an esquire of the king	*Tenor*
Iago, an esquire of Don Silva	*Bass*
Elvira, betrothed to Don Silva	*Soprano*
Giovanna, maid to Elvira	*Mezzo-Soprano*

Mountaineers, bandits, courtiers, lords and ladies, both Spanish and German, electors, and pages.

John of Aragon, under the name of "Ernani," has become a brigand since his estates were confiscated, and has the camp of his followers in the mountains of Aragon.

Act I. In the mountain fastnesses Ernani's men are in camp, drinking and playing, when their chief appears on a rock above them, looking down in an attitude of melancholy and despair. He tells them that Elvira, who was betrothed to him, is to be married to the aged Don Silva on the morrow. The brigands pledge him their loyalty and assistance in rescuing her that very night. Ernani bursts into a song of praise of the beautiful and loved Elvira, and he and his men go away in the direction of Silva's castle.

Elvira is sitting alone in her apartment at Don Silva's

castle in Saragossa. She is lamenting the near approach of her marriage day, and wondering where Ernani is that he does not come and deliver her. Her ladies-in-waiting enter, bringing her wedding gifts. She receives them graciously, accepting their congratulations with apparent warmth. As they go out she leaves with them, but soon returns.

Meanwhile Don Carlos, who is secretly in love with her, enters. She is alarmed to find him there and begs him to leave her. But the king, when he cannot win her, tries to drag her away by force. She snatches a dagger from Carlos' belt and threatens to kill them both if he does not go. He is about to summon his men when a secret panel opens and Ernani enters. The king recognizes him, and the rivals prepare to fight when suddenly Don Silva enters. He does not recognize the king, but summons his squires and soldiers and turns to Elvira to know what the presence of these two men in her room means. Without giving opportunity for explanation he bitterly reproaches her, and tells her that his heart is cold against her. Then he prepares to fight and demands that the intruders withdraw with him to a suitable place. The king's men enter and salute him, and Don Silva, astounded, is obliged to kneel before his king. He forgives him his intrusion because he is sovereign. Carlos asks Don Silva to let Ernani depart. The latter, though furious to receive any favor from so stained a hand, at Elvira's plea consents to make his escape, while Silva conceals his great wrath toward the king and acts the part of a loyal subject.

ACT II. In a great hall of Don Silva's castle preparations for the wedding are going forward as Elvira, hearing nothing from Ernani, believes the rumor of his death. Silva in rich attire enters, and, while the attending knights and ladies are uttering praise of the beautiful bride and lordly groom,

Iago announces that a holy man comes seeking hospitality. Ernani in the disguise of a pilgrim enters and, once in the presence of Don Silva and Elvira, reveals his identity. He says that his followers are routed and that his enemies are without the castle, so he comes to deliver himself into the hands of his archenemy, Don Silva. But Don Silva respects the obligations of hospitality, and does not fail to protect one who is a guest under his roof.

When it is announced that the king and his army are demanding admittance, Silva hides Ernani in a secret passage and then admits the king. The king demands Ernani, and when Silva refuses to give him up, the castle is searched. He is not found, and the king commands that Silva be tortured in order that they may find out where Ernani is, but Elvira upon her knees begs mercy of the king. He then makes love to her and, promising her a happy future as his queen, departs taking her with him. When they are gone Silva releases Ernani, and handing him a sword tells him to defend himself. But Ernani refuses to fight the man who at the risk of his own has saved his life, and when Silva persists Ernani asks that he may bid Elvira farewell. He learns that she has gone with the king. Ernani stirs Don Silva at once to action against their common foe, that they both may follow and rescue her. He gives Don Silva his own hunting-horn, and says that whenever Don Silva shall demand his life, at the sound of the hunting-horn he will give it up. So they hasten to overtake the king and his troops.

Act III. Within the tomb of Charlemagne at Aix-la-Chapelle the conspirators against the king are about to assemble. Don Carlos enters and conceals himself, in order to witness their meeting. Aware in that solemn place of his own evil deeds, and that the conspirators have just cause for vengeance against him, he is very melancholy; but he resolves that if the electors, who are then in session, shall make him emperor, he will cease his evil deeds and henceforth live nobly. The conspirators enter, denounce the king, and choose the man who shall assassinate him. The choice falls upon Ernani, who exults, now seeing opportunity to avenge the death of his father. But the booming of the cannon announces to the king that he is emperor, and he discloses himself, to the consternation of the conspirators. The electors and courtiers enter at the same moment, and the king reveals the plot and condemns the conspirators to death.

Elvira rushes in, and kneeling before the king, again begs him to show mercy. Acting upon his new resolves, the emperor heeds her request, pardons them all, restores his estates to Ernani, and gives him Elvira to wed. The emperor's magnanimity is joyously acclaimed by all but Don Silva, who is secretly enraged at his rival's good fortune.

Act IV. At Ernani's castle in Aragon the lovers are receiving the homage and congratulations of their attendant knights and ladies. Then as they walk alone upon the terrace, rejoicing in their happiness, the sound of the hunting-horn is heard. Amazed and distressed Ernani recognizes it as his own, and remembers his promise to Don Silva. Silva, obdurate and revengeful, enters, and Elvira pleads with him to spare her husband and not make him fulfill his pledge. But Silva will not listen. Ernani mournfully bids her farewell, and for the honor of his word, stabs himself. As he dies, Elvira, broken-hearted, falls also lifeless upon his body, while Don Silva remorselessly looks on.

EURYANTHE
(*Yew-rĭ-anth′-thā*)

GERMAN sentimental grand opera, founded upon an old French romance, from which one of Boccaccio's tales and Shakespeare's "Cymbeline" are derived, and which was remodeled by Count Tressan in 1780, and translated into German in 1804 by the librettist of the opera, under the title "The History of the Faithful Euryanthe of Savoy." Music by Carl Maria von Weber. Book by Helmine von Chezy. First production, Vienna, 1823. The scene is France at the beginning of the twelfth century.

CHARACTERS

KING LOUIS	*Bass*
ADOLAR, Count of Nevers	*Tenor*
LYSIART, Count of Forest	*Bass*
RUDOLPH, a Knight	*Tenor*
EURYANTHE OF SAVOY	*Soprano*
EGLANTINE OF PUISET	*Soprano*
BERTHA, a Lady	*Soprano*

Ladies, nobles, knights, hunters, and peasants.

ACT I. In a gallery of the royal castle at Préméry a brilliant assembly of ladies and nobles is welcoming the knights returning from war. The ladies crown all the warriors but Adolar and Lysiart, who have drawn apart from the others. When the king learns that Adolar is yearning for his betrothed, Euryanthe, he promises to send to Nevers for her. He then requests Adolar to sing. In his song the young lover celebrates the beauty and the constancy of his lady. The song is warmly applauded, and Adolar is crowned while Lysiart stands by bitterly jealous. Veiling his insult in compliment, Lysiart criticizes the song, speaking sneeringly of woman's faith. Adolar is angered and challenges Lysiart to a duel. Lysiart disdains to fight in a cause so worthless, and taunts the lover by boasting that he himself can readily win from Adolar his sweetheart's love. Adolar insists on fighting, but Lysiart demands instead that Adolar allow Euryanthe's love to be put to the test. Adolar pledges his life, honor, and inheritance against Lysiart's inheritance, and each gives to the king his ring as gauge, while Lysiart swears that he will bring to the king a token of Euryanthe's love.

At the entrance of a vault at Nevers Castle Euryanthe stands in the early evening thinking with love and yearning of Adolar. Eglantine comes upon her and asks her why she lingers there. Euryanthe evades answering, but speaks of Adolar and tells how he came to love her while she was an orphan in a convent. Eglantine, jealous because she had known and loved Adolar before he met Euryanthe, curses them both in her heart. Euryanthe, however, quite unsuspicious of the other's hostility, tells of the great pleasure she has found in her companionship since Adolar has been gone, and offers sympathy and comfort to Eglantine when the latter tells of the sorrows of her life, the destruction of her home and the banishment of her father. But Eglantine pretends to be hurt because Euryanthe does not trust her with her secret reason for visiting this gloomy vault at midnight. Gradually Euryanthe is prevailed upon by the wily Eglantine to prove her trust by confiding in her.

Adolar's sister, Emma, committed suicide by taking poison from an envenomed ring upon the death in battle of her lover. Buried in this vault her spirit still grieves, for her deed has closed the gate of heaven to her. One night she appeared to Adolar and Euryanthe, and told them that nothing could give her rest until the poisoned ring had been bathed in the tears of innocence in utmost suffering and fidelity had rewarded evil with good. Eglantine rejoices that she knows the secret, but Euryanthe is disconsolate that she has violated Adolar's confidence, and fears that retribution will come upon her. The women renew their vows of friendship, and descend to the chapel together. Soon Eglantine rushes back exultant. Now she can obtain the ring and, showing it to Adolar, prove that Euryanthe is untrustworthy and win back his love to herself.

In an open space before the castle Rudolph and Bertha, a knight and a lady of Adolar's household, together with the peasants meet Lysiart and his attendant knights when they come to conduct Euryanthe to the court. Eglantine summons Euryanthe from the tomb, and peasants and knights joyfully greet her. She welcomes Lysiart so graciously that Eglantine wishes Adolar might be there to be stirred with jealousy, and Lysiart thinks he has an easy task before him. But Euryanthe's joy is only because she is going to Adolar, and when Eglantine realizes that, her hatred is increased.

Act II. In the garden of Nevers Castle Lysiart paces in despair. All his efforts to win Euryanthe have been futile and he is passionately in love with her. He plots the death of Adolar, by which only now can he be saved from losing his inheritance as well as Euryanthe. As Eglantine comes rushing in he hides. She has been to the vault and obtained the fateful ring. Lysiart, overhearing her plot against Adolar and Euryanthe's happiness, discloses himself, pledges his hand to her in marriage and these very lands to rule if she will make him the instrument of her revenge and give him the ring. She consents and they make a solemn compact, each gloating over the thought of Adolar's ruin.

In the king's palace Adolar awaits the coming of Euryanthe. He is exultant, for the fact that she comes means that all is well. Euryanthe enters, accompanied by her ladies, and hastens to her lover, who rapturously embraces her. Soon the nobles and the ladies enter, and lastly the king. All greet Euryanthe, and the king receives her respects and shows his high regard for her. As Lysiart also enters and makes obeisance, Euryanthe is seized with foreboding, but both the king and Adolar reassure her. Lysiart claims the lands of Adolar, saying that he took Euryanthe's heart by storm. Euryanthe exclaims that it is a lie, but Lysiart hands her the ring, which he claims she gave him as a pledge of love. She falls on her knees praying for vindication. Adolar charges Lysiart with getting the ring by fraud, but when the latter starts to tell the story of the ring Adolar stops him, tells him to take his lands and inheritance and life itself, for he has won the wager. The nobles and the ladies turn in scorn upon the forsworn Euryanthe, who prays in great anguish of spirit. The king reluctantly grants to Lysiart the land and rule of Adolar. Euryanthe and Adolar go out together, she glad to follow him until death, while the knights wish that they might go with him, and only Lysiart, unsated in his jealousy, wishes to see him die.

Act III. To a rocky mountain gorge lit by the moonlight Adolar and Euryanthe have come in their wanderings. She is weary and asks him to pause there. She beseeches him to speak but one word of pity or tenderness to her. With naked sword in his hand he tells her that she must now end her disgrace in death. She feels no shame, but begs him to take her life if he will not forgive her. As a monstrous serpent approaches she flings herself before it that she may shield Adolar. He does not permit her sacrifice, but fights the serpent and at last kills it. Again she begs him to kill her, but he will not, and turns and leaves her to Heaven's protection.

There are distant sounds of a hunt, and soon the king's party enters. The king sees the slain serpent and the maiden, and promises her aid. Then he recognizes Euryanthe, and it is in reply to his words of reproach that she denies guilt of the sin with which she has been charged. She tells him how she disclosed the secret of the ring to Eglantine. The king, rejoicing in Euryanthe's innocence, promises to vindicate her and restore her to her lover. She springs to her feet and bids them follow where he has gone, but sinks in a swoon and is borne away by the attendants.

In an open space in the village at Nevers Rudolph and Bertha and the villagers are bringing flowers for a bridal as Adolar enters. His visor is down and at first he is not recognized. When he is known the peasants crowd around him with joy and beseech him to lead them, that they may free their land. Touched by their affection he tells them that he believes in their faithfulness, although he can no longer believe in Euryanthe's. They pledge their assured faith that Euryanthe is true. As a bridal procession comes from Nevers Castle he learns that Lysiart and Eglantine are to be married that day. When it passes where Adolar and the villagers stand silently Eglantine, who has been very pale and leaning upon her attendants, is overcome with terror and cries out that the spirit of Emma has arisen from the tomb and is demanding her ring. Adolar, listening to Eglantine's ravings, begins to understand what she did, and stepping forward demands a hearing. Lysiart orders him seized, but when Adolar raises his visor and the members of the wedding party and the soldiers recognize him, they as well as the villagers pledge him their loyalty.

Adolar and Lysiart are about to fight when the king rushes in between them. Adolar tells the king of Euryanthe's innocence, and asks that aid may be sent her speedily as she wanders in the desert alone. The king replies that Euryanthe endured the scorn of all, only blessing her lover, until her heart broke. Eglantine, who has been dumb with terror, hearing the king's words now turns to Adolar and glories in the revenge she has had for his neglect of her. She tells how she herself stole the ring, and so fully vindicates Euryanthe. When she turns upon Lysiart and taunts him with the shame now come upon him, he stabs her and she dies. The king orders the murderer led to execution, and the prisoner and the corpse are both taken away. Adolar prays the king that Lysiart be set free and that he himself be killed because it is he who is most guilty in destroying the one who loved him. He is plunged in despair until the king's attendants come bearing Euryanthe, who has but swooned. She recovers and the lovers fly to each other's arms. Adolar catches a vision of Emma, who is now forgiven of Heaven and restored to her lover.

DER EVANGELIMANN
(*Der Ē-vahn-ghel'-ĭ-mahn*)
(THE EVANGELIST)

GERMAN sentimental grand opera, founded on a story from "The Papers of a Police Commissioner," by Dr. Leopold Florian Meissner. Both music and book by William Kienzl. First production, Berlin, 1895. The scene is Nether Austria in 1820 and Vienna in 1850.

CHARACTERS

FRIEDRICH ENGEL, justiciary in the cloister of St. Othmar, ...Bass
JOHANNES FREUDHOFER, school teacher at St. Othmar, ...Baritone
MATTHIAS FREUDHOFER, younger brother of Johannes, amanuensis .... Tenor
XAVIER ZITTERBART, tailor.......................... Tenor
ANTON SCHNAPPAUF, gun-maker..................... Bass
FRIEDRICH AIBLER, an aged burgher................. Bass
HANS, a country lad............................... Tenor
MARTHA, niece and ward of Friedrich Engel...... Soprano
MAGDALENA, friend of Martha....................... Alto
MRS. AIBLER, wife of Friedrich Aibler........ Mezzo-Soprano
MRS. HUBER..................................... Soprano

Voices of the night-watchman and the skittle-boy, a woman ragpicker, a boy, an old organ-grinder, a Benedictine, the abbot, citizens, peasants, servants, and children.

ACT I. In the Benedictine cloister of St. Othmar dwell two brothers; the older, Johannes, a teacher in the school, is a hypocrite and scoundrel, while the younger, Matthias, an amanuensis to the officials of the cloister, is a frank, open-hearted young man. Both of the brothers are much attached to Martha, the niece and ward of Friedrich Engel. She is in love with Matthias, and unmistakably shows her dislike and scorn of Johannes when he makes advances to her. When he finds that it is his own brother whom she loves and who loves her, he is fired with bitter jealousy. He goes to her guardian, who is sufficiently influential with the administration of the cloister to bring about the dismissal of Matthias from his position as amanuensis. The angry guardian does not stop there, but demands that he be sent from the cloister.

When the lovers find that the secret of their love is known and that Matthias is being sent away because of it, they plan a final meeting by night in an old arbor which was part of the cloister buildings. As twilight deepens the country people are gathered at the hostelry near the cloister for their evening recreation. They are drinking wine, gossiping, and bowling. The lovers steal away to their tryst.

Johannes, who has spied on their movements, himself witnesses their meeting, hears the frank declaration of their love for each other and their vows of fidelity though separated. Frantically he realizes that the girl's affections are lost to him, and fiercely determines to ruin his brother. He sets fire to a large barn belonging to the cloister, near the spot where the lovers are lingering. When the fire is discovered Matthias is caught in the immediate vicinity. He is brought to trial. When Friedrich Engel testifies how much cause for spite against the cloister administration the young man had, and accuses him of setting the fire in revenge, he is convicted of the crime. Only Johannes, who villainously aids in the conviction, Martha, and her friend and confidant, Magdalena, know of Matthias' innocence. In spite of the distress of the pretty and loving Martha, the legal action takes its course, and Matthias is sentenced to twenty years in state's prison.

Act II. Thirty years later in a street of Vienna an "evangelist," or one of a class of mendicants who read aloud portions of the Gospels to the crowds, or teach Scripture to the children, for whatever alms may be given them, comes upon a group of children who are playing around a linden tree and dancing to the music of a street piano. Near them sits Magdalena, a kindly and capable woman now middle-aged, who nurses the sick. The mendicant preacher approaches the children, engages them in conversation, and with interested and approving mothers near, reads to them a portion of the Gospel of Matthew. He reads to the children the verse, "Blessed are they which are persecuted for righteousness' sake, for theirs is the kingdom of Heaven," and leads them in singing some hymns.

As Magdalena watches the scene she recognizes in the old and dispirited man in his somewhat clerical garb the young and ardent Matthias. He also recognizes her as the friend of the girl he loved, and inquires with a trace of his old passionate fondness for Martha. Magdalena can only tell him that soon after he was taken away by the officers, Martha in grief and despair jumped into the Danube and was drowned. Though hope of seeing her had long since died, yet he is shocked by the news,—as is Magdalena when he tells her that for twenty years he has lain in prison for a crime of which he was innocent.

Within a room of the house before which Matthias had been reading and singing with the children lies an old man dying. The incurable disease from which he suffers gives him more peace than the remorse that is in his soul. Something in the tones of the voice of the wandering preacher stirs the sick man, and he asks his nurse, who is Magdalena, to summon the preacher. The mendicant is brought in, and the sin-haunted invalid relates to him the story of his life, and of his setting fire to the barn and permitting his brother to be accused and convicted of his crime.

As he talks the evangelist recognizes his brother and learns to whom he owes his life's sorrow. Christian feelings struggle with his natural indignation, and when the sick man gradually recognizes in his confessor the brother whom he has wronged, and begs for his forgiveness, the younger man forgives him. Johannes expires in his arms, while through the triumphant spirit of Matthias ring the words. "Blessed are they which are persecuted for righteousness' sake, for theirs is the kingdom of Heaven."

FAIRYLAND

AMERICAN allegorical grand opera. Music by Horatio Parker. Book by Brian Hooker. First production, Los Angeles, 1915. The scene is a picturesque valley in a hill country of Central Europe, about the thirteenth century. "The action takes place Once Upon a Time and within the interval of a Year and a Day, in the Valley of Shadows, also called the World, which seen in a certain light is also Fairyland."

CHARACTERS

AUBURN, the King, afterward Prince of Fairyland......*Tenor*
CORVAIN, brother of Auburn........................*Bass*
MYRIEL, the Abbess........................*Mezzo-Soprano*
ROSAMUND ....*Soprano*
ROBIN, surnamed Goodfellow, a villager..............*Tenor*

Nuns, men-at-arms, and common folk (the people of the hills, who are also fairies).

ACT I. Early one autumn evening the peasants of a valley village are returning after their day's work in the forests on the hills. As they pass an ivy-covered abbey a young novice, Rosamund, clad in white, comes out on the balcony and gazes afar over the valley. The passers-by pay reverence to her, but she is oblivious of their presence and reaches out her arms as if she longed to escape into the beautiful world. The peasants go on their way and Rosamund still stands gazing, when suddenly she sees in the distance the figure of a horseman. Fascinated by his appearance she leans over the balcony, following him with her eyes and stretching out her arms toward him, then buries her face in her hands. The voices of the peasants die away and the Angelus rings. Rosamund crosses herself and disappears within the convent.

Corvain comes up the path, over a frail bridge crossing a chasm, and pauses before the abbey door. Robin comes from the forest and goes along the other side of the chasm. Corvain hails him arrogantly and asks which way the king went. Robin answers tauntingly, and hints that if the king is absent it is necessary to find him or make some plausible excuse, otherwise men will say that his brother has murdered him for the sake of the crown. Corvain is fiercely angry as Robin goes unconcernedly off.

The nuns are heard chanting in the abbey and soon they come forth, two and two, headed by the abbess and with Rosamund in the rear, all carrying garlands which they lay upon the wayside shrine near the chasm. Corvain, who stands almost in their path, does not make way until the abbess confronts him. When the last of the nuns have re-entered the abbey and Rosamund lingers at the door, Myriel asks Corvain what he does there. He says that he seeks the king, and his contemptuous words reveal the hatred in his heart for his saintly brother. He boasts that if the king is long absent he may himself be king. Myriel scorns the thought, and is about to go into the abbey when Rosamund says that at sunset she saw a very beautiful man in golden armor ride down the valley and into the forest. Myriel rebukes Rosamund for wandering thoughts, but Rosamund defends her impulse to see how beautiful the world is and asks if the glory and the gladness of it are evil. Corvain starts to reply, when the abbess tells Rosamund that she has her answer,—that such as he are those who love the earth. Rosamund murmurs that she has sinned, and as Myriel tells her to go seek forgiveness, she meekly asks where lies the road to Fairyland. Just then Corvain points out Auburn approaching, and the abbess fairly drives the reluctant Rosamund into the abbey.

Auburn is a poet and an idealist, brimming with enthusiasm, and when Corvain asks him who shall have the crown in his absence, he values the rule so little that he is about to bestow it upon Corvain when the abbess interposes. She covets it for the church, while Corvain is so eager that he says he may take life to get it. The righteous scorn of the abbess causes Corvain to retreat across the chasm. At her command Auburn destroys the bridge with his sword. Then he offers the crown to Myriel, but with a gesture toward the wayside shrine she goes into the abbey.

Auburn kneels before the shrine holding the crown on high, as Corvain disappears in the darkness. While Auburn is praying that his quest for the meaning of life may be successful, Corvain clambers up from the gulf and creeping stealthily behind him seizes the crown and strikes him senseless. At the same moment the red Rose within the shrine lights up, and Corvain shrinks back before gleaming lights, which appear everywhere as fairy voices are heard singing. At last he flings away the crown and rushes off.

Many fairies enter and the whole place glows with the strange lights that they kindle from the Rose of the shrine. Robin comes in with a great cup in his hands, and standing before the prostrate Auburn, he drinks to the health of the King and Queen of Fairyland, and scatters the last drops of the wine on Auburn's head. He rises and looks about him dazed. Turning to the shrine, which is suddenly illumined, he sees within, not the image of the Virgin, but Rosamund enthroned. She and Auburn look in wonder upon each other, realizing now the beauty and the joy of life, and as they acknowledge their love they know they are in Fairyland. Auburn is seated beside Rosamund, and the fairies crown them King and Queen, while Robin sings the Song of the Rose, and the lovers have their first revelation, which they do not yet quite comprehend, that the Fairyland of the child and the dreamer is one with the idealism of human souls that aspire.

Act II. In the courtyard of his castle Corvain stands dressed in royal splendor. He haughtily grants an audience to Robin and a half dozen miserable-looking peasants. Robin asks justice, and shows how the peasants have been maimed in punishment for petty crimes caused by their hunger, and says that the Abbess Myriel, claiming the land for the church, takes taxes as well as the king. Corvain sends them to the abbess, for he will not release his claim. The peasants are driven out by the men-at-arms as soldiers enter bringing Rosamund, who is footsore and frightened. Corvain recognizes her and dismisses the soldiers. She tells him that she seeks the king in Fairyland. When he tells her that he is king she turns from him and says that she has known the prince of faery in a waking dream and that she will follow and find him or die. He tells her that if the nuns find her she shall surely die, and invites her to stay with him. She looks at him questioningly, for he somewhat resembles his brother, but as he draws her closer she knows instantly that he is not the one she seeks, and repulses him. He makes love to her and when she tries to flee his soldiers appear. She sees that she cannot escape and falls fainting upon a seat. She recalls her glimpse of Fairyland and sings the Song of the Rose as she remembers Robin's singing it.

Robin, hearing, reënters, followed by Auburn, who is dressed as a pilgrim, tattered and disheveled and prematurely aged. She recognizes him at once, and rushes forward as if to throw herself in his arms, but meets only his questioning stare. In pain of soul she sinks at his feet. Auburn asks Robin who she is, and he says it is one who knows him. Auburn claims that he is king there in the palace, but Rosamund murmurs that he is king in Fairyland. At the word Auburn is alert and bids Robin summon his people and he will establish his claim by showing to them the light that burns in the Rose he wears, for it is the Rose of Fairyland. When Robin doubts Auburn's power to make the Rose burn, Rosamund bids him do as the king commands, and he goes out.

Rosamund asks Auburn if he does not remember her, but he, intent upon his thoughts, seats himself and tells of his dream, how he was king in Fairyland and yet that here his people do not recognize him. Rosamund kneels at his feet and tries to make him remember. He tells how the queen sat beside him and on her breast was the Rose of all the World, and how when the abbey bell clanged the fire died from the heart of the Rose, and thunder and lightning broke the vision. As Rosamund raises her eyes and arms to him, the Abbess Myriel, who, dressed in purple and gold and with her train of black-gowned nuns, has entered the palace in search of Rosamund, comes toward them though the two are oblivious of her. A red light gleams for a moment in the Rose that Auburn wears and recognition dawns in his face, only to die out as Myriel towering above them commands "Forbear!" The nuns surround Rosamund that she may not escape, and though Auburn protests, Myriel, who takes him for a holy saint, will not brook his interference. He says that presently he will be king, and withdraws.

Corvain enters followed by his men-at-arms. He laughs as he sees that Rosamund is a prisoner. When Myriel says that she came only to take her and that now they will go, he tells her that Rosamund is beyond her power, and summons his soldiers. Corvain and the abbess face each other for a moment in a silence tense with anger and defiance, then

Auburn with a resumption of his kingly authority advances between them. All are astonished, especially Corvain. He calls his soldiers about him, and Auburn his people. The peasants flock in, a mob threatening violence. Auburn demands his crown but Corvain tries to discredit this stranger, so unlike the old Auburn, and the people begin to doubt. Auburn, perfectly confident, takes the Rose from his breast and holds it up, bidding them watch. The Rose remains unlighted; the fairy power does not come at his incantation. At last Corvain laughs aloud. The people catch up the laughter. The petals of the Rose fall to the ground while Auburn stands holding the empty stem. At length he sits down among the scattered petals and gathers them up, and Rosamund flings herself down beside him and tries to look into his face. The peasants laugh in mockery, ridiculing Auburn and thinking him mad. Rosamund springs up resenting their insults, and drives them back. At length she is face to face with Corvain, who holds out his arms to her. Fear seizes her and she shrinks toward Myriel, who with the nuns departs, taking Rosamund. Auburn still sits crouched by the petals, and Corvain taunts him as he goes out. Auburn murmurs to himself, "I have been king in Fairyland."

ACT III. In an open space in the midst of the village as day dawns Rosamund is seen fastened to a stake, while four soldiers keep guard over her. When the sun rises the abbey bell is heard and Myriel enters, somberly dressed. She approaches Rosamund with sympathy and kindness. Rosamund tells her that the nuns cannot understand the choice she has made, and therefore they destroy her. Myriel strives to understand, and thinks that Rosamund has mistaken human love for spiritual righteousness. But Rosamund says that is not so, that it was not heaven she chose but Fairyland. Myriel offers her life, absolution, and sainthood if she will repent, but Rosamund chooses her dream instead.

Myriel goes away and Auburn approaches stealthily and tries vainly to free Rosamund. The chains that bind her shatter his sword. He tells Rosamund that she shall not die while he lives, though he has no power to release her. When she asks him if he recognizes her, he says that she was the one friend when all people mocked him. He kneels before her and she looks at him happily. Slowly as her hands rest upon his head the memory of the first time he saw her in the shrine comes to him, and he exclaims, "My Queen in Fairyland!" Then they realize that through all life's changes they have seen one light.

It is now broad daylight and the village has awakened. The people wander around and finally gather in the tavern. Soldiers set up two thrones, one on each side, for Corvain and Myriel. Auburn goes among the peasants inciting them to rebellion. When Robin enters Auburn asks him to announce him as the rightful king, and, inspired by Rosamund's faith, Robin thinks well of the idea and asks Auburn to go with him to the tavern. Auburn meets Corvain and his soldiers entering, and thinks rebellion is now impossible. Myriel and her nuns have already entered, and she and Corvain each accuse the other of having murdered the rightful king, Auburn. As Corvain orders his soldiers to seize this pilgrim who claims the throne, Auburn, despairing of the people's support, takes the crozier from Myriel and strikes Corvain down, half stunning him. The soldiers overpower Auburn and chain him to the stake beside Rosamund, then pile fagots about them.

Myriel makes one final appeal to Rosamund, who though Auburn's life too is endangered is still firm and fearless. Corvain also gives Rosamund a last chance, picturing the torment she will endure from the flame. Rosamund turns utterly unshaken, almost amused, to Auburn and tells him that Corvain thinks they are afraid. As Corvain and Myriel return to their thrones muffled shouts of laughter come from the peasants in the tavern, to which the victims listen intently while the fagots are being piled high. As the flames begin to crackle a drinking song from the tavern drowns all other sounds. Rosamund has recognized the fairy music and understands now that it is the common people who are the fairies and that the world is one with her dream.

She bids Auburn listen to the song, but he turns to her, and clutches at the withered Rose at his breast. She slips her hand upon his, and then suddenly the Rose blooms and lights up within. The doors of the tavern fly open and Robin is seen lifting the cup as when he first drank to the King and Queen of Fairyland. As the Rose burns in Auburn's hand the peasants come out of the tavern and change to fairies in the unearthly light. Rosamund is singing the Song of the Rose. Nuns and soldiers give way before the fairies as before a powerful spell. Robin comes and standing before the stake drinks to the health of the King and Queen and throws the last drops upon the fire, which immediately subsides. Their chains fall away and Auburn and Rosamund are surrounded by the fairies, who deck them in costly robes and place them upon the thrones side by side. All join together in the Song of the Rose, which voices their belief that here and now is Fairyland.

FALSTAFF

ITALIAN comic grand opera, after the adventures of Falstaff in Shakespeare's "The Merry Wives of Windsor," supplemented by some passages from his "Henry IV." Music by Giuseppe Verdi. Book by Arrigo Boito. First production, Milan, 1893. The scene is Windsor in the reign of Henry IV, early in the fifteenth century.

CHARACTERS

SIR JOHN FALSTAFF	Baritone
FENTON, a young gentleman	Tenor
FORD, a wealthy burgher	Baritone
DOCTOR CAIUS, a physician	Tenor
BARDOLF } followers of Falstaff	{ Tenor
PISTOL }	{ Bass
MRS. ALICE FORD	Soprano
NANETTA, her daughter	Soprano
MRS. QUICKLY	Contralto
MRS. MEG PAGE	Mezzo-Soprano

Pages, innkeeper, servants, and townspeople.

ACT I. Sir John Falstaff, a portly and conceited knight, who believes himself irresistible to the ladies, is sitting in a room at the Garter Inn at Windsor, writing two love letters, or rather the same letter addressed to two different ladies who have taken his fancy. One is Mrs. Meg Page, the other Mrs. Alice Ford. He asks his followers, Bardolf and Pistol, to deliver the notes, but they both object, so he is obliged to send them by a page. Doctor Caius comes to complain that Bardolf and Pistol have emptied his purse while he slept, and a battle of words takes place to which Falstaff listens with such complacency as to suggest that the contents of the purse repose in his own pockets.

In the garden of the wealthy Ford his wife and daughter,

Mrs. Page, and Mrs. Quickly are gathered. The two recipients of Falstaff's favors compare the letters, and seeing them identical determine to punish him. They send Mrs. Quickly to him with an invitation for him to call. Meanwhile Bardolf and Pistol have come to Ford's house and told him of the intentions of the amorous knight.

ACT II. Falstaff is drinking his favorite sack at the Garter Inn when Mrs. Quickly arrives. She delivers the message and has scarcely gone when Ford, disguised, comes in and, feigning friendship and producing a bottle of wine, succeeds in getting from Falstaff an admission of his engagement with Mrs. Ford, and even of the hour.

At Ford's home the ladies are gathered expectant of Falstaff's coming, and Nanetta confides in her mother that her father is determined to marry her to Doctor Caius, but that she would rather die than marry him. Her mother promises to help her evade her father's choice and attain her own, Fenton. As Falstaff is announced all but Mrs. Ford hide conveniently near. The gay but fat knight is full of honeyed speeches, but is shortly interrupted by Mrs. Quickly's entering to say that Ford is coming in great anger. Falstaff is very much frightened, and when the women suggest that he get into a clothes basket and be there concealed, he willingly does so. The house is searched, but he is not found. While the search is proceeding the sound of a kiss startles the irate Ford, and he removes a screen and finds his blushing daughter in Fenton's arms. Shortly two servants at the women's orders carry the clothes basket to the river and empty out the clothes, giving Falstaff also a salutary ducking.

ACT III. At the Garter Inn Falstaff is recovering from his immersion by drinking sack. Mrs. Quickly comes and says that the basket episode was no fault of Mrs. Ford's and that she would fain see him again. So a midnight meeting in Windsor Forest is agreed upon. When he arrives all the conspirators are present, but hidden and in grotesque disguise. As he greets Mrs. Ford Bardolf gives the signal, and they all fall upon him and pinch and claw and maul him until he, terrified by this proof that the forest is haunted, cries for mercy and they reveal to him who they are and invite him to join their masked revel. Ford promised Doctor Caius that he would give him Nanetta in marriage that night and instructed him to disguise himself as a monk. The ceremony now takes place, Nanetta humbly consenting, and when the masks are removed the monk is found to be Fenton. Ford is reconciled to his daughter's having outwitted him, and all go off to supper in great good spirits.

FAUST

FRENCH tragic grand opera, after Goethe's "Faust." Music by Charles Gounod. Book by Jules Barbier and Michel Carré. First production, Paris, 1859. The scene is a German village in the eighteenth century.

CHARACTERS

FAUST, a philosopher	*Tenor*
MEPHISTOPHELES, the evil one	*Bass*
VALENTINE, brother of Marguerite	*Baritone*
WAGNER, once a student, now a soldier	*Baritone*
SIEBEL, a student	*Soprano*
MARGUERITE, a village girl	*Soprano*
MARTHA SCHWERLEIN, her duenna	*Contralto*

Students, soldiers, villagers, fiends, and angels.

ACT I. The aged Doctor Faust, philosopher and alchemist, who has sought his whole life long to solve the mysteries of life and death, is seated in his library before a table covered with heavy folios and rude scientific apparatus. As his light flickers and goes out he closes his book and going to the window pulls back the curtain and sees that another day is dawning. Full of despair at the futility of his study he is about to mix a vial of poison with which to end his life, when he hears a merry chorus of maids singing of the joys of life and love. The song awakens no response in his heart. As he again lifts the poison to his lips he hears the song of laborers going to their work in the fields. This recalls to him the days of his youth and strength, of his hope in life and trust in God, and at the thought of his wasted years he defiantly calls aloud upon the infernal king. Mephistopheles, the evil one, enters, clad gaily as a cavalier. He obsequiously salutes the terrified Dr. Faust, and offers him youth, fame, and power. Each of these gifts Faust spurns and seeks a way to rid himself of the evil spirit. But the latter craftily insinuates himself into the old man's confidence so that he unburdens his heart, and expresses his longing for youth, the vigor of manhood, and the pleasures of living.

Mephistopheles promises to grant his desires upon one condition,—that Faust shall sign a contract to serve him hereafter as faithfully as he now agrees to serve the doctor. While Faust hesitates, Mephistopheles causes the vision of a beautiful peasant girl to appear. Mephistopheles promises that the maiden shall be his if he will but sign the contract. Faust agrees and signs, and the evil one hands him the cup of poison. He drinks it and is immediately transformed into a young man.

Act II. The people are assembled for a fair in a square before the inn of Bacchus, near the city gates. A group of students are drinking. Soldiers stand about boasting of their conquests in love and war, and attentive to the young women in the company, who bring upon themselves the rebukes of the older women for their frivolity. Among the students Wagner, a former pupil of Faust's but now enlisted in the army, is rallying Siebel, who is greatly in love with Marguerite, a village maiden. Valentine enters, dispirited because his going leaves his sister alone and unprotected. He commends her to Siebel's care, who promises to protect her.

Mephistopheles enters with Faust and speaks lightly the name of Marguerite. Valentine is startled and ready to draw his sword when Mephistopheles notes his palm and prophesies that he will die at the hand of a friend. Revealing more of his sinister knowledge, he tells Wagner that he shall fall in his first engagement, and Siebel that he shall not pluck

© Aimé Dupont

NELLIE MELBA
AS MARGUERITE, IN "FAUST"

a flower but it shall fade. All drink and Mephistopheles, objecting to the poor wine, says he will obtain better. Leaping upon the table, which brings him up to the signboard of the inn—the god Bacchus seated upon a cask—he calls upon the god and proceeds to draw wine from the cask. Again the name of Marguerite is light upon his lips, and Valentine and his friends draw their swords to avenge the insult. Mephistopheles draws with his blade a magic circle, and each assailant as he approaches is baffled and opposed as by a wall. Believing that he is evil and withal powerful, they reverse their swords and present the hilts, each of which is in the form of a cross, and advancing upon him make him shudderingly retreat.

Scarcely have they left the square when Faust and Mephistopheles reappear. Faust is very impatient to be shown the maiden that has been promised him, and Mephistopheles says she will come to them there. Siebel enters and stands waiting for Marguerite's return from church. As she approaches Mephistopheles hails Siebel and engages him in conversation, giving Faust a chance to accost her and offer his arm, which she, a humble peasant girl, considers too great an honor, and refuses. Faust and Mephistopheles follow her as she goes out.

ACT III. Into an enclosed garden before Marguerite's house Siebel enters to serenade her. Thinking to give her a bouquet, he starts to pick the flowers and finds that, because of the spell cast upon his hands by the evil stranger, the flowers wither as he touches them. Disconsolate, he perceives the font of holy water before Marguerite's door, and having dipped his hands therein is purged of the spell. The flowers he now picks lose none of their freshness and he leaves the bouquet where Marguerite will find it. Mean-

revels Mephistopheles has brought Faust, but in the midst of the wild gaiety Faust catches a vision of Marguerite, pale, disheveled, despairing, almost dying, and he takes Mephistopheles aside, reminds him of his promise to serve him, and compels him to take him at once to Marguerite.

To the prison where Marguerite is confined in punishment for the murder of her child, Mephistopheles, having procured the keys, admits Faust while he remains outside keeping guard. Faust falls upon his knees beside the pallet of straw on which the sadly changed Marguerite lies asleep, and calling upon her name, wakens her. She recognizes him joyfully, but her memories and rambling talk, although she is still most affectionate, show him plainly that her mind is deranged. He begs her to come with him and swears that he will save her. She is about to go when she catches a glimpse of Mephistopheles without, and the remembrance of his taunts and dire predictions throws her into a frenzy of fear. She begins frantically to pray and falls upon her knees in a dying state. As she prays the heavens open and a company of angels is heard welcoming the repentant woman. Mephistopheles, with a derisive laugh, sinks with Faust through the earth into a fiery abyss.

LA FAVORITA
(*Lah Fah-vō-rē'-tah*)
(THE KING'S FAVORITE)

ITALIAN tragic grand opera, after the drama "Le Comte de Commingues," by Baculard-Darnaud. Music by Gaetano Donizetti. Book by Alphonse Royer and Jean Gustave Waëz. First production, Paris, 1840. The scene is Castile, Spain, about 1340.

CHARACTERS

ALPHONSO XI, King of Castile.....................*Baritone*
FERDINAND, a young novice of the Convent of St. James of
   Compostella ....*Tenor*
DON GASPAR, the king's minister....................*Tenor*
BALTHAZAR, superior of the Convent of St. James......*Bass*
LEONORA DI GUSMANN, the king's favorite..........*Soprano*
INEZ, her confidant...............................*Soprano*

Courtiers, guards, monks, pilgrims, ladies of the court, and attendants.

ACT I. In the cloister of the monastery of St. James of Compostella, opening on a secluded garden and giving a glimpse of the distant city, Ferdinand, the novice, confesses to Balthazar, the prior, that he has seen a very beautiful woman and has fallen in love with her. Balthazar is greatly troubled and urges the young novice to repent of his sin and give himself wholly up to a life of prayer. His personal affection for Ferdinand makes his sorrow very great when the young man, though he confesses that he does not even know her name, is impelled to forsake the holy life of the cloister and follow her. Balthazar, finding him obstinate, spurns him and tells him to be gone. As Ferdinand goes he turns and stretches out his arms beseechingly toward Balthazar, whom he loves and admires, but the disappointed prior is obdurate and only turns away his head.

In a castle on the island of Leon, where Leonora dwells, Inez, her confidant, is telling the maiden attendants of the love her mistress feels for an unknown youth, whom she saw but once and whose boat now draws near. Having disembarked, he inquires of Inez the name of the lady who sent for him, but she replies that her mistress will disclose all. She and the maidens go away as Leonora enters. The lovers greet each other fondly, but Leonora is fearful lest Ferdinand should discover her name and that she is mistress to the king. She therefore begs of him that he will leave her forever, and places in his hand a parchment which she says will insure his future. Inez tells Leonora that the king has arrived, and the favorite urges her lover's speedy departure. Ferdinand opens the parchment and finds that it is a captain's commission in the army. He is then willing to go that he may win honors for her.

ACT II. The king is walking in the gardens of the Alcazar Palace, which has just been acquired by the crown through the victory of the young captain, Ferdinand, over the Moors. A message comes from his father-in-law, who is none other than Balthazar, the superior of the convent and the head of the powerful Church party, declaring that the wrath of the Pope and the Church will fall upon him if he does not give up Leonora. He is not daunted and as Leonora enters, quite evidently melancholy, he asks her sorrow. She says that she can no longer endure her position at the court and asks that she may leave. She relates how he took her from her father's home, having deceived and betrayed her, how he promised to marry her but did not, and how she lives in sorrow and retirement. Now she only asks that he let her go.

Balthazar enters bringing the mandate of the Pope, and the king, moved to remorse by Leonora's words and his love for her, defies the Pope and the Church and declares that he will wed Leonora. Balthazar solemnly adjures the king that he bring not down upon himself the wrath of God, and when he finds that his words have no effect he turns to the frightened Leonora and denounces her.

Act III. In the royal palace the king is receiving the young but victorious captain. When Ferdinand is asked to name a boon of the king as his reward he requests the hand of the noble lady to whom he owes his distinction, and, not being able to name her, points to Leonora among the court ladies. The king is then jealous and, sorrowfully and gravely spurning her, decrees that they be married within an hour. When he and Ferdinand go out Leonora, left alone, determines that she will tell Ferdinand all about her life and await his judgment. She summons Inez and gives her the message to take in person, then retires to prepare for her wedding. Inez starts to carry out her commission, but on her way is intercepted by the servants of the king.

When all are gathered in the hall of state Leonora enters. She is overjoyed to see Ferdinand, now Count of Zamora, who still regards her lovingly although he already knows her dread secret, she believes. When the ceremony has been performed, the pair are presented to the court, but meet only with coldness and slights. Ferdinand draws his sword in resentment of such treatment as Balthazar enters and demands a hearing. He is told of the wedding, then he announces to Ferdinand that he has married the king's mistress. Ferdinand denounces the king, who in remorse tries to justify himself, but Ferdinand throws down his broken sword and his badge of honor, and leaves. The unhappy Leonora faints, and Balthazar follows Ferdinand.

ACT IV. It is early morning in the cloister of the convent. The heartbroken Ferdinand is about to renew his vows in the presence of the monks, who are assembled to welcome him back. Balthazar urges the prodigal to forget the world and think only of heaven. Ferdinand looks once again at the distant city, then enters the chapel, and at the altar takes the vows renouncing the world forever. He lingers as the others go out, and then turning to go sees that a young novice has fallen before the altar. He starts to assist him and to his amazement and consternation recognizes Leonora. He bids her go, but she begs his mercy, tells him of the undelivered message she sent him, and pleads for forgiveness. The sight of her stirs his love, and he begs her to flee with him and be happy. But she reminds him of the terrible vows he has taken, and tells him that she is dying. Even as she speaks she falls from weakness and privation, and expires.

FIDELIO
(*Fē-dä´-lē-ō*)

(OR, CONJUGAL LOVE)

GERMAN sentimental grand opera, after Bouilly's "Léonore, ou l'Amour conjugal." Music by Ludwig van Beethoven,—his only opera. Book by Joseph Sonnleithner. First production, Vienna, 1805. The scene is the state prison near Seville, Spain, in the eighteenth century

CHARACTERS

DON FERNANDO DE ZELVA, minister	Baritone
DON PIZARRO, governor of the state prison	Baritone
DON FLORESTAN, an imprisoned Spanish nobleman	Tenor
ROCCO, jailer	Bass
JAQUINO, gatekeeper	Tenor
LEONORA, wife of Florestan, known as "Fidelio"	Soprano
MARCELLINA, daughter of Rocco	Soprano

Captain of the guard, a lieutenant, soldiers, prisoners, and people.

For two years Don Florestan has been imprisoned in a subterranean dungeon by his enemy, Don Pizarro, who has given out word that he is dead.

ACT I. In the courtyard of the state prison near Seville Jaquino is on guard and is watching Marcellina, whom he loves, who is working near the door of her father's house. Jaquino is anxious to talk with her, as he wishes to ask her to marry him without further delay. Marcellina, however, is much attached to Fidelio, the young assistant, so puts Jaquino off and welcomes each knock that calls him to the gate. At last impatient with the interruptions, he declares that he will not go until she answers him, but just then Rocco is heard calling him, and he is obliged to respond. In her heart Marcellina is pitying Jaquino, because before Fidelio came she had intended to marry him, but now she is enamored of the latter and makes plans for their home.

Her father and Jaquino come in, and the former is very much disturbed that Fidelio has not yet returned from the city, to which he went on errands. Just then Fidelio enters, burdened by a heavy basket, some fetters, and the dispatch box. Both the jailer and his daughter hasten to relieve the young man of his burden, much to Jaquino's discomfort. Fidelio gives account of his purchases and receives Rocco's approval for his thrifty buying. When Fidelio replies that it was not for the money he cared, both Rocco and Marcellina interpret his remark to mean that it was their favor he sought. Fidelio sees Marcellina's affection and laments that he is obliged to resort to so much deception to gain access to the prisoner Florestan. Especially does he become apprehensive, when Rocco promises soon to give him Marcellina.

Rocco commends thrift to the young people, saying that gold is requisite to happiness. Fidelio replies that perfect trust is better, and intimates that Rocco does not trust him completely or he would permit him to assist in the care of all the prisoners. Rocco says that he is ordered to admit no one, but when Marcellina and Fidelio both urge him to let the latter assist him with all, as he is getting old and soon cannot himself go, he says that he will, to all except one cell. This is the information for which Fidelio has been longing, and adroitly he questions him and finds out that the man so distinguished from the other prisoners seems not to be guilty of any special crime but only to have powerful foes, for he is being subjected to slow starvation. Fidelio's interest and sympathy is so marked that Rocco assures him

© Mishkin

MELANIE KURT
AS "FIDELIO"

that if he is to take up such duties he must harden his heart, and Fidelio promises that he will not falter. The jailer then plans to ask the governor to appoint Fidelio as his assistant.

The governor now enters and Rocco, having sent the young people away, presents him with the dispatch box. The governor is alarmed at a letter which announces that the minister is already on his way to examine the prison, having been told that some prisoners were being held without cause. The governor then realizes that he must kill Florestan at once, who was so long since supposed to be dead. He orders a trumpeter to give notice at the first appearance of a carriage from the city. He hands a large purse to Rocco, whom he summons, and tells him to kill Florestan. But Rocco refuses, and when the governor cannot by any means prevail upon him to do it, he tells him to dig a grave in an old cistern in Florestan's cell and he will himself come and do the deed.

As the governor and Rocco leave the courtyard Fidelio, having overheard the plan in part, passes through. Then Marcellina and Jaquino enter. Jaquino is still trying to persuade her to love him, and as Rocco enters and finds them still disputing, he announces that he is about to give his daughter's hand to Fidelio. Fidelio suggests that it would be well to celebrate this, the day of their betrothal, by giving the prisoners a few minutes' freedom in the open air. He is anxious to find out if Florestan is not among the other prisoners, so is rejoiced when Rocco finally consents to this plan.

Rocco hurries off to obtain the governor's endorsement to Fidelio's appointment. When he returns he tells Fidelio that the governor has consented, but has ordered that both of them go into the dungeon to dig the grave for the unfortunate prisoner. Fidelio grows exceedingly apprehensive, because he does not find Florestan among the prisoners, and so believes he must be the one appointed to die. Fidelio asks if the one for whom the grave is to be made is already dead, and is told that he is not. Rocco offers to do it alone, but Fidelio will not consent to that. Marcellina announces that the governor is very angry that the prisoners have been let out, and Rocco hastens away to appease him. Pizarro appears, wild with wrath, and the prisoners are hastily sent back to their cells.

Act II. In the dungeon Florestan is sitting on a huge stone near the wall to which his chain is fastened. It is cold and dark save for a feeble lamp. He is meditating over his long unjust imprisonment, and is thankful that he is not guilty. He dreams of the past, sees as in a vision his loved wife, Leonora, then exhausted he sinks back unconscious. He is so lying when Fidelio and Rocco enter. They dig the grave, and the anxious Fidelio, who is none other than Leonora, tries to see whether the man is indeed her husband. Florestan recovers consciousness and Rocco goes to him, saying he will have to tell him that he is to die. Florestan's voice discloses to Leonora that it is he, and she sinks down almost fainting on the edge of the grave. When Florestan hears from Rocco's lips the name of the keeper of the fortress he knows that it is his mortal foe and begs Rocco to send word immediately to his wife, Leonora, at Seville.

When Florestan asks for water she, having recovered her strength and courage, brings the pitcher and a crust of bread to Rocco, who gives it to the prisoner. She is so overwhelmed by emotion that both notice it, and Rocco explains that the young man is soon to marry his daughter. Then Florestan beseeches them both that some means be found of restoring him to his wife. The jailer's whistle sounds, and they know that the governor is approaching.

Pizarro enters wrapped in a dark mantle. He orders that the lad be dismissed, and Leonora is forced to retreat, but hides in the shadows close to Florestan. She overhears Pizarro say to himself, as he throws off his mantle, that he must get rid of both the jailers that day. Before Florestan has a chance for defence he tries to stab him with his dagger, but Fidelio flings himself before the prisoner. Pizarro is checked for a moment, then he tries to pull him away. Then a woman's voice tells him that he shall not kill Florestan until he has first killed her, Leonora, his wife. The prisoner exclaims joyously, while both Rocco and Pizarro are forced to admire her spirit. But the governor soon realizes that he must kill them both, and is about to strike again when Leonora presents a pistol at him and threatens to kill him if he moves.

The trumpet call announcing the visit of the minister is heard, and the governor and Rocco hasten away, while Florestan and his faithful wife cling close to each other. Soon Rocco reappears to lead them into the presence of the minister, and says that, as Florestan's name is not among the guilty, he will shortly be released.

In the principal court of the castle the minister is reviewing the prisoners and the officers. He is releasing all state or political prisoners, having an order from the king, who he says is no tyrant. Soon Rocco and Leonora come supporting Florestan. The governor tries to prevent their appearing, but Rocco calls the minister's attention. Recognizing Florestan, who was a valiant and virtuous man and had long been thought dead, the minister is moved with mingled delight and pity. Then Rocco tells the story of Leonora's disguise, of the attack by Pizarro, and how the minister's arrival balked the governor's plans. The minister bids the faithful wife herself remove her husband's chains, and Pizarro when he tries to protest is silenced. The people applaud the wife and Florestan is exceedingly happy, but Leonora notes nothing except that her husband is freed and restored to her. Marcellina, who has been greatly surprised by the turn affairs have taken, meets Jaquino's look in a way that makes him happy, and the rejoicing is general.

THE FLYING DUTCHMAN

(DER FLIEGENDE HOLLAENDER)

GERMAN tragic grand opera, after Heinrich Heine's poetical version of the legend of the Flying Dutchman. Music and book both by Richard Wagner. First production, Dresden, 1843. The scene is a Norwegian fishing village in the eighteenth century.

CHARACTERS

DALAND, a Norwegian sea captain....................*Bass*
THE DUTCHMAN................................*Baritone*
ERIC, a huntsman, a lover of Senta................*Tenor*
DALAND'S STEERSMAN............................*Tenor*
SENTA, daughter of Daland......................*Soprano*
MARY, Senta's nurse............................*Contralto*

Sailors, maidens, hunters, and villagers.

ACT I. Near the shore of the rocky coast of Norway Daland's ship is anchored. The crew furl the sails and Daland, going ashore, climbs a cliff and discovers that his home is only seven miles away. They must wait, however, for a change of wind, and he commands his crew to go below and sleep. The steersman only is on deck, and he has fallen asleep, when a vessel, the *Flying Dutchman,* heaves in sight, approaches the harbor, and drops anchor. The sails of the ship are blood-red, the masts black, and a spectral crew mans the vessel as the Dutchman on her deck gives his orders. In cruises seven years in length he is compelled to sail the sea, which has no dangers for his vessel as he is doomed to perpetual sailing unless he shall be so fortunate as to find a woman who will be true in her love for him until death.

He believes this sole hope is fruitless, but he is now coming ashore to try once again to find such a woman.

Daland, coming on deck, is amazed to see the strange vessel, and as he arouses the steersman and they hail the ship, the Dutchman himself responds and asks if Daland will take him to his home, promising to pay him well. Daland tells him of his family, and when he mentions his daughter, the Dutchman promptly proposes to marry her. As the stranger is evidently a man of great wealth, Daland acquiesces if his daughter consents. As the wind has now changed Daland sails for home, and the Dutchman follows.

ACT II. Within Daland's house a group of maidens are busily spinning. But Senta, his daughter, sits idly dreaming, with her eyes fixed on a picture of the Dutchman that hangs on the wall, and her thoughts on the story of his fruitless effort to pass the Cape of Good Hope, of his rash vow to make the effort forever unless he succeeded, and of the decree that he should roam the seas until some woman would love him faithfully unto death, in search of whom he could land only once in seven years. Forgetting the women about her, Senta sings the ballad and, running to the picture, stretches her arms passionately toward it, praying that Heaven may take pity upon the Dutchman and grant him soon to find the faithful wife. The maidens, alarmed at Senta's fervor, rush out just as Eric enters with the news of the arrival of the *Flying Dutchman*. When the others have gone to the shore to see the ship, Eric reproves Senta for her emotion over the picture, but she will not listen to him, so he leaves.

While she is still alone the Dutchman himself enters, accompanied by Daland. She looks from the stranger to the portrait and then back again. As they silently gaze at each other, Daland goes out unobserved, and the Dutchman approaches her. To him she appears as the woman of his dreams; to her he seems the world-worn traveler who is to be redeemed from eternal sorrow and wandering by a woman's love. He tells her of her father's approval of their marriage and asks her consent. She joyfully yields, and together they rejoice at his deliverance from the curse. Daland reënters and invites the Dutchman to a fête that evening in celebration of the arrival of the Norwegian ship. In his presence they plight their troth, and all are very happy.

Act III. In the bay near Daland's home both vessels are anchored, the one gay with lanterns, the other dark and silent. Maidens bring baskets of food for the crews and, having given to the sailors of Daland's vessel, they approach the other and call out, but there is only silence. When they have left, the sea rises about the Dutchman's vessel and weird lights shine about the ship. The crew appears and begins a chant so sepulchral that the crew of Daland's ship are frightened, and crossing themselves go below. At last the crew of the Dutchman's vessel laugh mockingly and disappear, while the lights die out.

Senta and Eric come to the shore, the man angry with her for he has heard of her engagement to the strange sea captain. He kneels before her, and the Dutchman, entering, is dismayed to see them and to hear the man's impassioned pleading. He believes her to be false, and with a farewell cry that all is lost, starts to go away. The villagers come; both crews are aroused; the Dutchman declares to them all who he is, and that because of Senta's faithlessness he is forever cursed; then he springs upon his ship and as if by magic it sets sail, while the crew chants the weird song.

Senta, terrified yet exultant, breaks from those who would

hold her and, rushing to the highest rock, cries out to the disappearing vessel that she is faithful, and throws herself into the sea. Immediately the ship vanishes into the water, and from the wreckage the forms of Senta and the Dutchman can be seen clasped in each other's arms. Thus the curse is lifted.

LA FORÊT BLEUE
(*Lah Foh-rāi Blur*)
(THE BLUE FOREST)

FRENCH fairy grand opera, founded upon the three fairy tales, "Little Red Riding-Hood," "Hop-o'-my-Thumb," and "Sleeping Beauty," by Charles Perrault. Music by Louis François Marie Aubert. Book by Jacques Chenevière. First productions, Geneva, 1912; Boston, 1913. The scene is fairyland, and the "atmosphere, that of a dream," symbolized by the color blue.

CHARACTERS

PRINCE CHARMING	Tenor
THE FATHER OF HOP-O'-MY-THUMB	Baritone
THE OGRE	Baritone
HOP-O'-MY-THUMB	Soprano
LITTLE RED RIDING-HOOD	Soprano
THE PRINCESS	Soprano
THE FAIRY	Soprano
THE MOTHER OF HOP-O'-MY-THUMB	Contralto
THE MOTHER OF RED RIDING-HOOD	Mezzo-Soprano

A servant, the baker's wife, the brothers of Hop-o'-my-Thumb, fairies, reapers, villagers, spinners, servants, a page, and an equerry.

ACT I. While the stars are twinkling in the darkness just before dawn, the fairies are dancing and singing, and the fairy queen is promising protection to children. As day breaks they disappear and a village square becomes visible, upon which front the homes of little Red Riding-Hood and her mother and the poverty-stricken house of Hop-o'-my-Thumb. A bell sounds and the villagers awaken and appear. The song of reapers going into the harvest fields is heard. At the tavern in the square a waitress pours wine for the reapers before they leave. Red Riding-Hood comes from her house as Hop-o'-my-Thumb enters bringing a titmouse which he has captured. He very gallantly gives it to Red Riding-Hood as a present. Her mother appears and, angry to see them talking together, dismisses Hop.

The baker's wife brings some loaves of bread from her kitchen, and is met by Hop-o'-my-Thumb's father, who asks some of her, but she will not give him any. The father then talks with his wife about their poverty, and tells her that he has decided to take the children into the wood and give them into the keeping of a good fairy he has seen there. Then the father and Hop's brothers disappear in the wood.

When little Red Riding-Hood comes out of her house she has upon her arm a basket of goodies and gives Hop a cake. He starts eagerly to eat it, then recollects himself and decides to follow his father and brothers into the woods, dropping bits of the cake by the way in order to trace his path out. When Hop-o'-my-Thumb and Red Riding-Hood have gone, the Princess, announced by her pages, comes into the village in her coach. She gives the villagers flowers and presents. Prince Charming, wrapped in a dark mantle, mingles with the crowd, attended only by his faithful equerry, to whom he cannot but express the great love for the Princess that is consuming him.

Well does the Princess know the old prophecy that when she shall take a spindle into her hands to spin, she shall prick her finger and thereupon shall immediately fall asleep, only to be awakened by the kiss of a lover. As she is telling the prophecy the Prince approaches and addresses her, offering her his love and his life. She replies graciously, neither accepting nor refusing his devotion.

As the village women bring their spinning-wheels to the doors of their houses and begin their work, the Princess is fascinated by the sight and, undeterred by the prophecy, asks to take a spindle in her hands. As she does so she pricks her finger, and immediately the magic spell falls upon her. Her attendants bear her off fast asleep, while the Prince, much distressed, reproaches the spinners for allowing her to touch a spindle.

Act II. Meanwhile within the forest the father of Hop-o'-my-Thumb has carried out his plan and left the children in the care of the fairies. Hop, who has followed the others, has no means of finding his way back because the birds have eaten the pieces of cake he dropped. The children rush by him, running away from the Ogre who is pursuing them. Hop hides behind a tree and after they have all gone on, he hears the voice of Red Riding-Hood. He joins her, and as they wander about night comes on and they lie down to sleep. The fairies then appear and spread branches over the sleeping children. As their voices die away the Ogre enters growling. Seeing the children he approaches them, when suddenly from out a tree gushes a stream of wine. Of this the monster drinks eagerly, and finally falls down in a drunken stupor. As dawn comes the birds awaken and sing, and the sun floods the forest. The children open their eyes and Red Riding-Hood tells of a beautiful dream she has had. When they espy the Ogre they plan to pull off his seven-league boots and thus prevent him from following them. They do so without awaking him. When he awakens he tries to catch them, but the fairies cast thorns under his feet and fetter him with garlands of leaves, and while the children are dancing about him the trumpets of the Prince and his train are heard, and they enter and take the Ogre captive. The Prince is very sad as he is bemoaning the absent Princess, who has been carried away to an enchanted castle. Suddenly through the trees the walls of the castle are seen, and the Prince hastens off to find his loved one.

Act III. Preceding the Prince and his train Hop-o'-my-Thumb and Red Riding-Hood steal into the castle of the Sleeping Beauty and find her and her attendants all asleep. Soon the Prince appears, and Hop-o'-my-Thumb and Red Riding-Hood stand silently by while he approaches the Princess and, after contemplation of her beauty, kisses her first upon the forehead, then upon the lips. The Princess slowly awakens, and recognizing the Prince greets him graciously and lovingly. At length all the castle is awakened from the magic sleep. The Prince and Princess, and Hop-o'-my-Thumb and Red Riding-Hood, are married, and while the royal pair stay in their castle, the humble villagers go happily through the woods to their home.

FRA DIAVOLO
(*Frah Dē-ah'-vō-lō*)
(OR, THE INN OF TERRACINA)

FRENCH comic grand opera. Music by Daniel François Esprit Auber. Book by Augustin Eugène Scribe. First production, Paris, 1830. The scene is Terracina, Italy, in the ninteenth century.

CHARACTERS

FRA DIAVOLO, calling himself "Marquis of San Marco"..*Tenor*
LORD ROCBURG ("Lord Allcash"), an English traveler..*Tenor*
LORENZO, chief of the carbineers.....................*Tenor*
MATTEO, an innkeeper...............................*Bass*
GIACOMO } companions of Fra Diavolo.............. { *Bass*
BEPPO } { *Tenor*
LADY PAMELA ("Lady Allcash"), wife of Lord Rocburg, *Soprano*
ZERLINA, daughter of Matteo.....................*Soprano*

Bandits, villagers, servants, and carbineers.

ACT I. From Matteo's inn near Terracina Lorenzo with his carbineers is starting out to capture a notorious bandit, Fra Diavolo, who with his band of brigands has been terrorizing the countryside, and for whose arrest a large reward is offered. Lorenzo hopes to win the reward and also the hand of Zerlina, which has been promised by her father to Francesco, a rich peasant. Shortly after he leaves, there arrive Lord Rocburg and his wife, Lady Pamela, who are traveling under the names of Lord and Lady Allcash. They have been robbed on the road, and Lord Allcash is also irate over the attentions that a fellow traveler, the Marquis of San Marco, has paid Lady Allcash.

The marquis enters, is greeted by the landlord and his

daughter, and orders his dinner. Zerlina entertains the party with tales of the bandit's exploits, and the marquis listens interestedly and continues his devotion of Lady Allcash, at the same time deftly purloining her jewels. Lorenzo returns, having dispersed the bandits and recovered the Englishman's property.

Act II. Within Zerlina's bedchamber, which adjoins that of Lord and Lady Allcash, Fra Diavolo hides his two companions, Giacomo and Beppo, whom he has admitted to the inn by the window. Zerlina soon enters, having conducted the guests to their room, and prepares to retire. She is very happy over the prospect that Lorenzo, whom she loves, will find and arrest the chief and claim the reward. She composes herself for the night quite unconscious of the hiding thieves.

When all are asleep the men steal into the room of the Englishman and again rob him. A cry is raised, and Lorenzo and his guards enter. He would have seized Giacomo and Beppo but that the Marquis of San Marco covered their retreat. His prompt appearance in the sleeping apartments arouses the jealousy of both the Englishman and Lorenzo, especially when he pretends to have had a rendezvous with a lady, and hints that it was Zerlina. Lorenzo challenges him to a duel and he accepts.

Act III. In the forest Lorenzo awaits the coming of the marquis, while he, now in his brigand's costume as Fra Diavolo, rejoices in his freedom and keeps out of the way. A wedding procession passes, and Lorenzo sorrowfully recognizes Zerlina and her rich lover, Francesco. He espies among the crowd Giacomo and Beppo, and arrests them for the robbery at the inn. He forces them to lure their chief into ambush, and Fra Diavolo is there shot, but not until he is recognized as the Marquis of San Marco and has cleared Zerlina from all suspicion. Lorenzo, now having won the reward, is rich, and receives the hand of Zerlina, so nearly lost to him. Lady Allcash is amazed at the perfidy of her gallant admirer, and Lord Allcash is happy to have his possessions and his wife's affection both restored to him.

FRANCESCA DA RIMINI
(*Frahnd-shĕs'-kah dah Rē̆-mĕ-nē*)

ITALIAN tragic grand opera, based on a drama of the same name by Gabriele d'Annunzio. Music by Riccardo Zandonai. Book by Tito Riccordi. First production, Turin, 1914. The scene is Ravenna and Rimini in Italy, during the thirteenth century.

CHARACTERS

GIOVANNI, the Lame	} sons of Malatesta da Verucchio {	Baritone
PAOLO, the Beautiful		Tenor
MALATESTINO, the One-Eyed		Tenor

OSTASIO, son of Guido Minore da Polenta..........*Baritone*
SER TOLDO BERARDENGO.............................*Tenor*
THE JESTER..*Bass*
THE BOWMAN.......................................*Tenor*
THE TOWER-WARDEN................................*Baritone*
FRANCESCA, daughter of Guido Minore da Polenta...*Soprano*
SAMARITANA, sister of Francesca and Ostasio.......*Soprano*

BIANCOFIORE	} the women of Francesca.. {	Soprano
GARSENDA		Soprano
ALTICHIARA		Mezzo-Soprano
DONELLA		Mezzo-Soprano

SMARAGDI, the slave............................*Contralto*

Bowmen, archers, and musicians.

ACT I. In a court of the house of the Polentani at Ravenna four women attendants of Francesca are chatting with a jester who has just come to the castle. They tell him that Messer Guido da Polenta is going to give his daughter Francesca in marriage to one of the Malatesta, and he says that he has come to sing at the wedding, and begs that they give him a piece of scarlet with which to mend his jerkin. While the jester is singing them a song the voice of Ostasio is heard and the women hastily retreat up the stairs to their quarters. Ostasio enters accompanied by Ser Toldo Berardengo, the notary. Seeing the jester, Ostasio flies into a great rage and handles him roughly, fearing that he has come from Rimini and knows the Malatesta and has been gossiping about them with the women. When he finds that he has no knowledge of the family, he dismisses him, and explains to Ser Toldo that had the man been a jester from the house of the Malatesta their plans for the marriage of Francesca would have been in vain.

In order that the Polentani, who are Guelphs, may obtain from the Malatesta a hundred infantrymen, a union is sought for the beautiful Francesca with the house of Malatesta. Gianciotto, lame and bent and with the eyes of an angry devil, is the one whom she must marry. And as they would never get Francesca's consent to the marriage if she should see her intended husband, his brother, Paolo, a handsome and attractive man, already married to Orabile, is to come as representative of Gianciotto with full power to contract the marriage. So, as the scheming notary points out, Francesca will not know until the morning after her wedding day that she is not married to Paolo.

Ostasio, though unscrupulous and hardhearted, has some misgivings, knowing how high-spirited his sister is, lest some scandal come of the marriage, so he urges speed and secrecy. His compunctions of conscience are chiefly because he thinks the prize too great for the advantage gained, and he accuses the notary of poisoning his father's mind. They discuss at great length the situation of their faction in the feudal wars now raging, and in how great straits they are for lack of resources, and other possible alliances for Francesca. The thought of her beauty haunts Ostasio until Ser Toldo fires his ambition again and he becomes a man of blood and of war, reckless of his sister's happiness.

When they have gone out Francesca and Samaritano enter. Her women are keeping watch as if expecting some one, and are singing as they wait. Francesca tells her sister that she is about to go away, and Samaritana begs that she will not, but will still stay with her that they may never be parted. Francesca is full of foreboding and melancholy, and her sister sorrows with her. Smaragdi, the slave, stands near a sarcophagus in which plants are growing, among them red roses. Francesca turns to her and asks what she will do when her mistress is gone, and the slave expresses her sorrow so bitterly that Francesca promises to take her with her. As they talk the women call Francesca, saying that her betrothed has come. She catches only a glimpse of him, but Smaragdi slips out into the garden and soon returns guiding him. Francesca through fear wishes not to see him, and as she is about to take refuge in flight, she sees him standing near at hand beyond a marble screen. They face each other silent and motionless. Then Francesca turns, goes to the sarcophagus, and picking a large red rose offers it to Paolo Malatesta across the bars.

ACT II. On the ramparts of a tower in the castle of the Malatesta warriors are preparing to wage battle between their faction, which is Guelph, and the Parcitade faction, which is Ghibelline. Francesca has been now some time married to Gianciotto and is living with him and his young brother, Malatestino, here at Rimini amid the blood and furor of war. She does not love her husband, but is without hope of release. She cannot pardon, or believes she cannot, Paolo for his part in the fraudulent marriage, which was that of silence rather than active deception. She has come upon the tower anxious to forget the cares which oppress her. She talks with the tower-warden, who is preparing Greek fire, asks him about it, and herself plays with it, recklessly, the warden thinks, fearing that she may burn the tower.

Paolo comes, and as she seeks to avoid him he follows and speaks with her. He tells her of the shame and horror he feels at his part in her betrayal, and she tells him of the despair in which she dwells. She is bitter in her resentment and he is conscience-stricken; but under the veil of their hostility gleams a strong attraction. In expiation of the wrong he has done her, Francesca would have him fight without his helmet or shield, thus leaving his punishment to the judgment of God. The battle has already begun, and as it waxes more and more fierce he fights fully exposed upon the battlements, while she watching imperils her life because she will not leave him. When, holding a shield before her, he has drawn her out of range of the firing, she begs him not so to expose himself again. Firing from a window while she holds the portcullis he sends an arrow straight into the throat of an archenemy, greatly to Gianciotto's pleasure when he learns of it. When the forces on horseback under Gianciotto have driven off the enemy and the firing ceases, Paolo is found not to have suffered a wound, and to Francesca it means that he is pardoned and she may therefore hold him in honor in her heart. He, overcome by her presence with him in his danger, avows his great love for her, but she thinks him mad and commands him never again to speak thus.

Gianciotto enters, bent and limping, and fiercely railing against his men. Francesca commands Smaragdi to bring wine, and offers it to her husband and to Paolo. The latter drinks it with his eyes upon her, and though Gianciotto makes no comment upon his finding them there together, he announces not without pleasure that envoys have arrived from Florence saying that Paolo has been made Captain of the People and Commune of the city, and that he must leave for his post within three days. Suddenly Malatestino is brought in apparently dead. As they bend over him they discover that he lives, but that he has been wounded in one eye. He revives and though weak and feverish returns with the others to take part in the fighting, which still wages.

Act III. Within her sumptuously furnished apartment Francesca is reading aloud to her women the story of Lancelot and Quinevere. After a time she dismisses them and soon Paolo enters. He has returned from Florence after some months, because he can no longer refrain from seeing her. They strive to conceal their love, yet each subject brings them to the same silent acknowledgment. At last they start to read from the book together, each taking one of the parts. They come to the words, "She takes him by the chin and slowly kisses him on the mouth," and, overwhelmed by their longing, they "read no more that day."

Act IV. In a hall of the castle Malatestino is talking with Francesca. Suddenly he avows his passion for her, fostered by her presence during his illness when she tended him. He knows that she does not love her husband, and he offers to put poison in Gianciotto's food, and thus free her. Horrified at his violence and frightened at his cruelty, but pitying his youth, she starts to go, when she hears a terrible cry. He tells her that the son of the chief of the Parcitade is confined in the dungeon awaiting ransom; and to vent his anger at the repuse he has received, he takes a weapon and goes out promising to silence the cries that have disturbed her.

She stands shuddering with great dread when Gianciotto enters. From her pallor and trembling and unguarded words he gathers that Malatestino has not treated her with due respect. As the youth is heard returning she goes out. He enters dragging the head of his enemy wrapped in a cloth. Gianciotto upbraids him for disobeying his father's orders and killing the Parcitade, and then asks him how he has offended Francesca. Malatestino is frightened for fear she has betrayed him, and to cover his confusion strives to throw suspicion upon Paolo and Francesca. So greatly does he stir Gianciotto's jealousy, by taunts as to both his own and Gianciotto's personal appearance as contrasted with Paolo's, that at length Gianciotto agrees only to pretend that he leaves that night for Pesaro and to return and surprise Francesca and Paolo. Malatestino promises to have Smaragdi out of the way. In accordance with that plan Gianciotto bids Francesca a tender and trustful farewell, commending her to Paolo's care.

Act V. Within Francesca's room late that night the women are still watching, for Francesca is restless and distressed because Smaragdi has not returned. She lies quite dressed upon her bed and fitfully sleeping. She wakes in terror and then recovering herself dismisses the women. To the last, Biancofiore, she almost betrays her foreboding as she bids her a tender good-night and speaks of her sister, Samaritana. At last she is alone. She knows that Paolo waits outside, for the women have said that they saw him there. Calling Smaragdi she opens the door and as Paolo appears she flings herself in his arms. He kisses her passionately and they go into the room and shut the door. They read together and talk of their love.

Suddenly the voice of Gianciotto is heard outside demanding admission. Paolo starts up, lifts a trap-door, and bidding Francesca be courageous, goes down the steps as she opens the door. Gianciotto comes in searching for Paolo. Suddenly he catches sight of him where he stands with head and shoulders above the floor, having caught the corner of his cloak in the bolt of the trap-door. He pulls him up by the hair of his head, and unsheathing his sword rushes upon him. Francesca dashes between them and the sword pierces her breast. Paolo flings aside his dagger and catches her in his arms as she falls, while Gianciotto mad with rage and sorrow stabs his brother a deadly thrust. The two bodies sway together and fall. Gianciotto breaks his blood-stained sword upon his knee.

DER FREISCHÜTZ

(*Der Fri'-shewts*)

(THE FREE SHOT)

GERMAN sentimental grand opera, based on an old Teutonic legend. Music by Carl Maria von Weber. Book by Johann Friedrich Kind. First production, Berlin, 1821. The scene is Bohemia shortly after the Seven Years' War.

CHARACTERS

PRINCE OTTOKAR, Duke of Bohemia	*Baritone*
CUNO, head ranger	*Bass*
CASPAR } two young foresters	{ *Bass*
MAX }	{ *Tenor*
KILIAN, a rich peasant	*Tenor*
A HERMIT	*Bass*
AGATHA, daughter of Cuno	*Soprano*
ANNIE, cousin of Agatha	*Soprano*

Hunters, peasants, bridesmaids, and spirits.

The free shot is any rifleman who has sold his soul to the demon huntsman, Zamiel, for seven magic bullets, six of which surely hit the mark aimed at, but the seventh Zamiel guides. If any man shall bring another to barter for the bullets he will obtain a second lot and an extension of his life.

ACT I. At a target-shooting range in the forest several marksmen are gathered about Kilian, who has won the title of King of the Marksmen. At one side the young Max sits sullenly at a table. As the huntsmen pass by and jeer at him because of his ill luck at the shoot, he jumps up and seizing Kilian, is about to fight him when Cuno and Caspar enter. Kilian explains that the taunting was good-natured and customary when one failed to hit the target and so lost the right to try for the kingship.

Max's failure is of great moment, for he is to wed Agatha, Cuno's daughter, on the morrow, and if he succeeds at the wedding in his trial shot he is to inherit his father-in-law's office. Cuno warns Max that unless he succeeds he will not give him the hand of Agatha. Max is much disheartened because his shots have recently been going wild though he used to be one of the best marksmen. He fears that some evil influence is over him.

All go out to dance, but Caspar soon returns to tell Max that there is a way to insure success. He bids him take his rifle and shoot at a bird quite out of range overhead. Max does so and, though aiming at random, brings down an immense eagle. He asks Caspar if he has more of such bullets, and Caspar says that was his last, but that if Max will meet him at midnight at the Wolf's Glen he will give him some magic bullets with which to win his bride. Max's scruples are quite overcome by his need and much to Caspar's delight he promises to be there.

Act II. Within her home Agatha is anxiously awaiting her lover while her cousin, Annie, tries to cheer her. But Agatha has a strong premonition of trouble, and when it grows late and Annie goes to rest, she lingers on, praying for his safety. At last he comes and shows her the eagle's feather in his hat. When he says he must go that night to the Wolf's Glen to bring back a stag which he has shot, she is greatly alarmed and begs him not to go, because the place is haunted by evil spirits. Nevertheless he goes out.

Already at the Wolf's Glen Caspar as midnight struck has invoked the Black Huntsman, who appears. Caspar promises the fiend another customer for the magic bullets. Zamiel says that he may have six to do his will, but that the seventh shall do harm. As Caspar begins casting the magic bullets, Max appears on a crag overlooking the glen. Though warned by a vision, he goes down. The moon is eclipsed and Caspar casts the bullets within a magic circle amid many horrifying portents. During a hurricane, while meteors fall, the Black Huntsman himself appears and tries to grasp Max's hand, but the terrified youth crosses himself and falls to the earth, where Caspar also lies unconscious. As the tempest ceases Zamiel disappears.

Act III. At dawn of her wedding day Agatha, dressed in her bridal gown, kneels in prayer. Annie enters and Agatha relates how in a dream she was a white dove flying from tree to tree and Max shot at and wounded her, but she speedily recovered. Even with her bridesmaids about her she is apprehensive because other omens occur.

Prince Ottokar and his retainers are present at the festival. Max had four of the bullets, but he has already used three in unnecessary shots, and the last seems too heavy as he weighs it in his hand. He decides to shoot before Agatha comes, and the prince points out a white dove for the mark. As Max lifts his gun Agatha runs forward crying to him not to shoot. Leveling his gun at the dove, which has flown to a tree that Caspar has climbed to watch the shot, he fires. Both Agatha and Caspar fall, the girl unharmed, but Caspar mortally wounded. He dies with curses on his lips. The prince requires an explanation from Max, and he confesses how he obtained the magic bullets. The prince banishes him, but at Cuno's and Agatha's intercession, the sentence is changed to a year of probation after which he may marry Agatha. The trial shot for the succession is abolished.

LA GIOCONDA
(*Lah Jō-kon'-dah*)

ITALIAN tragic grand opera, based on Victor Hugo's drama, "Angelo, the Tyrant of Padua." Music by Amilcare Ponchielli. Book by Arrigo Boito. First production, Milan, 1876. The scene is Venice in the seventeenth century.

CHARACTERS

ENZO GRIMALDO, a Genoese nobleman.................Tenor
ALVISE BADOERO, one of the heads of the State Inquisition..Bass
BARNABA, chief of police and a spy of the Inquisition..Baritone
ZUANE, a boatman....................................Bass
LAURA, wife of Alvise......................Mezzo-Soprano
LA GIOCONDA, a ballad singer.....................Soprano
LA CIECA, her blind mother.....................Contralto

Isepo, who is a public letter-writer; a pilot, monks, senators, sailors, shipwrights, ladies, gentlemen, masquers, and the populace.

ACT I. In Venice near the Adriatic the people are gathered on a holiday. Barnaba announces the opening of the regatta and the people hasten off to the shore, leaving him alone. He is in love with Gioconda, who supports herself and her blind mother by singing in the streets. He is planning how he shall win her, for she has given her love to Enzo Grimaldo, a Genoese nobleman and captain of a sailing vessel now in the harbor. Gioconda and her mother enter, and he conceals himself behind a pillar. Gioconda leaves her mother and starts to seek Enzo, when Barnaba stops her, declares his love for her, and when she repulses him, tries to seize her, but unsuccessfully. Thoroughly angered at her aversion, he determines on revenge.

The people return from the regatta bearing the victor on

© Mishkin

RICCARDO MARTIN
AS ENZO, IN "LA GIOCONDA"

their shoulders. Barnaba tells Zuane, the defeated contestant, that Cieca is a witch and has cast over him a spell that caused his defeat. Zuane and his friends then set upon her, and she is being roughly handled when Enzo appears and defends her. Just then Alvise, head of the Inquisitorial Council, comes along with his wife, Laura, who before her marriage was engaged to Enzo. They see the disturbance and, learning the cause, Laura pleads for the old blind woman and Alvise affords her protection. Cieca in gratitude presents Laura with her rosary.

Alvise and the people go into the church, leaving Enzo standing alone looking after Laura, whom he has recognized as his former love. Barnaba accosts him, tells him his real name and city, and when Enzo denies both, declares that he was proscribed by Venice and is in danger of arrest. Revealing further knowledge, he tells of Enzo's love for Laura and then gives him a message from her to the effect that she will be at his ship that night. Enzo's love is revived and, forgetting Gioconda, he is about to go to his ship when he asks Barnaba who he is. The latter reveals the fact that he is a member of the Council of Ten, tells of his love for Gioconda and that he is determined to win her, and threatens Enzo, who goes off. Barnaba writes Alvise, telling him that his wife is about to elope with Enzo, and is reading the note aloud when Gioconda, entering, hears and, overcome with sorrow at her lover's faithlessness, enters the church with her mother to pray.

ACT II. That night in the lagoon near Venice Enzo's ship is riding at anchor when a fisherman (Barnaba in disguise) comes along and hails the crew. He takes note of their number, then passes on, meanwhile sending for the police galleys. Enzo appears and is greeted by the sailors, whom he sends below while he keeps watch. Laura comes and the lovers plan to set sail when the wind arises. While Enzo is below arousing his men, Gioconda comes and denounces Laura. They both declare their love for Enzo, and Gioconda is about to stab Laura when she recognizes her mother's rosary. Just then Laura's husband appears in great anger, and Gioconda helps Laura to escape. Enzo reappearing finds Gioconda, who reproaches him and tells him that Barnaba's galleys are about to seize the ship. Then Enzo sets his boat on fire.

ACT III. At night in his palace Alvise sits alone brooding over the attempted elopement of his wife with Enzo, while in an adjoining room nobles and their ladies are dancing at a masked ball. He declares that for the honor of his name Laura must die, and determines to poison her that night. He sends for her, denounces her, hands her the poison, and leaves, ordering her to take it. She is about to do so, when Gioconda, who is hidden in the room, gives her an opiate instead, and leaves. Alvise sees the empty vial and Laura's stupor and thinks she has fulfilled his orders.

Enzo is among the masquers when Barnaba whispers to him that Laura is dead. Horrified he tears off his mask and denounces Alvise. The police officers seize him and he, grief-stricken, rejoices that the doom he is awaiting will take him to her. Meanwhile Barnaba, who has been watching Gioconda as she hears Enzo's lament over his lost love, demands that she give herself to him under threat of great ill. Gioconda promises to, if he will deliver Enzo to her at a certain place. He promises, and the blind old mother is comforting her heartbroken daughter when Alvise draws aside a curtain and reveals to the horrified guests the apparently lifeless Laura and acknowledges that he killed her.

Enzo struggles to kill Alvise, but is bound and led away to prison.

Act IV. Into a ruined palace on an island in the Adriatic two men are bearing the still insensible Laura at Gioconda's direction. She bids them on their return find her mother and care for her. Alone she takes up the glass of poison. She knows that suicide only remains, but is for the moment tempted to give the poison to Laura. Enzo, who has been released by Barnaba and whom she has sent for, arrives. She bitterly reproaches him for his faithlessness. As they talk Laura's voice is heard. The lovers are joyously reunited, and Gioconda helps them escape. She is about to swallow the poison, when Barnaba arrives. As he approaches her exulting that she cannot escape, she puts him off, feigning to adorn herself, and unobserved seizes a dagger. She turns to him as if yielding, and stabbing herself dies. Barnaba, furious with anger, in a last effort to harm her, screams into her ear that last night he strangled her mother, and then, wild that she is already dead and does not hear, rushes off.

THE GIRL OF THE GOLDEN WEST

(LA FANCIULLA DEL WEST)

ITALIAN sentimental grand opera, founded upon the drama of the same name by David Belasco. Music by Giacomo Puccini. Book by Carlo Zangarini and Guelfo Civinini. First production, New York, 1910. The scene is laid in a mining camp at the foot of the Cloudy Mountains in California, in the days of the gold fever, 1849 and 1850.

CHARACTERS

JACK RANCE, sheriff	Baritone
DICK JOHNSON (Ramerrez)	Tenor
NICK, bartender at the "Polka"	Tenor
ASHBY, agent of the Wells-Fargo Transport Company	Bass
BILLY JACKRABBIT, an Indian	Bass
JAKE WALLACE, a traveling camp-minstrel	Baritone
JOSÉ CASTRO, a greaser from Ramerrez's gang	Bass
MINNIE	Soprano
WOWKLE, Billy's squaw	Mezzo-Soprano

Sonora, Trin, Sid, Handsome, Harry, Joe, Happy, Larkens (all miners); a postilion, and men of the camp.

ACT I. In the barroom of the "Polka" a number of miners are gathered and also Rance, the sheriff. Ashby enters and says that after three months of tracking, his men are rounding up Ramerrez and his band of Mexican "greasers." Minnie, a comely young woman who has been brought up among the miners and since her father's death continues to run his business, enters in time to stop a fight between the sheriff and a miner who resented Rance's boast that Minnie would soon be his wife. Rance makes love to Minnie but she repulses him, even showing him a revolver that she carries. After a time a stranger appears. He gives his name as Dick

Johnson, from Sacramento, and when the sheriff threatens him, Minnie acknowledges that she has met him before. She and the stranger recall their chance meeting on the road, when each fell in love with the other, and Johnson (who is no other than Ramerrez, the outlaw, and who has come to rob the saloon, knowing that the miners leave their gold in Minnie's charge) finds himself so attracted by the girl that he relinquishes his plan.

When Minnie has gone with him and the miners into the dance hall, Ashby's men bring in José Castro. They are for hanging him, and Castro, though he sees his chief's saddle and thinks him captured, soon finds from the talk that Ramerrez is still free, and offers to conduct them to him. The miners go with the sheriff and Ashby's men to seize the outlaw, leaving their barrel of gold in Minnie's charge, with only Nick and Billy to protect her and it. Nick reports that a greaser is skulking around, and Johnson knows that his men are only awaiting his whistle to come and seize the gold. Minnie declares valiantly that he who takes the gold will have to kill her first, and he admires her spirit. She invites him to call on her at her cabin after the miners come back, and he, accepting the invitation, goes out.

ACT II. At Minnie's dwelling Wowkle is sitting on the floor before the fire rocking her baby in her arms. Billy comes in and Minnie soon follows. She puts on what finery she possesses and when Johnson arrives entertains him graciously. They both acknowledge their love, and when a severe snowstorm comes up Minnie invites him to remain for the night. Pistol shots are heard and Johnson, knowing himself to be in grave danger, determines to stay with Minnie and vows that he will never give her up. Johnson is lying on Minnie's bed and she is resting on the hearth rug when shouts are heard without, and Nick hails Minnie. She insists that Johnson hide, and then she admits Nick, Rance, Ashby, and some of the miners. They tell her that Dick Johnson is Ramerrez, and is near, and that they were worried about her. They say also that Johnson came to the saloon to take their gold, though he left without it, which they cannot understand. She is overwhelmed by their revelations, especially when Johnson's photograph, obtained from a notorious woman at a nearby ranch, is shown her.

She sends the men off, and will not listen to having any one stay with her. When they are gone she confronts Johnson with the photograph and he confesses who he is and tells her how he was brought up to the life of an outlaw. Minnie cannot forgive him for deceiving her when she gave him her love, and she sends him off. Johnson goes out, desperate and willing to die. A shot is heard and Minnie opens the door, drags him in wounded, and hides him in the loft. Rance enters and Minnie has almost convinced him that the outlaw escaped and is not there, when a drop of blood falls on his hand. He drags the wounded man down from the loft. Minnie, knowing that the sheriff has the gambler's passion, offers to play a game of poker with him, her life and Johnson's to be the stake. If she loses she will marry him and he may do what he will with Johnson. They play while Johnson lies unconscious near, and Rance is winning when Minnie cleverly cheats and so wins the game. Rance, dumbfounded, but true to his word, goes out.

ACT III. On the edge of the great California forest in the early dawn, Rance, Ashby, and Nick are waiting. Rance tells of his chagrin that Johnson's wound was not fatal, and that Minnie has nursed him back to life at her cabin. Ashby's men come on the scene, having captured Johnson after an exciting chase. He is brought in, bound and wounded and his clothing torn. The men gather about him like animals about their prey, and taunt him savagely. Johnson confronts them defiantly, even when they name many of the robberies and murders that he and his gang have committed. As they are about to hang him he asks one favor—that they will never tell Minnie how he died.

At the last moment Minnie dashes in on horseback. She places herself in front of Johnson and presents her pistol to the crowd, and in spite of Rance's orders no one dares to push her aside and pull the noose taut. Minnie appeals to them, reminds them of what she has done for them, and at last in spite of Rance the miners cut the noose and restore Johnson to Minnie. The two go off together amid the affectionate farewells of the men.

GWENDOLINE

FRENCH tragic grand opera. Music by Emmanuel Chabrier. Book by Catulle Mendès. First production, Brussels, 1886. The scene is the shore of Great Britain at the end of the eighth century.

CHARACTERS

HARALD, Danish sea king.
ARMEL, Saxon king.
ERICK.
ÆLLA.
GWENDOLINE, daughter of Armel.

Danes, Saxons, both men and women.

ACT I. It is early morning in a Saxon seacoast village. As the day dawns the villagers stir, windows are thrown open, and the people come out upon the highways and join in a song of greeting to the day. Gwendoline, a beautiful fair-haired girl of sixteen years, appears with her father, and she calls to the young people to take their sickles and iron harpoons and go, the girls to the fields and the boys to the sea. Her father approves her orders, and tells her that he will command upon the waves while she rules over the golden fields. She confides in him that she has had a fearful dream and that the Danes threaten them. He quiets her fears, saying that his ship is strong and sails well. The men and boys go away to their fishing.

Gwendoline, left alone with her girl companions, relates to them her dream that a Dane carried her away with him upon the sea. They try to quiet her fears and ask her what sort of man he was. She tells them not to laugh but to fear the dark rovers of the beach, which she so plainly saw in her dream, for they are rude and strong like famished wolves; in the horror which followed their army the fields were covered with dead and the skies were filled with smoke. She cries out, asking if they do not hear them—the barbarians with the red locks. Her companions think she still dreams, while she murmurs to herself that yet she pities them somewhat, those sad young men, ever far from the beautiful and peaceful valleys, without wives, and knowing nothing of love. Then she tells how hideous their ships are, like somber ravens or dragons breathing flame. She cries again, "Do you not hear them?"

Suddenly are heard distant shouts of alarm followed by fierce cries of rage and hate. Saxon men come rushing in great fright from the direction of the shore, followed by savage Danes. The women take refuge in the house of Armel. The Danes have utterly routed the Saxons, who unarmed and under the menace of swords are quickly brought to terms. Harald, the sea king, enters with naked sword in his hand and his warriors gather about him as he shouts their fierce war song. Armel is pointed out to him and he demands of him all his treasure, saying that it is theirs, for the chances of war have made them conquerors.

Armel proudly replies that they shall have the treasure if they take it. Harald then threatens to loot and to burn the whole farm and village. Armel replies that they shall then have only firebrands. Terribly angry Harald tells Armel that he shall die, and orders him to cover his head. Armel refuses and Harald says that, covered or not, it shall fall.

Gwendoline rushes from the house and, flinging herself at Harald's feet, begs him to spare her father's life. He, amazed at her appearance and fascinated by her beauty, orders the soldiers off and the Saxon men and women t¤

disperse. He grants her request, and lingers by her instead of continuing to pillage the town,—much to the derision and disgust of his men.

He commands Gwendoline to come to him, and as she hesitates, he, after a moment's fierceness, supplicatingly asks her to come. He tells her not to fear him, that he has never seen women and thinks that she must be a Valkyrie with her golden helmet. At length winning her confidence by his gentleness, he asks her to become his wife. He summons Armel and her people, and makes his request. Her father, though his hatred is bitter against the Danes, consents perforce to the marriage. He sees therein an opportunity to avenge himself upon his enemies. Surreptitiously he gives Gwendoline a dagger, commanding her to stab Harald during the bridal night, when she hears the sound of fighting, that all the Danes may die together. Gwendoline, however, is much attracted by the manly strength of the Danish sea king, and because of her love for him intends to save him from the wrath of her father.

Act II. Armel sits in the nuptial hall, thoughtful and gloomy, while the hymeneal chorus is being sung by the Saxon women. Ælla enters and Armel asks if all is ready, if the oil and pitch and the incendiary torches are hidden near the foreign vessels. Then as Erick enters he inquires if the Danes have left their arms outside the hall and are quite without defense. Learning that they have, he rejoices with great delight, while Erick protests that nevertheless the Danes are their guests and the laws of hospitality should hold. Soon the whole company of Saxons and Danes enter for the merrymaking.

At length the bridal couple are alone together in their chamber. Gwendoline cautiously and securely closes the door, then she prays Harald to go away speedily, saying that she foresees danger threatening him and his men. But he realizes that she loves him and he will not listen to her protests, and in his love for her but clasps her closer. After a time loud cries are heard without. The Danes, outnumbered, are being slain by the Saxons and call upon their king for help. He flies to their aid, armed only with the dagger which had been given his bride for his own slaughter.

Hastening with the handful remaining of his men to the seashore, they find their ships aflame, and taking a last stand they are cut down by the Saxons. Armel himself strikes the blow which fatally wounds Harald, but the doughty Dane, wishing to die standing, leans against a tree trunk facing his foes. Gwendoline, unable to save her lover, comes rushing toward him, and seeing that he is dying, stabs herself, and the two lovers die in each other's arms, raised by the ecstacy of their passion into faith in their reception together at the banquet of the gods in Valhalla.

LA HABANERA
(*Lah Ah-bah-nä´-rah*)

FRENCH tragic grand opera. Both music and book by Raoul Laparra. First production, Paris, 1908. The scene is in Castile, Spain, at the present time.

CHARACTERS
PILAR.
RAMON.
PEDRO.

Four jolly fellows, an old man, three blind men, two betrothed women, a girl, a serving man, a middle-aged man, a young man, who is the son of the middle-aged man, two Andalusians, a *madrilène*, a man, a small boy, a small girl, and Castilian peasants—both men and women.

ACT I. In an upper room of a village tavern on the high plateau of Castile four jolly fellows sit at a table drinking and dining, while at another table Ramon, morose and gloomy, sits brooding and viciously hacking at the table with his knife. He drinks deep drafts of wine and stares impatiently about him, with mingled grief, hatred, and tenderness in his eyes, as he hears the sounds of merriment which come to him through the open windows. The four men go out, and soon Pilar enters, dressed in the Castilian fashion for a betrothed girl, for she is to marry Pedro, Ramon's brother. Ramon, whose disappointment, for he too is in love with her, has made him plan suicide, takes her passionately in his arms when she tells him of her engagement. Pedro enters, and as Ramon releases her, the favored lover lavishes caresses upon her. She soon goes out, leaving the two brothers together, and shortly her voice is heard, with the strains of the passionate *La Habanera* dance, inviting

Pedro to come and dance it with her. The thought of her choice of Pedro for the intimacies of the wild dance adds the final flame to Ramon's jealousy, and as his brother starts down the stairs to join her, he plunges his knife into his back. Pedro reels and falls; then realizing that he is about to die, he crawls up the steps to where Ramon stands and tells him that if he does not confess the murder to Pilar his spirit will return within a year and will have its revenge. He then falls dead.

An outcry is raised, and the old blind father of the two brothers comes together with Pilar. Ramon enters among the bystanders, and his father, whose hands are wet with the blood of his murdered son, fumbles for Ramon and beseeches him to avenge his brother's murder.

ACT II. In the courtyard of an old farm, illuminated only by pale moonlight, Ramon and Pilar, who are soon to be married, are gathered with the old father and their friends and servants. It is a year lacking one day since Pedro was murdered, and Ramon, who has never confessed the crime, is exceedingly apprehensive and does not respond to the gaiety about him, even when Pilar begs him to join them in the dance, *La Habanera*. There is a knocking at the outer gate, which Ramon at first ignores, then at Pilar's request he opens the door. Three blind men, wandering minstrels, enter, each with his guitar. With them Ramon sees glide in a fourth figure—Pedro, ghostly and threatening—but neither Pilar nor a small boy whom Ramon asks sees anything unusual. Nevertheless Ramon is overcome with fear and remorse, yet cannot bring himself to tell Pilar of his crime.

ACT III. Within the cemetery on the morrow Ramon and Pilar are praying at the grave of the murdered Pedro. It is night, and as they kneel there a funeral procession passes by with its weird laments and the flashing of the torches. Ramon, stricken with remorse, and yet eager to wed Pilar, hears in the strains of the funeral march echoes of the fateful *La Habanera* dance, which so stirred his jealousy. As the procession goes away and they are left alone, he notices that Pilar is crouching lower and lower toward the grave. He speaks to her and she does not answer, seeming unconscious of his presence. Lights appear, the earth of the grave seems to open, Pilar sinks into it, and a hoarse, exultant laugh is heard. Ramon stretches out his arms to seize Pilar, but cannot grasp her. She has vanished. With a wild shriek his sanity leaves him, and he, throwing his dark mantle over his head, rushes off into the night.

HAMLET

FRENCH tragic grand opera, based on Shakespeare's drama of the same name. Music by Charles Louis Ambroise Thomas. Book by Jules Barbier and Michel Carré. First production, Paris, 1868. The scene is Elsinore Castle, Denmark, and the time is about 1600.

CHARACTERS

HAMLET, Prince of Denmark	Baritone
CLAUDIUS, King of Denmark	Bass
GHOST OF THE DEAD KING, Hamlet's father	Bass
POLONIUS, Chancellor	Bass
LAERTES, son of Polonius	Tenor
GERTRUDE, Hamlet's mother, Queen of Denmark,	Mezzo-Soprano
OPHELIA, daughter of Polonius	Soprano

Horatio and Marcellus, who are friends of Hamlet; lords, ladies, officers, actors, peasants, pages, and soldiers.

ACT I. In the room of state in the palace the Queen of Denmark and her husband, Claudius, the brother of the late king, are holding court. The queen is angry because her son, Prince Hamlet, is not present. When the ceremony is over and all have left, he enters and sits musing as Ophelia, his betrothed, comes in. She tells him that she hears he is to leave the court, and asks him if he no longer loves her. He assures her that he does, and they renew their vows of affection.

On the esplanade of the palace late at night Horatio and Marcellus are watching and talking about an apparition of the dead king that has been seen there. Hamlet enters and they tell him of the vision. He is much alarmed and wonders what the significance of it may be. As they talk the clock strikes twelve and the ghost enters. Hamlet speaks to it and asks why it does not remain within the sepulcher. The ghost motions Hamlet to draw apart from the others and then tells him that he was murdered by his brother. Claudius, incited by desire for the queen. He leaves with Hamlet the task of avenging his death, but stipulates that his mother's punishment be left to God. The ghost vanishes and Hamlet undertakes the task of vengeance, bidding farewell to all hopes of happiness.

Act II. In the garden of the palace Ophelia is weeping because Hamlet neglects her. The queen comes in and tries to comfort her, telling her that Hamlet's strange actions make her fear that his reason is affected. The king enters and shortly after Hamlet comes in, asking them all to a play which a company of strolling players will give. They are glad that Hamlet is interested in such amusement, and consent to attend. As all but Hamlet go out the players enter and he instructs them in their parts, arranging a play by which he hopes to trap the guilty king into confession of his brother's murder.

In the palace hall a stage has been erected. The court assembles to watch the play, and Hamlet takes his stand where he can observe the king. A murder is enacted exactly like the one that Hamlet believes to have been committed on his father. The king is strangely agitated and at the climax orders the players away. Hamlet, thoroughly convinced of the king's guilt, denounces him as a murderer in the presence of the court. The members of the court think that Hamlet's charge is but the raving of a madman. He is left alone with Horatio and faints in his arms.

Act III. In the apartments of the queen Hamlet soliloquizes upon life and death. The queen and Ophelia enter and both plead with him to cease his wild ravings. He turns to Ophelia and urges her to enter a convent, then he accuses his mother of being an accomplice in his father's murder. As he speaks the ghost again appears, warning Hamlet to spare his mother. The prince conducts her to the door of her room, urging her to pray and to repent.

Act IV. By the shore of the lake Ophelia, driven insane by her sorrow at the loss of Hamlet's love, is playing with flowers and singing to herself. She speaks to the peasants and the shepherds, and then, following the lure of a siren's voice, wanders away. Finally she plunges into the water, singing Hamlet's vow of love.

Act V. Into the churchyard where Ophelia is to be buried Hamlet comes, burdened with grief at her death. He determines to end his own life upon her grave. The funeral cortège arrives, the queen and the king among the mourners. The ghost of his father appears to Hamlet, looking reproachfully at him. As the mourners turn away from the grave, Hamlet stabs the king. The people, who now believe Hamlet's charge against his uncle, acclaim Hamlet as their new king.

HÄNSEL UND GRETEL

(*Hahn'-sĕl ōōndt Grä'-tĕl*)

(HANSEL AND GRETEL)

GERMAN fairy grand opera, adapted from the tale "The Babes in the Wood," by Jacob and William Grimm. Music by Engelbert Humperdinck. Book by Adelheid Wette, the sister of the composer. First production, Munich, 1893. The scene is a forest in Germany in the seventeenth century.

CHARACTERS

PETER, a broom-maker	Baritone
GERTRUDE, his wife	Mezzo-Soprano
HANSEL } their children	{ Mezzo-Soprano
GRETEL }	{ Soprano
THE WITCH, who eats children	Mezzo-Soprano
SANDMAN, the Sleep Fairy	Soprano
DEWMAN, the Dawn Fairy	Soprano

Children, fairies, and angels.

ACT I. Hansel and Gretel are busily working in their home, Hansel making brooms and Gretel knitting a stocking. Gretel is singing, but Hansel, who is hungry, asks when they are going to have something to eat. Gretel tells him that a neighbor has sent in a jug of milk and Hansel is delighted. He sings and Gretel teaches him a little dance. As they are dancing together their mother, tired and hungry, comes in, and when she finds that they have neglected their work she is very angry. In attempting to punish them she overturns the jug of milk. Thrice angry, she gives them a basket and sends them out into the woods to pick strawberries, with the threat of a terrible beating if they do not bring home a big basketful for supper. When they have gone she falls asleep by the hearth, but soon Peter comes in with a basket loaded with food and provisions. When he finds the children gone he alarms his wife by telling her of the Crust-Witch, who lives in a gingerbread house, and who entices little children into her house and bakes them into gingerbread. Much frightened they both rush into the forest hoping to overtake their children.

Act II. The children have wandered into the depths of the woods. They pick berries and weave garlands of flowers. Hearing a cuckoo's call they imitate it and, playing that the strawberries are eggs and they are cuckoos, eat up the berries. Frightened when they realize that the basket is empty and that they must bring it home full, they try to find more, but wander around, and at last twilight overtakes them. They are frightened and cling closely to each other. After a time Sandman, the Sleep Fairy, comes along and sprinkles sleep-sand into their eyes. They say their prayers and lie down side by side. While they slumber angels descend from the clouds by a golden stairway and keep watch over them.

Act III. Hansel and Gretel are still fast asleep in the woods when Dewman, the Dawn Fairy, comes along and shakes dewdrops on them. They wake up and see near them the gingerbread house of the witch. They approach it very cautiously, and seeing that the fence is made of gingerbread children, they begin to nibble at it, for they are very hungry. Thereupon the witch comes out. When they try to run away, she waves her wand and puts a spell upon them that prevents their moving. A moment later the witch, who wants Gretel to do something for her, disenchants her.

Within the house the witch makes a big fire in her stove, so that she can bake the children into gingerbread. As it burns she rides around the room on her broomstick, chuckling with delight. Gretel uses the countercharm over Hansel, and together the two children push the witch into the oven and close the door tight. They dance around the room gleefully while the witch burns. An explosion destroys the oven and shatters the covering from the children about the cottage. As the children have no power to move Hansel repeats the countercharm and the children dance around and thank their benefactors. From the ruins of the oven they drag the body of the witch, now baked into gingerbread, and there is great rejoicing. Peter and Gertrude now arrive, and great is their joy when they find their children unharmed.

HÉRODIADE
(*Ā-rōd-yahdd*)
(HERODIAS)

FRENCH tragic grand opera, based upon Gustave Flaubert's novelette, "Herodias." Music by Jules Massenet. Book by Paul Milliet and Henri Grémont. First production, Brussels, 1881. The scene is Jerusalem about A. D. 30.

CHARACTERS

JOHN THE PROPHET	Tenor
HEROD, King of Galilee	Baritone
PHANUEL, a Chaldean	Bass
VITELLIUS, a Roman proconsul	Baritone
THE HIGH PRIEST	Baritone
A VOICE IN THE TEMPLE	Bass
SALOME	Soprano
HERODIAS	Contralto

A young Babylonian woman, merchants, Hebrew and Roman soldiers, priests, Levites, temple servitors, seamen, scribes, Pharisees, Galileans, Samaritans, Sadducees, Ethiopians, Nubians, Arabs, and Romans.

ACT I. In the court of Herod's palace at Jerusalem a caravan bearing gifts is awaiting the appearance of the king. The servants quarrel among themselves and Phanuel silences them. Salome enters and Phanuel is much astonished that she should be within the palace and wonders if she does not know who her mother is. She is seeking the prophet, who she says was very kind to her when she was a child. She and Phanuel go out just as Herod enters in search of her. Herodias rushes in, very angry with the prophet John, who has rebuked her. She demands that he be killed, but Herod will not consent. John enters the court and his denunciation of the wicked king and his queen is so stern that they both slink away, terrified and conscience-stricken. Salome returns and, seeing John, expresses her admiration and love for him. He coldly repulses her and tells her to turn to God.

Act II. Within his chamber Herod lies upon his couch longing for the beautiful Salome. Attendants sing and dance before him, and a slave gives him a love potion, saying that it will make him see a vision of the one he loves. Vowing that he would give his soul to win Salome, Herod drinks the opiate and lies in heavy sleep.

Inspired to action by Phanuel, who urges him not to give himself up to following a woman while his people are under the Roman yoke, Herod is addressing the people gathered in a public square of Jerusalem and receiving messengers from the various parties which will support him in a revolt. All are thrown into consternation, however, by the news which Herodias brings of the arrival of the Roman proconsul, Vitellius. When he appears Herod speaks for the people and asks that the sacred Temple on Mount Zion be restored to them. Vitellius grants their request. Suddenly from among the crowd appears John the Prophet. Salome also enters, and hangs eagerly upon his words, while Herod, forgetting affairs of state, watches her, fascinated with her beauty, and Herodias with jealous eyes watches him. Vitellius is surprised at the deference the people pay the prophet. John comes into the presence of the proconsul, and in words of no uncertain sound rebukes his arrogance and display of power, saying that power is only from God.

Act III. On the balcony of his house Phanuel, who has been much impressed by the words of John, seeks by means of astrology to find out who the man is and whence his authority. Herodias appears, having come to ask him to read her future and to tell her how she may regain Herod's love. Phanuel foresees nothing but disaster for her. She asks him where her child is, who has long been lost to her. From the balcony he points out Salome, who is just entering the Temple, but Herodias exclaims that that is not her child but her rival.

At the entrance of the Temple Salome is overcome with sorrow on hearing that John has been cast into prison. Herod comes and, seeing Salome, pours out his love and begs her favor. She is startled, and repulsing him confesses that she loves another. He is exceedingly angry and vows that he will kill his rival. They have gone away when the proconsul enters and is met by a body of the priests with John. They demand of him that the prophet be condemned to death, but he refers them to Herod. When the latter enters John is brought forward and questioned. Salome falls on her knees before Herod, asking him to spare the prophet, and Herod, realizing that it is John whom Salome loves, condemns them both to death.

ACT IV. Within a dungeon John sits awaiting execution when Salome enters. He admires her courageous devotion to his safety, and advises her to flee to escape Herod's wrath. She refuses to go and declares her purpose of dying with him. The High Priest enters and offers John pardon if he will take sides with Herod against Rome. When the prophet refuses he is led away to death and the guards seize Salome to bear her to the palace of Herod.

In the audience chamber of the palace a festival is in progress. The proconsul, Herod, and Herodias are being entertained by dancers when Salome enters. Again she pleads that John be spared, and begs that at least she be allowed to die with him. When Herod refuses both requests she turns to Herodias and renews her plea, saying, "If thou wert ever a mother, pity me!" Herodias trembles with fear and is about to speak when an executioner appears with a dripping sword in his hand. Salome gazes upon it in horror, and then turning to Herodias, for she knows that it is her deed because of her hatred of John, tries to kill her. Herodias cries for mercy and tells Salome that she is her mother. The girl shrinks back in horror, and exclaiming, "Take back the life you gave me!" stabs herself.

LES HUGUENOTS
(*Lăz Hew-gno*)
(THE HUGUENOTS)

FRENCH tragic grand opera, based upon the massacre of St. Bartholomew's Eve. Music by Giacomo Meyerbeer. Book by Eugene Scribe and Emile Deschamps. First production, Paris, 1836. The scene is laid in Paris and Touraine in August, 1572.

CHARACTERS
COUNT DE ST. BRIS } Catholic noblemen......... { *Baritone*
COUNT DE NEVERS } .... { *Baritone*
RAOUL DE NANGIS, a Huguenot nobleman.............*Tenor*
MARCEL, a Huguenot, servant to Raoul...............*Bass*
MARGARET OF VALOIS, betrothed to Henry IV of Navarre,
Soprano
VALENTINE, daughter of St. Bris...................*Soprano*
URBAN, page to Margaret....................*Mezzo-Soprano*

Ladies and gentlemen of the court, both Catholic and Huguenot; pages, citizens, soldiers, the night-watch, students, monks, and the people.

ACT I. In a salon of the house of Count de Nevers Catholic noblemen are dining when Raoul, a Huguenot, arrives at the count's invitation and is treated with great courtesy. For entertainment it is proposed that each guest relate an adventure with a lady. Raoul tells of his rescue of an unknown but beautiful lady from a band of drunken revelers, and of his avowal of love to her. Suddenly Marcel enters and rebukes his master for being in the company of Catholics. Raoul apologizes for his old servant, who loves him as a father, and the guests request a song of the old man. He sings a Huguenot battle hymn, which expresses bitter hatred of the Romanists. A servant announces to De Nevers that a lady wishes to see him and he goes to an adjoining room. Raoul catches sight of the lady and is surprised and grieved to recognize her as the one to whom he pledged his devotion and whom the count now greets affectionately. A page enters with a note for Raoul, which requests him to return with the guide, blindfolded and without questioning. Raoul shows the message to the others, and the seal of Queen Margaret of Valois is recognized, so Raoul goes out envied by all.

In the gardens of her castle at Chenonceaux Queen Margaret sits surrounded by her maids. She voices her distress at the bitter hatred between the Catholics and the Huguenots, and her desire that peace and love should reign. Her maids go out as Valentine enters, having just returned from her interview with Count de Nevers, and tells the queen that the count has released her from her engagement to him. The queen says that she has planned a better marriage for her.

Valentine goes out as Raoul is led in. Delighted with the royal favor, he pays his devotions to the queen, who is charmed that the man whom Valentine has chosen is so gallant a courtier. The nobles of the court assemble, having been summoned by the queen, who asks them to put aside their religious differences, and as brothers support the crown. She announces that she has arranged a marriage that will unite the two parties. They take the oath of good fellowship. Valentine is led in by her father and presented to Raoul. He recognizes her as the lady to whom he had given his love, but whom he now believes to be engaged to Count de Nevers. Therefore he loyally refuses her hand. The reason of his action is misunderstood. Her father challenges him to a duel, and all the Catholics are deeply angered and can scarcely be restrained from striking him down on the

© Aimé Dupont

JEAN de RESZKE
AS RAOUL, IN "LES HUGUENOTS"

spot. Only Marcel rejoices at his master's escape from marriage with a Catholic.

ACT II. In a public square in Paris Catholic students are singing and drinking outside an inn, opposite one where Huguenot soldiers are gathered. The wedding procession of Count de Nevers, who has repersuaded Valentine to marry him, enters a nearby chapel. When they return after the ceremony Valentine is not with them, as she has requested to be left there until nightfall to pray. St. Bris lingers after De Nevers has hastened away, and Marcel approaches him, bearing a challenge from Raoul. St. Bris is eager to accept, and takes a companion aside into the chapel to tell him of the plan to assassinate Raoul.

Valentine overhears his disclosure and, hastening from the chapel to warn Raoul, meets Marcel and tells him of the plot. She returns to the chapel and Marcel sees his master enter the square with his seconds for the duel. Raoul is immediately surrounded by Catholics, and Marcel, rushing to his aid, alarms the Huguenots within the inn. Immediately the square is filled with the warring parties. Queen Margaret arrives suddenly and in time to prevent bloodshed. While Raoul and St. Bris each accuse the other of treachery, Marcel explains that Valentine, who now appears upon the church steps, overheard the plot against Raoul and sought to warn him. The queen tells Raoul that Valentine, to whom he now owes his life, visited Count de Nevers to obtain release from her engagement to him. Raoul is filled with remorse and sorrow that Valentine is now married to another. A boat comes on the river and De Nevers conducts his bride to it, while all the people wish them joy.

ACT III. In a room in the castle of Count de Nevers Valentine sits alone when Raoul comes in, having braved death to speak again with her whom he loves. As Valentine hears her father's voice she hides Raoul. St. Bris and De Nevers with a large party of Catholic noblemen enter, and the plot for the massacre of all Huguenots that very night is disclosed. St. Bris requires the conspirators to pledge their assistance in carrying out the plan. De Nevers alone protests, as he will not become an assassin, and is led away under guard. Then the Catholic lords, inspired by the fanatic zeal of three monks who enter and address them, pledge themselves to kill without mercy at the ringing of the bells all Huguenots, and promise secrecy.

When they leave Raoul comes forth from his hiding-place, eager to warn his coreligionists and friends. Valentine fears for his safety and tells him that she loves him. Raoul cannot then consent to leave her and urges her to flee with him, while she, fearful for his safety, would detain him. As he hesitates the fateful bells begin to ring. He is remorseful over his selfish delay and, finding the door locked, escapes by the window as Valentine faints.

ACT IV. In a ballroom in the Tower of Nesle the nobles are assembled celebrating the marriage of Queen Margaret to King Henry. The alarm-bell rings and nearer and nearer comes the sound of guns, the cries of the assassins, and the groans of the wounded. Raoul dashes in and announces the wholesale slaughter of the Huguenots.

In a cemetery near a church, to which women and children are fleeing for refuge, Raoul and Marcel meet. Suddenly Valentine appears, seeking Raoul. She tells him that De Nevers is killed, and begs Raoul not to leave her, saying that she would rather die with him than be safe among her people. At length Raoul consents, and bids Marcel marry them. Scarcely is the ceremony finished when the assassins rush upon the people within the church and slay all who will not abjure their faith.

Raoul, mortally wounded, is being supported by Valentine and Marcel as they seek to escape under cover of night. St. Bris with his musketeers comes upon them and challenges them. Raoul valiantly answers "Huguenots!" The soldiers fire, and all fall. St. Bris is horrified to hear his daughter's voice as, dying, she recognizes him, and he rushes forward only to clasp her lifeless body.

IRIS
(Ī'-rĭs)

ITALIAN tragic grand opera. Music by Pietro Mascagni. Book by Luigi Illica. First production, Rome 1898. The scene is Japan in the nineteenth century.

CHARACTERS

THE BLIND FATHER OF IRIS	Bass
OSAKA	Tenor
KYOTO	Baritone
IRIS	Soprano
GEISHA	Soprano
A RAGPICKER	Tenor

A young girl; three women representing Beauty, Death, and the Vampire; three geisha girls, a huckster, traveling musicians, mountebanks, samurai, citizens, and ragpickers.

ACT I. At the break of day, as all nature wakens slowly to life, are heard the multitudinous voices of the sun, proclaiming itself the source of life, love, and all existing things. As the light shines upon Fujiyama Iris, who lives in a house in the country with her blind and poverty-stricken father, comes out into the garden. She is young and very beautiful, and of a childish innocence. She carries her doll and, when she herself has made her obeisance to the sun, she raises it in her arms three times in salutation to the god of morn. She is troubled by a terrible dream of monsters from which she has just awakened. Her father comes out into the garden to pray in the sunlight, whose cheer he can only feel, and to him she tells her dream. He and the bright day and the beauty of the garden reassure her, and soon she is again the joyous, happy girl she has been all her life.

As she plays contentedly about she is seen by Osaka, a

wealthy and dissolute young nobleman. He is greatly attracted by her beauty and her innocence, and longs to make her his own at all costs. With him is Kyoto, a crafty and villainous man, a procurer. They plot together how best to obtain her. Kyoto thinks that the only way is abduction, and they go off to further their plans. Young girls pass by singing on their way to wash in the stream. Workmen go by to their work. Still the joyous Iris takes her delight in the sunlight and the flowers.

Osaka and Kyoto come back in the disguise of strolling players. Iris's curiosity is aroused by their appearance, and when they set up a puppet show near by she leaves her father for a moment to watch them. In their marionette theater are three women masked as Beauty, Death, and the Vampire. The plot is the story of a young girl who is lured to her death,—a truly prophetic plot for poor little Iris to see. While she is absorbed in it she is seized and borne away and that without the knowledge of the bystanders, who disperse. The blind father soon misses his daughter and calls for her, but gets no answer. When his distress and anxiety draw the attention of some merchants who are passing, they search in vain for her, but find near the father a bag of money and a paper explaining that Iris has gone to the Yoshiwara, a place of ill repute. His grief and anger at her are unbounded, and wildly railing he goes to seek her.

Act II. In a room of the Yoshiwara Iris lies sleeping. Osaka and Kyoto stand gazing at her and admiring her beauty, and the nobleman is so pleased with the prize he has obtained that he pays Kyoto liberally. As she awakens they go out. Iris finds herself in such gaudy splendor and luxury that she thinks she must be in paradise. She has jewels and beautiful garments to wear and she hears the sounds of music and dancing. From a window she sees guests arriving in their jinrikishas. As she believes that in paradise one is capable of doing everything that one wishes, she tries to paint, but her clumsy fingers succeed in making only a colored daub. She takes a cittern and tries to play upon it while she sings, but she can make only discord. This throws her into a childish rage.

Soon Osaka comes. He admires her greatly and seeks to woo her, but she does not understand in the least what his protestations mean or what her being there denotes. When he kisses her she bursts into tears and sobbing wishes to go back to her garden. Osaka's patience is exhausted and he commands Kyoto to take her back home. But the wily trader does not propose to lose her so, and dressing her in transparent garments opens the doors to a gaping crowd. She is amused by this maneuver, which she does not understand. Osaka is among the crowd and as he hears the comments upon her beauty, his own desire for her is inflamed and he offers Kyoto any price for her. He approaches her again with tender words just as a wild cry is heard and her father appears calling her name. She answers him. The blind father, thinking she has come to this place of her own accord, is beside himself with anger and shame. She runs toward him, but he strikes at her and taking up the mud of the street flings it upon her, cursing her. She understands then, suddenly, clearly, what it all means. Immediately she rushes to a raised balcony and throws herself down into an open sewer.

Act III. Blackest night lies over an abyss outside the city, where some ragpickers are searching. For in the slime and filth of the sewer one has found a jewel. They come across the body of Iris, whom they believe to be dead. As they quarrel among themselves and tear her clothing in their eagerness to get the jewelry she wears, she moves and they rush away in terror. Her mind is wandering in delirium, beset by fearful dreams and tormented by wondering thoughts. She thinks she hears the voices of the three men who have in one day ruined her life,—Osaka, Kyoto, and her father,—and the maledictions that they each cast upon her. She cannot understand at all how this fate can be hers, and she asks of the world, of destiny, and of Heaven the question, "Why?" She does not long suffer, for the rising sun comes with its message of life and drives away the darkness and the mists. The abyss and its terrors slowly disappear, and Iris's soul is caught up into a wonderful country of flowers and beauty, and she mounts above the earth to take her place in the sun, which with its multitudinous voices welcomes her.

THE JEWELS OF THE MADONNA
(I GIOJELLI DELLA MADONNA)

ITALIAN tragic grand opera. Music by Ermanno Wolf-Ferrari. Book by Carlo Zangarini and E. Golisciani. First production, Berlin, 1911. The scene is laid in Naples at the present time.

CHARACTERS

GENNARO, in love with Maliella	Tenor
RAFAELE, leader of the Cammorists	Baritone
BIASO	Tenor
CICCILLO	Tenor
ROCCO	Bass
MALIELLA, in love with Rafaele	Soprano
CARMELA	Soprano
STELLA	Soprano
CONCETTA	Soprano
SERENE	Soprano

Grazia the dancer, Totonno, vendors, monks, and the people.

ACT I. In Naples on a festal day the people are gathered in a public square when Maliella, beautiful and wayward, rushes out from the house of her foster-mother and mingles with the festal crowd. Gennaro, her foster-brother, who loves her, is vainly trying to restrain her reckless gaiety, but she willfully resents interference. When accosted by the dashing Rafaele, leader of the Cammorists and a man of lawless instincts, she is infatuated. He makes love to the spirited girl, but when he attempts to kiss her, she stabs him. Instead of resenting the blow he kisses the wound, and to prove his devotion to her, boasts that he would even steal the jewels that deck the statue of the Madonna, which is then being borne by in a procession, that he might give them to her. Terrified at the proposed sacrilege she recoils from him.

Act II. In the garden of her foster-mother's home Maliella sits thinking of Rafaele, whose bravado she admires and whom she longs to meet again. When she tells Gennaro that she is restless to go out into the world, he declares his love for her. She only laughs and taunts him with lacking the spirit to dare steal the jewels of the Madonna. Gennaro, recklessly eager to prove his devotion, vows that he will bring her the jewels and goes out, locking the gate of the garden. As Maliella awaits his return Rafaele comes with his guitar and serenades her. Overjoyed to see him, she declares her love for him and when he pledges his devotion to her, she promises to join him on the morrow at the stronghold of the Cammorists. With this promise he leaves, and soon Gennaro returns. He presents to her the jewels, and she, fascinated with them and remembering that Rafaele wanted her to have them, puts them on.

Act III. Early the next day in a stronghold by the sea the Cammorists are holding high carnival. None is more jubilant than Rafaele, who awaits the coming of Maliella. When she enters, adorned with the jewels, Rafaele is wildly jealous and believes that she has sold herself for them. But Maliella cries out that Gennaro brought them to her, and that they are the jewels of the Madonna. The people fall back from her in horror, and, fearful of punishment, sink to their knees in prayer. Maliella then realizes how great a sacrilege has been committed, and when they spurn her as evil and accursed she snatches off the jewels and flings herself from the high cliff into the sea.

Gennaro, who has followed Maliella to the stronghold and witnessed her death, now in remorse and despair replaces the fateful jewels on the altar before the Madonna and, praying for mercy, stabs himself just as the people, seeking vengeance, enter the church.

THE JUGGLER OF NOTRE-DAME
(LE JONGLEUR DE NÔTRE-DAME)

FRENCH musical miracle play. Music by Jules Massenet. Book by Maurice Léna. First production, Monte Carlo, 1902. The scene is Cluny, near Paris, in the fourteenth century.

CHARACTERS

JEAN THE JUGGLER	Tenor
BONIFACE, cook of the monastery	Baritone
THE PRIOR	Bass
THE MONK PAINTER	Baritone
THE MONK MUSICIAN	Baritone
THE MONK POET	Tenor
THE MONK SCULPTOR	Bass

An apparition of the Virgin, two angels, a knight, a jovial fellow, a drunken man, a monk crier, monks, knights, citizens, peasants, merchants and their wives, clergymen, and beggars.

ACT I. On Mayday in a square of Cluny, where all the people are assembled for market-day and the dance of the children, Jean the Juggler, whom because of his lean appearance the crowd call "King Famine," is playing his hurdy-gurdy, singing his songs, and doing his tricks and dances. The crowd demand of him a rollicking song in praise of wine, and with obeisance to the statue of the Virgin he begins to sing. The Prior of the monastery close by comes out and, hearing the blasphemous song, frowns upon the crowd, which slinks away leaving Jean to meet the Prior's righteous rebuke. The indignant Prior urges Jean to repent. When Boniface enters to announce that dinner is ready he speaks kindly to the abashed Jean, who at his invitation follows the monks into the monastery.

Act II. Within the cloister the monks are gathered, each busy with his special work and all with the one ambition to do something in honor of the Virgin. One monk is painting a wonderful picture, another has made a statue of her, another has written a hymn. Jean sits disconsolate because his talents are not worthy of presenting to the Virgin, for his songs are all secular and frivolous, and his tricks foolish. Boniface, kindly and humble, tries to cheer him by telling him the legend of the humble sagebrush bush that better than its proud sister, the rose, sheltered the infant Jesus and so was blessed of the Mother Mary.

Act III. One day Jean steals into the chapel when he thinks he will be quite alone, and standing before the statue of the Virgin, doffs his monk's garb and discloses beneath his juggler's suit. He begins to go through his dances, his tricks, and to sing his songs, playing upon his hurdy-gurdy, and doing all to the very best of his ability in honor of the Holy Virgin. The painter monk, when he comes to work upon his picture, discovers Jean, and seeing what he is doing, summons the other monks, and they all are standing round, quietly witnessing the sacrilegious performance, as they think it. At length they can permit it no longer and seize him, surprising him out of his absorption and making him cringe before their denunciation. But Boniface stops them, crying out, "A miracle!" and points to the statue of the Virgin. A halo of light surrounds her face and angelic voices are heard. Jean, who falls on his knees begging forgiveness for his presumption, is transported by the light that streams upon him from the features of the statue, and seeing the light, the other monks kneel to him and beseech him to pray for them. Jean is enraptured with the divine favor, and as angelic voices sound his soul takes flight.

JULIEN

(OR, THE LIFE OF THE POET)

FRENCH allegorical grand opera, second in a projected trilogy of which "Louise" was the first. Both music and book by Gustave Charpentier. First production, Paris, 1913. The scene is Rome, Paris, and elsewhere, but the environment chiefly is the mind of a poet of the present day.

CHARACTERS

JULIEN, the poet.
LOUISE, his wife.
THE GRANDMOTHER ⎫
THE PEASANT GIRL ⎬ Louise in different incarnations.
BEAUTY ⎮
A STREET-GIRL ⎭

A high priest, fakir, officiating minister, a bell-ringer, an acolyte, a stone-breaker, a workman, dauber, student, a middle-class woman, four companions of Julien, two waiters, six dream maidens, six chimeras, three fairies, voices from the abyss, Levites, augurs, sages, servants of Beauty, Muses, lovers, sweethearts, elect poets, lost poets, woodcutters, excavators, Bohemians, Bretons, dancers, peasant men and women, and the crowds at the fête and at the carnival.

PROLOGUE. In the Villa Medici at Rome Julien, who has received the *Prix de Rome* and is ripening into a poet, is living with his wife, Louise. It is evening and Louise lies on a couch in their room, having fallen asleep while waiting his return. As he enters the farewells of his four companions are heard. He sits by the table and idly fingers the sheets of the poem he is writing, which he plans as his masterpiece. While meditating upon it and his high ambition for it, he falls asleep. Louise, awaking, stands beside him and in her affection gently caresses him, thinking of his great poem and how absorbed in it he is, and that she is content and happy though she knows that she is second in his heart to his work. While he sleeps he passes through visions which symbolize the passage of the poet's soul through the experiences of enthusiasm, doubt, impotence, and intoxication.

Act I. It is the country of dreams, and Julien finds himself with Louise by his side, on his way to the Temple of Beauty, which is set high on the distant Holy Mount. He goes to dedicate himself to the worship of the Beautiful and the True, and in the happiness of Louise's love and companionship upon this high pilgrimage he clasps her fervently in his arms. Other pilgrims and other lovers travel the same way. The ascent is steep, but dream maidens, singing of love and beauty and wreathed with dew-wet flowers, run among the rocks that border the path. They are poets' fancies and are fair as the light.

Julien and Louise have to pass the Accurst Valley, which is halfway to the temple. This alley is peopled with disappointed mortals. A voice from the dark abyss wails of lost dreams. Chimeras waving mystical veils tell of deceits and lying dreams, while lost and disillusioned poets stretch their arms up toward the mount and pray for the restoration of their lost hopes. This so stirs the heart of Julien that he believes it his mission to help his brothers.

Arriving at the temple Julien avows his purpose and Louise joyfully seconds him. Surrounded by the worshipers of Beauty, by Levites, augurs, sages, dream maidens, the servants of Beauty, sacred dancers, and elect poets, Julien is asked if he will sacrifice everything to the high ideal he seeks. Enthusiastically he pledges himself to the service of Truth, Beauty, and Humanity. In prophetic and warning words the high priest tells him of the sneers and indifference he must encounter, the humiliation he must endure, and that his sacrifice will be in vain, his effort result only in failure. Yet more ardently does he consecrate himself. Among the bystanders a bell-ringer and an acolyte laugh mockingly at his delusion, and deride the priest as a pretender. Louise, daunted by the fateful words of the high priest, takes refuge among the dream maidens, and henceforth becomes one of them. The ceremony continues. Julien prostrates himself before the altar. The temple grows dark, lightning flashes, and amid a peculiar splendor the Goddess of Beauty appears. Her face is the face of Louise. He addresses her, and she speaks to him words of counsel and wisdom: "Love! Fear pride and human reason!"

Act II. In a picturesque Slovaque valley in Hungary Julien lies sleeping on a mound not far from a peasant's cottage. Having wandered far he is very weary, and he moves restlessly. The old peasant woman in the cottage says that his soul is fixed by a dream. Reapers are reaping in the fields near by, woodcutters are chopping, and all are singing as they work. Julien awakes and hears the chorus of hard, burdensome toil that comes from all the land. He is discouraged by his failure to make the wretched world listen to his message and believe in the beauty of love and the love of beauty. Worn out he has come here seeking peace, but here he has found misery,—all are too much bowed down by toil to see visions. The old peasant farmer, as he sits on his bench by the door, watches Julien, and his daughter, a peasant girl whose beauty of face is strangely like that of Louise, looks compassionately at him.

Night falls and the peasant speaks hospitably to him. The girl bids him linger and seeks to relieve his dejection. She offers him her love, bidding him renounce his dream of world regeneration and find happiness in dwelling apart from the world. As they stand together in the moonlight, she timidly inviting him, the old peasant speaks to him from the open door, and it is with the same voice as that of the high priest of the temple when he warned him against treating Beauty lightly. The tones recall haunting memories, and he turns from the peasant girl and drawn by the voices of the night fares forth alone upon his wanderings.

ACT III. On the storm-tossed coast of Brittany, under its cold gray skies, which cast weird lights on rocks and sea, near the cottages and church of the village in which he was born sits Julien. He sees women, brown and bent, silently threading their way from gloomy houses to the dark and forbidding church. Burdened with sorrow at the ugliness, the unrelieved toil of a world grown blind of heart, and wild with despair at the fruitlessness of all his efforts to speak the life-giving message, he is beyond all hoping. His old grandmother, whose features and face are, strangely enough, those of Louise, comes from a cottage and would minister to him. She caresses him and bids him remain with her. For his comfort she tries to restore to him his childhood faith in Christ and His teaching, and responding to old emotions Julien kneels at a wayside shrine. But again comes the thought of his failure, and he tastes the bitterness of a sense of utter impotence. The old grandmother asks him what are the halting figures that creep by upon the highway, and he tells her that they are disillusioned poets. He hears their voices, their sardonic taunts, and their laments for their lost dreams. She bids him beware of pride and in her tone and words he hears again the voice of the high priest. "Who told you that?" he questions, and then, his rising faith checked by the mocking laughter of the lost poets, he cries aloud, cursing her God and all gods.

Act IV. It is a dark and misty night as into a deserted street in the Montmartre district of Paris Julien rushes pursued by the Furies. Rejected by a world that has chosen animal pleasure, he too will be an animal like the rest. The memory of his consecration to Beauty and Love is bitter to him. As he falls upon a seat sounds of merrymaking are heard, and there comes from the Cabaret of the Muses a bold street-girl, who offers him wine and bids him drink with her. Again in her features and the tones of her voice he sees and hears Louise; the Goddess of Beauty from the Holy Mount has now become degraded with him to the gutter. The dream maidens, the vanished chimeras, now sad-looking creatures, are seen dimly in the distance, as they sing of the mists of oblivion. Julien weeps, and the street-girl offers him drink. Her voice haunts him, and he demands who she is, for if Louise were not dead he would think her she. She says she is the muse of bagpipe tunes, the beauty who makes the beast. He attempts to seize her but she goes laughingly off into the cabaret. Julien bows his head and confesses that all he has done has been inspired by pride and ambition. He is now ruined and it is only left for him to die.

Suddenly a boisterous crowd comes to celebrate the fête of Shrove Tuesday, and the street is transformed into a square before the Moulin Rouge, with cabarets and side shows brilliantly lighted. Everywhere there is singing and dancing and drinking. The street-girl comes again to him and he and she dance and revel with the rest. In mad orgy they recklessly and drunkenly riot together. Fronting the square is a theater, called the Theater of the Ideal, and before it a priestlike old man sells for two sous admission to view the splendors of Beauty. He resembles, to Julien's vision, the high priest of the temple on the Holy Mount; and in the mad crowd Julien recognizes the dream maidens, the bell-ringer, the acolyte, dream pilgrims, and chimeras, and others who were present at the ceremony of his consecration. They are transformed now into bestial beings. The crowd makes a rush into the theater, he and the street-girl with them. In great derision they wreck it, and suddenly as it falls a strange darkness descends and in the midst of it there is a dim light and a vision of the holy temple and the sacred service appears. The street-girl, at whose knees Julien has sunk in drunken abandon, laughs horribly as she watches the agony of remorse upon the poet's face. The aspirations of his youth scorch his soul. In complete despair he turns passionately to the street-girl, and while she still horribly laughs he falls dead at her feet.

KÖNIGSKINDER
(Koé-nigs-kĭn-der)
(KINGLY CHILDREN)

GERMAN allegorical fairy opera. Music by Engelbert Humperdinck. Book by Elsa Bernstein ("Ernst Rosmer"). First production, New York, 1910. The scene is Hellabrunn in the mountains of Germany during the Middle Ages.

CHARACTERS

THE KING'S SON	Tenor
THE FIDDLER	Baritone
THE WOODCUTTER	Bass
THE BROOM-MAKER	Tenor
THE SENIOR COUNCILOR	Baritone
THE INNKEEPER	Bass
THE GOOSE-GIRL	Soprano
THE WITCH	Contralto
THE INNKEEPER'S DAUGHTER	Mezzo-Soprano

Tailor, stablemaid, two gatekeepers, citizens, councilors, burghers and their wives, artisans, girls, lads, and children.

ACT I. Under a linden tree near a witch's hut in the wooded hills above the town of Hellabrunn a beautiful golden-haired Goose-Girl is tending her flock. The witch commands her to make a poisoned loaf of bread and she is obliged to obey. She is lonely and begs the witch to allow her to go to the town, but the witch refuses and goes off to gather herbs. The girl views herself in the waters of a nearby pool and, weaving a garland of flowers for her head, calls her geese to admire her. She is startled by footsteps and turns to find a man watching her. Amazed at her shyness and innocence, and much attracted by her beauty, he wins her confidence. He tells her that he is a wandering prince, the son of a distant king, and has left home to seek adventure because he tired of court life. They sit beneath the linden and, falling in love, kiss each other. She promises to go away with him. When the wind blows her garland from her head, he seizes it and puts it within his blouse and gives her his golden crown instead. She prefers the flowers and will not take the crown, so he casts it from him. They are about to go off together when she finds that the witch's spell keeps her feet from moving, and she sinks down in terror. He thinks that her heart fails her, and angrily spurns her, telling her that she is not worthy to be a king's mate and that she shall never see him again until a star falls from the sky into a lily. Deeply hurt, she bids him go. Hearing the witch approaching she hides the crown.

The witch notes her startled appearance and learns that a man has been there. She shuts the Goose-Girl into the hut as the fiddler comes out of the woods with two companions, the broom-maker and the woodcutter. They have come from the people of Hellabrunn to the witch for a prophecy. The old king has died, and they want a new king, one of royal blood, to reign over them. Where shall they find him? The witch tells them that the first person who enters the town gates after the clock has struck twelve the next noon, though he be clad like a common beggar, shall be worthy to wear the crown. The woodcutter and broom-maker go away, but the fiddler has caught a glimpse of the beautiful girl within the house, and lingers. At nightfall he knocks at the door and the witch reluctantly lets him speak with the girl. The fiddler laughs when she says that the witch is her grandmother. She tells him that she fears the cruel witch, and relates how the King's Son came, and how they loved each other, but she could not go away with him because of the witch's enchantment. He finds her fair and good, and wonders why she and the King's Son should not reign over the people of Hellabrunn. He promises to set her free and marry her to the King's Son, if she will help him find him. The witch ridicules the idea of the beggarmaid's wedding the King's Son, and tells the girl of her ignoble parentage and the tragic death of her father and mother. But the fiddler says that he knew her father and mother, and that they were in their love and sorrow akin to kings. The Goose-Girl says that she will find her lover. When she asks the witch to release her, the witch refuses, and the fiddler tells the Goose-Girl that alone she must free herself from the witch's spell. She puts the crown upon her golden curls, and kneeling prays to her father and mother to help her. A star falls from the sky straight into the heart of a lily, and there glows. She jumps up and rushes for the wood, followed by her geese and the fiddler.

Act II. Within the gates of Hellabrunn stands an inn and opposite it are seats for the town councilors who are to welcome the king. The King's Son in his ragged garments comes to the inn, and overhearing a conversation between the innkeeper's daughter and a stablemaid, learns of the prophecy. The innkeeper's daughter is much taken with him and brings him food and drink, but even in his hunger he spurns them. He sits dreamily meditating upon the beautiful Goose-Girl, whom he sincerely loves, and the innkeeper's daughter, finding that he pays little attention to her, becomes very angry. The King's Son is about to leave the town in disgust when the Goose-Girl's wreath within his blouse whispers to him not to go. He then resolves to hire out to the innkeeper to gain a livelihood.

Many people enter the square. The innkeeper has no work for the poor King's Son except as a swineherd, but the lad accepts that. He is sitting under a tree thinking upon his lost love when the woodcutter comes and pretends to pay the innkeeper an old score, but pockets the money again when his host is not looking. The councilors enter and take their places, and everybody discusses the coming ruler. The woodcutter relates again how the witch said that whoever first entered the city gates after the stroke of twelve should be their king. The people declare that they will crown whoever so comes, but they show that they expect him to come in regal state. The King's Son asks them if the future king might not come in rags, but they laugh at him. He assures them that the regal state means kingly qualities, not robes. They jeer at him. The innkeeper's daughter accuses him of not paying for the food she got him, and the woodcutter of stealing the money he paid the innkeeper. The crowd are rushing at him when the hour strikes and they pause expectant. The gates are flung open and the amazed people see the Goose-Girl approaching with the golden crown on her bright curls and followed by her flock of geese and the fiddler. The King's Son rushes to her and kneels before her, calling her his queen. The crowd laughs in derision. As they surround and menace her the King's Son draws his sword in her defense. In spite of the fiddler's protests the people drive the pair back through the gates and away.

ACT III. The dark woods about the witch's hut are white with snow. The witch has been burned at the stake by the townspeople because they thought her prophecy false, but the fiddler, though imprisoned, has escaped and taken refuge here. He is feeding the pigeons as the woodcutter and broom-maker and a band of children from the town come to beg him to return, that he may again sing and play for them. He says that he has vowed never to return. When the children ask him to help them find the kingly young pair, whom they now believe to be their destined king and his queen, he starts off at once with them while the woodcutter and broom-maker wait in the hut.

After they are gone the King's Son comes in, bearing in his arms his weary and almost fainting sweetheart. He too is exhausted, and they cling to each other, worn out with hunger and cold, but loving and tender. They recognize the place, and go to the hut seeking food and shelter. The woodcutter will not admit them, and refuses them food. The Goose-Girl draws the King's Son away with her to the shelter of the linden tree. There they recall their wanderings, and rejoice that they still have the happiness of being together. To cheer him she throws off her cloak and shoes and dances before him, singing happily until she falls in a faint. As she recovers and he is trying to make her comfortable, his eye lights on the bundle wherein is his crown. In spite of her protests he breaks the crown in two and goes to offer it to the woodcutter in exchange for shelter. The broom-maker has just discovered a box containing an apparently fresh loaf of bread, so the men sell it for both pieces of the golden crown. The King's Son exultantly carries the bread to the Goose-Girl and together they eat it. But it is the poisoned loaf that the Goose-Girl made long ago, and the lovers, kissing passionately, fall into the sleep of death in each other's arms.

When the fiddler and the children return from their fruitless quest, the woodcutter exhibits the golden treasure he has obtained, and the fiddler recognizes it as the crown that the Goose-Girl wore. He starts out again, the children with him. A dove circles around his head and then flies to the linden tree. Following it he finds the lifeless bodies of the royal lovers. The children place them upon a bier, and weeping, bear back to Hellabrunn the kingly children.

DER KUHREIGEN
(Der Kōō-rīgh'-en)
(LE RANZ DES VACHES)

GERMAN tragic grand opera, founded on the story "Die Kleine Blanchefleure" by Rudolf Hans Bartsch. Music by William Kienzl. Book by Richard Batka. First production, Vienna, 1911. The scene is Paris and Versailles in the years 1792 and 1793.

CHARACTERS

LOUIS XVI..*Bass*
MARQUIS MASSIMELLE REOLE DE COURTROY, Commandant, *Bass*
CAPTAIN BRAYOLE....................................*Tenor*
MARQUIS DE CHÉZY..................................*Bass*
PRIMUS THALLER ⎱   ⎰ *Tenor*
DURSEL   ⎬ Corporals in a Swiss regiment ⎨ *Tenor*
MARION   ⎱   ⎰ *Bass*
FAVART, Sergeant of the Chasseurs................*Baritone*
BLANCHEFLEURE, Marquise Massimelle.............*Soprano*
CLEO, matron of honor of Marquise Massimelle..*Mezzo-Soprano*
DORIS, daughter of the quartermaster in the barracks of St. Honoré ....*Soprano*

The chancellor, Chanteclair, Jourdan, Duval, Epissier, Cartouche, the "Temple" warder, the chaplain, a girl, French soldiers, Swiss soldiers, hunters, officers, orderlies, gentlemen and ladies of the court, lackeys, and two sans-culottes.

ACT I. In the late afternoon in the barracks of St. Honoré in Paris groups of Swiss soldiers are gathered together, among them Sergeant Favart and Primus Thaller. The commandant, Marquis Massimelle, has just left the barracks. Favart is full of revolutionary spirit and ridicules the marquis. Thaller resents his remarks, and a quarrel starts. The other soldiers interfere and prevent the two from coming to blows, and the Swiss soldiers all sit down together to a glass of wine. Primus Thaller impulsively starts to sing the *Kuhreigen,* or *Ranz des Vaches,* the melody which the Alpine herdsmen use to call their cattle to pasture. The singing of this melody in the barracks has been forbidden on pain of death, because it recalled to the Swiss their homeland so vividly that they were sorely tempted to desert and return to the mountains to hear it once more. Favart, with his hostility toward Thaller not yet cool, sees an opportunity for revenge, and denounces the singer and orders him led away to prison for disobeying orders.

ACT II. In the chamber of the king, Louis XVI, at Versailles, the case of Thaller is brought up for decision and sentence. The facts are all attested and the sentence of death is the legal penalty, but the charming Marquise Blanchefleure, wife of the commandant, interposes in behalf of the young and sturdy Swiss, whose only crime is homesickness. The king grants the request of this favorite and pardons Thaller. The marquise is amused by the awkward but frank and ingenuous soldier and coyly flirts with him. But what is play to her is serious enough to him, who, although unversed in the ways of the court, is full of gratitude to the woman who has saved his life. So though he knows she is married he falls deeply in love with her, and will accept no patronage but hopes that the time may come when he shall rise to the position that her husband holds.

ACT III. The French Revolution has broken out and the aristocrats are in danger. Marquis Massimelle has been beheaded and his beautiful wife is in prison expecting a like fate. The fortunes of the time have promoted Thaller to the rank of general, and he has it now in his power to save the woman whom he has so long and faithfully loved. As his wife she will be free. In the dungeons of the "Temple," a large prison, many aristocrats are gathered awaiting their doom. General Thaller seeks the fair Blanchefleure, tells her of his love, and makes his proposal to her. She is very grateful to him for his devotion, but she does not really love him, and she cannot bring herself to marry a revolutionist and become merely Mrs. Thaller instead of being a marquise,—so she prefers to go to the scaffold.

It is customary for the aristocrats to spend their time of waiting for death in singing and dancing. So to prove her gratitude the Marquise Massimelle promises that she will give her last dance to Thaller. La Blanchefleure outshines all of that doomed but brave throng in beauty and grace. True to her word she gives the worthy Thaller the last dance, and dances until the officers at the door summon her to lay her head upon the guillotine. Primus Thaller turns away from her vanishing face heartbroken.

LAKMÉ
(Lăk-mā)

FRENCH tragic grand opera, founded upon the story, "Le Mariage de Loti," which appeared in the *Nouvelle Revue* about 1880. Music by Clément Philibert Léo Delibes. Book by Edmond Gondinet and Philippe Gille. First production, Paris, 1883. The scene is India at about 1880.

CHARACTERS

GERALD } officers of the British army in India { Tenor
FREDERICK } { Baritone
NILAKANTHA, a Brahman priest......................Bass
HADJI, a Hindu slave..............................Tenor
LAKMÉ, daughter of Nilakantha..................Soprano
ELLEN, daughter of the Viceroy..................Soprano
ROSE, friend of Ellen............................Soprano
MRS. BENTSON, governess of Ellen and Rose...Mezzo-Soprano
MALLIKA, slave of Lakmé....................Mezzo-Soprano

A fortune-teller, a Chinese merchant, a Sepoy, Hindus, both men and women; English officers and ladies, sailors, bayaderes, Chinamen, musicians, Brahmans, and snake charmers.

ACT I. At sunrise in the garden of Ganesa, the Goddess of Wisdom, Nilakantha, a Brahman priest, bids his two slaves, Hadji and Mallika, open the gates to a company of Hindu worshipers. As Nilakantha comes from his dwelling in the midst of the garden, he greets the worshipers and tells them that though the foreign victors have defied the gods and cast down their images in the temples, he believes that Brahma will avenge the wrongs of his people. Lakmé appears on the threshold of the priest's home, and joins the Hindus in their prayers. Her father gives them his benediction and they go off to their day's work. He bids fare-

© White

MARIA BARRIENTOS
AS "LAKMÉ"

well to Lakmé, as he must go to an important conference, and commends her to the care of the slaves. As Hadji goes away into the house Lakmé takes off some of her jewels and lays them upon a stone table. She and Mallika then take a light boat and go up the brook.

The garden is deserted until suddenly there is the sound of English voices and laughter, and two English officers with the daughter of the Viceroy, her governess, and a friend enter, lured by the beauties of the garden. Frederick, one of the officers, recognizes the place as the home of Nilakantha, the fanatic Brahman priest who is constantly counseling resistance against the invaders. He tells the party of the beautiful Lakmé, how she is regarded as a goddess and is kept hidden from the sight of all but the devoted. The women are curious and anxious to catch a glimpse of her, but Frederick is cautious and insists that they not linger longer as their intrusion would be considered sacrilege, which the Hindus do not easily forgive. The ladies espy the jewels, but Frederick succeeds in persuading them to leave. Not so Gerald, whose fancy is touched and who takes out drawing materials to get the design of the jewelry. As he examines the pieces he is seized with a strange premonition and also a romantic longing to see the famed beauty whose hand and arm and neck the jewelry has encircled. Lakmé and Mallika return, and he hides.

Lakmé brings flowers which she places before the statue of Ganesa. As she pensively lingers alone she catches sight of Gerald and utters a cry. Mallika and Hadji come running in, but Lakmé, realizing that it will mean death to the man if she discloses his hiding-place, excuses her outcry as an idle fear due to her great anxiety for her father. When they have gone she goes directly to Gerald and bids him be gone and forget what he has seen. But he, entranced by her beauty, tells her that he cannot forget her. She, though angered, is softened by his unfeigned admiration, and admires his courage in thus braving death to linger with her. Her beauty inspires his love, and as he avows it she feels an answering passion stir in her heart. Deeply attracted they rejoice in youth and in each other until suddenly Nilakantha approaches. While Lakmé stands by terrified Gerald makes good his escape, though not before the angry father has seen him.

Act II. In a public square of the city, upon which open shops and restaurants, sailors, Hindu vendors of all sorts, Chinamen, and musicians are making holiday. Mrs. Bentson enters alone and is accosted by the vendors, and by a Sepoy, who steals her watch. She is angry and insulted when Frederick and Rose hasten up just as the market bell rings and the shops are closed. They stand at one side as dancers enter, dance, and pass on. They are joined by Gerald and Ellen, his betrothed, and soon the English party, after watching the crowds, among whom they notice an aged beggar leaning on the arm of his daughter, pass on.

The beggar was no other than Nilakantha, who seeks the intruding English officer. Lakmé is compelled to go with him and sing sacred ballads, that the Englishman may betray himself by recognizing her. Lakmé begs her father to forgive the stranger's intrusion, but Nilakantha believes that the Englishman loves his daughter and that she is sad because her fancy has been stirred, so he thinks only of vengeance. At his command Lakmé sings, and a crowd gathers about them. Some officers join it, among them Frederick and Gerald. Lakmé's voice falters, and when Gerald draws near she utters a cry and seems about to fall. Gerald springs forward, calling her name. Nilakantha observes him and gives thanks to Brahma, as Frederick leads Gerald away.

Soon Lakmé is left alone with Hadji, and Gerald enters searching for her. She dismisses the slave and greets the officer. They avow their love for each other in spite of difference of race and faith, and Lakmé warns him of his danger, and tells him of a secret hut within a near-by forest where she will meet him. He says that duty and honor forbid him, but when she weeps he promises. He goes away as Nilakantha and Brahmans enter bearing the image of the Goddess Dourga, and go toward the pagoda. When the procession has passed on Nilakantha and the Hindu linger. As Gerald also lingers seeking a word with Lakmé, Nilakantha stabs him and runs away as he falls. Lakmé goes to him, smiles when she sees that the wound is not serious, and with Hadji's aid bears him away.

ACT III. Within an Indian forest embowered in flowers stands a hut under a large tree. Gerald lies on a bed of leaves, and Lakmé, half leaning over him, watches his sleep, singing softly of their love for each other. He stirs and, not seeing Lakmé, tries to recall where he is and what has happened. Lakmé tells him how Hadji bore him to this place, and how by her knowledge of healing herbs she has restored him. Gerald gives himself up to the rapture of their love and to Lakmé's plan that there they shall live, protected of Brahma and unknown of the world. He hears footsteps, which Lakmé tells him are those of lover pilgrims going to the springs sacred to lovers, to drink of the water. She goes to get some of that water that he and she may drink.

During her absence Frederick enters, searching for him, and pleads with him to break the spell that holds him and to return to his regiment and his betrothed. He exacts a promise from Gerald that he will return, and goes away content, as Lakmé reënters. She brings the holy water and is proffering it to him when she notices a different look on his face, and, overcome with terror and surprise, sets down the cup. She asks him if their destinies are not to be united, and reminds him of his vow to her. He starts up as he hears the marching chorus of English troops, not heeding Lakmé and listening attentively to the voices.

Lakmé, unnoticed, calmly and despairingly plucks a datura flower and bites it in two, smiling bitterly to herself. Gerald notices her with a start, and asks her what she has done. She tells him of her love for him and begs him to stay and end this dream of love with her, and he, alarmed by her strange calmness, when she begs him to drink the pledge of love with her, takes the cup and drinks it. A sadness comes over her and he tries to dispel it by renewing his vow and dwelling on the joys of their love. She, however, fails and droops from his embrace, defying the death he reads in her face by the bliss of his presence and love. She bids him farewell as Nilakantha comes rushing in to stab Gerald. The wounded man bravely bids him strike, but the dying girl tells her father that she has drunk with him from out the sacred cup, and Nilakantha's arm falls to his side. She says that if the gods must have a victim it shall be she, and dies breathing words of love, while Nilakantha in religious ecstacy seems to behold her entering the heaven of Brahma.

LOBETANZ

(Lō'-bĕ-tahnts)

(MERRY-DANCE)

GERMAN sentimental grand opera. Music by Ludwig Thuille. Book by Otto Julius Bierbaum. First production, Mannheim, Germany, 1898. The scene is Germany in the Middle Ages.

CHARACTERS

LOBETANZ	*Tenor*
THE KING	*Bass*
THE SECOND PRISONER	*Bass*
THE THIRD PRISONER	*Baritone*
THE OLDEST PRISONER	*Bass*
A YOUTH OF THE PEOPLE	*Tenor*
THE PRINCESS	*Soprano*
THE FIRST OF THE DARK GIRLS	*Soprano*
THE FIRST OF THE FAIR GIRLS	*Alto*

The minnesingers, who form a male quartette; the forester, the hangman, the judge, and the first of the prisoners; maidens, musicians, pikemen, prisoners, two heralds, two flower-girls, standard bearers, and the people.

ACT I. Within the rose garden at the King's palace the companions of the Princess are making ready for a fête. The Princess is ill, and in the hope of restoring her to health the King has appointed a day of festivity. Lobetanz, a wandering minstrel, with his fiddle slung from his shoulder, scales the garden wall and comes among the maidens, who are festooning a bower with roses. The first of the fair girls and the first of the dark girls shower questions upon him, to which he replies simply that his name is Lobetanz, and that he is of obscure parentage. The girls translate his name and call him "Merry-Dance," and, because of the merry gleam in his eye and his ready chivalry, they deck him with rose garlands to conceal his tattered garments. Meantime they tell him of the illness of the Princess, and how she lies sick (for love, they whisper) and none can heal her; and how the King has ordered the minnesingers, the poets and musicians of the court, to appear at the fête and play and sing to her, that the power of song may revive her.

While Lobetanz lingers the King, the Princess, and the court arrive, accompanied by the minnesingers, who are all of noble birth. At the King's bidding the Princess greets her maidens with a song of the awakening of spring and of budding roses. Then each of the minnesingers does his utmost to interest and delight the Princess and so bring her health. In their efforts to outrival one another they produce only horrible discord and confusion, while the maidens mock them, and the Princess turns her head away. Suddenly the music of a fiddle is heard coming from an arbor in the rear of the garden. The Princess is charmed with it and eager to hear more, and though the minnesingers are indignant and threaten the unknown intruder the Princess sends for him. Lobetanz comes forward and continues his song of two roses of the spring, which were like two young lovers, a boy and a girl, playing in the May-time. As he plays the Princess, from sheer delight and joy in the wonderful melody, revives. Her eyes brighten and she is almost well again. Whereat the minnesingers, jealous of his success in healing the Princess, and because the maidens and the people are for him, would seize him, but he is over the wall again and away, and has left with them only the memory of his tender song.

Act II. The minstrel wanders in the near-by forest, then sits beneath a linden tree within whose spreading branches seats have been built. He sings of the springtime and of the birds, and when an old forester passes on his way to the hunt he talks with him about the King and the Princess. Alone he thinks of his mother and how she used to smile at his fancies, and he wonders what she would think if she knew that these same fancies of his have been powerful enough to revive the Princess. He remembers the young girl's beauty, and how his voice had called her to life.

She is strolling alone through the woods, having dismissed her maidens, when she hears his song, and answers it with another. He comes to meet her, and together they clamber into the tree and sit conversing. He tells her a story of a knight who came for his sweetheart and found her among the roses and took her away with him. They sit dreaming of this knight, and of themselves, and of the love that has sprung up between them, when suddenly the King and his hunting party, and the court singers also, come upon them. The wandering minstrel is seized and dragged away by the pikemen at the King's command, on the charge of having enchanted the Princess by sorcery, while she, sore distressed, finds comfort only in the presence of the old forester, who alone believes in the nobility of the humble minstrel and who knows that they love each other.

Act III. Within a dungeon in semidarkness miserable prisoners await their doom. They are ragged and filthy men, just awakening from sleep. In one corner an old man sits motionless with his head in his hands. Removed from the others sits Lobetanz, heartbroken at the fate that awaits him. The prisoners, knowing that he is no criminal, jeer at him, and angrily he sings them a Ballad of Death,— the ballad of a drunkard who summons Death to drink with him and in the orgy dies in horrible agony. It is a wild, gruesome song, but musical, and the prisoners try to dance to it. All are gavotting around, even the half-witted old man, when the headsman with his flaring torch enters, seeking for Lobetanz. The prisoners are silent with dread, except the old man, who still dances.

The gallows, upon which Lobetanz is to be hanged at daybreak, are standing black and bare against the sky. The people are already gathering to witness the execution. The prisoner, bowed and silent, and the red-clad headsman enter to the beat of muffled drums. The minnesingers come with the grave old King, secretly rejoicing at this speedy removal of their rival in the favor of the Princess. She is borne in upon a bier in a dying state, attended by her mourning maidens. It is believed that the death of Lobetanz will exorcise the spells he has cast upon her and restore her.

The judge reads the sentence. The condemned man makes a last request,—that he be permitted once more to sing, to see if he cannot by that means restore again the Princess. His fiddle is given him, and as the sun breaks through the clouds, he sings of love and life. Speedily the red flush mounts the cheeks of the Princess. She opens her eyes, and stirs upon her couch, then begins to murmur the words after him. As he continues she rises to her feet and goes to meet him. And because the melody is a waltz, the people too stir, and even the minnesingers respond to its compelling rhythm, and all begin to dance. At length the King and all the people are joining the lovers in a merry love-dance. The sentence of death is forgotten and the future dawns bright with joy.

LOHENGRIN
(Lō'-ĕn-grēn)

GERMAN sentimental grand opera, based upon three legends, chief of which is that of King Arthur and the Knights of the Holy Grail. Both music and book by Richard Wagner. First production, Weimar, 1850, under the direction of Liszt. The scene is Antwerp and the Scheldt in Flanders, in the first half of the tenth century.

CHARACTERS

HENRY THE FOWLER, King of Germany	*Bass*
LOHENGRIN	*Tenor*
FREDERICK OF TELRAMUND, Count of Brabant	*Baritone*
GODFREY, the child Duke of Brabant, brother of Elsa.	
THE KING'S HERALD	*Bass*
ELSA	*Soprano*
ORTRUD, wife of Frederick	*Mezzo-Soprano*

Saxon, Thuringian, and Brabantian counts and nobles, ladies of honor, trumpeters, retainers, pages, and attendants.

ACT I. On the banks of the Scheldt Saxon, Thuringian, and Brabantian nobles are gathered in the presence of their king, Henry the Fowler, who announces that when he came to enlist them against the Hungarians, who threaten the eastern frontier of the empire, he found them at strife with one another, and he asks Frederick of Telramund to state the cause of the dissension. Frederick says that the Duke of Brabant, when dying, made him guardian of his children, the maiden Elsa and the young Godfrey, promising him the hand of Elsa in marriage. One day when Elsa and Godfrey were out walking together unattended the boy disappeared. Fruitless search was made, and in Elsa's grief and horror he read her crime. Therefore he relinquished his claim upon her, and has now taken in marriage Otrud, daughter of Radbod, whose house had long been rulers of the land, which he now claims, charging Elsa with the murder of her brother. The king and the nobles are amazed, and Frederick admits that the maiden scorned his offer of marriage, and that he believes she has some secret lover with whom she purposes to share the rule. The king summons Elsa, and asks her if she knows the charge and what is her defense. Distraught and bowed with grief, she cannot reply, and the king, impressed with her beauty and her apparent innocence, gently asks her to confide in him. She says that when she prayed Heaven for help she had a wonderful dream of one in shining armor, who came in clouds of light and brought her hope and life. For his coming she now waits.

The king urges Frederick not to press his charge, but the knight affirms its truth and challenges any one who dare attaint his honor. The Brabantians, who are his friends, will not fight with him, and the king, recalling how Frederick once saved his life, desires to make him guardian of the land. So he decrees that the matter shall be left to the judgment of Heaven, and asks Frederick if he will do battle for life or death in a holy ordeal. Frederick confidently consents, and Elsa prayerfully agrees to the appeal to Heaven. When the king tells her to choose her defender, Frederick murmurs that now she will disclose who is her lover and accomplice. Elsa declares that the knight of her dream is her champion, and that she will bestow upon him her hand and inheritance if he will accept it. All agree that the prize is noble and await the coming of the knight. The herald blows the summons. There is no answer, and Frederick claims that the failure of any one to appear in her behalf proves his cause is just. Elsa, however, asks that the herald may again sound the trumpet, and it is done.

Suddenly a skiff drawn by a swan is seen approaching on the river, and in it is a knight resplendent in gleaming armor. The skiff stops and the knight steps out. Frederick is amazed and Otrud seems horrified when she sees the swan. Elsa cries out with joy as she recognizes the knight of her vision, who bids farewell to his swan before making his obeisance to the king. Then he turns to Elsa and asks if she will entrust her cause to him with the gift of her hand in marriage if he shall conquer. Gladly she pledges herself. Then he solemnly exacts of her a promise—that she shall never ask of him his name or race. She vows perfect obedience to this his command. He then faces Frederick, who, already daunted, reluctantly stands forth for battle. The king offers a prayer, in which all but Otrud join, that the decision of the combat may be Heaven's decree. The two knights fight, and almost immediately Frederick is struck down, and though his opponent magnanimously spares his life, he is proved perjured and disgraced. All hail the unknown knight as victor, and Elsa joyfully accepts his homage as he kneels before her and promises to requite her for her past sorrows. Frederick laments his doom from Heaven, while Otrud wonders what has brought her evil spells to naught. The people raise the valiant knight and his beautiful betrothed upon their shields and bear them away to rejoicing and feasting.

Act II. Within the fortress of Antwerp that same night Otrud sits on the dark steps of the Minster, while near by Frederick stands impatient to be gone before dawn. Outcasts now and clad in the dark garments of beggars, they linger listening to the sounds of revelry that come from the castle. Bitterly he reproaches her for the deception that brought about this shame, for it was she who had said she witnessed the deed of which he had accused Elsa. When he bewails Heaven's harsh decree against him, she laughs to scorn his superstition, and says she knows a spell that even now can ruin his opponent. She tells him that shall anything compel the unknown knight to disclose his name and race his power will be gone, and therefore did he exact the promise of trust from Elsa, who alone now can bid him divulge his secret. Stirred by a dark hope of revenge they plot together how Elsa may be prevailed upon to break her promise.

While they speak Elsa in white garments appears alone upon the balcony of the Kemmenate, or dwelling of the women, and leans there blissfully happy and thinking of her lover. Otrud calls her name, and, feigning humility and sorrow, appeals to her pity. Elsa is greatly disturbed, and when Otrud tells of Frederick's repentance and contrasts her own misery with Elsa's great joy, the compassionate girl goes to her. When she appears at the door Otrud kneels before her. Elsa cannot withstand the appeal of the other's humiliation, and promises that, as she is to be married at morn, she will ask a boon of her husband for the two outcasts. Then she invites the evil woman to lodge with her and to attend her at the altar. Otrud tries to inspire distrust in Elsa's heart by saying that she hopes the lover who so mysteriously came to her may not as suddenly and as mysteriously depart, but Elsa rebukes her with words of faith and love.

Frederick, left alone in the shadows, vows that he will kill the unknown knight, and as day breaks hides in a niche in the Minster walls. Warders and servitors of the castle appear, and a herald proclaims the ban upon Frederick and upon any who shall harbor or companion him. He also proclaims that Elsa's champion is by the king invested with crown and scepter and takes the title of "Guardian of Brabant," and that to the royal espousal all the people are bidden. Pages clear the way as Elsa and her train of waiting-women come from the palace. Otrud, who with courtly robes has resumed her haughty bearing, accompanies her, and as they advance toward the Minster steps she claims the right of precedence by virtue of the rank she lately held. When Elsa, amazed at the change of tone, asks how she, the wife of an outcast, dare attempt to supersede her, Otrud answers that Frederick was until yesterday held in great honor throughout the land, while Elsa's knight is utterly unknown and without a name.

Elsa is proudly defending the honor of her champion as the king and his retinue approach. Noting the commotion King Henry and the bridegroom hasten forward. Elsa turns to her knight for protection as Frederick steps forth, begging audience of the king, who grants it. Then Frederick declares that the ordeal was won by sorcery, and demands that the unknown avow his name and station. All are taken aback at the charge, but the Guardian of Brabant defies him, and says that none can make him speak but only Elsa. She, though disturbed and trembling, clings trustfully to him, and the king and the people repledge him their faith. Frederick whispers to Elsa that if she but permit him to wound her knight ever so slightly, he will then declare his name and remain ever by her side; and the traitor adds that he will that night be near if she should call. Elsa's love, however, knows no doubt, and amid the plaudits of the people the bridal couple enter the Minster, Elsa alone seeing Otrud's gesture of malicious triumph.

ACT III. Into the bridal chamber knights and ladies come singing a joyful bridal chorus and escorting the bridegroom and the bride. When the lovers are left alone each tells the other how love, before ever they had met, drew them together in heart. Elsa, striving to express her affection, wonders if, like his name, it can never be spoken; and when he calls her by her name, she regrets that she may not use his. His tenderness silences her curiosity, and in impassioned words they pour forth their love. Yet upon their bliss falls a shadow, for Elsa thinks his trust not perfect if he does not confide in her his secret. She longs to share his past, whatever its sorrows, and when he says that he came from blest delights, she fears that he may sometime leave her and return to them. In her apprehension she fancies she sees the swan coming for him, but when he chides her she says that she will not be compelled to trust him, and demands to know his name. In sad silence he hears her eager questions. Suddenly Frederick with four accomplices bursts in the door. Then her love conquers and she hands him his sword, beseeching him to save himself. He strikes dead the traitorous knight, and the accomplices kneel abjectly before him. Elsa faints with fright. Long is the woeful silence until the sad lover bids the attendants bear Frederick's body to the king's judgment hall and lead Elsa there, saying that he will disclose all that she asks to know.

Over the banks of the Scheldt dawn is brightening as the Brabantians assemble. The king with his Saxon and Thuringian nobles enters. As they await the coming of the new ruler of Brabant the body of Frederick is brought in. Elsa, sad of countenance, enters with her ladies, and last and alone comes the Guardian of Brabant. King Henry tells him that all await his word to advance against their foe. He sorrowfully replies that it is not his to lead them forth. He asks judgment whether or not he was guilty of wrong in slaying Frederick when that one sought his life, and the king and his men avow that the dishonored one's doom was just. Then sadly he tells them that Elsa, who in their presence pledged herself not to ask his name or state, has been won from her allegiance and has questioned him. Now he will publicly declare who he is. The people listen breathlessly as he tells them of the city called Montsalvat, where the Holy Grail was borne by angels and is guarded by faithful knights, of the cleansing from sin and the enduement with power that the sight of the Grail bestows, and how one so favored can overcome all evil spells and champion men in their sore need; but that if he is doubted or his name known, he must depart. He then tells them that such a one is he, Lohengrin, son of Parsifal, king in Montsalvat and keeper of the Grail.

Elsa, at the revelation of all that he is and the knowledge that she has now lost him, is overwhelmed with repentance and grief. The swan is seen approaching, and Lohengrin, beholding it, says that he must obey the Grail. Sorrowfully he bids Elsa farewell, withstanding her passionate efforts to detain him and telling her that had she trusted him one short year he would have restored her brother and would himself have stayed with her. He leaves in her care, for Godfrey upon his return, his horn, his sword, and his ring, all possessing miraculous power. Otrud, who has been standing by, exclaims that it was she who by evil spells and magic changed Godfrey into a swan, and that now she triumphs. The people are dismayed and angrily threaten her. Lohengrin sinks to his knees in prayer and the people see the white dove of the Grail fly slowly down and hover over the skiff. Lohengrin rising looses a golden chain from the neck of the swan, which immediately sinks, and Godfrey, a fair boy in shining silver garments rises from the river. Lohengrin tells the people that this is the rightful ruler of Brabant. Godfrey makes obeisance to King Henry, then is clasped in his sister's arms as the people sink to their knees in reverence. Otrud, seeing the boy, falls dead. Lohengrin springs into the skiff, which the dove now draws along, and though the anguished Elsa stretches out pleading arms is borne away. All watch him go, as he stands leaning upon his shield with his head sorrowfully bowed. When he vanishes from sight Elsa falls lifeless.

LOUISE

FRENCH sentimental grand opera. Both music and book by Gustave Charpentier. First production, Paris, 1900. The scene is Paris at the present day.

CHARACTERS
JULIEN, an artist.................................*Tenor*
THE FATHER OF LOUISE........................*Baritone*
LOUISE ....*Soprano*
THE MOTHER OF LOUISE.......................*Contralto*

Girls of a dressmaking establishment, street peddlers, a ragpicker, scavenger, a song writer, a nightwalker and Father of Fools, who symbolizes the Pleasure of Paris, two philosophers, a painter, a young poet, a student, a sculptor, policemen, an apprentice, a group of Bohemians, another of grisettes, another of loafers, and the people.

ACT I. In a garret room of a workingmen's lodging-house in Paris Louise, the young and beautiful daughter of poor parents, is standing late one April afternoon by a window which opens upon a balcony, opposite which is a terrace fronting an artist's studio. She listens carefully, then opens the window and is greeted by the young artist. They are in love with each other, but her parents frown upon his suit because of his free and easy manners and his artist's mode of life, so they cannot marry, for in France a legal marriage requires the consent of the parents of both parties. She loves her father and mother, but she also loves Julien, so she tells him to write again and if her parents still withhold their consent she will go away with him. Julien pours forth his love, and speaks bitterly of their enemy, her mother, who would prevent his ever speaking with her. They recall the night when outside her father's door they exchanged their vows. Just then her mother, who having entered unnoticed has been listening, draws the girl back, closes the window, and lowers the shade.

While Louise trembling busies herself preparing supper her mother taunts her, mocking Julien's very words. When the girl begs her to let them marry she heaps accusations upon the man, but Louise defends him, defiantly saying that all the gibes cannot change her love. Her father enters with a letter in his hand. After supper he tells them of Julien's letter and says that he will make further inquiries and, if all is well, ask Julien to call. Her mother, however, is angry and renews her attack on Julien's character. Louise passionately protests and her father, greatly troubled, talks gently with her and tells her that they hoped she might begin at the end of the hard road they have traveled, and that she is not old enough yet to choose a husband. She avows her love for Julien and her faith in him. He wins from her the promise, however, that if he should refuse Julien's request she will be obedient and forget him. Torn between love for her father and for Julien, and longing for the joys that her lover and the great city offer her, Louise cannot be comforted, and when she tries to read aloud the evening paper she bursts into sobs over the word "Paris."

Act II. Early the next morning at the junction of streets below Montmartre housekeepers are hurrying by on their way to market, while street vendors and scavengers begin to ply their trades. A nightwalker, known as the Father of Fools, saunters along, and when questioned replies that he is the Pleasure of Paris, the soul of the great city. He is gone when Julien comes with four Bohemian companions. He points out to them the building where Louise works, and tells them that when she has come he will go in and seize her, and that if her parents do not then consent to their marriage, he will abduct her. He has Louise's promise that she will consent to it. The Bohemians agree to crown her as their muse. They go off leaving Julien to watch.

Girls come to their work in the dressmaking establishment, and soon Louise enters with her mother. The mother catches sight of Julien and angrily threatens Louise that she will have to work at home hereafter. When the mother has bidden her good-bye and gone away after watching the girl within the door, Julien comes forth cautiously, then rushes into the building and almost immediately returns dragging Louise by the arm. She begs him to let her go. He asks what was her parents' answer to his letter and, learning that it was unfavorable, begs her no longer to submit to them but to keep her promise and go with him. She pleads that she loves her father and cannot leave him. He tries to force her to yield, but she withstands him, promising that sometime she will be his wife, but not now, and Julien goes sadly away.

Within the building the workgirls are sewing around a table and talking of their work and their customers, of love and their lovers. They notice that Louise is sad and taunt her with being in love. Hearing a song in the street all but Louise flock to the window. She recognizes Julien's voice, but does not leave her work. After a little he strikes his guitar in rage at the gibes of the other girls and her silence. Louise rises trembling, but sits down again. Julien sings passionately of his love and then of his despair, and at last asks if she lied to him. When she is still silent he starts to curse her, much to the amusement of the girls. When the song ceases and they say that he is going away, Louise takes her hat and says that she must go home. The girls are amazed, but when some one from the window sees her talking with the singer, they laugh long and loud,—all but Gertrude, her one sympathetic friend, who clasps her hands in terror.

Act III. The following midsummer in a small garden at the apex of the Butte Montmartre, which affords a panorama of Paris, Julien sits in the twilight meditating. Louise comes and they talk together of their great happiness in each other. She recalls how her father could not believe that she was old enough to choose a husband, and Julien defends with poetic enthusiasm the right of every heart to be free to choose its own happiness. As evening falls and the lights of Paris appear, he tells her that she is the muse of the city, that the Town has given him the Girl. She, enthusiastic over his work, adds that the love of the Girl will give him the Town. Then they plan his conquest of the marvelous city, and kneeling they pray Paris to be kind to their loves. They rejoice in their freedom and ecstatically embrace, renewing their vows and saying that this is their wedding night.

They have entered the cottage when several Bohemians appear and drape it with flags and lanterns. Groups of Bohemians and grisettes come, and following them the fathers and mothers, the girls and boys who live on the Butte and who look with varying shades of disapproval and curiosity upon the doings of the merrymakers. When Lousie appears the grisettes and Bohemians joyously surround her, presenting flowers, and throwing over her shoulders the silver shawl of royalty, acclaiming her the Muse of Montmartre. The Father of Fools leads the dance. Louise, touched by the tribute of her friends, offers Julien a rose, which he accepts, taking her in his arms.

Suddenly the crowd falls back as the mother of Louise enters hesitatingly. The Father of Fools turns away laughing, and the musicians go off. Julien places himself in front of Louise, who is half fainting. When all have vanished but Louise, her mother, and her lover, the mother speaks and says that she comes only to tell Louise that her father is suffering and that she alone can save him, that they have mourned for her as dead, and that her father has grieved so that now only a great joy can restore him. She begs Louise to come back for a little time, promising to let her return soon. Julien doubts the mother's word but consents, and the lovers reluctantly part.

Act IV. In her father's house Louise has now been detained for twenty days, contrary to her mother's promise. It is about nine o'clock in the evening and her father, who has that day been to work for the first time since his illness, sits by the table watching her as she sews in her room. The wreckers have removed the old building where the artist's studio was, and in its place the lights of Paris may be seen. The father is very melancholy and his wife tries to cheer him, but he complains bitterly of the ingratitude of children, who though tenderly reared follow the voice of the stranger. Louise opens her window and looks out into the night, weeping. Her mother calls her, but she, pale and inanimate, passes her father's outstretched arms without response. She says that they promised to let her go back, else she would not have come, and that she longs for love that is free.

Her mother only taunts her, but when she bids her father good-night he takes her in his arms and plays at rocking her to sleep, and she humoring him asks him to let her have the handsome picture that she wants and not to be kept like a bird in a cage. When she reminds them of their own love time, her mother tells her that she had only the right to marry, nothing else, and that if her lover, satisfied, now talks of free love, she has what she deserves. Her father coaxes and beseeches her to stay with them for they have forgiven her. But she claims the right to her share of love. Then her father calls her wicked and denounces her as a stranger. She expresses the call of the city, and voices the longing of her heart for the man she loves, at last rushing to the door. Her father, furiously angry, intercepts her and when she calls for Julien starts to strike her, but instead opens the door and orders her to go. As she hesitates he threatens to throw her through the door. When he rushes at her she escapes with a cry. After she has gone he looks about him in a daze, his anger vanished, then rushes to the staircase calling her name, but there is no answer. He turns to the window, sees the lights of the city, and cries out in agony, "Oh, Paris! Paris!"

A LOVERS' QUARREL

(I DISPETTOSI AMANTI)

ITALIAN comic grand opera. Music by Attilio Parelli. Book by Enrico Comitti. First production, Philadelphia, 1912. The scene is Italy in the latter half of the eighteenth century.

CHARACTERS

FLORINDO, son of Donna Angelica.....................*Tenor*
DON FULGENZIO, brother of Donna Angelica.......*Baritone*
ROSAURA, daughter of Don Fulgenzio..............*Soprano*
DONNA ANGELICA.................................*Mezzo-Soprano*

In a gentleman's park, amid ancient trees, fountains, and statues, Rosaura and Florindo loiter, the girl embroidering with her back to the man, who is demanding a definite answer to his question. Deriding and mocking each other in turn, they at length attempt to decide when they shall have their formal and premeditated quarrel and thus end the comedy of their engagement. In mock earnest he says that when her father and his mother wished them to become engaged he thought, if she loved him, why not? When he seriously talked of marriage, however, she declared that she would never marry a rake under any consideration, implying that she thought him that. Rosaura retaliates that he said he would not marry a girl who was capricious and a featherhead like her. Florindo reminds her of the storm they stirred up when they told their parents that their love was a delusion, and how his mother became ill and was near to dying, so they patched up the engagement as if willing to listen to reason. Since then they had pretended to be lovers whenever their parents were by, but when alone they were lovers no more, and only awaited his mother's recovery to end the matter.

Rosaura is piqued when Florindo seriously affirms that the engagement bores him, and asks if he cannot spare her one kind word. He replies that he cannot allow love to move him since he well knows that she could never love him. She coquets with him and hints that, playing with fire, perhaps they have themselves got burned. The possibility has apparently not occurred to him. They pace up and down, she fuming, he mischievous, but suddenly when they hear some one coming he takes her hand and draws her to a seat beside him and they play at being lovers.

Don Fulgenzio and Donna Angelica step behind a clump of trees and observe the lovers, thinking that all opposition to the engagement has been happily ended. Florindo and Rosaura treat them to such impassioned words and gestures, all the while carrying on their quarrel in lower tones, that the fond parents determine on a speedy marriage. Florindo sings a very beautiful love song, which so touches Rosaura that she responds with genuine feeling, forgetting that she is acting a part. Just then Don Fulgenzio interrupts, and when he tells the lovers that he and Donna Angelica have been listening for some time, Florindo pretends great confusion. Don Fulgenzio draws him aside and announces to the prospective bridegroom that the marriage license has arrived from Rome. He hastens joyfully to Rosaura with the news. Aside she asks him if he is still flirting, and when he replies, "Surely," she angrily turns to her father and starts to speak. Florindo takes her hand and calls her his bride. Thoroughly angry she repulses him and acknowledges the deception that they have both been playing, and he confirms her words. Then Rosaura says she hates him and runs away, and he walks abruptly off in the opposite direction.

Don Fulgenzio and Donna Angelica look at each other as if stupefied, then walk up and down talking. They decide to try to get each of the lovers to confide in them, and as Florindo returns Don Fulgenzio leaves the mother with her son. Florindo tells her how they agreed to remain engaged until she was well. She protests that he does love Rosaura, and he acknowledges that that is the truth, but that he tried to make Rosaura love him by pretending indifference, so that she might be brought to sue for grace, and says that he was about to win her when they were interrupted. Donna Angelica reproves him for the game that he seems to have carried too far, for she thinks Rosaura's outburst of hate was quite genuine. Florindo is greatly dispirited, and agrees to confess all if after one more effort he cannot conquer Rosaura's pride.

Meanwhile Rosaura has stolen into the park and from behind a tree has heard his confession, but thinks him still deceiving. His sadness is convincing, however, and she exults in the fact that he loves her, but determines to take down his pride before she yields. When Florindo approaches her she laughs at him for being taken in by her acting, and pretends that just now in the quarrel she was carrying out their plan. He, with great misgiving, for now he is sure that she does not love him, takes her to task for being so angry when he proposed their parting, if she was willing to act so quickly. She taunts him with having fancied that she did love him, and he replies in the same words she had used to him. As she continues to mock him he sadly says goodbye. Before he goes out of hearing she expresses her hope that some youth will come who will care for her. He scornfully describes the dandy she would like, and she depicts an extravagantly ideal man. When his anger is overcoming him she again bids him farewell and seats herself on a bench with her back to him. He steals up behind her and kisses her hair repeatedly, then is about to run away when she draws him to her and acknowledges her love. They are joyfully embracing when Don Fulgenzio and Donna Angelica approach much surprised. Don Fulgenzio charges them with being up to the same old tricks, and only their united and repeated assurances convince their parents that they speak the truth.

LUCIA DI LAMMERMOOR

(Lōō-chēē'-ah de Lah-mair-moor')

(LUCY OF LAMMERMOOR)

ITALIAN tragic grand opera, based upon Scott's novel, "The Bride of Lammermoor." Music by Gaetano Donizetti. Book by Salvatore Cammarano. First production, Naples, 1835. The scene is Scotland in the latter part of the seventeenth century.

CHARACTERS

SIR HENRY ASHTON, Lord of Lammermoor........Baritone
SIR EDGAR OF RAVENSWOOD.........................Tenor
SIR ARTHUR BUCKLAW..............................Tenor
RAYMOND, chaplain to Lord Ashton and tutor to Lucy..Tenor
NORMAN, Captain of the Guard of Ravenswood......Tenor
LUCY, sister to Sir Henry Ashton.................Soprano
ALICE, companion to Lucy..................Mezzo-Soprano
Friends, relatives, and retainers of Sir Henry Ashton.

ACT I. At the entrance of the park of Lammermoor Castle, which formerly was the ancestral home of Sir Edgar of Ravenswood, but was forfeited by him and is now held by his political opponent, Sir Henry Ashton, Norman is directing his warriors to search the neighboring wood and the vaults of an old tower to find out whom Lucy secretly meets there. As Sir Henry and Raymond enter the knight is confiding in his chaplain that his power is menaced by Sir Edgar and that only a powerful alliance can prevent his overthrow; that he purposes to give his sister Lucy in marriage to Sir Arthur Bucklaw, who has great influence at court, but that Lucy refuses to accede to his wishes. Raymond suggests that the young woman is still mourning for the death of her mother, but Norman discloses that he knows she is already in love with some one who, one day when she was attacked by a furious bull, shot at the animal, killing it.

Sir Henry asks who it may be, and though Norman is far from sure, he says that he suspects the hereditary foe of the family, Sir Edgar of Ravenswood. This throws Sir Henry into great fury, which is changed to a murderous intent by the report of the hunters, who now return saying that in surrounding the tower they surprised a man, who dashed away upon his waiting horse, and was none other than Sir Edgar.

In the park Lucy and her faithful attendant, Alice, are awaiting the coming of the lover. Lucy looks with horror upon a fountain where it is said a Ravenswood, insane with jealousy, killed his sweetheart. She tells Alice that once she beheld the spirit of the unhappy lady, and she believes it was a warning to her to give up her lover, but that, try as she will, she cannot, for she loves him dearly. Edgar enters and tells her that he is sent to France on a mission of state, but that before he goes he will seek her brother and offer his hand in friendship, asking in return her hand in marriage. Lucy is much alarmed, for she knows her brother's nature, and begs Edgar still to conceal their love. Edgar sees in this only her solicitude for him and the acknowledgement that the enmity between the two houses is, indeed, past assuaging,—that Henry, having killed Edgar's father and usurped his heritage, is bent upon his death. Sir Edgar tells her how over the grave of his father he vowed warfare against the house of his slayer, and how, when he saw Lucy, he repented of his vow. Lucy begs of him that he will let the vows of love prove more holy than the vows of passion, and bids him for her sake temper his anger. Then he asks of her that she shall pledge him her hand in marriage, and solemnly they plight their troth to each other. They reluctantly bid farewell, and he promises to send her an occasional letter to shorten the tedium of their separation.

ACT II. Within an apartment in Lammermoor Castle Henry awaits the coming of his sister, whom Norman has just summoned. He tells his Captain of Guards how much trepidation he feels, because he has already assembled his friends for the nuptials and Sir Arthur will soon arrive. Norman reminds him that they have intercepted the letters from Sir Edgar and have ready the forged letter telling of his marriage to another.

Sir Henry dismisses Norman as Lucy, pale and rigid with sadness, enters. Again he urges her to give up her secret and guilty love and take the noble husband he has chosen for her. She replies that her faith is pledged. Then he gives her the forged letter. Overwhelmed with grief at the news of Edgar's base treachery toward her, she longs for death, but hears instead festal music. To her question her brother answers that her future husband has come. When she protests he tells her that a secret revolution against King William, in which he had part, has been discovered, and that only the union of their house with that of Sir Arthur Bucklaw can prevent her brother from dying as a traitor. His desperate pleadings and the fear of her own lasting remorse if she fails to save him from death, move her, and in dumb sorrow she consents to his plan.

Into the reception hall Sir Henry, knights and ladies, pages, retainers, and servants enter to joyous music. Sir Arthur comes conducted by Norman and his guards. The prospective bridegroom asks for Lucy, and Sir Henry warns him that she may seem sad, but that it is for her mother's recent death. Arthur asks the truth of the report that Sir Edgar has wooed her, and Henry acknowledges that it is true. Lucy, with Raymond and Alice, enters and is presented to Sir Arthur. Henry, anxious lest something should defeat his plans, urges the immediate signing of the marriage contract; so Lucy, reluctant and almost fainting, approaches the table and signs the paper.

Sir Henry breathes more freely, but there is immediate commotion at the door, and Sir Edgar rushes into the room. Lucy recognizes him and faints. Henry, seeing Lucy apparently lifeless, is stricken with remorse, and pauses with hand on sword before striking down the intruder. Edgar, also moved by her suffering and the love he has for her, stands motionless. Lucy, reviving, calls upon death to release her, and bemoans the fate that brought the news of her lover's constancy too late. All the company gather about their loved mistress in pity. Henry and Arthur bid Sir Edgar depart, but he defies them and is about to fight them all when Raymond intervenes and commands in Heaven's name that no blood be shed.

Henry demands of Edgar an explanation, and he says that he came for Lucy, who is betrothed to him. They then show him the marriage contract and he demands acknowledgement of it from Lucy's own lips. Hearing it, he returns her ring and, infuriated, demands his own, which when he receives he stamps upon, declaring her shameless like her kindred. Henry and Arthur and the knights and retainers of the house of Ashton vow that he must die for the insult he has given, and he boldly confronts them, courting the death they threaten. But Lucy, anguished beyond endurance, prays that Heaven may grant her one prayer,— that his life may be spared. Then Raymond and Alice and the ladies in Lucy's train urge flight upon Edgar, and prevail over him in the name of the bitter grief their lady feels.

ACT III. In the hall outside of Lucy's apartments the family friends and retainers are making merry when Raymond and Norman enter, commanding peace. Raymond an' nounces to the horrified guests that, hearing a groan of terror from the bridal chamber, he rushed in and found the bridegroom dead from a sword wound, while Lucy, bereft of reason and with the sword still in her hand, asked where was her husband. As he pauses Lucy enters. In her insanity she murmurs of Edgar and his love, thinks that she is again meeting him by the fountain, speaks of the horror that the spot inspires in her, then dreams that he is restored to her and that they are celebrating their marriage. Henry enters vowing revenge, but Raymond points out to him that her state is hopeless. Again she babbles of Edgar's scorning her, and begs his mercy because she is the victim of a most cruel plot. Henry rushes away wild with remorse.

To the burial ground of the castle, where are the tombs of the Ravenswood family, Edgar has come to end his unhappy life. His love for Lucy is so strong that because she is false he can no longer live. He pictures her within the castle, whose gleaming lights he can see, sharing in the festivities with her husband and without thought of him. He prays that she may never pass his grave with that husband, that she may at least respect the ashes of the man who died for her.

Suddenly the inhabitants of Lammermoor flock from the castle and pass near where he is. He catches their words of sorrow and despair and asks them of whom they speak. Then he is told that Lucy is dying in misery, and that in her ravings she talked of him and was true in her love. As they speak the passing bell rings and he knows she is dead. Raymond, who has come from the castle, seeks to comfort and restrain him, but he, with a calm beyond despair and rejoicing that soon he will be united with his love in heaven, plunges his poinard into his heart and dies.

MADAME BUTTERFLY

ITALIAN tragic grand opera, founded on a story by John Luther Long, which was dramatized by the author and David Belasco. Music by Giacomo Puccini. Italian text by Luigi Illica and Giuseppe Giacosa. First production, Milan, 1904. The scene is Nagasaki, Japan, at the present time.

CHARACTERS

B. F. PINKERTON, Lieutenant in the United States Navy, *Tenor*
SHARPLESS, United States Consul at Nagasaki....*Baritone*
GORO, a marriage-broker............................*Tenor*
PRINCE YAMADORI, suitor of Cho-Cho-San.........*Baritone*
THE BONZE, uncle of Cho-Cho-San....................*Bass*
CHO-CHO-SAN, Madame Butterfly..................*Soprano*
SUZUKI, servant of Cho-Cho-San.............*Mezzo-Soprano*
KATE PINKERTON, American wife of B. F. Pinkerton, *Mezzo-Soprano*
THE MOTHER OF CHO-CHO-SAN..............*Mezzo-Soprano*

Trouble, who is Cho-Cho-San's child, an aunt, a cousin, and various relations and friends of Cho-Cho-San, also servants.

ACT I. Goro, the Japanese marriage-broker, is showing Lieutenant Pinkerton a house which he has just purchased for him on a hill overlooking the city and harbor of Nagasaki. The lieutenant is pleased with the terraced garden filled with flowers, the sliding walls, the perfect appointments, and with the servants that Goro has hired. One of them, Suzuki, is the handmaid of Miss Butterfly, with whom the lieutenant is about to contract a Japanese marriage. The marriage-broker dilates upon the future wife, her honorable position, and her numerous relatives. Sharpless, the American consul, laboriously climbs the hill and Pinkerton greets him affectionately. The consul has misgivings about the projected marriage. He warns the light-hearted officer that what may be a happy adventure for him, may prove of grave moment to the bride, as this marriage will not be binding in the United States. Goro is sent to escort her hither, and Sharpless tells of a chance meeting with her, of her youth and her trustfulness, and once more almost sternly warns the young man. As they drink together Sharpless toasts the friends and relatives at home, but Pinkerton drinks to the day on which he will wed in real marriage an American wife.

Women's voices are heard as Butterfly and a bevy of her girl friends climb the steep ascent. When they enter Butterfly commands them all to make obeisance to the lieutenant. The couple exchange compliments, and Sharpless questions the bride as to her family. She says that she has a mother, who is very poor. When questioned about her father, she is silent a moment, then answers that he is dead. Pinkerton is talking enthusiastically with the consul of the charms of the bride when a large crowd of her relatives enter. They are introduced to the bridegroom-to-be, and refreshments are served.

Butterfly draws Pinkerton aside and shows him the few possessions she has brought with her. Among them is a long and narrow sheath, which she lays down very reverently. Goro whispers Pinkerton that it contains the dagger sent to her father by the emperor with the command of suicide. Butterfly shows him also some small figures, which she gravely says are the souls of her ancestors. He treats them respectfully, but very softly she tells him that yesterday she went to the mission church, because now she wishes to adopt the religion of his people, and taking up the images she throws them away. The Imperial Commissioner reads aloud the marriage certificate, which is then duly signed by the bridegroom and the bride. Sharpless and the other officials then take leave of Pinkerton, who is surrounded by his large new family connection, all joyfully drinking the health of the bridal couple.

Suddenly the festivities are interrupted by the coming of the Bonze, the priestly uncle of the bride, who enters in high dudgeon and, approaching Butterfly, stretches out threatening hands toward her. Her relatives shrink back as he tells them that she has been to the American mission church and has thereby renounced her religion and with it her family and friends. Incredulous at first, her relatives become angry when she does not deny it, and though Pinkerton tries to defend his bride from the wild denunciations of the Bonze, they follow the latter's command and leave her, hurling threats and curses at her. Butterfly, in tears at their harshness, is consoled by the tender words of Pinkerton, and as night comes on they realize only that they are alone together and very happy. They walk on the terrace, Pinkerton wooing her and at last drawing from her a confession of her great love for him.

ACT II, PART I. Three years later within the house on the hill Madame Butterfly awaits the return of her long-absent husband. The faithful Suzuki prays fervently to Buddha that her sorrowful mistress may again be happy. At the latter's command she brings their scanty store of coins and anxiously they count them over, and realize that unless Lieutenant Pinkerton comes soon they will be facing starvation. Suzuki doubts his coming, and Butterfly, furious at the doubt, forces her to affirm her own loyal expectation. They are surprised by Goro's entrance with the American consul. Madame Butterfly, overjoyed at the prospect of a message from her husband, entertains Sharpless hospitably, and can hardly compose herself to listen to the letter that he wishes to read her. She plies him with questions as to the health of the absent lieutenant, and asks when robins nest in America, for he promised to return at that season. Sharpless, pitying her for the sorrowful news he brings, tries in vain to tell it. Goro comes, bringing with him Prince Yamadori, an elderly and somewhat feeble-minded suitor. Butterfly makes fun of and flouts, and at last indignantly refuses the prince's offer of marriage, although Goro tells her that she is already divorced by her husband's desertion. Firmly Butterfly dismisses the obnoxious guest, and again Sharpless essays to read the letter, but the opening words, though only courteous, raise wild hopes in her heart.

At last he asks her what she would do if Lieutenant Pinkerton should never return. Stunned for the moment, she says she might go back to her former life and entertain with her songs, or better—die. When Sharpless urges her to accept the hand of Prince Yamadori she bids Suzuki show the consul to the door, but he apologizes. To prove that she could not be forgotten, she brings to him from an adjoining room her baby. Sharpless is greatly troubled that she has a child and at its strong resemblance to its father. Madame Butterfly begs him that he will write her husband of the child, whom she calls "Trouble," but whose name she says shall be changed to "Joy" on the day of his father's return. Scarcely has Sharpless left when Suzuki enters, dragging in Goro, whom she accuses of whispering scandal regarding Madame Butterfly. Goro defiantly declares that in America her baby would be considered an outcast. Butterfly threatens Goro with her father's dagger, but Suzuki intervenes and he rushes away.

A cannon shot is heard and they see from the terrace an American man-of-war entering the harbor. Butterfly takes a telescope, and with Suzuki's aid to steady her hand, makes out the words "Abraham Lincoln," the name of her husband's ship. Joyfully they prepare for his coming, decking the house with flowers and the mother and child in their best robes. Then they take their stand by the windows overlooking the terrace to watch for him.

ACT II, PART 2. The next morning the waiting wife still stands motionless, and as the sun comes up Suzuki rises from sleep and gently arouses her mistress. Butterfly takes the child in her arms and goes upstairs to rest. Soon Suzuki opens the door to Pinkerton and Sharpless, who bid her be quiet. She tells them of the long vigil and is about to call Butterfly when Pinkerton stops her. She catches sight of an American lady walking in the garden, and realizing that it is Pinkerton's American wife she falls on her knees in utter sorrow. Sharpless tries to calm her, telling her that she must help them arrange for the baby's future, and sends her into the garden. When he and Pinkerton are left alone, the latter, overcome with memories and remorse, gives him some funds to use for the little mother and goes out, unable to face the woman he has wronged.

Kate Pinkerton and Suzuki enter and the latter promises to try to persuade her mistress to give the child into the American wife's keeping. Butterfly calls and before Suzuki can prevent enters the room. Joyfully she greets Sharpless and seeks for Pinkerton, then espies Kate. Rapidly she questions who she is, why she has come, and why Suzuki weeps. Only a sad silence answers her. At last she gains from her maid the knowledge that Lieutenant Pinkerton lives, that he is well, but that he will come no more. Slowly it dawns upon her who the stranger is, and as Kate humbly approaches her and asks her forgiveness, Butterfly regains her composure, solemnly blesses the American wife, and sends the absent man the message that peace will come to her. She promises to give his son to Lieutenant Pinkerton if he will come in half an hour, and Sharpless and Kate go away.

The wretched woman gives her baby to the maid, bidding her play with him. When alone she bows before the once-repudiated Buddha, takes her father's dagger and, kissing it, reads the inscription—"To die with honor when one can no longer live with honor." She raises it to her throat, but lets it fall as Suzuki pushes the toddling child into the room. The frantic mother seizes little Trouble, fondles and prays over him, and bids him farewell. Then she seats him on a stool, puts his doll and an American flag into his hands, and gently bandages his eyes. Again she seizes the dagger and goes to another part of the room. Soon the dagger falls from her hand, and with her white, now crimsoning, veil wound around her throat, she gropes her way toward the child, gives him one last embrace, and falls to the floor beside him. Pinkerton, followed by Sharpless, enters, calling her name. She looks up, points to the child, and dies. Pinkerton falls on his knees beside her, while Sharpless, sobbing, catches up the child and kisses him.

MADAME SANS-GÊNE

(*Mă-dăm Săn-zhain*)

(MADAM FREE-AND-EASY)

ITALIAN comic grand opera, founded upon a play of the same name by Victorien Sardou and E. Moreau. Music by Umberto Giordano. Book by Renato Simoni. First production, New York, 1915. The scene is Paris and the time is August 10, 1792, and September, 1811.

CHARACTERS

NAPOLEON BUONAPARTE	Baritone
LEFEBVRE, Sergeant of the National Guards, later Marshal of France and Duke of Danzig	Tenor
FOUCHÉ, officer of the National Guards, later Minister of Police	Baritone
COUNT DE NEIPPERG	Tenor
VINAIGRE, drummer-boy	Tenor
DESPREAUX, dancing-master	Tenor
GELSOMINO, page	Baritone
LEROY, tailor	Baritone
DE BRIGODE, chamberlain	Baritone
ROUSTAN, head of the mamelukes	Baritone
CATHERINE HÜBSCHER, "Madame Sans-Gêne," laundress; later Duchess of Danzig	Soprano
TOINETTA ⎫	Soprano
JULIA ⎬ laundresses	Soprano
LA ROSSA ⎭	Soprano
QUEEN CAROLINE ⎫ sisters of Napoleon	Soprano
PRINCESS ELISA ⎭	Soprano
LADY DE BULOW, matron of honor to the empress	Soprano

Maturino, Constant, who is valet to Napoleon, the voice of the empress, citizens, shopkeepers, villagers, national guards, gunners, ladies of the court, officials, diplomats, academicians, hunters, pages, and two mamelukes.

ACT I. Within the laundry of Catherine Hübscher, in St. Anne's Street, Paris, the work of the day is going on as usual, although the revolution is in progress. The boom of cannon and the rattle of musketry are heard, and crowds are rushing by. The laundresses pause in their work, frightened at the uproar and anxious for the safety of their mistress Catherine, called "Madame Free-and-Easy" because of her frank and outspoken manner. She is a great favorite with every one, being young, pretty, graceful, and very kindhearted. She has been gone all the morning and the girls fear that she has been injured in the street fighting.

Fouché, a young officer in the National Guards, of priestlike appearance, calls for his laundry. He has his valise with him and says that he is leaving Paris because the forces of King Louis XVI seem to be successful, and if the revolution is overthrown he and his companions will be condemned for treason. Just then Catherine enters with her laundry basket over her arm and followed by an amused crowd. She is much put out because a soldier kissed her against her will. Triumphant shouts are heard and the news comes that the revolutionary forces are victorious and the king and queen, Marie Antoinette, have been taken prisoners. Catherine gives the girls the washing, which is put in soak, and then she declares a holiday because of the general rejoicing in the patriots' victory.

The girls go out, leaving her and Fouché alone, after she has sent a boy to summon Sergeant Lefebvre. Fouché remarks upon her affection for Lefebvre, and she rather pointedly extols the latter's courage, and says that he is a fellow-countryman of hers, an Alsatian, whom she met at a ball at Vauxhall. When she tries to hasten his going, he says that he will wait until the Tuileries is taken. She talks hopefully of the revolution and promises that when she is a Duchess he shall be Minister of Police. When she mentions his laundry, he says that there is another who, like himself, cannot pay her, and that it is one of the officers of the artillery, Napoleon Buonaparte, a man of no account. She declares that that man is a soldier and will be heard from.

The noise of the fighting increases, and Julia and Toinetta enter and rush to the rear of the shop, Catherine and Fouché following them, as soldiers fight in the street. Shouts of victory are heard and Catherine from the window cries out that the Tuileries is burning. Vinaigre rushes in, followed by a crowd, among whom is La Rossa. Soon all go out and Catherine is closing the windows when she hears a noise and a wounded royalist enters. He is Count de Neipperg. Catherine has compassion on the injured man, and when his pursuers, headed by her lover, Sergeant Lefebvre, are heard approaching, she sends de Neipperg into her own room, locks the door, and then at the command of Lefebvre opens the street door and admits him and his soldiers. They tell her of a royalist who is hiding somewhere near.

Lefebvre introduces Catherine to his companions, and when she brings them wine they drink her health, while Lefebvre vaunts their attachment to each other. His hands are stained with powder, and when he attempts to wash them at the tub where the clothes are, she protests. Then he starts to go into her room, and before she can prevent he has found out that her door is locked. This arouses his suspicion and jealousy, and fairly snatching the key from her pocket, he unlocks the door and enters. The young woman stands motionless with dread, until shortly Lefebvre returns pale, distressed, and grave, yet declaring that his suspicions were without cause. He dismisses his soldiers, and when they withdraw he blames Catherine for not telling him that she had a dead man in her room. Catherine, though surprised that the man is dead, reveals no affection, but only pity for him; so Lefebvre, who was only testing her, says that the man is not dead and that he will help her to keep secret the officer's escape. His comrades are calling for him, and he goes out and marches away with them.

Act II. Nineteen years later, in September, 1811, Madame Free-and-Easy, who is now wife of Lefebvre and Duchess of Danzig, is living in state at Compiègne. Lefebvre, the Duke of Danzig, is Marshal of France and Governor of the Palace, and, true to Catherine's old prophecy, Fouché is Minister of Police. The Duchess of Danzig, however, is not fitted either by nature or training for court life, and she makes many mistakes of etiquette and social blunders despite her good heart and fidelity. Within the great salon of her house Gelsomino and Leroy are talking when Despreaux enters and inquires for the duchess. The servants laugh at the thought of the duchess's taking dancing lessons, and make fun of her. Catherine enters, and eagerly follows the directions and imitates the motions of Despreaux, in the vain hope of acquiring a stately and dignified manner.

When Lefebvre enters she sees that he is troubled and dismisses the teacher. He says that the emperor is displeased with him because he permits himself to be humiliated in his position by his wife's mistakes, and has recommended to him that he divorce her and take another wife. Lefebvre has, with becoming firmness, answered the man who within so short a time has for reasons of state put away his own wife that he might take another, but both he and Catherine know that the emperor's wish is a command. Lefebvre takes her in his arms and caresses her, and they agree that they will not consent to separation for any reason. Lefebvre in a burst of humble tenderness is on his knees before her when Gelsomino announces the Count de Neipperg.

De Neipperg tells them that Napoleon has suspected him of daring to raise his eyes in affection toward the empress, Marie Louise, and has banished him from the court. His old friends, who once before saved his life, now wish to save his happiness, and when he confesses to them that he deeply loves the empress and cannot consent to leave without first bidding her farewell, they beg him to hasten away without seeing her. Catherine especially urges him not to compromise the one he loves by such a rash effort, but he goes out still determined to see the empress in secret that very night. Fouché, having learned of Napoleon's displeasure with the duchess, enters and begs her to treat important personages with more diplomacy and curb her too ready tongue. He says that the sisters of the emperor are to be at the social function which Lefebvre and Catherine are about to hold, and he counsels Catherine how to receive them. Lefebvre and Catherine are startled to find the guests arriving and Catherine hastens off to prepare.

A large crowd of people,—lords and ladies of the court, officials, academicians, and diplomats,—enters. They greet Lefebvre and Fouché. Soon after Gelsomino announces Queen Caroline and Princess Elisa. Lefebvre is distressed that Catherine does not come to receive them. They enter and take their places and there is a long pause, filled with great uneasiness on the part of the guests and increasing haughtiness on the part of Napoleon's sisters, before Catherine hastens in. She greets them courteously, but is frozen by their hauteur, and when they reply in cutting remarks she gives them cool answers. They soon withdraw offended. The guests are hospitably entertained, but there is an early breaking up of the party. When all are gone and Lefebvre and Catherine are again alone, De Brigode enters with a message from Napoleon summoning Catherine to him at once. Lefebvre takes her in his arms and tries to reassure her, pledging her his fidelity, and with head held high and brave countenance to cover her misgiving she goes to the emperor.

ACT III, PART 1. Within the apartments of the emperor Roustan and Constant are standing near their master, who is seated at his desk. Some officials are present, among them Fouché. Queen Caroline and Princess Elisa are seated in the room, for they have been relating to their brother the insults that they have suffered at the house of the Duchess of Danzig. Within an inner room, the door of which is open, the ladies-in-waiting of the empress are seen. De Brigode announces Catherine. Before she is admitted Napoleon enters the room of the empress to bid her good-night, and his sisters withdraw. When he is again at his desk, all the officials dismissed, and the door of the empress's room closed, Napoleon, alone but for Roustan, receives Catherine.

He is stern and severe as he accepts her homage, but when he takes her to task for the way she spoke to Queen Caroline and Princess Elisa and she tells him what they also said, his face relaxes, and he sees adequate reason for her anger and humor in her sharp replies. Then in her direct and fearless way she meets his reproof by saying that she has an account against him. She takes from her dress a worn slip of paper and hands it to him. He looks at it and glances up in amazement. It is an old unpaid laundry bill of his, contracted when he was lieutenant in the artillery. He asks her if she is Madame Free-and-Easy, a name and a person which he well remembers, and when she acknowledges that she is, he greets her cordially. She shows that she expects him to pay the bill, which she claims now amounts, with principal and interest, to three napoleons. He searches in his pockets, but can find no money. She tells him that his credit is good with her, and so she takes his draft for that amount. She asks him if he would permit one of his soldiers to receive the treatment that his sisters have given her, and when he questions her, she tells of following the army, in order to be with Lefebvre, through several campaigns as vivandière, and of receiving a wound upon her shoulder. He approaches her, much touched, and kisses the scar, and taking her hand, acknowledges that Lefebvre is honored in having such a wife and promises that she shall receive due recognition at court.

While they are still talking a man is seen stealthily making his way toward the room of the empress. Roustan and two other mamelukes seize him, and Napoleon recognizes him as De Neipperg, whom he has already banished. The emperor is very angry and declares that the man shall be executed at dawn, and neither his own protests nor Catherine's pleas avail anything.

Act III, Part 2. Lefebvre and Catherine have tried to plan the rescue of De Neipperg, but Napoleon will brook no delay in the execution of the sentence. Nevertheless, as Napoleon paces his chamber Catherine asks audience, making another effort. She tells him that there is no proof that De Neipperg was guilty of any wrong, that he will die an innocent man. So she proposes that Napoleon make a test which will reveal whether there is any attachment between the empress and the prisoner, by causing some one to say that De Neipperg is waiting outside for a message. Then Napoleon can himself open any letter or package that may be sent to the count.

Napoleon is struck with the plan, and forces the reluctant Catherine to help him carry it out. He commands that she herself impersonate Lady de Bulow, the matron of honor, and give to the empress the message. So Catherine speaks the words just outside the empress's door, and after some waiting a letter is handed out. Napoleon seizes it and tears it open, then gives it to Catherine to read. It is addressed to the Emperor of Austria, the father of Marie Louise, and it begs him to detain Count de Neipperg in Vienna, because his attentions to the empress are annoying. Relieved beyond measure at this proof of his wife's fidelity, Napoleon orders the release of De Neipperg and his speedy departure, and thanks Catherine for preventing him from doing a great wrong.

MADELEINE
(*Mahd-lān*)
(MADELINE)

AMERICAN comic grand opera, adapted from the French of Decourcelles and Thibaut. Music by Victor Herbert. Book by Grant Stewart. First production, New York, 1914. The scene is Paris about 1760.

CHARACTERS

CHEVALIER DE MAUPRAT..........................*Tenor*
FRANÇOIS, Duke d'Esterre...........................*Bass*
DIDIER, a painter....................................*Bass*
MADELINE FLEURY, of the *Opéra*................*Soprano*
NICHETTE, her maid............................*Contralto*
GERMAIN, a servant.

A stewart, lackeys, retainers, etc.

In the late afternoon of New Year's Day the servants of Madeline Fleury, of the *Opéra,* are still receiving the gifts that have been sent to their mistress, and Nichette is arranging them. They go out as Madeline enters with the Chevalier de Mauprat. She is admiring the bracelet that he has just given her. She invites him to dine with her, but he goes off to dine with his mother. In a joyous mood she talks with Nichette of Didier, the painter, who was a childhood playmate of hers, of the position, wealth, and prizes that her career has given her, and she tells Nichette to announce to the servants that she will double their wages. Left alone, she acknowledges to herself that she has everything that life can offer, even love, and tenderly dwells upon her mother's memory.

She hears shouts and cries and the sound of galloping

hoofs, and Nichette announces the Duke d'Esterre, who comes in laughing heartily. He tells Madeline that he has turned her horses out and given her four English thoroughbreds as a New Year's gift. Soon servants enter to set the table for dinner and Madeline invites him to dine with her, but he tells her that is impossible, as he dines with his mother. Madeline is very insistent, but he declares that he must go, for though he is not a very good son, this one attention of dining with his mother on New Year's Day he never omits. Madeline makes it a test of his love for herself, and he protests, but does not yield. As proof of his love he tells her that he challenged De Fontages when the latter averred that she sang off the key, and that he is to fight him on the morrow. Still perverse Madeline forbids him to go, saying that if he goes her door will be barred to him henceforth. He is firm, and she vows that she will not dine alone, but with the first who comes, and hopes that it may be Baron de Fontages, to whom she wishes success on the morrow. Silently the Duke d'Esterre goes out.

Madeline writes a note inviting the baron to dine alone with her, and sends it by Germain. The baron sends regrets and the explanation that he is dining with his mother. She then thinks of Didier, but first asks Nichette to dine with her. Nichette, surprised, says that she told her she might be free that afternoon and evening, and she has promised to dine at home with her mother. When Nichette refuses to stay and even threatens to resign, Madeline very angrily discharges her. She summons the lackeys and has them throw all the flowers into the street, then discharges them all, saying that she is ever in fear of death from their treachery.

As she lies upon her sofa weeping Didier enters, bringing her mother's portrait. Without seeming to notice her emotion, he talks of the picture, then humorously gives her an orange for his New Year's gift. When she continues to cry he treats her as a big brother might, reminding her of the days when each studied his own art in two adjoining attic rooms. She tells him that no one will dine with her, and he starts to explain that he, too, dines with his mother, when she stops him, and he invites her to dine with him at his home, even though the fare be poor. He bids her put on a plain dress, and says that he will tell his mother that she is a sewing girl, who makes only a pittance.

Nichette comes with tear-stained eyes to say good-bye, and Didier tells her that she is not discharged. Then Madeline borrows a gown of Nichette, and while they are gone Didier muses how small a thing will stir Madeline to the depths, though she is courted, caressed, and envied by all, and that success does not bring happiness. He has misgivings about his invitation, but trusts to her kindness and loyalty. Madeline sends Nichette joyously home, after she shall have told the servants that they are not discharged, but that they receive double salary beginning that very day.

Didier thinks Madeline looks beautiful in the plain gown, and, half laughing and half confused, tells her that his parents are both old and dote on him overmuch, so she will hear too much about him; and it will not be easy for her to eat their coarse food perhaps, but that they will be hurt if she does not eat; and he asks her not to laugh at them—till afterward. She asks him if he really means to take her to his home. When he replies that he does, she thanks him and says that she is quite satisfied. She tells him that she cannot come, not to deceive them, and she cannot let him tell them who she is, so she will dine at home. Much touched, he weeps and embraces her, saying she has a heart of gold, then goes hastily out. Madeline, left alone, repents that she treated poor François as she did, and is about to sit down alone at her table with her mother's portrait opposite her, when Nichette reënters, saying that her mother has permitted her to come back and dine with her mistress. Madeline, however, again sends Nichette off, saying that she does not dine alone, but she, too, dines with her mother.

THE MAGIC FLUTE
(DIE ZAUBERFLOETE) (IL FLAUTO MAGICO)

GERMAN allegorical grand opera, adapted from a tale by Wieland, called "Lulu, or The Magic Flute." Music by Johann Wolfgang Amadeus Mozart. Book by Emanuel Johann Schikaneder. First production, Vienna, 1791. The scene is within and in the vicinity of the Temple of Isis at Memphis, Egypt, about the time of Ramses I.

CHARACTERS

SARASTRO, High Priest of Isis......................*Bass*
TAMINO, an Egyptian prince.......................*Tenor*
PAPAGENO, a bird-catcher.........................*Baritone*
MONOSTATOS, a Moor, chief of the slaves of the Temple, *Baritone*
PAMINA, daughter of the Queen of Night............*Soprano*
ASTRIFIAMMANTE, the Queen of Night..............*Soprano*
PAPAGENA ....*Soprano*

Three lady attendants of the Queen of Night, three boys belonging to the Temple and serving Sarastro, priests and priestesses, slaves both male and female, warriors, and attendants.

ACT I. Near the temple of Isis Prince Tamino is pursued by a huge serpent. As he faints from fright three lady attendants of the Goddess of Night come to his rescue and stab the serpent with their javelins, then return to tell Astrifiammante of the young and handsome man. Tamino awakens and finds that the serpent is dead just as Papageno, a merry fellow grotesquely decked out in feathers to aid in his trade as bird-catcher, enters, playing a flute. Tamino thinks that Papageno killed the serpent, and the bird-catcher, frightened until he makes sure that the serpent is dead, assumes the honor. The three ladies, however, return and, rebuking him for his deception, put a padlock upon his lips. The Queen of Night has sent Tamino a portrait of her

© Aimé Dupont

MARCELLA SEMBRICH
AS ASTRIFIAMMANTE, QUEEN OF NIGHT, IN "THE MAGIC FLUTE"

daughter, Pamina, whom Sarastro has taken from her mother. Tamino is immediately impressed by Pamina's beauty and the story of the mother's distress, and vows to rescue the princess. The queen herself comes with solemn music and thunder, and promises him a rich reward. When she leaves her ladies remove the padlock from Papageno's lips, present Tamino with a golden flute whose music will guide him to safety when he is in danger, and give Papageno a set of musical bells having the same property. Then the two set off together to the palace of the High Priest.

In Sarastro's palace Pamina is sitting, watched over by Monostatos, a Moor, who is now so faithless to his trust as to oppress her with his attentions. When she repulses him, he orders slaves to put chains upon her. Papageno enters, and the Moor and he, suddenly face to face, each think the other the devil and run in different directions. Papageno courageously returns and, identifying Pamina by her portrait which he carries, tells her of Prince Tamino's love for her, and together they go in search of him.

Tamino is still outside the palace walls. He has tried two of the ponderous gates and been warned back from each by mysterious voices within. At the third an aged priest reveals to him that Sarastro is no pitiless robber, but the High Priest of the Temple of Wisdom. He enters the gate and the mysterious voices, in answer to his questions, tell him that his night of ignorance will be soon or never lifted, and that Pamina still lives. He plays upon his flute and, hearing Papageno answer, hastens off toward him for news of Pamina.

Meanwhile not far off the princess and the bird-catcher are searching for him and seeking to escape from Monostatos. But the latter overtakes them and his slaves have bound them when Papageno bethinks himself to play upon his magic bells. The slaves draw back and dance and sing, and then all go away as Sarastro and his retinue enter. Pamina, resolved to speak the truth, tells of the persecutions of the Moor, and of her grief for her mother, to which the High Priest listens compassionately. He orders Monostatos scourged, and as Tamino comes upon the scene and the lovers fly into each other's arms in joyous recognition, he decrees that Tamino and Papageno shall enter the temple of probation, and as the two novices are covered with veils, he himself takes Pamina away with him in his car.

Act II. At night in a forest thunder rumbles as Sarastro and his priests pray to Isis and Osiris for the two novices, and pass judgment upon them as worthy to enter the ranks of the elect. Tamino and Papageno are brought. They are warned of the testing that awaits them, and are told that they shall see each the woman whom he desires, but that he must not speak to her. Soon they are accosted by the three attendants of the queen, with whom appears Pamina also, and although Tamino has much difficulty in restraining the talkative Papageno, both novices come through the trial successfully.

Pamina is sleeping alone in a garden when Monostatos comes upon her. As he starts to kiss her the Queen of Night rises out of the ground and arouses her daughter, frightening the Moor away. The queen begs Pamina to avenge her mother's wrong by stabbing Sarastro with a dagger that she gives her, telling of the long feud between herself as the ruler of Night and Darkness, and Sarastro, the High Priest of Wisdom and Light, whose symbol is the sun. The queen tells her daughter that unless she fulfills this wish, never shall Tamino be hers and never again will her mother embrace her. As the goddess sinks into the earth, Monostatos returns and again presses his suit. Pamina tells him that she loves Tamino, and the Moor is about to strike her dead when Sarastro enters. The High Priest spurns the recreant, who goes off to make a traitorous bargain with Astrifiammante. Pamina pleads for her wretched mother, and Sarastro generously declares that he desires no better revenge for the murderous design of the Queen of Night than the happiness of her daughter through union with a victorious Tamino.

Meanwhile within a temple hall three boys have restored to Tamino his flute and to Papageno his set of bells, and have laid a royal table for them. Tamino is intent on playing upon his magic flute, but Papageno is quite absorbed in eating and drinking. The flute tones, however, have brought Pamina to the prince, and she stands sorrowfully by, watching him and weeping when he is silent to her entreaties. When she goes sadly away, eager only for death, Tamino rescues Papageno from the dangers of his gluttony, and they go off together. Pamina, when alone, starts to stab herself with the very dagger her mother had given her, and the three boys stay her purpose with the news that Tamino still loves her faithfully, and they promise to conduct her to him.

In a subterranean vault the High Priest and other priests and attendants are gathered when Tamino and Pamina are led in with their heads veiled. When the veils are removed, Pamina is told to take her last farewell of her lover. The moment's recognition does not suffice to break down Tamino's steadfast courage. Yet when Sarastro commands them, as one last test, to forget each other, they both declare that he that is capable of so forgetting never loved. In longing and yet obedience to the High Priest they part.

All have gone out when Papageno enters in search of

Tamino. He is diverted from his quest by a full wine cup, and a woman appears to him, to whom he impulsively makes love. When he notices her great age and lack of comeliness he still swears to be a good husband to her. Then she becomes a beautiful young woman, dressed in the same guise of feathers that he himself wears. He would embrace her, but she sinks into the earth.

Below an enormous mountain, down the sides of which run molten lava, Tamino is led by two knights in black armor into a deep cavern. It is now the extreme testing, the final purification before he is admitted into the mysteries of Isis. Courageously he approaches a prisonlike iron grating, and when he has passed through, an opposite one opens and Pamina stands before him. They rush into each other's arms, and though it is a place of great danger, she promises to go with him. They advance hand in hand, and go through raging flames and roaring torrents, and suddenly, when almost overwhelmed, find themselves within a temple in the inmost recesses of the mountain, kneeling safely before a shrine.

Papageno is still wandering about the garden, searching for his little Papagena. At last he sounds his bells and she appears, and they dance off happily together. The Queen of Night has pledged her daughter in marriage to Monostatos, and she with her attendants and the Moor come seeking her. As they plan to enter the temple and assault the kneeling worshipers, a tempest of thunder and lightning shakes the edifice and in its place rises the Temple of the Sun. Sarastro is seated on his throne, and Tamino and Pamina, clad in the garments of the initiated, move forward and take their stand before him. The Queen of Night and her minions suddenly sink with outcries and laments into the ground, as priests sing the nuptial hymn of the lovers.

MANON

FRENCH tragic grand opera, founded on Abbé Marcel Prévost's "Manon Lescaut." Music by Jules Massenet. Book by Henri Meilhac and Philippe Gille. First production, Paris, 1884. The scene is laid in Amiens, Paris, and Havre in 1721.

CHARACTERS

CHEVALIER DES GRIEUX............................. *Tenor*
COUNT DES GRIEUX, his father........................ *Bass*
LESCAUT, one of the Royal Guard, cousin to Manon.. *Baritone*
GUILLOT DE MORFONTAINE, Minister of Finance, an old
    beau .... *Bass*
DE BRÉTIGNY, a nobleman........................ *Baritone*
MANON, a school girl............................. *Soprano*
POUSETTE, JAVOTTE, ROSETTE, actresses............ *Sopranos*

Students, an innkeeper, a sergeant, a soldier, gamblers, merchants and their wives, croupiers, sharpers, guards, travelers, ladies, gentlemen, porters, postilions, an attendant at the monastery of St. Sulpice, and the people.

ACT I. In the courtyard of an inn at Amiens villagers are awaiting the coming of the coach. Guillot de Morfontaine, Minister of Finance, a wealthy and dissolute nobleman, has just arrived, accompanied by De Brétigny and a company of actresses, and is giving orders for a dinner. Lescaut and two other guards enter. He finds that the coach from Arras is expected shortly, and he tells his companions that he must meet his cousin, but will join them later. The coach soon comes and among the passengers is Manon Lescaut, a young and beautiful girl, gay and pleasure-loving, who is on her way to a convent school. Lescaut greets her, then hastens off for her baggage, leaving her seated alone outside the door of the inn.

Guillot comes out calling an order to the landlord, and

espying the young girl, makes advances to her. She is much amused by his appearance and laughs at his ardent words. He tells her who he is and that he is very rich. De Brétigny, seeking Guillot, catches sight of Manon and is also charmed by her beauty and simplicity. Guillot hastily whispers to her that a postilion is coming soon with an empty carriage, which is at her service and which he begs her to take. Lescaut blusters in and asks what he is saying, but Guillot denies that he spoke to her and reënters the inn. Lescaut, thus reminded of his responsibility as escort, warns Manon against talking with the men whom she may meet. The two guards come for him and take him away to play cards with them. Manon, left alone, hears the laughter of the dinner party and, catching a glimpse of the actresses, envies them their gay life.

The young Chevalier des Grieux strolls into the courtyard, impatiently awaiting the next coach for Paris, where he is to meet his father. He sees Manon and is attracted by her beauty and her modest bearing. He addresses her respectfully, asking her name and showing his admiration of her. She likes his appearance and responds, after a little telling him that because she loves pleasure too much she is to be put into a convent. He is indignant that she should be thus immured and vows that he will not permit it. She says that then she would owe him more than life. Interest speedily changes to an affection that they frankly acknowledge to each other. He pledges her his protection, and, the carriage of Guillot now coming along, she suggests that they take it. So they speed away to Paris together, while Lescaut, searching for her, comes upon Guillot, also searching, and accuses him of having taken her off, whereat the landlord says that she went away in Guillot's carriage, it is true, but with a young man. The bystanders laugh

© Mishkin

FRANCES ALDA
AS "MANON"

heartily at Guillot's discomfiture, while Lescaut, who has been gambling, drunkenly vows vengeance for the double loss of coin and cousin.

Act II. Des Grieux has taken Manon to his apartments in Paris, and there is writing a letter to his father, telling him of Manon and their love for each other, and begging his consent to their marriage. He and Manon read the letter together and she is surprised at the glowing account of her beauty and at his impassioned love for her. He notices some flowers upon the table and asks who sent them. She says she does not know, as they were thrown through the window, but asks if he is jealous, and he assures her that he trusts her.

Lescaut, accompanied by De Brétigny, enters abruptly. While the rough soldier, representing the girl's family, demands satisfaction of Des Grieux for the abduction of Manon, De Brétigny draws her aside and urges his suit upon her. He tells her that he is very wealthy, while the chevalier is poor. He also tells her that the Count des Grieux is that night coming to take his son away, and he urges Manon that she come with him. She listens to his proposal, but will make no promise. Meanwhile the chevalier has shown Lescaut the letter to his father and has satisfied him of his honorable intentions.

When the two men are gone the chevalier goes out to post the letter, and Manon ponders over De Brétigny's words and, though mildly accepting the situation, yet grieves that her happy times with the chevalier are over. When he returns he sees the traces of her tears, and to comfort her tells of a dream he had of a cottage in the depths of woods, where they two could pass their lives in happiness, but strangely enough she was not there. So he urges her to promise to marry him. While they talk a knock is heard at the door, and Manon, well knowing what it means, tries remorsefully to prevent him from answering. He insists upon going, however, and when he opens the door is seized and borne away. Manon is overwhelmed with grief as she hears a carriage driving off.

Act III. On a festival day in Paris among the crowds the actresses—Pousette, Javotte, and Rosette—with their gallants are making merry, having escaped the jealous eyes of Guillot. Lescaut comes along, buying extravagantly of the street vendors and boasting of his large winnings at gambling. Guillot encounters the actresses, is very angry at seeing all three of them, and is reviling them and all women as De Brétigny accosts him. De Brétigny tauntingly asks the old beau not to take Manon from him. Guillot replies that he heard that De Brétigny refused Manon an opera performance for which she begged with tears. De Brétigny acknowledges the fact, and Guillot goes away, prophesying that some one will win Manon from him.

With De Brétigny and a party of gallants Manon comes, singing a love song, which is much applauded. Count des Grieux, who is among the people, accosts De Brétigny and to the latter's question replies that the chevalier is now an abbot, having taken holy orders at the monastery of St. Sulpice. Manon overhears the words and, absorbed in thought, draws apart from the gay crowd. The count tells De Brétigny that he was responsible for the step by breaking off the chevalier's attachment to a certain person. De Brétigny points out Manon to the count, who stands aside watching her. She comes with a request that takes De Brétigny away, and then timidly addresses the count, telling him that his son once loved a friend of hers and asking if he has forgotten that friend. When the count parries her questions, Manon with deep emotion asks if the chevalier has suffered. The count says that the wound has closed and that his son has done as her friend has—forgotten it.

He leaves her weeping and De Brétigny returns just as Guillot enters with some friends. Guillot tells Manon that he will give her the opera that De Brétigny refused, and he orders a chorus of singers and dancers to produce a new ballet. As it goes on De Brétigny is rejoicing that the expense will ruin Guillot, and the latter is delighted because he has outdone his rival. Manon, however, summons Lescaut and asks him to take her to St. Sulpice, and when Guillot sees her sad and troubled and asks what she thinks of the ballet, she says that she has seen nothing.

Count des Grieux, waiting in the reception room of the monastery of St. Sulpice, hears the enthusiastic comments of devout women, as they go from the chapel after a service, on his son's eloquence and fervor. They think him indeed a saint and as he approaches show him great reverence. Alone with the young abbot, the count sarcastically congratulates him on his success, saying that their house should be proud to have another Bossuet. The young man begs his father not to taunt him and expresses disgust with the world and with life. His father asks him what right he has to think life finished, and tells him it is his duty to marry some good girl and become the father of a family. The son is firm in his renunciation, however, and the count goes away only saying in parting that he will send him that evening a considerable sum of money, which has come to him from his mother's estate. Left alone, the young man rejoices in the calm faith that supports him, though he devoutly prays to be delivered from the image of the one face that haunts him and the sad shadow that lies on his heart.

Manon seeks audience with the young abbot and is shown into the reception room. She shudders at its gloomy walls, and when she hears voices in the chapel chanting a prayer, she, too, prays for forgiveness and mercy—and for the heart of Des Grieux. As he enters and, recognizing her, asks why she comes, she is speechless with emotion. When she approaches him he bids her keep her distance. She acknowledges her cruelty and wickedness, and asks him if he cannot pardon her. He is very stern, but she kneels at his feet and tries to recall his former love, asking if she is not the same Manon. He prays to be sustained in this trial, but when she in an agony of longing confesses her love for him, saying she will not leave him and begging him to come with her, he relents, owning that he cannot cast out of his heart the memory of her. Then in great exaltation and abandon he declares that he still loves her and asks her to come away with him.

Act IV. In a gambling-room of the Hotel Transylvania in Paris is gathered a gay party of men and women, among whom are Lescaut and the three actresses. Guillot de Morfontaine enters, and soon Manon comes, accompanied by Des Grieux. Lescaut comments that Guillot changes color, and the latter acknowledges that he adores Manon, but that she loves another. Des Grieux seems troubled and sad, and when Manon begs him to take courage he, torn between his love of her and his disapproval of her desire for wealth and pleasure, says in one breath that he loves and he hates her.

When she urges him to play because their money is gone and he must find a fortune, he vows that he never will. Lescaut remarks that Manon does not love poverty, and Manon says that if he loves her he will play that they may be rich. When she promises him her love and her life, he surrenders, and, assured by Lescaut that it is easy to win, accepts Guillot's challenge to a game to see whether Des Grieux can always take Manon from him. While they are playing for high stakes Manon sings a passionate song of love for the gold and for the pleasure it brings. Lescaut and Guillot both lose heavily, while Des Grieux wins. Manon comes to him and he shows her the gold and they speak lovingly to each other. At last Guillot, jealous and furious over his loss, accuses Des Grieux of stealing and calls the bystanders to witness, then threatening revenge, goes out. Manon tries to persuade Des Grieux to flee, but he will not, for it would seem a confession of guilt. Soon a loud knock is heard at the door and officers of the law enter. Guillot is with them and denounces both Des Grieux and Manon. Des Grieux is wild with anger, but can do nothing. His father appears and tells him that it is necessary to submit to arrest, but he will come later to free him and save their name from dishonor. Manon in great grief cries out that they are to be separated, and her lover is overwhelmed with remorse. When the officers start to take her he makes a desperate attempt to protect her, but is not permitted to interfere, and Manon is led away.

ACT V. The count has obtained the release of his son, but Manon has been ordered deported as a dissolute woman, and is being taken with other prisoners to a vessel lying at Havre. The young chevalier is heartbroken, but will not give up his efforts to save her. He plans with Lescaut to have a band of hired men lie in wait on the road and deliver her from the guards. He is in the woods by the roadside when Lescaut comes up and reports that their plan has failed, for the men fled when they saw that the guards were armed. Des Grieux is distracted and starts to rush forth himself and free Manon, but Lescaut holds him back. Concealed in the bushes, they see the archers pass, and gain from their talk as they stop near them to drink that Manon is very ill. Lescaut asks Des Grieux for his purse, and going to the officer, who recognizes him as a fellow-soldier, says that he is of Manon's family and asks that she be left in his charge at this place. When, therefore, the archers and their prisoners have gone on, Manon comes weak and trembling to her lover, who is enraptured to see her and freely gives her the pardon she asks. He plans how they may get away and live together in seclusion. She is very ill and weak and realizes that death is near. He cannot believe it until, with words of love for him, she expires in his arms.

MANON LESCAUT
(*Man-on Les-koh*)

ITALIAN tragic grand opera, founded upon Abbé Marcel Prévost's novel of the same name. (It is in reality four scenes taken from this, rather than a connected plot.) Music by Giacomo Puccini. Book by the composer and a committee of friends. First production, Turin, 1893. The scene is Amiens, Paris and its vicinity, and the vicinity of New Orleans, Louisiana, in the second half of the eighteenth century.

CHARACTERS

LESCAUT, Sergeant of the King's Guards, brother of Manon .... *Baritone*
CHEVALIER DES GRIEUX .... *Tenor*
GERONTE DE RAVOIR, Treasurer-General .... *Bass*
EDMUND, a student .... *Tenor*
MANON LESCAUT .... *Soprano*

An innkeeper, a dancing-master, a sergeant of the royal archers, a captain in the navy, a lamplighter, singers, old beaus and abbots, girls, citizens, villagers, a hair-dresser, students, courtesans, archers, sailors, and the people.

ACT I. In a square of Amiens, where the post chaises depart for Paris, Edmund and other students are strolling when the Chevalier des Grieux, dressed as a student, joins them. They greet him jovially, and when he plays the melancholy lover and accosts the girls that are passing, they shout with merriment. A coach draws up and from it alights Manon Lescaut, her brother, and Geronte de Ravoir, the Treasurer-General, who chances to be their traveling companion. Manon is a very beautiful young girl, who is being taken to a convent school to finish her education. Her brother is a sergeant in the King's Guards, and an irresponsible fellow, fond of wine and gambling. Geronte, an old beau, is greatly taken with Manon, and intends to thwart the brother's plans. While Geronte and Lescaut are in the inn, Des Grieux accosts Manon, and in answer to his questions she tells him her name and destination. He is much impressed with her beauty and asks her to meet him later, and she half promises to do so. Lescaut calls her and she goes into the inn. Edmund and the students, who have been watching, banter Des Grieux on his seriousness, but he is now in no mood for fun and goes off. Shortly Lescaut reappears, accompanied by some fellow-soldiers, who urge him to a game of cards, and he goes off with them.

Geronte and the landlord come into the courtyard. Geronte is ordering a carriage with fleet horses, and inquires about the rear door of the inn, at the same time instructing the landlord to keep Lescaut engaged with wine and the game. Edmund overhears the conversation and tells it to Des Grieux, who is lingering about to meet Manon. When he learns the old Treasurer-General's plans, he determines to persuade Manon to go away with him. So when she comes he is very ardent in his protestations and very urgent in his pleas. She is much taken with him and of a thoughtless and adventurous spirit, so the plan appeals to her. The carriage for Geronte is waiting, and as he comes seeking her the lovers appropriate it and drive off toward Paris. Geronte arouses Lescaut to follow his sister and confesses his liking for her. But Lescaut will not fall in with Geronte's plan until the latter has promised to make him also one of the family.

ACT II. Manon is now established in the luxurious apartments of Geronte, having left Des Grieux and the humble cottage to which he had taken her. She has every-

© Mishkin

LUCREZIA BORI
AS "MANON LESCAUT"

thing that her gay heart can wish,—costly dresses and jewels in abundance. Her hair-dresser attends her, and her dancing-master awaits her leisure. Lescaut, quite one of the family, enters and as they talk reminds her that her change in fortune is due to him. She asks after Des Grieux and whether he has forgotten her. Lescaut tells her that the young man is gambling madly to get money enough to win her back to him. Touched by this sign of his affection, she looks at the rich hangings about her and longs for the simple home that Des Grieux gave her and the happiness she knew there. A company of madrigal singers, whom Geronte has sent to amuse her, come and entertain her. Afterward, while she is having her dancing lesson, Geronte and several of his friends come in and watch her admiringly. She sings to them and coquets with them, much to Geronte's amusement. They leave after making her promise to join them soon on the boulevards.

Suddenly Des Grieux enters, Lescaut having told him of Manon's pensive inquiry for him. He heaps reproaches on her, but she declares that she loves him, humbly confessing that she has wronged him, and weeps that he loves her no more. He tells her of his suffering, and when on her knees she begs his forgiveness, he bewails the weakness that still makes him feel the power of her charms. He is overcome by her tenderness and, quite reconciled, is caressing her, when suddenly the door opens and Geronte stands there amazed. The older man sarcastically taunts Manon, and when Des Grieux would defend her he silences him. He reminds Manon of his gifts, of his love, but she, taking a mirror from the table, bids him look in it and then at them. He ironically bids her good-bye and goes out threatening.

Des Grieux, alarmed, urges Manon to come away with him, but she hesitates, sorry to leave all the splendor, and he laments that nothing can change her. She again asks his forgiveness as Lescaut enters, saying that Geronte has denounced them and that the police are at hand. He urges them to hasten away, but Manon strives to gather together some of the jewels that Geronte has given her. She picks up everything of value that she can put her hands on and hides them in her cloak, although Des Grieux and Lescaut both deplore the delay and try to stop her. At last Lescaut announces that the house is surrounded and escape is impossible. In a panic of fear Manon hides in an alcove as Geronte enters, followed by guards. When the sergeant demands her surrender Manon comes forth, and in her terror lets slip the cloak and the jewels fall upon the floor. Geronte laughs long and loud. Des Grieux draws his sword, but Lescaut holds him back, asking who will save Manon if he is arrested. So Manon is led away alone, while Des Grieux cries out her name in heartbroken tones.

(Here occurs an intermezzo expressive of Manon's horror and grief at her imprisonment, at the order that she be deported, and of her experiences on the journey to Havre; also of Des Grieux' despair when, having done his utmost to obtain her release, he fails in an attempt to take her by force from the guards on the road to Havre.)

Act III. In a square of Havre near the harbor Des Grieux is impatiently waiting. Lescaut comes and tells him that soon the guard he has bribed will be on duty and that he may speak with Manon. He also says that Manon knows of the signal for her to come forth when his own trusty comrades attempt her rescue. Des Grieux can scarcely hope that Manon may be free, so many efforts have failed. The sentinel comes and the guard is changed. Lescaut goes to the barracks and gives a signal, at which the sentinel retires. Lescaut taps on the window and Manon appears and holds out her hands through the bars to Des Grieux, who ardently kisses them. The lovers talk together, exchanging vows and promises. A lamplighter sings gaily as he goes his rounds.

At last Des Grieux is obliged to bid Manon farewell, and they each encourage the other. As he goes away a shout is heard and he knows that Lescaut's attempt has failed. Manon comes again to the window and begs Des Grieux, if he loves her, to go away. The commotion increases and citizens rush in at the report that a woman has tried to escape. Shortly the guards enter the square, conducting the band of women in chains. The captain of a man-of-war comes to take over the prisoners after the roll is called. As each woman replies to her name, Manon, the last, attracts much attention because of her beauty and her great sadness. Lescaut in a crowd of men tells her story—that she was abducted from the arms of her lover. Des Grieux tries to follow Manon, hiding behind her, while she begs his forgiveness and says that now they must part. When the sergeant would drive the women before him Des Grieux suddenly wrenches Manon from his grasp and defies him. The men who have heard Manon's story run to Des Grieux' support. The captain appears and Des Grieux looses his hold upon Manon and bursts into sobs, declaring that he is mad. On his knees he begs the captain to take him as a servant. The captain consents, and in her joy Manon stretches out her arms to her lover, who rushes to her. As the exiles depart, Lescaut goes off sadly shaking his head.

ACT IV. In a vast plain near New Orleans Manon and Des Grieux wander. She, worn and fatigued, leans on him and he tries to cheer her, but in spite of her effort she sinks fainting and begging for a moment's rest. Des Grieux is in despair and weeps over her suffering. She slowly revives and begs for water. He rushes off, but soon returns, for there is none in sight. They pray for help, and then she bids him go ahead in search of shelter while she rests, and he reluctantly leaves her. Alone, she is distraught with terror and fatigue, and prays that she may not die. She recalls how her beauty ever surrounded her with enemies, and how, when they would have separated her from her lover, the two of them sought this barren region as a haven. Burdened with remorse and fear, she raves wildly. Des Grieux returns, running, and she falls in his arms. Recovering, she tells him again how much she loves him and that she is dying. He feels the chill of death upon her cheek and says that he cannot live without her. Commanding him to live and breathing words of love, she dies, and he falls senseless upon her body.

THE MARRIAGE OF FIGARO
(LE NOZZE DI FIGARO)

ITALIAN comic grand opera, a continuation in its story of Rossini's "The Barber of Seville," and founded upon Beaumarchais' "La Folle Journée, ou Le Mariage de Figaro." Music by Johann Wolfgang Amadeus Mozart. Book by Lorenzo da Ponte. First production, Vienna, 1786. The scene is the chateau of Aguas Frescas, three leagues from Seville, Spain, in the seventeenth century.

CHARACTERS

COUNT ALMAVIVA, Grand Corregidor of Andalusia..*Baritone*
FIGARO, valet to Count Almaviva and major-domo of the chateau............*Bass*
DOCTOR BARTOLO, a physician of Seville............*Bass*
DON BASILIO, music-master to the Countess.........*Tenor*
ANTONIO, gardener of the chateau, uncle to Susanna..*Bass*
DON CURZIO, counselor-at-law.................*Tenor*
CHERUBINO, head page to the Count.............*Soprano*
COUNTESS ALMAVIVA............................*Soprano*
SUSANNA, head waiting-woman of the Countess, betrothed to Figaro..........*Soprano*
MARCELLINA, a duenna........................*Contralto*
BARBARINA, daughter of Antonio.................*Soprano*

Servants, officers of the court, and peasants both men and women.

Figaro, in his gayer and less prosperous days, gave a written promise of marriage to Marcellina, who is many years his senior and who, in expectation of its fulfillment, gave him various sums of money. He is now in love with Susanna and engaged to marry her upon the very day appointed to wed Marcellina. The duenna, with the aid of Doctor Bartolo, has planned a surprise for the ex-barber.

ACT I. Figaro is telling Susanna that the count has given them that room for theirs. Susanna, disturbed, tells him that the count, though less than a year married, is unpleasantly attentive to her, and when Susanna goes away, Figaro plans his revenge. He goes off as Bartolo and Marcellina enter, plotting how they may gain the count's ear for their scheme against Figaro. Bartolo chuckles to himself over foisting upon Figaro the cross old duenna. Susanna, at the door, overhears their plan, and when Bartolo takes his leave, enters with a gown of her mistress's in her hand. Marcellina taunts Susanna with the count's attentions, then goes out. Susanna throws the gown over a chair as Cherubino enters. He tells her that the count found him alone with Barbarina that morning and dismissed him from his service. He comes to ask the countess to intercede for him, that he may not have to go away. Suddenly the count comes in and Cherubino hides behind an armchair.

The count announces that he has been made ambassador to London and intends taking Figaro with him. When he makes love to her Susanna asks him to leave her alone, but the count will not, and says that he has already sent her a message through Basilio that he wishes to meet her that night within the orange bower. Basilio's voice is heard, saying that he will seek the count with his lady. The count starts to hide behind the armchair, much to Susanna's distress, but Cherubino slips around and into it and Susanna conceals him under the gown as Basilio enters.

Basilio also taunts Susanna with the count's attentions, and asks whether it is she or the countess that keeps Cherubino hanging around, saying that the count would be very angry if he knew what was being talked on all sides. Susanna wrathfully accuses him of slander, and the count, more curious about his wife than fearful for his own repu-

© Mishkin

FRIEDA HEMPEL
AS SUSANNA, IN "THE MARRIAGE OF FIGARO"

tation, comes from his hiding-place, much to Basilio's enjoyment. When Cherubino is mentioned, Susanna pleads in his behalf, but the count relates how he himself came to Antonio's cottage and found the door locked, then, when Barbarina opened to him, he was sure some one was lurking about, and lifting the table cover he found the head page. Suiting action to word, he lifts the gown from the armchair—and finds the head page. He angrily accuses Susanna, and starts to send for Figaro, but remembers his own predicament. Susanna explains, and the count realizes that Cherubino has heard his conversation with Susanna and the appointment for that evening. Figaro enters and is told that the page has been ordered to quit the castle. He pleads for him, and the count, because it is Figaro and Susanna's wedding day, makes Cherubino ensign in his own regiment, but orders him to be off immediately. The count and Basilio go out together, and Figaro and Susanna bid Cherubino farewell.

In her chamber the countess sits pensively hoping that her husband's love may be restored to her. Susanna enters, and while disclosing the count's attentions to her, assures the countess that his jealousy proves his love for his wife. Figaro comes, saying that through Basilio he has sent the count a note to the effect that the countess has made an engagement for that evening. They then plan that Marcellina shall keep the appointment of the countess, and Cherubino, dressed as a woman, shall keep the appointment that the count wishes to make with Susanna. As the count is now off hunting, Cherubino is to come at once and get his costume.

When the page appears, languishing with love of the countess, the two women have much fun at his expense. He shows the countess his commission, which she notes lacks the seal. Susanna has just taken away his coat and waistcoat and gone to fetch the gown he is to wear, when the count demands admission. Cherubino hides in the cabinet, and the countess locks the door and takes the key before admitting her husband, who is very suspicious of the voices and the delay. He gives her the note that Figaro sent him concerning her appointment as Cherubino knocks over a chair. The count demands an explanation of the noise, and the countess now tells him that Susanna is within the cabinet, although she had just said that she had gone to her room. Susanna is about entering the room when she stops in the doorway, listening, and hears the count commanding her to come out of the cabinet. The count goes off to get a crowbar, taking the countess with him, and Susanna aids Cherubino to open the door and then locks herself in the room as he, in a panic, jumps from the window and escapes.

The count and countess return, and before giving him the key, she tells him that Cherubino is within. More jealous than ever, he opens the door and finds Susanna. The maid quietly tells the countess that the page is off. The count is forced to apologize to his wife, who forgives him and satisfies him about the note by saying that Figaro made it up. Figaro comes, announcing the wedding chorus, and, confronted with the note, denies it, in spite of the countess and Susanna's efforts to make him own it. Antonio, drunk and with a pot of broken flowers in his hands, enters and says that a man was thrown from the window, but got away. Figaro explains that it was he himself who, surprised by the count while waiting to see Susanna, in his excitement jumped from the window, thereby spraining his ankle, which he then thinks to rub. Antonio hands him papers which fell from his pocket, and Figaro, undaunted, though one is Cherubino's commission, at a hint from the countess says that the page left it with him, as it lacked the seal. All seems well until suddenly Marcellina, Basilio, and Bartolo enter, presenting the count with Figaro's promise to marry Marcellina and asking him to give decision. The count takes the paper, saying that he will read it over.

Act II. The count is walking up and down the cabinet, thinking about Marcellina's claim upon Figaro, when Susanna enters, presumably on an errand for her mistress. When he, fearing that she has betrayed him to the countess, hints that she may lose her lover even on this their wedding day, she accuses him of planning to give Marcellina her dowry. He repudiates his promise of dowry unless she will do as he wishes, so she consents to meet him in the grove that night. Figaro enters as the count goes, and the latter is again made suspicious and furious by Susanna's words to Figaro as she runs away.

Don Curzio, Marcellina, Bartolo, and Figaro enter for the decision, and the count, still angry with Susanna, says that Figaro must either pay Marcellina or wed her. Figaro, saying that he was well-born and will, therefore, first have to gain the permission of his parents to marry, tells how as a child he was stolen by robbers, who took the rich garments and jewels that were upon him, so he has only a mark upon his arm as identification. Marcellina eagerly asks if it is a spatula on his right arm. He demands how she knows it. She exclaims that he is then Rafaello, the child whom thieves stole and of whose story Bartolo and Basilio both know. Basilio then tells Figaro that Marcellina is his mother, while she tells him that Bartolo is his father. There is joyous recognition and embracing, Bartolo foregoing his hostility to him and Marcellina relinquishing her claim to marriage.

The count is starting off when Susanna meets him and offers a purse of her own money to pay Marcellina's claim upon Figaro. Just then she sees her betrothed embracing Marcellina, and angrily bids Figaro good-bye. He detains her and explains, and Marcellina embraces her also. The count and Don Curzio, both disappointed at the turn of affairs, go out. Marcellina gives Figaro a receipt for the money he owes her, Susanna offers him the purse she had made ready, and Bartolo adds a gift, all of which Figaro accepts.

The countess enters seeking Susanna, and shortly the count comes in with Antonio, who brings Cherubino's regimental hat and declares that the lad has not gone to Seville, but is at his cottage dressed in woman's clothes. They go out to seek him, and the countess and Susanna write a note for the count, and in place of a seal pin it with a needle. Barbarina and some peasant girls, among them Cherubino in disguise, enter and present garlands to the countess. The count and Antonio come and seize Cherubino, take off his bonnet and put his regimental hat upon him, laughing at the gallant soldier. Figaro enters, asking that the maidens may hasten, so that the wedding festivities may begin, and all go out, leaving the count and countess alone.

Almost immediately the wedding party returns to be received by them. As Susanna kneels before the count, while he puts on her head the wedding wreath, she slips a note into his hand. He throws the needle away, but is obliged to hunt for it, as it is to be returned to the sender. Figaro, watching him search, whispers to Susanna that the count has received a love note. Shortly after, in a small room, Figaro and Marcellina come upon Barbarina, who is looking for a needle she has lost, which she says the count gave her to take to Susanna. Figaro is wild with rage and jealousy, and goes out stormily.

That evening within the garden, where is a pavilion on

either side, Cherubino, searching for Barbarina, comes upon the supposed Susanna, in reality the countess, and fondly takes her hand just as the count comes through the iron gates and sees them. The real Susanna is hiding opposite Figaro, and they both see the encounter. When Cherubino tries to kiss the supposed Susanna, each one of the three watchers is for a different reason angry. Cherubino meets only with coldness, and saying that she is usually not so shy with the count, he ardently bestows the kiss—upon the count, who has stepped between them. Figaro has come forward and received upon the ear the count's blow intended for Cherubino. Both Figaro and Cherubino retire, and the count addresses the supposed Susanna in tender tones. The countess, simulating Susanna's voice, succeeds in deceiving him until he has avowed his love and bestowed upon her a diamond ring. The countess takes alarm and the count leads her to a near-by grove, but when Figaro appears close at hand they separate. Susanna herself comes forward and speaks with Figaro. He is taken in by the disguise and confesses his fury that Susanna is with the count. In her indignation at his distrust, she forgets her part and demands that she be vindicated. He then recognizes her voice and assures her that he knew who she was before. They are both elated that their plot is succeeding, and Figaro is kneeling before her, declaring his love, as the count returns from his search for the supposed Susanna. He seizes Figaro, but the supposed countess escapes into the pavilion, where the real countess is.

The count raises an alarm, and Basilio, Antonio, Curzio, Bartolo, servants, and peasants enter with torches. The count goes to the pavilion and first drags out Cherubino, then rushes off again and leads in the supposed Susanna, who hides her face with her hands. She begs him to forgive her, but he is obdurate, although the bystanders plead for her. Then the real Susanna comes and kneels before the count. He is taken aback with amazement. He turns to the real countess and asks her forgiveness, which she freely gives. Then all the lovers and their friends go off happily together to the banquet.

MARTHA

(OR, THE FAIR AT RICHMOND)

GERMAN comic grand opera. Music by Friedrich von Flotow. Book by Jules H. Vernoy, Marquis St. Georges, and Wilhelm Friedrich Riese. First production, Vienna, 1847. The scene is Richmond, England, during the reign of Queen Anne, about 1710.

CHARACTERS

SIR TRISTAN MICKELFORD, cousin to Lady Harriet.......*Bass*
PLUNKETT, a wealthy young farmer..................*Bass*
LIONEL, his adopted brother, afterwards Earl of Derby *Tenor*
THE SHERIFF OF RICHMOND..........................*Bass*
LADY HARRIET DURHAM, Maid-of-Honor to Queen Anne,
                                                Soprano
NANCY, waiting-maid to Lady Harriet................*Alto*

Courtiers, servants both men and women, ladies, farmers, hunters, huntresses, pages, and peasants.

ACT I. In her boudoir Lady Harriet Durham sits surrounded by her ladies, but overwhelmed with ennui. Nancy, her faithful maid and companion, tries to arouse her, but she looks at the gifts of her admirers indifferently. Nancy says there is but one cure for her, and that is to fall hopelessly in love. Sir Tristan Mickelford, a gay but no longer young man, who is unavailingly devoted to Lady Harriet, comes with fruitless plans for her amusement. When, however, she hears the joyous songs of servant girls on their way to the fair at Richmond, she envies them. She and Nancy at once decide to put on peasant's dress and, unknown, mingle with them, taking Sir Tristan along as escort. He is shocked, but still devoted, and capers about as they teach him the peasants' dance.

In the market place at Richmond merchants, shopkeepers, townspeople, farmers, peasants, and servants are gathering for the fair. Plunkett and Lionel enter. They propose to hire a servant to help them run the farm that Plunkett's mother has left him. They speak tenderly of her, recalling how she has made them share everything equally, although she treated Lionel with special kindness, because he was frailer than her own country boy. They recall also how Lionel's father came, a lost, proscribed, and dying stranger, to their cottage, bearing in his arms his infant son, and that when he died he left no account of his rank or station except what might be revealed by the ring he left for his son to present to the Queen if ever fate sorely threatened him. The two young men wander off among the crowds, rejoicing in their friendship and the tie almost of brotherhood that binds them.

As the clock strikes midday the sheriff opens the fair by announcing the rules on which the servants' contracts shall be given, chief of which is that when money has been given and taken the contract is closed and shall be binding for a year and that neither party shall be able to break it. Soon Lady Harriet and Nancy, with Sir Tristan, all in peasant's dress, enter. The reluctant lord is torn between distaste for his part and fear of offending Lady Harriet. Lionel and Plunkett enter, and when they see the disguised party, they are much attracted to them, but think that the women are too young and fair for the heavy work they wish done. Sir Tristan is taken for a farmer seeking help, and is surrounded by a crowd of importunate servants. At last the two young men summon courage to address the girls and ask if they will take service with them. Plunkett apportions the prospective work,—to Nancy the care of the geese, pigs, and chickens, to Lady Harriet the work in the field and garden with harrow and shovel. At Lionel's protest the latter's is changed to housework and darning the socks. The offer of fifty crowns a year is accepted, and the women roguishly shake hands with the men over the contract and accept part of the money. Sir Tristan returns, and when the ladies would go away with him, Plunkett appeals to the sheriff, and they find that they are bound to the contract for a year. Lady Harriet forbids Sir Tristan to disclose who they are, and she and Nancy go off with the two men.

Act II. Arrived at the farmhouse, Plunkett announces that the day's work begins at dawn. When he shows them their room, the adventurous young women say good-night, but he calls them back, for supper is to be prepared. Lionel protests that they may be weary, but Plunkett says that it will never do to be too easy. Lady Harriet gives her name as Martha, and Nancy as Julia. Both refuse to hang up the men's coats and hats, and the men are puzzled and indignant over their impertinence. Plunkett tells them to fetch the spinning wheels and begin to spin, and the girls laugh at the idea. But when he threatens not to pay them their wages, they realize that he has a claim upon them and bring the wheels. They cannot run them, and the men have to show them how. Nancy mischievously tips over Plunkett's wheel and rushes from the room, he after her.

Lionel, who is much attracted by Lady Harriet's beauty, speaks kindlily to her and she acknowledges that she does not know how to work or to earn the bread he would give her, and asks him to let her go. He says that he cannot, for his heart would break, but asks her to sing to him, which she does. Then he makes love to her, and when he grows more earnest and proposes marriage, telling her that with their marriage all differences of birth would cease, she cannot but laugh, and because she cannot answer him seriously, though she also is in truth much attracted, she continues to laugh. He is deeply wounded, yet cannot but care for her. Plunkett and Nancy return, and Plunkett says that he found her in the kitchen breaking every dish she could lay her hands on, yet, he confesses, he likes her spirit. Midnight strikes and all say good-night. When the men have gone into their room, locking the door, the girls return to the living-room and are talking over their plight when they hear a noise at the window. It is Sir Tristan, who tells them that a carriage is waiting, and with him they make their escape.

ACT III. Outside an inn on the edge of a small forest Plunkett and Lionel sit drinking, when sounds of the Queen's hunting party are heard. The men separate and Plunkett goes into the inn, as a band of huntresses pass through. Following them comes Nancy, searching for her mistress. She is melancholy herself and is thinking how sad Lady Harriet has been ever since their escapade. Plunkett comes out of the inn and recognizes her. He calls her Julia, and commands her to come and fulfill her contract with him. The huntresses reënter and she calls to them, saying that she has found game. When they surround him and threaten him with their lances, he goes away hastily.

Lionel, also very melancholy, is walking up and down thinking of the beautiful lady he loves, who so heartlessly left him, when Lady Harriet and Sir Tristan enter. He reproaches her with leaving the Queen alone, and she dismisses him and gives herself up to longing for her absent lover. Lionel recognizes her voice and approaches, addressing her as Martha and most tenderly expressing his love for her, kissing her hand in the fervor of his devotion. She, however, is forced to pretend that she does not know him, and when at last he commands her to return to the farmhouse with him, she calls for help and Sir Tristan rushes in, followed by the huntresses. Plunkett and Nancy come upon the scene from different directions. As Nancy whispers to Lady Harriet to keep up her courage and calls her "My Lady," Lionel hears, and realizes all, and knows that the whole encounter was but a jest. When Sir Tristan would have him arrested, he states his case and demands his right. Lady Harriet persists in her denial that she knows him, and says that he has evidently lost his senses. The Queen and her attendants approach, and Lionel takes the ring from his finger and gives it to Plunkett, reminding him how it was to be used, and is led away heartbroken.

ACT IV. Plunkett, sitting alone in his farmhouse, is lamenting over Lionel, who is pining away with melancholy and unrequited love, and whom he greatly fears will shortly die. Plunkett is himself sad, because he is haunted by thoughts of the teasing but beautiful Nancy. Lady Harriet and Nancy enter, and the former promises yet to save Lionel. The others leave her and soon Lionel enters. Immediately he recognizes her, he spurns her. In tears she acknowledges her remorse, and tells him that she herself presented his ring to the Queen and that he is the son of the Count of Derby, who was unjustly banished; that he inherits the title and estates of that house, and that the Queen is anxious to make reparation for his father's wrong. Then Lady Harriet offers him her own hand in marriage. Even so great good news does not move his melancholy, and he remembers that the hand now offered him was the same that brought him the anguish and dishonor; so in spite of her repentance, he goes off, saying that hatred now rules in his heart. Plunkett and Nancy return and Lady Harriet goes away, saying that she will try yet another scheme. The farmer and the maid show their affection for each other, but will make no promises or plans until their friends are happier.

Within Lady Harriet's park she and Nancy sit dressed at servants. Lionel approaches, still brooding over his lost love. The clock strikes and servants enter, just as at the fair at Richmond. Plunkett accosts Lionel and brings Martha to him for hire. He recognizes her and is overcome with joy. She is gracious to him and his love and tenderness for her soon return, while Plunkett and Nancy quickly plan to unite their fortunes, and all is joy and merriment.

THE MASKED BALL
(UN BALLO IN MASCHERA)

ITALIAN tragic grand opera, first called "Gustavo III," after an assassinated Swedish monarch, with scene in Stockholm. Music by Giuseppe Verdi. Book by M. Somma. First production, Rome, 1859. The scene is in or near Boston, Massachusetts, in one version of the opera, and the time at about the end of the seventeenth century; in another the scene is Naples, Italy, in the first half of the eighteenth century, with the names of characters those given in parentheses. The Neapolitan setting is usually given as more consistent with the plot.

CHARACTERS

RICHARD, Count of Warwick and Governor of Boston...*Tenor*
  (Riccardo, Duke of Olivaies and Governor of Naples)
REINHART, secretary to Richard and husband of
  Amelia (Renato) ....*Baritone*
SAMUEL } enemies to the Governor.......... { *Bass*
TOM (Tommaso) }   { *Bass*
SYLVAN, a sailor (Silvano)..........................*Bass*
OSCAR, a page (Edgar)..........................*Soprano*
AMELIA (Adelia)..............................*Soprano*
ULRICA, a negress astrologer....................*Contralto*

A judge, a servant of Amelia, deputies, officials, sailors, guards, men, women, and children of the people, partisans of Samuel and Tom, servants, masks, and dancing couples.

ACT I. In the hall of the governor's house deputies, gentlemen, officials, and various representatives of the people are gathered, both adherents and opponents being present. The governor enters and the people cheer him. As he takes up the business of the day the bystanders depart. Oscar admits the deputies, and the governor gives them audience. The page presents a list of the guests for a proposed masked ball, and Richard ponders happily over the name of Amelia, to whom, although she is the wife of his secretary, his heart has gone out. His meditation is broken by the entrance of her husband, who informs him of a plot against his life, begging him to take precautions and have the conspirators watched. But the governor will make no move against them, and Reinhart is very anxious.

Oscar admits a judge who wishes the governor's signature to the sentence of exile of a negro sorceress, who has been seducing the people with her superstition. Richard wishes to look into the justice of the charge before approving the sentence, and when Oscar says that she reads the stars and predicts the future, the governor calls in the people and says that he himself, disguised as a fisherman, will go to the hut of Ulrica and test the truth of her claims. He invites them to meet him there at three o'clock. Reinhart sees Sam and Tom nod significantly to each other, and he determines to guard the governor even against his will.

At the hut of Ulrica the tripod smokes and the prophetess, surrounded by credulous women and gaping children, evokes the dark spirit. Richard has come in advance of the others and is observing the scene. Sylvan enters and tells the sorceress that he has long been a sailor in the governor's service, has even saved his life, and yet receives no advancement. Ulrica predicts that he will soon receive promotion and reward. Richard has meanwhile, unobserved, written a promise on a slip of paper, signed it, and put it into the sailor's pocket. Soon Sylvan finds it, and great is the wonder at this speedy verification of prophecy.

A servant, whom Richard recognizes as a page of Amelia's, enters with a request, and the prophetess, dismissing the crowd, opens a secret door to Amelia. Richard has hidden himself, so he hears her confession to the sorceress of a great and secret love from which she would be delivered. She acknowledges that it is for the governor, and asks how she may obtain forgetfulness of it. Ulrica tells her that a potion made of certain herbs, which she herself must gather at midnight at the foot of the gallows where criminals have died, will bring her rest from this unholy love. Burdened with dread of the terrible spot to which she must go, she leaves, determined to accomplish her task that very night. Richard is exultant over her love for him, but determined that she shall not go alone and unprotected to such a place.

The people, headed by Sam and Tom, enter. Richard asks Ulrica to tell his fortune and whether he will have storms or fair weather on his next voyage. She rebukes him for his scorn of fate, takes his hand, saying that it is the hand of a noble, then bids him go away without knowing more. He protests. She tells him that his death is nigh, at the hand of a friend. Richard mocks at the prophecy. Sam and Tom shrink back, thinking that their murderous plot has been detected. Oscar laments, frightened at the idea of assassination. Richard asks whose hand it will be, and Ulrica replies that it will be the hand that is first locked in his. He offers to shake hands with any of them, but they all shrink back. Reinhart appears at the door, having in his anxiety come seeking the governor, and Richard hastens to him, stretching out his hand, which Reinhart in his relief heartily grasps, calling him by name. Richard says he has no friend who is more devoted to him than Reinhart, and again laughs at the prophecy, and taunts the sorceress with not knowing who he was and that she herself had been doomed to exile. He gives her money and she thanks him, yet repeats her warning, while the people cheer him and voice their love and loyalty for him.

ACT II. At midnight to a bleak hilltop Amelia comes. In fear, she kneels and prays, then descends the hill, terrified, yet determined to gather the plant that will quiet the storm of passion in her heart. Richard discloses himself to her, and she asks him to go and leave her, but he fears for her safety in such a place at such an hour, and will not go. She confesses her love for him and they both realize the hopelessness of their passion and the obligation that Reinhart's faithful devotion to Richard puts doubly upon them.

As they linger Reinhart appears. Amelia draws her veil, and in the darkness he does not recognize her. He tells Richard that the conspirators are following him to this place, exchanges cloaks with him, and bids him fly while yet there is chance. Richard hesitates to leave Amelia thus, but she urges it, even threatening to reveal who she is if he stays. He makes Reinhart promise to conduct the veiled lady within the city in safety, without speaking to her or looking at her, and then hastens off, remorseful that because he is a traitor to his friend he must flee from traitors whom he otherwise would face with scorn.

Scarcely has he gone when Sam and Tom and other conspirators come upon the couple, surrounding them. They are chagrined when they find it is Reinhart, and Tom would brutally tear the veil from Amelia's face, but Reinhart interposes with drawn sword. They are about to do him harm when Amelia, fearing for him, puts aside her veil, to the horror of her husband and the amusement of the bystanders. Reinhart grieves over his dishonored name, and with bitter hate in his heart for the man who, he thinks, has wronged him, he turns to Sam and Tom and tells them to meet him at his house on the morrow. The conspirators leave the scene, and Amelia tremblingly goes with her husband back to their home.

Act III. Arrived at their house, Reinhart tells Amelia that for this crime only blood can atone, and she must die. She confesses that, though her heart went out to Richard for a time, she has done no wrong. He is relentless, and she begs only to bid farewell to her son. He grants her wish and she goes out. Soon Sam and Tom appear, and Reinhart confronts them with his knowledge of their conspiracy and with the papers that prove it. Then he tells them that he would unite with them in bringing about the death of Richard. They are incredulous that he is siding with them, but he offers his son as hostage until the act is accomplished. Each man wishes himself to slay the governor, and they decide to draw lots. Amelia, happening to enter the room, is forced to draw the fateful lot, which falls upon Reinhart, much to his joy. Oscar brings invitations to a masked ball to be given by the governor that very evening, and Reinhart, thinking the occasion will offer a good opportunity for their deed, says that they will all go. Amelia, heartsick with suspicion of their plot, determines to warn the governor.

Within his cabinet Richard sits writing. He has decided to send Reinhart away on a mission of state, and thus remove Amelia from his own presence and put an end to the temptation of their love. Oscar brings him a letter from an unknown woman, which warns him that an attempt upon his life will be made at the ball. He decides, nevertheless, to go.

Within the hall the masks are gathered dancing. Among them are the three conspirators, eagerly awaiting the coming of the governor. When Reinhart finds out from Oscar that the governor is present, he tries also to learn what is his mask. Finally, when Reinhart threatens him, under pretext that important matters claim the governor's attention, the page discloses what the costume is.

Richard is in black domino, and accosts Amelia, who is in white. They soon recognize each other, and she warns him that his life is in danger, and he thanks her for her care. On her knees she pleads with him to hasten away. He tells her that he has arranged for her and her husband to return to England on the morrow, and they are bidding each other a heartbroken farewell when Reinhart, unobserved, comes up and stabs Richard. All is confusion as Oscar, ladies, officials, and guards rush in, demanding who the traitor is, and unmasking Reinhart, who is recognized with horror and execration by all. The wounded man himself pleads for them not to condemn his slayer. Drawing from his pocket the dispatches he had already prepared, he tells Reinhart that his wife is pure and blameless, and that he himself, even in his love, would never have wronged her, and that he was sending them away in honor. Reinhart is overwhelmed with remorse and shame as the dying governor forgives all for the wrong that has been done him, and amid their laments and prayers, expires.

MEFISTOFELE
(*May-fee-stoh-feh-leh*)
(MEPHISTOPHELES)

ITALIAN tragic grand opera, a paraphrase taken from both parts of Goethe's "Faust," with additional incidents from the Faust legend. Both music and book by Arrigo Boito. First production, Milan, 1868. The scene is mainly in Frankfort, Germany, and also in the upper world and in classic Greece. The setting is medieval.

CHARACTERS

MEPHISTOPHELES	Bass
FAUST	Tenor
WAGNER	Tenor
NEREUS	Tenor
MARGARET	Soprano
MARTHA	Contralto
HELEN	Soprano
PANTALIS	Contralto

Celestial phalanxes, the mystic choir, twenty-four boys as cherubs, penitents, wayfarers, men-at-arms, huntsmen, students, citizens, the populace, witches, wizards, Greek chorus, sirens, naiads, Greek dancers, and warriors.

PROLOGUE. In the regions of space celestial phalanxes, invisible behind clouds and led by the solemn tones of seven trumpets, unite with cherubs and penitents in a hymn of praise to the Sovereign Lord of the universe. Soon Mephistopheles, the spirit of evil, standing alone in the shadows, also addresses the Deity, mockingly apologizing for his own dark, unspiritual appearance and his purposed irreverence, and derisively points out what a puny creature man, the acme of creation, has become, declaring that he is no longer content to tempt him, because of his frailty. The mystic choir challenges him with the question, "Knowest thou Faust?" Mephistopheles sneers at that maddest of men, with his unquenchable desire to know, and defiantly boasts that he can entice the soul of this lover of wisdom with the sweet fruits of vice, and so win an easy victory over goodness. The mystic chorus permits the soul of Faust to be so tested, and Mephistopheles vanishes to begin his machinations. The cherubs resume their chorus of adoration, while with it mingle the songs of penitents from the earth.

Act I. It is Easter Sunday, and through the gates of Frankfort-on-the-Main crowds of people of all classes are passing out. Bells are ringing and everywhere is festivity. Students and hunters mingle with the townspeople, while halberdiers and peasants drink together. Among the groups passes a gray friar with his hood over his face. Some shun him, others kneel to him. A cavalcade, headed by the Prince, the Elector, and dignitaries, passes amid the homage of the people.

The aged Faust and his pupil Wagner come down a hillside and watch the crowd, Faust commenting upon their gaiety. As twilight comes on they seat themselves and meditate, Faust intent on the beauty of the scene, and Wagner thinking of the phantoms that lie in wait to trap the unwary footsteps of men. As they start homeward the gray friar appears, and slowly and spectrally approaches Faust. Wagner sees him, too, but does not think his appearance strange, although Faust wonders who he may be. Wagner thinks him a begging friar making his rounds, but Faust tells him to note that the friar moves in wide circles, that his tracks upon the ground are flame, and that he seems to be laying snares about them. In spite of Wagner's failure to notice

© Mishkin

MAURICE RENAUD
AS "MEFISTOFELE"

anything strange about the man, Faust realizes that the circle is closing around him and that the friar is nigh. As they go away the friar follows them, and when Faust arrives alone at his laboratory and enters, the gray friar, unobserved, slips in and hides in an alcove.

In the evening hour Faust sits meditating upon spiritual mysteries, and has just placed the sacred volume of the Evangelist upon the lectern and begun to read when he is startled by a shriek and the sight of the friar coming forth from the alcove. He bids the intruder be more quiet. The friar stands motionless looking at him, and seems to Faust, who in his wisdom discerns the innate ugliness, a horrid phantom.

Not frightened, for his knowledge has given him power, Faust makes the all-potent sign of Solomon and compels the demon to reveal himself. The friar throws off his disguise, and Mephistopheles appears clad as a gay cavalier and with a black cloak upon his arm. He places himself at Faust's service and acknowledges that he is the spirit that denies all things, that by sneers and strife causes ruin and death. He invites Faust to be his companion, and offers him willing service. Faust asks his terms, and he says that he will meet all his wishes here on earth, but beyond, their relations shall be changed. Faust has no concern for the future, so he tells the spirit of evil that if he can bestow upon him one hour of peace, if he will unveil the mysteries of his own soul and of the world, if he can make him "say to the flying moment, 'Stay, for thou art blissful,'" then he will consent to die and be engulfed in hell. The evil one and he grasp hands over the contract, and Mephistopheles pledges himself that from that night on Faust shall be his master and he the servant. When Faust is eager to start forth, Mephistopheles says that he has but to stretch his cloak and they can journey through the air.

Act II. In a garden Mephistopheles and Martha, Faust, who is now a gay young cavalier by the name of Henry, and Margaret are walking and talking together. Faust makes love to the simple village maiden, who is much attracted to him, though coy of his attentions and flattery. Faust shows her great devotion, and begs her pardon for his daring words when first he saw her. Margaret, who is devout, asks him if he has faith in true religion, and though he denies belief as the pious know it, yet he calms her distrust and turns all her thoughts to love.

When she would hasten away, he asks her if he may never see her alone, and she tells him that it is impossible, for her mother sleeps but lightly, and she cannot risk her finding him there. Then he gives her a phial containing a liquid, and tells her that but three drops of it will make her mother sleep sounder, but do her no harm. The young lovers part reluctantly, and Mephistopheles also detains Martha, but at length the women enter the house.

To a wild, lonely spot in the valley of Schirk, among the higher summits of the Brocken, come Faust and Mephistopheles. The evil one urges him ever on, up a dreary road to the abode of Satan, while lambent flames fly before them. At last they come out upon an eminence, high and solitary, and hear the clashing pines of the forest and a thousand shrill voices shouting loudly. It is the Walpurgis Night, or the Sabbath of the Witches, and Faust watches the wild dance of the wizards. As they whirl Mephistopheles cleaves through the throng and bids them bow to their king. They kneel in a circle about him. After the witches dance, Mephistopheles, seated upon a thronelike rock, addresses them, and tells them that he would fain rule the whole world. The witches and wizards circle about a large dark cauldron, stirring its contents, then bring to their king a globe of glass, a world entire. Taking it, he meditates upon the mean race of men that inhabit the world, who laugh at hell and scorn his power. Then in derision he dashes the globe in pieces.

Surrounded by the wild revelers, Faust sees in a vision against the sky the form of a maiden, pale and sorrowful, whose features are those of his poor, dead Margaret. Mephistopheles tells him that it is but a phantom, but Faust continues to dwell upon it, and at length cries out in a great passion of sadness and longing. Mephistopheles rails at him, but Faust asks in horror what the red stain about her throat can mean. The evil one coldly answers that apparently she was decapitated. The witches continue their Bacchanalian riot, while Faust, almost swooning at the thought of Margaret's death, heeds them not.

Act III. Within a prison Margaret lies delirious upon a heap of straw, in darkness broken by a single light. She is singing to herself of her babe, who was taken from her and thrown into the sea, and whom they say she killed; of her mother, who fell into a deadly slumber, from which she never awoke, and whom they say she poisoned. Faust appears outside the grating of the door, having bidden Mephistopheles bring him to her. He frantically demands of the evil spirit that her life be saved, and Mephistopheles hands him the key of her cell, saying that the coursers stand ready for instant flight, and that the jailers are sleeping.

Faust enters, but Margaret does not recognize him. She begs him to save her, and when he calls her by name her wandering mind returns to the first time they met. She is willing to go away with him, but asks one kiss, and when he embraces her she prattles of his love, and of the crimes with which she is charged, and begs him lay her in a grave by the side of her mother and lay her baby on her bosom. In great agitation, he urges her to come or it will be too late, but she catches sight of Mephistopheles and refuses to go. Mephistopheles warns them that day has come and that the trumpet of death has sounded. Margaret sees visions of the axe falling upon her head and feels the terror of death, but will not go with Mephistopheles, whom she sees as an accursed fiend waiting for her. Faust struggles to calm her, and in the torture of his soul curses the day on which he was born. Margaret, lying in the arms of her lover, prays for pardon and dies. Suddenly the voices of the celestial phalanx are heard exultantly crying that she is saved. Faust and Mephistopheles escape as the executioner appears.

ACT IV. Mephistopheles takes Faust to the shores of the Peneus in the Vale of Tempe in Greece. Faust lies sleeping on a flowery bank while Helen and Pantalis converse, and a band of sirens near by sings softly. Faust murmurs Helen's name in his slumbers. Mephistopheles enters and awakens him, and tells him that it is the night of the classical Sabbath and that he now stands in an old land of fable. They agree to part for a time, and Faust, the spell of the land upon him and athrill with love, wanders away in delight. Mephistopheles, however, longs for the terrible vapors of the Hartz Mountains and the hags of the Brocken, and as a band of Greek maidens approaches, dancing, he retires.

Helen of Troy enters, absorbed in a terrifying vision of the night when Ilium burned. As the vision passes from her eyes, Faust enters, clad as a knight of the fifteenth century, followed by Mephistopheles, Nereus, and Pantalis, with little fauns and sirens. He kneels before Helen, giving her homage. She listens to him; the others comment on their mutual love and leave them together. They languish with love of each other, and exchange happy vows and visions of a life of love together.

EPILOGUE. Within his laboratory once more Faust sits meditating, while the lamp burns dimly. The holy volume is open where he has been reading, but mystical voices are in the air, and behind Faust's chair stands Mephistopheles like an incubus. Faust starts from an ecstatic vision of memory and ponders how he has wandered through the world, has seen its mysteries of the Ideal and the Real, and how, in the love of a simple maiden and then of a higher goddess, he found that the Real was sorrow and that the dream is the Ideal. He remembers, too, how he came upon a faithful people, who made him their king and whom he benefited by his wise rule. He wishes that that might be his last vision, as to him heaven in its splendor seems opening and he already feels its peace in his soul.

Mephistopheles, however, stands by, whispering of the longings, the enjoyments, and questioning whether he has not said to some moment, "Stay, for thou art blissful." As Faust is rapt in his vision of heaven, Mephistopheles arouses the forces of evil for battle with the good, and says menacingly that he has only to spread his cloak and it will again take them through the air. As the voices of the celestial phalanx burst on the ear of Faust, Mephistopheles throws spells around the alcove, and sirens appear singing of love. When the sirens vanish, the evil one seeks to draw near to Faust, but the philosopher tears himself away and with great effort goes to the holy book, and falling on his knees upon it, prays. A heavenly vision appears to him, and in an ecstacy of holy love and faith he dies. A shower of roses falls upon his body, and Mephistopheles gradually sinks into the earth, while the heavenly chorus sings of celestial joys.

DIE MEISTERSINGER VON NÜRNBERG
(*Dēē Mī'-ster-sing-er fon Nuern'-berg*)
(THE MASTER-SINGERS OF NUREMBURG)

GERMAN comic grand opera—the only comic opera of this composer—suggested by Hoffmann's novel, "Sängerkrieg," and planned as the counterpart of the Minnesinger contest in "Tannhäuser." Both music and book by Richard Wagner. First production, Munich, 1868. The scene is laid at Nuremburg in the middle of the sixteenth century.

CHARACTERS

Hans Sachs, cobbler		Bass
Veit Pogner, goldsmith		Bass
Kunz Vogelgesang, furrier		Tenor
Conrad Nachtigal, buckle-maker		Bass
Sixtus Beckmesser, town clerk		Bass
Fritz Kothner, baker	Master-singers.	Bass
Balthazar Zorn, pewterer		Tenor
Ulrich Eisslinger, grocer		Tenor
Augustus Moser, tailor		Tenor
Herman Ortel, soap-boiler		Bass
Hans Schwarz, stocking-weaver		Bass
Hans Folz, coppersmith		Bass
Sir Walter von Stolzing, a young Franconian knight		Tenor
David, apprentice to Hans Sachs		Tenor
A Night Watchman		Bass
Eva, daughter of Pogner		Soprano
Magdalena, nurse to Eva		Soprano

Burghers of all guilds, journeymen, apprentices, girls, and the people.

In the twelfth and thirteenth centuries in Germany the cultivation of the poetical and musical arts was in the hands of the Minnesingers, men usually of noble birth, who wandered from court to court. From the fourteenth to the nineteenth centuries the growth of these arts was mainly in the

© Aimé Dupont

EMIL FISCHER
AS HANS SACHS, IN "DIE MEISTERSINGER VON NÜRNBURG"

hands of burghers and artisans. Thence rose the order of the Master-singers. They formed the schools and guilds, and according to rigid rules taught versification in all its branches. Nuremburg was the center of these activities. In this opera Wagner satirizes the sacrifice of matter to form, and the conventionalism and pedantry that grow out of such a method.

The burghers were ranked according to proficiency, candidates being "apprentices," those who had mastered a certain number of tunes being "singers," those who could compose verses to a given air being "poets," and those who could write both words and music on a given theme being "Mastersingers." The rules and prohibitions were called the "Tabulatur." Candidates were rigidly examined and allowed only seven mistakes or infringements of the Tabulatur, a chief examiner, called a "marker," keeping a record of errors.

Act I. Within St. Katherine's Church the service on the feast of the Vigil of St. John is ending. In a rear pew Eva, the beautiful, golden-haired daughter of the wealthy goldsmith, Pogner, and Magdalena, her nurse, are standing. The young girl's attention is distracted from the service by a handsome young knight, Walter von Stolzing, who has been watching her and now presses forward to speak with her. She is nothing loath, and to gain time sends Magdalena back to the pew for her handkerchief, again for her brooch, and lastly for her prayer-book, all of which have been forgotten. The young man is eager to learn whether she is betrothed or free, and the maid, returning, hears the question and answer that her mistress is promised in marriage. Eva, however, hastens to explain that she does not yet know who the bridegroom is to be, and that her father, in his devotion to the cause of music, has promised her hand in marriage and his fortune to the Master-singer who shall, upon the morrow, win the song contest. The maiden may refuse the winner of the contest if she so wishes, and Eva impulsively assures the ardent young man, who avows his love for her and his determination to enter the contest and win, that she will accept no other for her betrothed. He says that she will inspire him to be both poet and musician. Magdalena turns to David, who is arranging the seats for a meeting of the guild, and bids him instruct the knight in the rules of the contest, promising to save a basket of dainties from her larder for him as his reward. David, who is in love with Magdalena, when she has hurried Eva off bids Walter remain, for the Master-singers are now to examine the candidates.

Shortly apprentices enter and arrange chairs and benches, adjusting the curtains which conceal the box where the marker sits. The Master-singers appear, Eva's father among them. Beckmesser, an old widower, who is the marker, is telling Pogner that he expects to win the prize, and wants Pogner to promise that, whether or not Eva consents, the victor may have her hand in marriage. He intends, however, to woo her and purposes to serenade her that very night. Sir Walter von Stolzing comes forward and Pogner cordially greets him, much pleased that he desires to enter the contest. Beckmesser is disturbed at having so young and handsome a rival, and determines to prevent his entrance into the lists.

The other members of the guild are now assembled, among them Hans Sachs, the poet-shoemaker. Beckmesser calls the roll, and Pogner again announces the morrow's contest and the prize to be obtained. The meeting then proceeds to the examination of candidates. Sir Walter announces Love as his theme, and sings a song the words and music of which are very beautiful, but so original that the usual methods of judging cannot be applied. Beckmesser, who is fiercely marking down infringements of the rules, soon interrupts the measures, showing his slate all covered over, and declares the candidate outsung and outdone. The Master-singers agree with him, for they judge of the song as he does,—all except Hans Sachs, who appreciates its unique beauty. He protests against the general condemnation and valiantly champions the young knight's ability. Beckmesser rudely silences him, saying that he had better stick to his last, and taunts him with having long had a pair of his shoes that he has not yet finished. Hans Sachs replies good-humoredly, promising that the shoes shall be ready for him on the morrow. Walter finishes his song, but the Master-singers have no appreciation of it, and he rushes away in despair, believing that he has now no chance of winning Eva with her father's consent. Discussion of the song waxes so heated that the meeting soon breaks up.

ACT II. At the intersection of a straggling alley and a wide street, where Pogner's imposing house and Hans Sachs's humble shop and home oppose each other, David is that evening putting up the shutters on the shop, and other apprentices down the alley are doing the same. Magdalena comes, offering David the promised basket of dainties and asking the outcome of the song trial. When David tells her that Sir Walter was rejected, she is very much concerned and angrily snatches the basket from his grasp and hastens back into the house, wringing her hands. The other apprentices surround David and tauntingly congratulate him on his successful wooing. David starts to fight them when Hans Sachs enters, reproves him for fighting, and sends him off to bed, after he shall have put the shoes on the lasts for mending. They both go into the workshop and then into the house by an inner door. Pogner and Eva come down the street and seat themselves on the bench by their door. Eva anxiously inquires if none but a Master-singer can win the contest, and Pogner firmly insists on that condition. As they go into the house Magdalena appears and detains Eva to tell the disappointing result of Sir Walter's trial.

Hans Sachs comes into his workshop and sends David off to bed. Then he sits down by the door, the lower half of which is closed, and meditates upon the strange new song that the young knight sang that day. He could find no fault with it, for it seemed as natural as the birds' songs and as if the singer sang because he must. Eva comes over to learn, if possible, more of the meeting of the guild, and sits down on a stone by his door. He tells her that the shoes he is working on are for Master Beckmesser, who expects on the morrow to win her, there being few bachelors to compete. Eva coquettishly asks him why he, who is a widower, does not enter the contest. He says that, though he loves her, he is too old for her, and tries to find out how she feels toward the young knight. He voices the jealous and bigoted opinion of the other masters regarding the knight's song. She takes it to be his own, and as Magdalena calls her she goes away, very cross with the shoemaker, who nods his head wisely, seeing in her girlish betrayal of her feelings the love he suspected. He closes the upper half of his door, leaving only a thin streak of light visible and being quite out of sight himself.

Magdalena tells Eva that Beckmesser is going to serenade her that evening, if she will be at her window, with the song he intends to sing on the morrow. As they whisper at the door, some one draws near. Eva tells Magdalena to stand at the window in her stead when Beckmesser comes, and

Magdalena consents, anticipating fun if David, whose room is on the street side of Hans Sachs's house, shall see her. Walter turns the corner of the alley, and with a cry Eva rushes toward him. He is very sad, for he has lost all hope of winning her, but she declares her love for him, her hero-poet, though he disclaims the title, as the masters have refused him fellowship. Eva says that her hand alone awards the prize and that she will give it only to him. Then Walter reminds her that her father said none but a Master-singer should wed her, and that, though he sang his best, he failed to win the title. The night watchman's cowhorn sounds and Walter starts up, but Eva tells him to hide beneath the linden, then, as Magdalena calls her, she goes into the house.

The watchman passes, and Sachs, who has been all the time listening from his shop door, now opens it wider, having shaded his lamp, for he fears that an elopement is being planned and intends to prevent it. To Walter's surprise, Eva returns dressed in Magdalena's clothes, and suggests that they hasten away, but as they try to turn up the alley, Sachs throws a broad stream of light across the street. They draw back, fearing detection, just as Beckmesser, also disconcerted by the light, tunes up his lute to begin his serenade. Hans Sachs, comprehending the marker's purpose, starts singing lustily a folk-song and beats time with his hammer as he works on the shoes. Beckmesser angrily asks him why he works at such an hour, and Sachs replies that he must finish shoes about which he has been twitted in public. Beckmesser suggests that Sachs listen to his song, that he may give an opinion of it, and Sachs consents, saying that he will pound his hammer when the singer makes a mistake.

Beckmesser is greatly agitated, however, especially when the cobbler keeps up a constant hammering, and he sings ever louder and less musically. Magdalena, impersonating Eva at her window, motions Beckmesser to go away. David, who has recognized Magdalena, thinks she is approving the marker's song and he jealously attacks Beckmesser with a cudgel. Thereupon the whole neighborhood is aroused and the factions of journeymen and apprentices, ever warring, take up their old quarrel. Sachs, as the fight begins, closes his shutters, and going into the street, pretends to mistake Eva for Magdalena and pushes her into Pogner's house, then drags Walter with him into his shop just as the night watch is heard approaching. The men stop fighting, hurriedly reënter their houses, put out the lights, and all is quiet when the watch turns the corner.

Act III. Within Hans Sachs's shop the next morning the cobbler sits reading when David enters with a basket of dainties that Magdalena has given him. Thinking to appease his master for his part in the brawl of the previous evening, he offers him the basket, but Sachs good-naturedly declines it, makes David rehearse the song of the day, and sends him off to dress for the festival. Walter, who has spent the night with the cobbler, comes in and relates a dream he had. The cobbler realizes that it is part of a beautiful song, and he sets down the words and bids Walter remember the tune.

When they have left the room Beckmesser comes in limping. He sees the song, likes it, and takes it. When Sachs returns and says that he does not intend to take part in the day's program, Beckmesser asks him about the song. He lets Beckmesser keep the verses, saying that he will never lay claim to its authorship. Beckmesser goes off and soon Eva enters in bridal attire. Under the pretext that her shoe troubles her, she has come to learn where Sir Walter is. Sachs is kneeling before her, trying to find out the difficulty, when, from her confused answers, he perceives that Walter has entered the room. He takes the shoe off and goes to his bench, pretending to fix it, while Walter approaches Eva and declares his love for her in a song that Sachs realizes is the third and final stanza of the earlier song. The cobbler announces that Walter has composed a master-song, and, as David now enters, calls him and Eva to witness that the young knight is the author and composer of it, and then says that he has a plan which will enable Sir Walter to win the prize and Eva to marry the man she loves. Eva realizes then the depth of the cobbler's affection for her, and declares that were she still heart-free she would marry none but him. Sachs makes David a journeyman, so that he can be a witness, and as Magdalena enters, they rejoice that now they can marry, while Eva and Walter try to realize their happiness, and Sachs seals within his own heart the secret of his renunciation.

In a field on the shores of the Pegnitz River the various guilds are gathered with the families of the members. All take their places, the Master-singers marching in stately procession to the platform. Hans Sachs addresses the assembly, announcing the conditions of the contest and the prize to be obtained, and at length calls upon Beckmesser to sing his song. The elderly marker ascends the platform, limping painfully because of the cudgeling he received the night before, and in great agitation, for he has not yet had time to commit to memory the words of the song that he obtained from Sachs and that he intends to pass off for his own. He tries to adapt the new words to the melody of his old song and makes a miserable failure of it, producing neither music nor sense. The laughter of the people forces him to stop, and he wrathfully acknowledges that the song is Hans Sachs's and accuses him of having plotted to defeat him. Sachs disclaims the authorship, and Beckmesser flings down the scroll and rushes off. Sachs takes it up and, examining it, declares that the song is a masterpiece. The Master-singers are incredulous, but Sachs says that if it were properly rendered, they would like it, and that the author alone could so sing it, and he says that, though accused, he is not the author. He calls upon any one present who knows that he is right to appear.

Sir Walter comes forward and the people murmur with surprise, but are much taken with him, while the Master-singers, seeing through Sachs's scheme, yet allow the young man the privilege of being heard. Sachs bids him sing, and Walter springs up the platform and proudly and joyously sings the song. Soon the masters forget to follow the scroll, and all are absorbed in the wonderful melody and the beautiful words of the song of love and homage to Eva. The people think it very different from Beckmesser's attempt, and at its end stir as if from a dream and declare that he has won the prize. The masters proudly acclaim him victor, and as the unanimous verdict is given, Eva rises and places on Walter's head, as he kneels before her, the crown of laurel and myrtle. Pogner gives him the badge of the guild and the hand of his daughter. Then all, Master-singers and people, turn to Hans Sachs, whose ability to recognize the genius of the singer has brought about the happy outcome, and acclaim him their honored head.

MIGNON

(French, Mēēn-yohn; English, Mĭn'yon)

FRENCH sentimental grand opera, based upon Goethe's "Wilhelm Meister." Music by Ambroise Thomas. Book by Jules Barbier and Michel Carré. First production, Paris, 1866. The scene is laid in both Germany and Italy, and the time is about 1790.

CHARACTERS

WILHELM MEISTER, a student	Tenor
LOTHARIO, a half-demented old man, wandering as a minstrel	Bass
LAERTES, an actor	Tenor
GIARNO, chief of the gypsies	Bass
ANTONIO, a servant	Bass
FREDERICK, a young nobleman, lover of Filina	Contralto
MIGNON, a young girl stolen by the gypsies	Mezzo-Soprano
FILINA, a young actress	Soprano

Townsfolk, peasants, gypsies, actors, and actresses.

ACT I. In the courtyard of a German inn, amid townsfolk, peasants, and waiters, comes Lothario, the half-demented old minstrel, who sings a song of his wanderings in search of a long-lost daughter, and accompanies himself on his harp. More peasants and a band of gypsies, with Giarno, their chieftain, enter. Filina and Laertes, from a balcony, watch the scene, and as the crowd gathers, Giarno announces that Mignon will perform the famous dance of the eggs. A carpet is spread and Giarno goes to the cart to get Mignon. At his call a wistful and beautiful young girl of about seventeen years of age comes forth, dressed in ragged garments, but instead of obeying the command to dance, she refuses. Giarno is very angry and threatens to whip her, but she is still defiant. The crowd stands agape and Giarno is in a towering rage. Lothario comes forward and offers the girl his protection, but the chief raises his whip to strike. Wilhelm Meister rushes in and seizes Giarno's arm, drawing his pistol and forcing the ruffian to desist. The bystanders pity the girl and Filina throws Giarno her purse to appease his wrath. Mignon gratefully divides her bouquet of wild flowers between Lothario and Wilhelm, the crowd disperses, and Giarno retires to the shed.

Filina has been taken with Wilhelm's appearance, arousing the jealousy of Laertes, to whom she tells a plan and whom she sends to make the acquaintance of the student. The two men are talking together, Laertes disclosing the plight of their company, stranded at this inn and out of employment, when Filina comes and makes herself agreeable to Wilhelm, who is not blind to her attractiveness. The actor and actress are gone when Mignon comes to Wilhelm. She tells him of her longing for the land of her childhood, a land of beauty and mildness. He is touched by her evident refinement and by the cruel fate that has placed her in Giarno's power. As the latter enters, Wilhelm takes him into the inn to make a bargain for Mignon's freedom. When Lothario comes, Mignon runs to him and tells him of her hope of freedom, and the old man fondly caresses her and they sing together.

They have gone away when Filina enters with Frederick, a young nobleman, and soon Wilhelm and Giarno return and the young student announces that Mignon is free. A note from Frederick's uncle is given Filina, asking her presence and that of her troupe at his castle. She asks Wilhelm to join them in the rôle of poet, but Laertes bids the student go his way, and saying good-bye, enters the tavern. Mignon comes joyfully to Wilhelm and he tells her that he plans to place her with some honest folks in the town, but she wants to go with him upon his wanderings, and suggests that she be dressed in his livery in the garb of a boy. When he says that it is impossible, she tells him that then she will go with Lothario, who now enters, hastens to Mignon, and embraces her. Wilhelm stops him from leading Mignon away, and tells her to remain with him.

The comedians enter, ready for the journey, and Filina again asks Wilhelm to go with them, and he promises to be there by evening. She takes his bouquet, which Mignon had given him, and the young girl is hurt, but says nothing, and bids good-bye to the gypsies as they go out.

Act II. In an elegant apartment of the castle of Frederick's uncle Filina sits when Laertes enters and taunts and compliments her in turn. He withdraws when Wilhelm appears, accompanied by Mignon dressed as a page. Wilhelm leads Mignon to a chair by the fire, while Filina laughs at them for their attentions to each other. Wilhelm expresses his devotion for the actress, and as they talk together, Mignon pretends to be asleep. As the others go out, Mignon decides that, as Wilhelm has granted her prayer that she might follow him, she will now submit, though he should love Filina.

She goes to the toilet table and touches up her face to make it beautiful. Then she opens the door of the dressing-room, and while she is within Frederick enters. Wilhelm comes, calling Mignon, and after a few words the two men start to fight for jealousy of Filina's favor, when Mignon, attired in one of Filina's dresses, intervenes. Frederick goes off, and Mignon is afraid that Wilhelm is very angry with her and that he will not let her stay with him, but he is silent and thoughtful, because, seeing her thus dressed as a woman, he finds her beautiful and knows that they can no longer continue their arrangement of master and page. She thinks, however, that Filina has persuaded him to send her away. He bids her farewell, and when he offers her money to take with her, she asks only to kiss his hand, which he permits. Filina enters with Frederick, and surprised at the girl's appearance, gives her the dress. But Mignon will not accept it, and picking up the package containing her own garb, runs into the dressing-room. Filina tries to arouse Wilhelm, and asks him if he is not still her lover. He starts up from thoughts of Mignon, and tells the actress that he adores her. Frederick jealously watches them go out, and when Mignon enters dressed in her gyspy garb, she, too, shows her jealousy.

In the park adjoining the baron's castle, where a conservatory stands near a lake, Mignon comes and lingers, listening to the music and applause from the brilliantly lighted building. She thinks of Filina within, near to Wilhelm, and she wandering in the garden. She grieves and looks long at the lake, but turns away, for she desires to live. Lothario comes and finds her, and gazes at her tenderly, calling her Sperata. Then he recognizes her as Mignon and tells her how he has followed her. He opens his arms to her, that she may rest there and tell him all her grief. She asks him if he has known loneliness and wandering as she has, and he replies that he has. The applause for Filina again startles her, and, fiercely angry, she asks why God does not launch his lightnings, rend the palace, and overwhelm all in it, setting it on fire. She rushes away, for she can bear no more. Lothario catches her last words and goes out with them ringing in his dazed brain,—"On fire! On fire!"

The prince, the baron and baroness, Filina and comedians, ladies and gentlemen, and servants bringing torches come from the conservatory. Filina is singing, and as Wilhelm comes seeking Mignon, she gaily hails him. The girl, however, is in the shadows at one side, listening to what Lothario is telling her—how he has avenged her and that the palace is on fire. As Wilhelm discovers Mignon, Filina asks her to prove her willingness to serve by seeking upon the stage a bouquet that Wilhelm had presented her. Mignon enters the conservatory just as Laertes comes out shouting that the stage is on fire. Wilhelm starts up aghast, and though Laertes tries to stop him, he rushes off. Filina exclaims that she knew of no danger, and all watch in horror as the fire advances. The wall falls, but soon Wilhelm comes forth bearing Mignon in his arms and lays her upon a bank. She still holds the withered bouquet.

Act III. In a gallery adorned with statues within the Italian castle of the Cipriani Wilhelm sits as Lothario comes, saying that the fever has left Mignon and she slumbers. Antonio enters and sets a lamp upon the table. He tells Wilhelm how to-morrow at the Fête of the Lake all the palaces will be lighted up, save this one, which has never been festive since the master went away. Wilhelm says he heard the tale, how a child perished in the lake long ago, the mother soon died, and the father then left his native land forever. He has heard, too, that the mansion is to be sold. Antonio goes out and Wilhelm lays his hand on Lothario's shoulder and they rejoice together that her native air has restored Mignon to health. Wilhelm declares his purpose of purchasing on the morrow this abode of the Cipriani. Lothario rises, trembling, and repeats the word. He goes to a great door at the back and tries to open it. Wilhelm tells him that it has been closed for fifteen years. He goes silently out, and the student ponders the look on the man's face, and thinks how he comforted Mignon for the sorrow that she had concealed in her heart and that Wilhelm has just discovered.

Antonio enters with a letter from Laertes, saying that Filina has followed Wilhelm. He goes toward Mignon's chamber as she comes forth, asking where she is, and saying that she has seen this palace in a vision. She tells him that it was he whom she longed for and that her heart no more pines forsaken. Wilhelm tells her that she shall live to know his love, and woos her, though Mignon can scarcely believe that he loves her and not Filina. Just as he assures her that Filina is far away, the actress's voice is heard singing. They both recognize it, and Mignon thinks that she must again hide the secret of her love, and is silent. Wilhelm fears that she loves him no more, and as she sinks fainting upon a seat, he tries to revive her, but she, recovering, calls for Lothario.

Just then she hears a step, but Wilhelm says that no one can come in through the door before them. The door, however, flies open and Lothario, richly attired, enters, bearing a small box. He bids them welcome in his house and tells them that once he was the master here. They think he raves, but he bids Mignon open the box. She takes out a child's girdle broidered in gold and silver. He says it was Sperata's. The name calls up memories to Mignon, as does a coral bracelet, which he says the little girl could not wait a day to put on. Mignon trembles and weeps, then takes a book, opens it, starts to read, and finishes from memory. She is much stirred and rushes with a cry through the door, returning almost immediately, saying that there is a portrait of her mother, but her chamber is empty. There is then no doubt that she is Sperata, and Lothario clasps his daughter in his arms, while she rejoices in her father and her lover, both of whom her heart had long since recognized.

MONA

AMERICAN tragic grand opera, which won the ten-thousand-dollar prize offered by the Metropolitan Opera House, New York, in 1912. Music by Horatio Parker. Book by Brian Hooker. First production, New York, 1912. The scene is southwestern Britain, about 100 A.D.

CHARACTERS

THE ROMAN GOVERNOR OF BRITAIN	Baritone
QUINTUS, his son, known among the Britons as Gwynn	Tenor
ARTH, a British tribesman	Bass
ENYA, wife of Arth	Soprano
GLOOM, son of Arth and Enya, a druid	Baritone
CARADOC, the chief Bard of Britain	Baritone
NIAL, a changeling	Tenor
MONA, Princess of Britain, last of the line of Boadicea, foster-child of Arth and Enya	Mezzo-Soprano

Roman soldiers, Britons—druids, bards, and tribesmen, both men and women.

ACT I. One midsummer morning within the primitive hut of Arth, Enya is busy with her household tasks. Nial lies by the hearth, while Mona and Gwynn stand near, talking earnestly together. He is pleading with her to fulfill her vow and marry him, but she tells him that while he has been away she has been planning to help her people to overthrow the Roman power in their land. She shows him the druidic sign upon her breast,—that of the Unspeakable Name,—which signifies that she is set apart for some holy mission other than the common destiny of woman. She tells him of a dream she had, wherein she walked between a dark forest and a deep sea, carrying a naked sword, with which she pushed back the waves. There came a veiled figure, who strove to take the sword from her, but she killed the unknown one with it. Then the trees of the forest and the waves of the sea overwhelmed her.

Arth, entering, throws at Enya's feet a Roman sword, taken from a Roman soldier he has killed. Gwynn rebukes him for so breaking the peace between the two peoples, and Arth bursts out into a tirade against Rome, in which the women excitedly join. Gwynn quiets Arth, however, and the latter goes out to bury the body, while Gwynn takes up the sword and shows how it is used. Mona cries out that he looks just like a Roman soldier, and in snatching it away from him, cuts him. They are noting the omen superstitiously when Gloom enters, and sends the women away as Arth and Caradoc enter. The men pledge themselves, with solemn oath of union and secrecy, to common cause against the Romans, although Gwynn would fain protest, were it not that the fact of his Roman birth might thereby be revealed. They lay plans for a universal uprising, of which Mona, because of her royal descent, is to be the leader. Mona is summoned and asked to choose between her love for Gwynn and her solemn mission. Gwynn strives unsuccessfully to hold her by his affection, as Gloom plays upon her superstition and the impression left by her dream. She consents to head the revolt, but as Gwynn, driven away, vanishes in the forest, she drops the sword, cries out his name, and bursts into tears.

ACT II. One evening a month later at the cromlech in the forest, Nial is dancing, joyfully exulting in his freedom from the cares that burden others. The Roman Governor, out with a scouting party, surprises him and takes him prisoner, expecting to find out whether or not a large meeting of the tribes of Britons has recently taken place there. But Nial, in his simplicity, does not answer their questions, and they are about to torture him when Gwynn appears. He is accused of treachery in siding with the Britons, but he declares that the peace of the past years has been really his work and that now, through Mona's influence and his own as bard, he hopes to quiet the people. He offers to conduct his father and the party back to the garrison.

Nial is again alone as Gloom and Mona enter. They have been out among all the tribes stirring up the people, and that very night an attack is to be made upon the Roman town. Gloom throws off his mask of brotherliness and priesthood, and declares to Mona his love for her, but she tells him that she is set apart for a holy mission and not for love, as he himself has said. Arth and Enya enter, and after a short talk the others go out together, leaving Mona alone to pray. Gwynn comes back, and by his love and persuasions prevails upon her so that she forgets all but him. He reveals the secret of his birth and tells her how their union shall unite the two races. When she realizes that he is the son of the Roman Governor and, therefore, an enemy, she instinctively cries out for help. The Britons rush to her, and Gwynn is about to be torn in pieces when Mona intervenes, saying that, as he is a bard, he can only be taken prisoner. Then all turn their attention to making ready for the attack, and at last go out, leaving Enya sobbing alone at the altar.

Act III. On a plateau at the edge of the forest just before dawn the next day, Enya and Nial are waiting for tidings. Mona, stung with shame at the defeat of the Britons, comes in, assisting Gloom, who is mortally wounded. A large Roman garrison under arms was awaiting the attack, and the rout was complete. Arth is dead. Mona blames herself for the terrible disaster, and searches her heart for the fault that caused it. Gloom, dying, says that their desire for power misled them; but Mona is convinced that, had she not saved Gwynn's life when she knew him to be a Roman, all would have been well. For she thinks it was he who informed the garrison.

Gwynn, having escaped from his guards, enters and tells her that he has power to treat with the Britons for peace. But neither she, who sees in his escape proof of his treachery, nor Gloom will believe him. At last she feigns yielding to his pleadings, and as he takes her in his arms, stabs him with her sword. The Roman Governor enters and, discovering Gwynn's body, tells them that they have destroyed their last hope of mercy. Fearing the utter ruin of her people, Mona confesses her deed, and he tells her that she will be a long time repenting it. At last she understands all that Gwynn has done, his nobility and truth, and broken-heartedly she lays the sword across his breast and says farewell to him. Disillusioned as to the higher holiness of any mission other than that common to womanhood, she faces the expiation of her deed, and, giving herself up to be bound, is led away captive.

MONNA VANNA
(*Mawn'-nah Vahn'nah*)

FRENCH sentimental grand opera. Music by Henry Février. Book by Maurice Maeterlinck. First production, Paris, 1909. The scene is Pisa, Italy, at the end of the fifteenth century.

CHARACTERS

GUIDO COLONNA, commander of the garrison of Pisa..Baritone
MARCO COLONNA, father of Guido.....................Bass
BORSO   } lieutenants of Guido................. { Tenor
TORELLO   Bass
PRINZIVALLE, captain of the Florentine troops........Tenor
VEDIO, secretary to Prinzivalle...................Baritone
TRIVULZIO, envoy from Florence.......................Bass
MONNA VANNA, wife of Guido Colonna............Soprano

Nobles, soldiers, peasants, men and women of the city.

ACT I. The people of Pisa, made desperate by starvation through their long siege by Florentine troops, are gathered before the palace of Guido Colonna, clamoring for his death because he brought about the war. Within he hears their cries. When Torello and Borso report that the ammunition is exhausted, he says that he has already sent his father to make terms with Prinzivalle. Marco returns, announcing that Prinzivalle will send a convoy of food and ammunition to Pisa on condition that Guido, in token of submission, send his wife to the tent of Prinzivalle that night, unarmed, alone, and naked under her cloak, to remain there until dawn. Guido, aghast, asks why his wife is chosen. Marco replies that it is because Prinzivalle loves her. When Guido insists that Prinzivalle has never seen her, Marco tells him that he has, but will not say when, and that Vanna, whom he has told of the condition, does not remember ever to have seen the commander, but will consent to go if her husband will permit her. Vanna enters, and with the people's clamors for her husband's death ringing in her ears, declares herself willing to go to save the city. Guido cannot believe that that is her motive, and is consumed with jealousy. He protests, but finding her resolute, coldly puts her from him, believing that her love for him is dead, and declaring that he no longer loves her.

Act II. Within his tent Prinzivalle is awaiting her as Vedio enters with a letter, which orders the commander to assault the city at daybreak or submit to arrest for treason. Trivulzio, jealous and suspicious, enters as Prinzivalle, from the door of his tent, sees the beacon light that heralds the approach of Guido's wife. Trivulzio asks what the signal means. Without replying, Prinzivalle confronts him with three letters in his own hand, which have been intercepted and which reveal his conspiracy with the citizens of Florence against Prinzivalle, to accomplish his death even should he return victorious. Trivulzio sees certainty of exposure and strikes at Prinzivalle with his dagger, but succeeds only in wounding his face. Prinzivalle gives Trivulzio into the charge of officers, to be carefully guarded.

As Vedio bandages the commander's wound, and warns him that so many are in the plot it will succeed, Prinzivalle is light-hearted, but directs Vedio to take possession of his property when he is gone. A shot is heard, and Vedio goes out as Vanna enters. Blood is on her hand, and Prinzivalle asks where she is wounded. She opens slightly the long cloak in which she is wrapped, and he sees a small flesh wound above her left breast. Assured that she does not suffer, he gives her another chance to draw back from the agreement, but she refuses. Asked why she comes, she says because the people are dying. He asks her if she has fulfilled all the conditions. She says yes; but when she starts to prove her word, he stops her with a gesture. From the tent door he shows her the wagons laden with food and ammunition for the besieged city, and orders the train to start.

He leads her to a seat on his soldier's couch, and kneeling before her, seizes her hand and calls her by name. Gradually she recognizes him, in spite of the bandages on his face, as a childhood playmate. He tells her that he has loved her all the years, and she is touched, but unconvinced of the sincerity of his love, since he did not constantly seek her. He lets go her hand and promises not to touch it or kiss it again. But she, though she does not pretend that she loves him, is tender toward her old friend, and surrenders it to him. He covers it with kisses. Vedio enters with the news that an officer and a company of Florentines have entered the camp and are proclaiming Prinzivalle a traitor. Realizing that he must flee, Vanna urges him to go back to Pisa with her, pledging her husband's hospitality and protection from his enemies, and they go away together.

Act III. In the hall of state of his palace Guido sits planning vengeance. Because his father counseled Vanna's going, he is about to drive him away forever when welcoming shouts are heard. Vanna comes, lauded by the garrison, acclaimed as their savior by the people. As she enters, Marco receives her in his embrace. She goes to Guido, but he repulses her. Vanna cries out that she comes back unsullied, but he will not listen and drives out the exultant people who follow her.

Espying a man with her, he is about to lay rough hands on him when Vanna intervenes. When Guido realizes that the man is Prinzivalle, he falls into a terrible passion of rage and jealousy. Suddenly he thinks that Vanna has planned to deliver Prinzivalle into his hands for revenge, and he takes her in his arms and plentifully forgives her. He gloats over his plans of torture. Before Vanna can prevent it, he has called back the people and told them who the prisoner is. Vanna makes a desperate appeal to be heard, first to him and then to the people, but Guido seizes her in his arms and demands that she kiss him. She refuses and threatens never again to kiss him unless he listens to her. Then she tells her story; but when she gives as Prinzivalle's reason for sparing her honor the fact that he loves her, Guido is more incredulous than ever. He appeals to the crowd, and among them all only Marco avows faith in Vanna's story. Guido accuses her of loving the man, and says that a single night has changed her heart.

When he prepares to find out the truth from Prinzivalle by torturing him to death, Vanna suddenly repudiates her first story, avows that he has treated her shamefully, and demands that he be given into her hands for her to wreak her wrath upon him. Prinzivalle, hitherto silent, will not countenance such a lie even to save his life, and denounces it; but she, feigning a fury of cruelty and bidding him be silent, herself ties the cords about him, orders him to be cast into the dungeon, and demands the key of his prison. Marco alone understands her strategy and approves. To him Vanna commits the prisoner, and, gloating over the fateful key, she faints in the arms of the now-reconciled Guido.

Act IV. In the dungeon Prinzivalle awaits her coming. Easily he slips his bonds when she at last appears. She rapturously embraces him, assuring him that admiration and love for him have taken the place in her heart that Guido's cruelty made empty. She opens the prison doors, and silently they hasten out to seek a new life together.

NATOMAH

(*Nah-to-'mah*)

AMERICAN tragic grand opera. Music by Victor Herbert. Book by Joseph D. Redding. First production, Philadelphia, 1911. The scene is southern California during the Spanish occupation in 1820.

CHARACTERS

Don Francisco de la Guerra, a noble Spaniard of the
    old régime .... *Bass*
Father Peralta, Padre of the Mission Church .... *Bass*
Juan Bautista Alvarado, a young Spaniard ...... *Baritone*
José Castro, a half-breed .... *Baritone*
Paul Merrill, lieutenant on the United States brig
    "Liberty" .... *Tenor*
Kagama ⎱ Spanish bravos, comrades of Castro .... ⎰ *Tenor*
Pico   ⎰   ⎱ *Bass*
Natoma, an Indian girl .... *Soprano*
Barbara de la Guerra, daughter of Don Francisco .. *Soprano*

Chiquita, who is a dancing girl, Bruzzo the innkeeper, two American officers, sergeant, alcalde, milk-boy, ladies, dignitaries, soldiers, friars, acolytes, nuns, convent girls, vaqueros, market-women, Spanish dancers, reapers, vineyardists, shepherdesses, and sailors.

Act I. From the porch of his hacienda on the island of Vera Cruz, two hours' sail across the bay from Santa Barbara, California, Don Francisco de la Guerra waits in the late afternoon for the coming of his daughter Barbara, who is returning home after school days spent in the convent of the Mission Church in the town. Alvarado, a young Spaniard, who is Barbara's cousin and is desirous of marrying her that he may share the estates inherited from her mother, comes with Castro, Pico, and Kagama ostensibly for a wild-boar hunt, but really to be present when Barbara returns.

Welcomed by Don Francisco they are off to the hunt, and he enters the hacienda for a siesta.

Natoma, a pure-blooded Indian girl from the mountains, who has been Barbara's companion from childhood, comes toward the house with Lieutenant Paul Merrill, whose vessel, the "Liberty," lies in the harbor, and whom she has already met several times. She is showing him an amulet she wears, a small abalone shell hung upon a necklace of pearls. She tells him of the legend connected with it, how when his people were starving her father came to the seashore, praying to the Spirit of the Waters, and there was tossed up at his feet abalone in great numbers, rich with meat, and thus the famine was broken; and how he called her, the strongest and eldest, to him and bade her succeed to his dominion, and hung about her neck the abalone shell as a token of the "deed of gift and plenty from the Spirit to his people," and told her to guard it jealously. She is the last of her race, for her people have vanished and a stranger is chieftain. When the young lieutenant listens with interest to her glowing account of her young mistress's beauty and charm, she suddenly realizes that he may care for Barbara and forget her, and kneeling at his feet, she begs him to make her his slave.

Barbara arrives, conducted by Father Peralta and the convent girls, and is greeted by her father, who invites tnem all into the hacienda. When the eyes of Paul and Barbara meet, the two fall deeply in love with each other. Natoma, who introduces them, watches him searchingly. Later, as Natoma goes toward the well with a water jar upon her shoulder, she is dwelling fondly on Paul's tender words to her, when Castro, who has been lurking near, suddenly confronts her and taunts her with playing the servant to white people, tells her that her own people are waiting in the mountains for a chieftain, and asks her to come with him.

She spurns him, calling him a half-breed, and he taunts her with caring for Paul, who, now that Barbara has come, has eyes only for her.

The hunters return, and Castro reports to Alvarado what has taken place, especially that Barbara seems much impressed with the American officer, at which Alvarado laughs. Castro again hides, and the Spaniard serenades Barbara, who comes upon the porch calling his name. She tells him that his song is the same that he has sung to other girls, and parries his earnestness until he bluntly proposes to her. She refuses to listen. He accuses her of caring for another, and she goes into the hacienda very angry, while Alvarado swears that he will kill the American.

Natoma, who is secreted in the arbor, now sees Castro come from his hiding-place and hears him propose that Alvarado seize Barbara the next day at the festivities, when hundreds of their friends will be present, and bear her away to the mountains. He says that because of the dislike for the Americans there will be no uprising, and promises to have swift horses ready. Alvarado approves of the plan. Soon Natoma is seen coming from the arbor with the water jar on her shoulder and going into the hacienda, and the men leave.

At nightfall the convent girls bid Barbara farewell and depart. When the guests are all gone, Don Francisco embraces his daughter and goes into the hacienda, while Barbara lingers on the porch and softly whispers to the moon the secret of her sudden love for the young officer. Paul comes and pours out his heart's affection for her and she cannot deny her own feeling for him. As a light appears in the window, Barbara bids him good-night and hastens in. Natoma comes to the window with a lighted candle in her hand and looks long out into the night.

Act II. Very early the next morning Natoma enters the plaza before the Mission Church in Santa Barbara. She starts to touch the holy water, but draws back and turns rapidly away. She thinks of her loved mistress tenderly and prays that she may be crowned queen of the land. She remembers how Paul's love was hers for one short hour, and that all her heart is his, and of the happy dreams of their going together through her country, ever alone together. Laughter from the inn reminds her of her plan to frustrate the cruel plot against Barbara. The church bells remind her of the padre's warning that she must turn from the faith of her people or else suffer eternal torture. Proudly she flings out her defiance, and humbly prays the Great Manitou, the spirit of the hills, to aid her, and goes away.

Spanish soldiers enter, and to the music of trumpets and drums raise the Spanish flag. Townspeople, vendors, rancheros, and vacqueros come into the square. Pico sings a dashing song and all join in the chorus. When Alvarado and his friends enter, the people greet him with lusty shouts. Chiquita and other dancing girls come, and Alvarado dances the *Habanera* with her. Kagama announces that Don Francisco and his daughter are coming, and the Spanish soldiers stand at salute, while Castro scolds Alvarado for wasting his time with Chiquita, and tells him the horses are waiting.

A procession of convent girls comes, followed by Don Francisco and Barbara on horseback, with Natoma on foot at her mistress's side. As they take their places upon the grandstand there is loud cheering, to which the Spaniard makes response. He then takes from Natoma's hands the royal lace, which, according to the ancient custom, is bequeathed to her who succeeds to title and estates, and places it upon Barbara's head, and the people acclaim her as ruler. Alvarado offers her name as a toast and all drink. He requests her to dance with him and she consents. Scarcely have they begun when cannon boom and an envoy of sailors from the American ship enters, and Lieutenant Merrill presents to Don Francisco the compliments of his commander and the good will of his government. As he starts to speak with Barbara Alvarado claims her for the dance. The crowd is expectant and at her father's bidding she joins her cousin. Many couples now take part, and soon it changes to the panuelo or handkerchief dance, a dance of declaration, at the climax of which each gallant places his hat upon the head of his lady-love. When Alvarado puts his hat upon Barbara's head, she tosses it to one side and joins her father. The crowd murmurs that he is refused, and he stalks off furiously angry.

Immediately Castro affects disdain for the simple dances, and sticks his dagger in the ground and dares any one to dance with him the ancient dagger dance of the Californians. The people are alarmed. Slowly Natoma advances to the center of the plaza, takes a dagger from her belt, and sticks it next to Castro's. At first he refuses, but she points to the daggers, and he is obliged to dance it with her. More and more wild become their movements, and while the eyes of all are fixed on them, Alvarado and Kagama creep up to where Barbara is seated. Alvarado throws a serape over her head as Natoma, having simultaneously with Castro snatched her dagger from the ground, makes a lunge at him and receives his parry, then passes by him and plunges her dagger into Alvarado.

Immediately the music of the dance stops with a crash and Alvarado drops dead. The crowd cries out that Natoma be killed, and as Castro springs toward her, Paul draws his sword and with his sailors keeps the crowd off. Now wild, the people make a rush at Natoma just as the doors of the Mission Church open and Father Peralta appears, bearing on high the crucifix. As he cries, "Hold, in the name of Christ!" the people fall on their knees. He motions to Natoma and she drops the dagger, staggers toward the priest, and falls at his feet. He exclaims, "Vengeance is mine, saith the Lord," and reënters the church, followed by Natoma.

Act III. Within the Mission Church that afternoon Natoma is crouching before the altar dazedly crooning a lullaby. She begins to think clearly of her situation, and arising, stands before the altar rail meditating. She thinks of her loneliness, of the love that for so short a time was hers. Then she thinks of her people, and repents that she has thought only of herself. She cries out, beseeching them to forgive her, and vows that she will go to them and rouse them to defiance and vengeance that they may retake their ancient land. Remembering the amulet, she prays to the Great Spirit to give her power to avenge their wrong.

Father Peralta appears on the steps of the altar and commands peace in the house of God. When she starts to defy him, he speaks to her tenderly, gently telling her of the one God, who shields and protects his people. She desires to go her own way, but he reminds her of Barbara, of the love they two had through their childhood, and then he tells her of the love that the pitying Madonna has for her, and that she will guide and protect her until Natoma's spirit shall meet that of her father in the skies. Natoma is greatly touched, and saying that "love shall be repaid by love," and that there is one whom she wishes to make happy, she promises to do the padre's bidding.

The church doors are thrown open for the service and the people come in. Don Francisco and Barbara enter last, and take seats across the aisle from Paul. Natoma stands as in a trance before the altar, recognizing no one. Nuns enter from the neighboring convent, and form a path from the altar to the garden of the convent. Natoma slowly enters the aisle. When she comes to Barbara and Paul, they both, as if moved by a single impulse, come and kneel before her. Natoma takes the amulet, the symbol of the "deed of gift and plenty," from her own neck and puts it about Barbara's. She then turns and, passing between the kneeling nuns, goes into the convent garden and the gates close upon her.

NOËL
(NOEL)

FRENCH tragic grand opera. Music by Frédéric d'Erlanger. Book by Jeanne and Paul Ferrier. First production, Paris, 1910. The scene is Cholet, a small town in southwestern France, and the time is a Christmas of the present era.

CHARACTERS

JACQUES HERBLET	Tenor
THE CURÉ	Baritone
FATHER VINCENT	Baritone
THE SACRISTAN	Tenor
MADELINE	Soprano
MADAME HERBLET	Mezzo-Soprano
BERTHA	Soprano
THE NURSE	Mezzo-Soprano

Working men and women, citizens, and children.

ACT I. In the open square before a church, the ground is covered with snow, and it is snowing as the Curé, accompanied by the sacristan, walks slowly toward the church. The Curé tells the sacristan to see that the candles are lighted on the altar, as it is time for the midnight mass. As they go into the church, Madeline, a poorly clad young woman, bearing in her arms a newly born infant wrapped in rags, enters the square. Although no longer snowing, it is bitter cold. She pauses on the bridge, then walks resolutely toward the house of Madame Herblet at one side of the square. Madeline knocks, and when Madame Herblet answers, she asks that she may speak with Jacques. But the woman refuses to call him. Madeline pleads for pity for her child. But Madame Herblet is pitiless and closes the door. Madeline kisses the child passionately, then starts toward the bridge to throw herself into the water, but falls fainting near the door of the church. The bell sounds the midnight hour, and some working men and women with their children arrive, carrying lanterns. The children are singing carols, and the sound arouses Madeline, who goes toward the door of the church and, with a prayer on her lips, enters.

Act II. Within the church stands the high, white altar, ablaze with candles, and at one side in the Chapel of the Virgin lighted candles stand before the statue of the Holy Mother and the wax figure of the Christ-child in a cradle. Madeline crouches on her knees in the shadow of a pillar, while Father Vincent, Madame Herblet, Jacques, and Bertha are kneeling before the altar. As the music of the service is sounding, Jacques turns to Bertha, to whom he is betrothed, and asks her if she is dreaming, so rapt she seems. She says that she is praying the Virgin to bless their union and that they may have a little son as beautiful as the Christ-child in the cradle. All go out as the service ends, and Madeline is left alone. She approaches the altar and kneels before the statue. She notes the resemblance between her own child and the waxen image, and prays for hers, the child of no heritage; then she takes the little living one and places it in the cradle, and wrapping the image in the rags and rocking it in her arms, leaves the church. The Curé and the sacristan enter the chapel, and the latter, seeing the living child, cries out that a miracle has taken place. But the Curé knows that some woman has abandoned her baby to the Virgin's protection.

Act III. In a small room of a hospital lies Madeline with the wax figure of the Christ-child clasped in her arms. She is delirious and is singing a lullaby to it when the Curé softly enters. Jacques and Bertha enter also, and tell the Curé that they have followed him from their wedding feast in order that they may bless some poor unfortunate. Madeline's voice is heard as she croons a lullaby. The Curé asks Bertha to go get the living child and bring it to the sick mother. When Bertha goes out, Jacques recognizes Madeline, and says that he had hoped to make her his wife, but that she was false to him. They approach the bed, and the Curé places Jacques' hand in Madeline's. Madeline recognizes him and asks his pardon for deceiving him. He gives it, and when she bewails her sins and says she is dying, the Curé ministers to her soul. She calls for her child, and Bertha enters, bringing it, but the mother is already dead. Bertha tells the Curé that the child shall be christened Noel, and that she and Jacques will bring it up as their own.

NORMA

ITALIAN tragic grand opera, founded on an old French story. Music by Vincenzo Bellini. Book by Felice Romani. First production, Milan, 1831. The scene is laid in druidical Gaul about 50 B.C., shortly after its occupation by the Romans.

CHARACTERS

POLLIONE, Roman proconsul in Gaul.................*Tenor*
FLAVIUS, a centurion..............................*Tenor*
OROVESO, the archdruid, father of Norma.............*Bass*
NORMA, high priestess of the druidical temple of Esus,
Soprano
ADALGISA, a virgin of the Temple of Esus..........*Soprano*
CLOTILDE, confidant of Norma.....................*Soprano*

Priests and officers of the temple, Gallic warriors, priestesses and virgins of the temple, and two children of Norma and Pollione.

ACT I. It is night in the sacred druid forest. The oak of Irminsul stands in the center, and beneath it is the cromlech, or druidical altar. Oroveso and a procession of Gallic soldiery, druids, and bards enter. The archdruid bids them away to the mountains to await the rising of the new moon, when they shall return to gather the sacred mistletoe. They ask if Norma, the mighty prophetess, will not soon be with them, and if they may not soon rise up against the Romans and scatter them. Oroveso replies that Norma will indeed come and the yoke of Rome be broken.

When they have gone out Pollione, the Roman proconsul, and his centurion, Flavius, enter. Pollione is conscience-stricken over the thought that his heart's loyalty has departed from his devoted and loving Norma, and that he burns with passion for the virgin priestess Adalgisa. Flavius urges him to keep the fact from Norma, and Pollione confesses that the fear of her anger haunts him even in sleep. The sacred bronze bell is heard and they know that Norma has sounded it for the sacrifice. Flavius senses danger and urges Pollione away, and as they go the proconsul vows to lay that grove and altar low, because it is her religion that stands between him and Adalgisa.

Oroveso and the druidical procession reënter, preceding Norma, of whose sanctity they sing, prophesying that Rome's red star shall tremble because of the god Esus, whose priestess she is. Norma silences their impatience by saying that while Rome is strong is not the time to strike, and that it is written that Rome shall fall by her own hand, self-destroyed by her crime and guilt. Then in deep silence she gathers the mistletoe and raises her arms toward the moon in prayer for peace. She dismisses the worshipers, saying that when the god shall decree she will, by striking the bronze shield, arouse them for the Roman slaughter, and promises that the proconsul shall fall by her hand. As she speaks she shudders, for her heart loves him.

Act II. By the altar in the grove, where she has before met Pollione, Adalgisa lingers, weighed down by remorse, for she loves the Roman. He comes upon her, and she bids him go, as she fears for his life if he is discovered. She laments her broken vows, and he asks her to flee with him to Rome, where they may safely enjoy their love. She feels such responsive passion that the holy vows seem as nothing, yet she bids him go. When he doubts her love, however, she yields and promises to meet him at the same hour to-morrow and go with him.

Within her dwelling Norma embraces her two children fervently, then gives them into Clotilde's keeping, revealing to her the fact that she is their mother. Clotilde is alarmed, for Norma seems on the verge of madness. The priestess explains that the Roman emperor has recalled his proconsul, and because she has not heard from Pollione what are his plans, she fears that he means to leave her and his children. Adalgisa enters as Clotilde leads the children away.

The young woman approaches reverently, believing in Norma's power as a prophetess and trembling with her guilty secret. Contrite of heart, she confesses her love, against which she has striven, but which now would lead her far from her home and nation. Norma, remembering her own heart's woe, is compassionate and questions her. Adalgisa says that when in prayer at the foot of the altar in the sacred grove she beheld him, she thought him a god, and his tender glances opened to her another heaven. Norma is lost in her memories as Adalgisa continues the story of her love, and when the young girl begs her to save her from her own heart, Norma takes her in her arms in sisterly sympathy, and gives her consent to her marriage.

Pollione enters, and Adalgisa confesses that he is the lover of whom she spoke. Norma, astounded, bids her deny it, but the girl cannot. Pollione is alarmed at seeing the two women together, and asks Adalgisa what she has been saying. Norma turns upon him fiercely, telling him that he need not tremble for the guiltless maiden, but for himself, for his children, and for her,—his wife. Adalgisa, understanding, calls him traitor and bids him depart. Norma denounces Pollione for his double crime, and Adalgisa turns to her with the same tender sympathy that Norma first extended. Pollione declares that he alone is guilty, and that he deeply loves Adalgisa. Norma is tortured by his admission, but the maiden turns from the husband of Norma. He, however, repeats his vows to her and begs her to go away with him. To Adalgisa's amazement, Norma bids them both be gone. Adalgisa will not leave Norma and the two women turn against the man, calling him traitor. Pollione defies Norma's vengeance, and again offering Adalgisa his love and devotion, goes away.

Act III. Upon a couch in Norma's dwelling her two children lie sleeping when she enters with a lamp and a dagger in her hands. Fainting with horror of the deed she contemplates, she is about to strike them dead when she thinks of another expedient, and sends Clotilde for Adalgisa. When the maiden comes, Norma points to her children, and then on her knees begs Adalgisa to grant her one boon. When she has promised Norma says that to expiate her own crime and to cleanse the temples that have been so polluted she is to die, so she desires Adalgisa to take her two children and go with them to the Roman camp, seeking their father and bearing Norma's pardon to him and the hope that he may more kindlily treat his new love.

Adalgisa protests that she cannot bereave her of her children, and more than that, she will never leave her. Then she determines to go to Pollione and plead for Norma, that he may restore his wife to her former sway in his heart. Norma at first will not consent, but when Adalgisa pleads in the name of her children, the priestess seems to come back from the shores of death and hope stirs. Adalgisa assures her that her husband will again love her, and that she herself repents her passion and will take again, and this time irrevocably, the vow to renounce all human love.

Oroveso has gathered the Gauls, their chiefs, the druids, and the bards, about him in an open place, and to their impatient inquiries why the legions of Rome have not yet marched, and how much longer they must endure the yoke of Cæsar, replies that a more cruel proconsul than the accursed Pollione has been sent and will arrive on the morrow. They ask if Norma knows this and does not yet give them the signal for war. Oroveso says that she keeps a deep and awful silence, and that, therefore, they must obey the will of the gods as she interprets it, and wait yet longer. They nurse their rebellion, nevertheless, and continue to plot the destruction of their foes.

In the center of the druidical temple stands the stone of sacrifice, and against it a bronze shield hangs. Norma enters, bright with the hope that through Adalgisa's intercession her husband's love for her may again awaken. Clotilde comes, announcing that Adalgisa has returned, pale and weeping, to the temple, her mission vain, and that Pollione has sworn that he will take the maiden back to Rome with him.

Norma, wrathful at her husband's defiance, strikes the sacred shield violently. Oroveso, the druids, and the warriors rush in. Norma declares that now there shall be the war and the carnage for which they have waited. They sing a terrible war chorus, and to Oroveso's questions Norma replies that a sacrificial victim is prepared. Clotilde comes, announcing that the proconsul has entered the sacred forest. At Oroveso's command, Pollione is dragged in. Oroveso gloats over his archenemy as prey, and Norma demands the privilege of striking the fatal blow. Her hand is raised above him, but she trembles and cannot strike. So she decrees that the victim be questioned before he dies as to the motive of his crime, and bids them leave the prisoner with her.

Alone together, he again disdains her, but she tells him that if he will swear by his gods to relinquish Adalgisa, she will spare his life. He will not swear and braves her anger. She tells him how she meditated killing their children, and at the thought that they were in danger he blanches, and baring his bosom, begs her to kill him. When she threatens to kill Adalgisa, he kneels before her and in desperation begs that she will spare the maiden.

Roused to a fury of jealousy, she summons back the druids, and announces that a priestess has broken her vestal vow, been traitor to her people, and spurned her nation's god. All cry out that she shall die, and beseech her to name the offender. She bids that the sacrificial pile be lighted, and Pollione, still eager to spare Adalgisa, begs Norma not to speak the name of the priestess. Norma, unable to accuse another of the crime that is her own, acknowledges that she is the criminal. They will not believe her, but she tells them that, as ever, she speaks the truth. Norma turns to Pollione and tells him that they must go down to the grave together, and reassures him of her love for him. He, touched by her nobility when the life of her rival was in her hands, is won back by this moment of revelation to his former love for her, and in remorse he is content to share with her the terrors of death and the unknown life beyond.

Oroveso, her bereaved father, begs her to repudiate her confession, and all her people join him in supplicating her. She but reaffirms her guilt, and to her father commends her children. He vows they shall die, but she prays him, because his blood is theirs, to protect and cherish them. Oroveso, heartbroken, parts from her, while Pollione looks not fearfully at the glaring torches of what he chooses to call their bridal couch. A black veil is thrown over Norma, and at the same moment Pollione is seized by the Gallic warriors, and the flames of the funeral pile mount ever higher.

L'ORACOLO

(*L'O̯-rah'-kŏ-lŏ*)

(THE SAGE)

ITALIAN tragic grand opera, founded upon the melodrama, "The Child and the Cherub," by Chester B. Fernald. Music by Franco Leoni. Book by Camillo Zanoni. First production, London, 1905. The scene is the Chinese quarter of San Francisco, shortly before the fire of 1906.

CHARACTERS

WIN-SHE, an old wise man, called The Sage	Baritone
CHIM-FEN, an opium-den proprietor	Baritone
WIN-SAN-LUI, son of Win-She	Tenor
HU-TSIN, a rich merchant	Bass
HU-CHI, a child, son of Hu-Tsin.	
AH-JOE, niece of Hu-Tsin	Soprano
HUA-QUI, nurse of Hu-Chi	Contralto

Four gamblers, a policeman, a maniac from the abuse of opium, a soothsayer, distant voices, four vendors, Chinese men, women, and children.

Up the steps of an opium den comes an opium-crazed man, pushed by the proprietor, Chim-Fen, who vehemently execrates him and tells him it is such as he who ruin his business. As the maniac slinks away Chim-Fen sees the lighted windows of the house of Hu-Tsin and feels that his neighbor's prosperity insults his misery. Hua-Qui, the nurse of Hu-Tsin's son, Hu-Chi, comes and tells him that she is watched and dares not leave the house nor bring him the fan he wanted, the one upon which San-Lui wrote words of love to Ah-Joe. Chim-Fen is very angry indeed, for he himself desires Ah-Joe and he purposed to show the fan to her uncle, as evidence against her favored lover and proof that she was being taught cunning. He expresses his hatred of San-Lui, and Hua-Qui rebukes him for his passion for the young girl, but he spurns her, declaring that he will never run away with her nor marry her. She accuses him of wishing to leave her, and he says that she can remain a slave for all he cares. He threatens her and she goes sadly and tremblingly away. Four gamblers come out of the den one after the other, all drunk with opium, and as they salute Chim-Fen he responds with a gesture of contempt.

It is five o'clock of the morning of New Year's Day as Win-She, the Sage, a wise and holy man, comes along and is obsequiously greeted by Chim-Fen, with the formal wish that the hate of all Win-She's enemies may die—a wish which Win-She returns with the added words, "however much you may merit that hate." Chim-Fen seeks to prolong the conversation by asking counsel, and Win-She embraces the opportunity to admonish the opium-den keeper in regard to his vile life, after which Chim-Fen goes off to seek his usual consolation.

San-Lui comes along and sings a serenade to Ah-Joe, and she, hearing him, comes forth. When he begs her to remain, she says that she may not speak to him and that she did wrong to listen to his words of love. Passers-by and street vendors interrupt their talk, and the lovers part. All have gone away when Hu-Tsin comes out and Chim-Fen accosts him, gravely announcing that he is in love. Hu-Tsin advises him to consult a doctor, and Chim-Fen declares that he wants the promise of the hand of Ah-Joe, and offers to pay liberally for it. Hu-Tsin spurns him with great anger, saying that he is a disgrace to the whole Chinese Quarter. As Hu-Tsin goes indignantly off a fortune-teller's cry is heard, and the street crowds run to have their fortunes told. Chim-

Fen joins them and asks for his fortune. The conjurer replies oracularly, "A vile past, a future possessed of the devil. Wash you of your slime." Chim-Fen is angry and threatens the fortune-teller, whereat the crowd laughs, and taking up the accusing words, howls and jeers in derision.

Out of his house comes Hu-Tsin with his family and friends. He tells the joyous Ah-Joe that her little day of love draws near, and wonders what is in store for his little son, Hu-Chi, and hopes that the gods may preserve him from all harm. Win-She gathers a group of worshipers about him, and bids San-Lui prevent the crowd from disturbing them. He then leads in a solemn prayer with all the people kneeling. He then enters into a sort of trance. He says that he sees the heart of a father heavy with grief at the killing of a hope. At this all join in lamentations. Win-She continues, saying that he sees two souls free of the body, one light aspiring toward Nirvana, the other engulfing itself in Inferno. Then he adds, "Hu-Chi is safe."

When the service is ended and the worshipers have dispersed, Hu-Tsin, alarmed, asks about the vision, and Win-She recommends that they turn their minds away from visionary horrors. Hu-Tsin, however, directs the nurse to have extra care, while the procession of the Dragon is passing, of the little Hu-Chi, and raising the child in his arms, kisses him.

After the procession has gone by Hu-Tsin shouts to Hua-Qui that he does not see the boy. They call for him and search, but there is no response, and the merchant blames the nurse for her carelessness. Hua-Qui, in her terror, calls to Chim-Fen to aid in the search, but he taunts her. Hu-Tsin, wild with anxiety, offers to give the hand of Ah-Joe in marriage to whoever will find his son. San-Lui then confidently says that the divine power of his father will find the child, and rejoices at the prospect of obtaining Ah-Joe. Win-She sorrowfully bids his son beseech the gods that so much love may not be lost, and San-Lui, quite confident, bids an impatient good-bye to Ah-Joe, who cannot bear to part with him, for she fears that he goes to his death.

As he starts toward the den of Chim-Fen Hua-Qui tries to warn him, saying that the opium-den proprietor deceived her and purposed to betray him and Ah-Joe, and that he wishes the money of Hu-Tsin. The young man orders Chim-Fen, however, to go with him into the latter's cellar. Chim-Fen refuses and threatens San-Lui, but the intrepid youth is not to be deterred. They descend and there San-Lui finds Hu-Chi, and is about to seize him, rejoicing that now he has won the hand of Ah-Joe, when Chim-Fen strikes him in the back with a hatchet. He staggers to the street, and calling Ah-Joe's name, falls dead. She comes, and with wails and heartbroken laments, bends over his body, praying the gods to take her also. A crowd gathers and Hu-Tsin, seeing that a man has been assassinated before his door, comes forth and is horror-stricken to find that it is San-Lui. After a time Chim-Fen comes out, exclaiming, "What, an assassination! Gods of pity, where is the wretch that killed him?"

Later Win-She finds out from Hu-Tsin that nothing is known of who did the deed. The bereaved Sage tries to comfort the father, who is weeping over his lost boy, and as they talk the voice of Ah-Joe, who has gone insane with grief, is heard calling for San-Lui. Win-She calmly tells Hu-Tsin to wait within his house and to-morrow he will come to him there. He then goes over to the opium den and hears the cry of Hu-Chi coming from the cellar. Going down into the foul darkness, he finds the child and carries him to the house of Hu-Tsin. Only waiting to hear the joyful cry of the father that his child is restored, he returns to the door of the opium den and calls Chim-Fen, vowing that the gods shall have a human victim.

Chim-Fen comes trembling superstitiously, and when he sees Win-She, bursts out with indignation against the coward who killed the Sage's son, and says that he would gladly strangle him with his own hands. Win-She asks the other to sit down beside him just within the doorway there, for the word of a friend is comforting. Then the Sage sadly speaks of his age and of death, which he feels approaching. Chim-Fen protests that he is not yet aged, and at length sits down beside him, while the voice of Ah-Joe is heard still calling her lover's name.

Chim-Fen suggests that they two together seek the assassin. Something in Win-She's face surprises him and he asks if the murderer has been found, for he has not a single suspicion. Win-She coldly says that he has certainty, and Chim-Fen eagerly asks who it is, and wishes to start at once to take him, just they two alone. Win-She replies that they will be alone, and plunges a knife into Chim-Fen's back. Then, as he quietly prepares to strangle the wounded man with his own pigtail, he speaks slowly and tauntingly to him, asking why he used an iron hatchet, telling how his son came there, and he, the brute that had stolen Hu-Chi, assaulted him, then, like a snake, hid himself, and later came out by another door, and raising his hands in feigned horror, shouted, "An assassination! Gods of pity, where is the wretch that killed him?"

As Chim-Fen chokes, the calm Sage asks him if he feels the rumbling of the surging blood, if death leaps at his heart, if he rages with fright in agony. He terrifies him with visions of the demons that stretch forth their greedy claws to snatch him. Then in grief he asks the already dead man if he sees in the infinite spaces the sweet face of his innocent victim. He cries out in lamentation over his son, dead without a word of love. Addressing Chim-Fen again, he bids him suffocate in his poisoned blood.

Arousing himself, Win-She murmurs that his mission is finished, and hopes that when the news spreads it may be a warning to all luxury-loving men who desire gold and power. While he speaks in calm yet impassioned tones, a policeman saunters past. Win-She has propped the body with some cases, and so seated by his side he seems to be in conversation with the man. When the officer has gone, Win-She, his revenge accomplished, goes calmly off and the body falls to the floor.

ORFEO ED EURIDICE
(*Or'-fā-ō ād Yū-rē'-dē-chā*)
(ORPHEUS AND EURYDICE)

ITALIAN sentimental grand opera. Music by Christopher Wilibald von Gluck. Book by Raniero di Calzabigi. First production, Vienna, 1762. The scene is laid in the Greece of antiquity and in the lower world.

CHARACTERS
ORPHEUS .... *Contralto*
EURYDICE .... *Soprano*
AMOR, the god of love .... *Soprano*

Shepherds and shepherdesses, furies and demons, heroes and heroines in Hades.

ACT I. In the silence of a forest of laurels and cypresses, on a hillside bordering upon the sea, Orpheus and a band of shepherds and shepherdesses, his friends, are performing funeral rites at the tomb of Eurydice. They call upon her spirit, if still it lingers, to take pity upon her sorrowing husband. Orpheus calls her name, and then, finding the laments of his friends intolerable, bids them sacrifice their offerings to the manes of Eurydice and leave him there alone. He calls upon her, but with never an answer. He wonders where she is, and prays the gods to deliver her from Pluto's power, or else in mercy bring him death, that he may go hence and find her. When he execrates the dreadful gods of Acheron, who carry out the wishes of cruel Pluto, and threatens to follow them to the lowest hell and fight and subdue their rage, Amor comes to aid him.

Amor tells him that the gods are touched by his grief and

that, if he desires to go to Hades to find Eurydice and can, by the sweet music of his lyre and his song, appease the fury of the tyrants of that place, he may lead her back again from the dire darkness. Orpheus is exultant that he may see her again, and Amor tells him the single condition that Jupiter has decreed, namely, that he cast not upon her one look until he has brought her forth, else forever shall he be separated from her. Amor further counsels him to keep silent, to restrain his desire even to the point of harshness, that soon his torments may be over. When Amor has left him, Orpheus meditates with joy upon the assurance that Eurydice will live, and tries to realize what it will be to him. Then he remembers the inhuman condition, and foresees her suspicions and the terror that he will feel. He vows, however, that he will accomplish the deed, and bowing to the will of the powerful gods, he calls upon Amor to sustain him in the evils that shall befall him.

Act II. In the depths of a rocky chasm by the portals of the underworld stands Orpheus. About him dance furies and spirits, but he, by the beauty of his music, calms their mad revels. The furies challenge his right as a mortal to enter their abode, and the spirits take up the challenge, while Cerberus, frowning fiercely, stays his entrance. Orpheus, shuddering with horror, begs their mercy, but they ask him what he seeks of them, saying that there naught is heard but the cries of the condemned in the agonies of death. Orpheus answers that the flame that devours him is a hundredfold more terrible than the torments they feel. Then they respond to the strange influence of his music, and assuage their rage and hate. He abjures them by the love they have never known to abate their fury. Then with one voice they bid Cerberus open the portals wide and let him,

© Aimé Dupont

LOUISE HOMER
AS ORPHEUS, IN "ORFEO ED EURIDICE"

who has conquered them with his enchanting melody, enter among them, and he advances into their midst.

In the Elysian Fields the spirits of the blest wander in peace and happiness, Eurydice among them. With slow and dancelike steps they pass. Orpheus comes, alone and lost in wonder at the beauty and harmony that surround him. Not to him can this beauty and harmony minister; his soul's love alone can bring him peace. For her he longs even there, and will not be blest until he has found her. A band of spirits come and bid him bide with them, saying that Eurydice will come to him, new born with heavenly charms. As they dance about him he bids them hasten her coming, saying that they would if they but knew the fire that devours him. They call her, and she appears before him. Orpheus, without so much as a single look at her, seizes her hand and draws her away with him.

Act III. Still within the Elysian Fields, but now passing through devious labyrinths among overhanging rocks, Orpheus leads her, speaking most tenderly, asking her to follow him. With great joy she recognizes him, and he tells her that he has come to take her away, that Jupiter has been touched by his grief for her and calls her again to the light of day, that no more is she a shade, for the god of love has united them forever. She is exultant and can scarcely believe his words. He lets go her hand, bidding her follow in his steps. She hesitates, however, noting that he does not meet her look when she would arrest his glance. She sadly says that his heart is now indifferent to her, and asks if the beauty of her features has for him vanished. He replies that time presses and they must flee, that he wishes to express his tenderness but cannot. She begs him for one little look, and he is terrified. She refuses to go with him, and asks if these are the caresses that his heart gives her. Orpheus extends his hand to lead her forward, begging her to cease from her suspicions. She draws her hand back and prays the gods to take away her life, which now burdens her, and bids her cruel husband leave her. He calls her cruel, bids her see his sorrow, and asks only that she follow him. When she demands an explanation, he replies that he may not speak. They each pray the gods to be propitious and succor them, for their torments are insupportable.

They stand apart, leaning against a tree or a rock. Eurydice wonders why he persists in silence, and what secrets he would hide from her. She thinks he has torn her from peace to overwhelm her with his indifference. Suddenly her strength leaves her and the veil of death falls before her eyes. She shudders and sinks down, trembling and pale, wondering if life was returned to her only for these torments. Orpheus rebukes her for her suspicions and tells her that they increase his own anguish. Hearing her frantic words, he longs to calm her and grief overcomes him. When Eurydice asks him if he abandons her, his resolution to keep his vow at all costs gives way and reason is lost in the excess of his love. He starts to go to her, but stops.

Eurydice sinks down upon a stone as he says that he will tell her all, and, fainting, bids him a last farewell. In anguish he asks the gods when shall his martyrdom end, and believing that heaven cannot demand so great a sacrifice, he turns and goes to her, his eyes fixed upon her. When he looks upon her, she sinks to the ground and dies. He cries out in terror of the deed his ill-starred love has made him commit. He calls her name and laments that she is lost beyond any possible return. His remorse is unbounded at this second death he has brought upon her. In despair, he believes that naught but death remains for him. The hope rises that his grief may end his life, and that when he reaches the gates of death he will again see his cherished wife. He calls to her, saying that he follows and bidding her wait for him. His faith and love triumph and he believes that in the land of spirits they will be reunited.

As Orpheus is about to kill himself in the happy hope of seeing his love again, Amor appears to him, staying his hand. Orpheus says that none shall now restrain him, but Amor bids him be calm and recognize the love that looks upon his destiny. Then the god of love announces that he has proved his constancy and his faith, and that now his martyrdom shall cease. Eurydice rises up as if from a deep sleep, and Orpheus and Eurydice face each other once more. Amor bids them no more doubt his power, but henceforth enjoy the pleasures of love.

Before the temple of love, a numerous crowd of shepherds and shepherdesses, with melody and joy, dance before Orpheus and Eurydice, to celebrate her return. They sing joyously of the triumph of love, and that its bonds are preferable to liberty. Amor enters, saying that in trouble and sadness he often causes hearts to languish, but that their woes are suddenly forgotten in joy and happiness. Orpheus and Eurydice join in his song and praise him for the transports and delights he brings.

OTELLO
(*Oh-tel'-loh*)
(OTHELLO)

ITALIAN tragic grand opera, founded on Shakespeare's drama of the same name. Music by Giuseppe Verdi. Book by Arrigo Boito. First production, Milan, 1887. The scene is a seaport on the island of Cyprus at the end of the fifteenth century.

CHARACTERS

OTHELLO, a Moor, general in the Venetian army.......*Tenor*
IAGO, ancient to Othello..........................*Baritone*
CASSIO, lieutenant to Othello.......................*Tenor*
RODERIGO, a Venetian gentleman....................*Tenor*
LODOVICO, Ambassador of the Venetian Republic........*Bass*
MONTANO, predecessor of Othello as Governor of the
  Island of Cyprus.................................*Bass*
A HERALD...*Bass*
DESDEMONA, wife of Othello.......................*Soprano*
EMILIA, wife of Iago.......................*Mezzo-Soprano*

Soldiers and sailors of the Venetian Republic; Venetian ladies and gentlemen; Cypriot men, women, and children; heralds; Greek, Dalmatian, and Albanian soldiers; an innkeeper, and four servants.

ACT I. In a square of a seaport on the island of Cyprus, near the quay and a castle, a group of Cypriots, Venetian soldiers and officials are striving, in spite of the night and a storm, to watch the governor's vessel make the harbor. Other citizens come, among them several women, who pray that the boat may not be lost. At last it arrives, and Othello, a Moor, governor of the island and general in the Venetian army, disembarks. He gives the watchers the joyous news that the wars with the Turks are ended. All is rejoicing

© Mishkin

LEO SLEZAK
AS "OTELLO"

and shouts of victory as he with Cassio, Montano, and soldiers enter the castle.

Iago and Roderigo stand at one side talking. Roderigo is ready to drown himself for love of Desdemona, Othello's wife, but Iago counsels patience. Iago confesses that he, too, hates the governor, for having appointed Cassio his lieutenant and himself only his ancient. They plot together, each for his own ends. As they talk the storm ceases and Cassio and his soldiers come out of the castle. Cassio, Iago, Roderigo, and other soldiers sit drinking at a table before the inn. Iago offers Cassio more wine, but the lieutenant refuses, saying that he has taken one glass, and more makes him unsteady. Iago proposes the health of Othello and Desdemona, and Cassio cannot help but drink. Iago plies him with wine and gets him to talk about Desdemona, meanwhile stirring up Roderigo's jealousy. Cassio becomes very drunk and at Iago's suggestion Roderigo provokes him to fight. Montano, trying to quiet the tumult, is wounded, while Roderigo raises the cry of mutiny.

Othello rushes in, followed by the people and by soldiers with torches. He asks Iago for an account of the trouble, and the smooth ancient feigns ignorance. When Desdemona appears, Othello is angry that she is disturbed, and degrades Cassio from his office as lieutenant, bids Iago quiet the town, Montano be carried off, and dismisses the others. He and Desdemona alone are left. They linger, embracing, and speaking of the years before they met, of the dangers through which he passed, and of the joy they now have in each other. At length they go into the castle.

Act II. Within a hall of the castle, which a glass partition separates from the garden, Iago comes, while Cassio stands on the terrace at one side. Iago assures him that if he follows his advice, he will soon be restored to his office and again be in the governor's favor; then he tells him to lay his petition before Desdemona, because she has now great influence over her husband and, being of a gentle nature, will plead for the lieutenant's pardon. Iago further says that Cassio will find her about noon in an arbor of the garden with his wife. As Cassio goes away Iago soliloquizes on the relentless fate that drives all men on, expressing his disbelief in aught of good or happiness in the universe.

As Desdemona and Emilia, Iago's wife, enter the garden Iago calls Cassio, who goes and humbly greets Desdemona. Iago starts to seek Othello, but hearing him coming, stealthily watches Desdemona and her companion. Othello catches sight of them, notes Iago's manner, and asks if the man is Cassio. Iago tries by every ruse to arouse Othello's jealousy, and soon gets him to thinking that his ancient knows a good deal about Cassio's visit, which disturbs him. Iago even warns his master against jealousy, and Othello avows that he believes only in proofs; once they have been given, then away with either love or jealousy. Then Iago tells Othello to observe Desdemona's attitude toward Cassio and his suit for pardon.

Desdemona reappears in the garden, surrounded by women and children, and Cypriot and Albanian sailors, who pay her homage. She is very gracious with them, and Othello's heart is stirred and he cannot suspect her of being in the least false. Soon Desdemona comes with Emilia into the hall, where Othello and Iago still stand. Approaching her husband, Desdemona's first words are of Cassio and his prayer for forgiveness, which she seconds out of pity for him. Othello tries to put her off, but she presses him to answer, and when she sees him disturbed, she inquires the cause. He feigns a pain in his forehead and she folds her handkerchief to put about it, but he snatches it away and throws it on the floor. Emilia picks it up, and Iago draws her aside and orders her to give it to him. She protests and accuses him of some wicked scheme, but he tears it from her hand. Desdemona, grieved at her husband's petulant act, begs to know wherein she has offended him, and asks his pardon and his favor. Othello, torn with jealousy, thinks only of his own disabilities—his age, his color, his lack of facile wit—and asks that she leave him. Iago bids Emilia keep silence, and the two women go out.

Othello sits brooding, while Iago, elated with his success, plots to leave the handkerchief in Cassio's house. Othello's mind has leaped from suspicion to certainty, and he does not doubt but that Desdemona and Cassio have indulged a guilty love. He sees his own disgrace, and his position and profession as soldier at once snatched from him. While he raves Iago tries to calm him, but he seizes the ancient by the throat and hurls him down, demanding proof of the suspicions that he has raised, and threatening him with death in failure of it. Iago feigns injured dignity, then tells him that if he wants proof he shall have it. He says that he recently slept with Cassio, who in his sleep murmured Desdemona's name. Othello is wild with rage, but demands other proofs. Then Iago recalls to him a certain handkerchief Desdemona had, one of fine texture and spotted with strawberries, which Othello acknowledges was his first gift to her. Thereupon Iago swears that that handkerchief was lately in the hands of Cassio. Othello is now beside himself with passion, and kneels and calls Heaven to witness that his hatred shall never cease until his own hand has wrought his vengeance. As he starts to rise, Iago, too, kneels and vows before Heaven that Othello's cause shall be his. Together, with hands uplifted, they solemnly repeat their oaths.

ACT III. Othello and Iago are alone within the great hall when a herald announces that the galley bringing the Venetian ambassadors has arrived. Iago tells Othello that he has bidden Cassio return, and counsels the Moor to hide himself and observe. Iago goes out just as Desdemona enters, and advancing to her husband, speaks lovingly. He answers her calmly and takes her hand, commenting upon it, and hinting that he knows her perfidy. She replies that it was the hand that gave away her heart, and then says that she must speak with him of Cassio. He asks her to lend him her handkerchief, the one he gave her, but she has not it about her. He then tells her that that handkerchief belonged to his mother and has a potent spell, so that if it were parted with harm would come. She is frightened, but when he asks her to go fetch it, she says she can, but thinks that he simply wants to put off her plea for Cassio. He is infuriated and forces her to look him in the eye and say what she is. She replies that she is his loyal wife, but he accuses her of being a strumpet. When he keeps accusing her, she falls on her knees before him and tells him that her face and soul lie open to him, and begs him not to break her heart. He, unbelieving and weeping, drives her away, and when she will not go, but reaffirms her innocence as he her guilt, he leads her to the door and pushes her out, ironically asking her pardon if he has wronged her.

Left alone, he is bitterly grieving when Iago announces that Cassio has come. Othello is hiding in the colonnade while Iago talks with Cassio, who says that he hoped to meet Desdemona. Iago cajoles him into telling laughingly of some amorous adventure, and Othello, from his vantage, hears his wife's name, the laughter, and an occasional word, and reads these to fit in with his suspicions until he can scarcely contain himself. Cassio draws from his doublet

Desdemona's handkerchief, saying that he knows nothing about it, but that some unknown hand must have placed it within his house. A gun is heard, and Iago tells Cassio that the ambassadors are coming, and bids him hasten away. Othello asks his ancient how he shall murder Cassio, and Iago very skillfully works his master up to an unconquerable passion, until he vows that Desdemona also must die that very night. When he asks for poison with which to kill her, Iago suggests that, instead, he strangle her in her bed. Othello, for his services, makes him lieutenant, and then as a flourish of trumpets is heard without, summons Desdemona, that with him she may receive the ambassadors.

Lodovico and Roderigo enter with other dignitaries of the Venetian Republic. Lodovico delivers to Othello a parchment from the Duke and State of Venice. While Othello reads it, Lodovico pays his respects to Desdemona. Iago approaches them, and when Lodovico asks after Lieutenant Cassio, replies that he has lost Othello's favor. Desdemona says that he will soon regain it, and Othello interrupts his reading long enough to question why she is so certain. As they continue talking Desdemona declares that she would do much for the love she bears to Cassio, and Othello excitedly bids her keep still. Desdemona has confided in Emilia that she believes Othello's mind is seriously affected, so she speaks humbly now to him and asks his pardon. This enrages him, and he starts as if to strike her, but Lodovico intervenes.

Othello sends for Cassio, while Lodovico, much puzzled that such should be the noble Moor that rules the island, asks Iago about him and receives a deceitful answer implying great censure of Othello. After quietly bidding Iago watch the effect upon Desdemona of Cassio's entrance, Othello announces that the Duke has recalled him to Venice and that Cassio is chosen to rule in Cyprus in his stead. Iago is greatly surprised and furious, but Othello bows to the mandate of the Duke, as does Cassio. Then Othello formally turns over to his successor the ships and fortresses, saying that he will sail to-morrow. Lodovico asks Othello to speak to Desdemona, for her heart is breaking. The Moor furiously forces Desdemona to her knees. Lodovico and Emilia raise her up and try to comfort her, but she, mourning the loss of her husband's reason and his love, cannot be comforted.

Roderigo, who loves Desdemona, regrets her going, while Lodovico pities her and desires to help her regain her husband's love. Cavaliers and ladies watch the unhappy couple and comment wonderingly. Aside Iago slyly urges Othello to finish his vengeance quickly before his wrath shall slacken, and promises himself to attend to Cassio. He stirs up Roderigo, who thinks that Cassio is also his rival in Desdemona's affections, to plot his ruin, Iago promising to follow the new governor's movements and be present when Roderigo shall strike the fatal blow. Othello furiously drives the people out. Desdemona rushes toward her husband beseechingly, and receives his curses upon her, then Emilia and Lodovico lead her away. Othello, left alone with Iago, becomes more and more excited and at length falls in convulsions and then swoons. Iago stands looking disdainfully down upon the man lying on the floor, and as he hears the crowds acclaiming Othello as the "Lion of Venice," he kicks the prostrate body with his foot, exclaiming, "See there, the Lion!"

ACT IV. Within her bedroom Desdemona is making ready for the night. She talks with Emilia of Othello, and says he seemed more gentle. But she cannot shake off her sadness and bids a bodeful good-night to her companion. Alone, she prays before a statue of the Madonna, then lies down upon the bed. Othello enters by a secret door, and placing his scimitar upon the table, furiously strides toward the bed. There he stops and gazes long at the sleeping Desdemona. He kisses her repeatedly and she awakes. When to his questions she answers that she has prayed, he tells her that he is about to kill her, but would not kill her soul. He charges her with loving Cassio, but she denies it, bidding him ask Cassio; but Othello tells her that Cassio is dead. Though she pleads for pity, he will not believe her, and seizing her, stifles her. She shrieks and a knock is heard at the door and Emilia demands to be let in. Entering, she announces that Cassio has killed Roderigo. Desdemona speaks from the bed, saying that she dies guiltless, and Emilia, horrified, demands who did this deed. Desdemona has strength to murmur that she herself did it, and commending herself unto her husband, dies. Othello acknowledges that he killed her, and in justification says that Desdemona loved Cassio, for Iago told him so. Emilia is heartbroken that he should have believed her husband, and when Othello threatens her, rushes to the door calling for help.

Lodovico, Cassio, and Iago enter, and Emilia accuses Iago of the lie that infuriated Othello. He says that he himself believed its truth, and Emilia tells how he came by the handkerchief which he had used as proof. Montano enters and declares that the dying Roderigo has revealed Iago's villainy, and though Iago flees, the servants start after him. Othello seizes his scimitar, but drops it when Lodovico would disarm him. He goes to the bed, and remorsefully acknowledging Desdemona's stainless purity, draws a dagger from his doublet, strikes himself repeatedly, and dies.

PAGLIACCI

(*Pahl-yaht'-chē*)

(PLAYERS)

ITALIAN tragic grand opera. Both music and book by Ruggiero Leoncavallo. First production, Milan, 1892. The scene is near Montalto, in Calabria, Italy, on the Feast of the Assumption (August 15), between 1865 and 1870.

CHARACTERS

CANIO (in the play "Pagliaccio" [Punchinello]), master of the troupe...*Tenor*
TONIO ("Taddeo"), the clown......................*Baritone*
PEPPE ("Harlequin")..............................*Tenor*
SILVIO, a villager...............................*Baritone*
NEDDA ("Columbine"), wife of Canio..............*Soprano*

Villagers and peasants.

ACT I. Tonio, the clown, appears before the curtain and announces that he is "Prologue," and would tell the audience, not that the play they are about to give is fiction and the actors but playing a part, but that it is life, and the author and actors men, who write and act out of memories or passions the most real. The curtain then rises on a scene near the small village of Montalto in Calabria, where a troupe of strolling players have placed their theater by the side of the road. It is three o'clock in the afternoon, and curious villagers are gathered around. Tonio, impatient of their stares, flings himself on the ground before the theater. Small boys shout that the players, having made a tour of the village with their cart, are returning. The crowd greets them with cheers, and asks Canio about the play. He an-

© Mishkin

ENRICO CARUSO
AS CANIO, IN "PAGLIACCI"

nounces the performance for seven o'clock that evening, promising a startling plot.

Canio steps down from the cart, and when Tonio would assist Nedda, he jealously resents the act and himself helps his wife to alight, while the clown goes off in ugly humor. A villager invites Canio to drink with him in the tavern, and the master summons Tonio, but the clown excuses himself. The villager jokes about the clown's staying behind to make love to Nedda, and Canio, serious and angry, warns Tonio not to try that game on him, for the stage and life are altogether different, and the outcome would be far from humorous or happy. Nedda catches his words and wonders whether he suspects her, as he kisses her affectionately and goes off. The crowd disperse, some to the church and some to the tavern.

Alone, Nedda thinks of the passion that burned in her husband's eyes, and trembles lest he discover her secret and act like the brute he is. She is singing, however, when she discovers that Tonio has come in. Knowing she is alone, he confesses that he, though ugly and deformed and inspiring only loathing, loves her. At first she laughs at him, but when he protests his affection, she replies insolently, threatening her husband's anger. He begs her for a kiss, and when he rushes toward her, she strikes him in the face with Canio's whip. He screams and goes out, vowing revenge.

Silvio, a young villager, comes over the wall, and Nedda greets him eagerly, but fears he will be seen. She tells him that Tonio has just gone, after having declared his love for her and received a blow of the whip when he tried to kiss her. Silvio is much disturbed, and asks if she will not go away with him instead of starting again on the morrow on her wanderings with Canio. She protests, and, acknowledging that she loves him, begs him not to tempt her. Tonio, who has entered unobserved, hears her confession, then stealthily goes out to fetch Canio. Nedda yields to Silvio's entreaties and promises to meet him that night. He is just disappearing over the wall when Canio enters and hears Nedda say, "Till night, then,—and forever I'll be thine."

Canio starts after the lover, but Nedda calls to him to hurry, so the husband does not get sight of him. Tonio laughs delightedly, and Nedda turns ghastly with horror at his malice. Canio returns furiously angry, and demands of Nedda the name of her lover. When she does not speak, he draws his dagger and threatens her with it. She is still silent, and he is about to stab her when Peppe enters, snatches the knife, and throws it away. He says that the people are coming for the performance, and goes with Nedda into the theater, while Tonio bids Canio calm himself and watch for the return of the man, who perhaps will come to see the play. Canio, tormented by his jealous thoughts, tries to gain self-control enough to play his part and to change his sobs into laughter.

Act II. As the villagers come Peppe and Tonio play trumpet and drum. Tonio goes out and Peppe helps the audience to find seats, while Nedda passes around the plate for money. Silvio comes in and approaches Nedda, who quietly tells him that Canio did not see him. He promises to wait for her that night, and she continues on her rounds.

On the stage a small living-room is represented, and Nedda, dressed as Columbine, is seated at a table. She watches the door expectantly, although her husband will not be home till late that evening and Taddeo also is absent. Soon she hears a guitar and rushes to the window. Harlequin, her lover, is serenading her. Columbine is again sitting at the table when Taddeo comes and watches her through the door, exclaiming on her beauty and his love for her. As he enters and in grotesquely loverly fashion presents her with the basket of provisions for which he had been sent, she signals from the window. Taddeo is kneeling before her, addressing her with great fervor, when Harlequin leaps in at the window and steals up behind him, and taking him by the ear, sends him away with a kick. Taddeo goes, realizing that Harlequin is her favored lover, yet determined to protect her. With exaggerated fondness the two sit down together to a repast. Harlequin hands her a sleeping draught to give her husband just as Taddeo rushes in, saying that Pagliaccio has returned and caught them, and is looking for a weapon. Taddeo makes off; Harlequin leaps from the window and disappears, and Columbine calls after him, "Till night, then,—and forever I'll be thine!"

Canio, who, as Pagliaccio, is about to come on the stage, recognizes the very words that his wife had said in actual promise, and is so vividly reminded of his own grievance that he addresses Nedda in earnest, accusing her of having a lover. She tries to recall him to his part, but the real and the fictitious run so nearly parallel that his passion is all too little feigned, and he faces her threateningly. When it seems as if he might continue the play, Tonio, no longer as Taddeo, sneers at Nedda. Canio shouts out to the spectators that he has the right to act as any other man, and begins again to question Nedda for the name of her lover. She tries to resume the play by calling him Pagliaccio, but he repudiates the title, and tells her how, when poor, he gave her his name and love and tried to save her. He sinks into a chair, overwhelmed by his emotions.

The spectators think the acting wonderfully lifelike and are greatly stirred. Canio tells how he hoped for love, believing in her purity, but now he contemptuously bids her go.

Nedda, pretending calmness, bows to his wish. Then he, bethinking himself, knows that that is just what she wants, and declares that she shall stay until she has told her lover's name. Nedda, with one last effort to restore the play, says that the man is Harlequin. The crowd of spectators laughs, but is immediately sobered by the deadly earnest of Canio's words and manner. He threatens her and she refuses to name the man, while the audience questions whether this is play or reality. Tonio, in his revenge, prevents Peppe from interfering. Nedda continues defiant, and declares her love, but not for her husband. When she tries to escape into the audience, he stabs her with his dagger. Silvio springs to the front, drawing his weapon, and while some of the people rush away and others, not understanding, seize Silvio and hold him, Canio springs upon him, and crying, " 'Twas you!" stabs him to the heart. Letting his knife fall, Canio, as if stupefied, exclaims, "The comedy is ended!"

PARSIFAL
(Pahr'-sĭ-fahl)

GERMAN sacred festival music-drama, founded upon a poem of the German Minnesinger, Wolfram von Eschenbach (1207), and dealing with the legend of the Holy Grail. Both music and book by Richard Wagner. First production, Bayreuth, 1882. The scene is laid in the domains and castle of Montsalvat, belonging to the guardians of the Grail, a region typical of the northern mountains of Gothic Spain; later at Klingsor's enchanted castle on the southern slope of the same mountains, supposed to face Moorish Spain. The time is the Middle Ages.

CHARACTERS

AMFORTAS, son of Titurel, present ruler of the Kingdom of the Grail..................................*Baritone*
TITUREL, first ruler of the Kingdom of the Grail......*Bass*
GURNEMANZ, a veteran Knight of the Grail..........*Bass*
KLINGSOR, a magician............................*Bass*
PARSIFAL ....*Tenor*
KUNDRY ....*Soprano*

First and Second Knights of the Grail (tenor and bass); four esquires (sopranos and tenors); Klingsor's flower-maidens (six solo sopranos, two choruses of sopranos and altos); the brotherhood of Knights of the Grail (tenors and basses); youths and boys (tenors, altos, and sopranos).

The Holy Grail was the legendary chalice from which Jesus Christ drank at the Last Supper, and in which were caught and preserved by Joseph of Arimathæa the last drops of the Saviour's blood when he was taken from the cross. The chalice was brought to earth by angels and placed in the keeping of a company of knights in the inaccessible temple-castle of Monsalvat. It is the symbol of the Divine

Presence and has miraculous properties of strength and good and bliss. The knights are men of spiritual attainment, devoted to the highest and purest ideals. They wear the white tunic and mantle, similar to the garb of the Knights Templars, with a white dove embroidered on escutcheon and mantle.

Titurel, first ruler of the Kingdom of the Grail, has builded a temple of marvelous and costly architecture, and within it a second temple of wonderful glories, where is enshrined the Holy Grail, in which every Friday a white dove, coming down from heaven, places the Host. Within this temple minister only such as are pure in heart, wise in mind, and gentle of spirit. All about the mountain height stands a magic wood, which only the pure and noble can penetrate. Besides the Grail, Titurel was also intrusted with the Sacred Spear with which Longinus pierced the side of Jesus as he hung upon the cross. Titurel has at an advanced age been succeeded in the kingly and high-priestly office by his son Amfortas.

ACT I. In a shadowy and solemn forest near Monsalvat Gurnemanz, an aged though yet vigorous Knight of the Grail, is lying asleep beneath a tree with two young esquires. The solemn morning trumpet call arouses them to prayer. Two knights from the castle enter, and say that King Amfortas is suffering greatly from his wound, and is being brought to bathe in the waters of the near-by lake. Kundry dashes up wildly on horseback, hair flying and black eyes blazing. She is a witchlike woman, dressed as a penitent and girdled with snake-skin. She gives Gurnemanz a small crystal vial, telling him that it contains balsam from Arabia for the king's wound. She casts herself wearily upon the ground as attendants bear in the king. He calls for Gawaine, and is told that the knight has gone on another search for a healing balm. Amfortas recalls the prophecy that a "fool yet pure, through pity guided," shall be the one to relieve his pain. When, however, Gurnemanz gives him the vial that Kundry brought, he takes it, thanking her, and is borne to the lake.

The esquires, seeing Kundry still lying upon the ground and suspicious of her good intentions, ask Gurnemanz for knowledge of her. He tells them of the times when she, undaunted, has brought back tidings of the Templars in battle and has succored them in danger; how Titurel found her sleeping in the wood, stiff and senseless as if **dead,** and he says that she seems to be a repentant sinner under some enchantment for past sins, who would fain break away, but cannot. The knights desire that if she be favorable to their cause, she be asked to search for the missing Spear.

Gurnemanz tells them of the bestowal of the Grail and the Spear upon Titurel; of the choice of saintly knights to guard them; how Klingsor, when he aspired to be among the number, was spurned by the Warder for some deep sin; how the knight, defiant, had withdrawn to the southern slope of the mountain and there built a castle, and filled it with beautiful and seductive maidens, that the knights might be won from holiness. He relates also how Amfortas, armed with the Sacred Spear, had gone forth to withstand Klingsor's enchantments, but had himself fallen by the wiles of Kundry, and while he lay in her arms, bewitched, Klingsor had seized the Spear and, laughing, borne it away, but not until the king, though guarded by Gurnemanz, had sustained a severe wound in his side; also how Amfortas has long lain ill of the unhealed wound and has been kept alive only by the strength-giving radiance of the Holy Grail, for, though torn by remorse and suffering, he is obliged to perform the rites of the Grail service. Not without hope, however, does the king languish, for it has been revealed to him that in the fullness of time a young and pure knight, having passed unscathed through temptation, shall come, bringing the holy lance, and with it touch and heal the king's side, and then succeed to the rule of the Kingdom of the Grail.

Shouts are heard from the lake, and Gurnemanz and the esquires see a wild swan with a broken wing struggle to continue its flight, then, dying, sink to the ground. Other esquires enter, inquiring who shot the bird, as Parsifal, with bow still in hand, is brought to Gurnemanz. The knight questions him, and he, with pride in his marksmanship, acknowledges the deed. Then Gurnemanz tells Parsifal that the forest is sacred, that no bird nor beast there knows fear, and taking the body of the bird, he impresses upon the youth the sin of wanton destruction. Parsifal, touched with pity and regret, breaks his bow and flings away his arrows, and says that he did not know the wrong he did.

Gurnemanz sends away the esquires and questions Parsifal as to who he is, and Parsifal answers that his mother was Heart-of-Sorrows, and that he used to wander about with her. To many questions the lad replies simply that he does not know. Kundry tells Gurnemanz that Parsifal's father was Gamuret, who died in battle, and that his mother would, therefore, not let her son know the arms of warriors, but brought him up in simplicity in the forest, and that all evil men and things feared him. When Gurnemanz asks further about the mother, Kundry says she is dead. Parsifal in grief and terror denies it, but Kundry tells him that she saw her die. Parsifal rushes to Kundry and seizes her by the throat, but Gurnemanz releases her, asking Parsifal if he would use force and saying that Kundry does not lie. Parsifal stands long, as if transfixed with sorrow, then trembles and grows faint. Kundry brings him water from the spring, then, as he revives, drags herself away. She cries out and trembles violently, but staggers on and sinks down senseless within a thicket.

The knights are seen bearing King Amfortas on his litter back to the castle, and Gurnemanz invites Parsifal to go there with him. As they go forward the forest disappears, a door opens in the rocks, and they ascend through passages until they come into a magnificent hall with high vaulted dome, from which comes the sound of chimes. Two long tables stand parallel to each other, on which are cups. The Knights of the Grail enter in solemn procession. Amfortas is borne in, while before him boys carry a veiled shrine, which is placed upon an altarlike marble table in front of the couch-bed, where the king is laid. The knights take their places at the tables, the chant ends, and a deep silence reigns.

From a vaulted alcove behind the couch of Amfortas comes the voice of Titurel, asking his son if he will not that day reveal the Grail, that his father may continue to live. Amfortas, bowed with a sense of his great unworthiness, asks that this be not required of him, for in the fulfillment of his office he is like to perish of remorse. Nevertheless, he raises himself up and bows before the chalice, praying in anguish of spirit until he falls unconscious. An ever-increasing twilight has been descending upon the temple, and boys' voices repeat the words of the prophecy of the coming of the pure fool who shall bring redemption. Amfortas, reviving, takes from the golden shrine an antique chalice of crystal and lifts it on high, while the words of Christ at the Last Supper are repeated. A blinding ray of light shines down from above and lights up the cup, which glows with increasing brightness. Amfortas gently waves the Grail from side to side, while all the knights, kneeling, lift their eyes to it, and the voice of Titurel is heard rejoicing. As Amfortas sets down the Grail and the boys restore it to its shrine, the light fades and slowly daylight returns.

The knights seat themselves at the tables and partake of the bread and wine there laid at each place. Gurnemanz motions Parsifal to an empty seat beside him, but the lad stands motionless and awestruck. The king's wound again begins to bleed, and at his cry of pain Parsifal is strangely moved. The boys and esquires bear away Amfortas and the golden shrine, and the knights leave the hall. Gurnemanz turns to Parsifal, much disappointed that he has not proved to be the long-awaited guileless one, and pushes him through an outer door, bidding him be gone.

Act II. Within his magic castle Klingsor sits awaiting the coming of Parsifal, whom from the ramparts he sees approaching, attracted by the castle towers. By fumes of incense and by mysterious gestures he arouses Kundry, whom he had sent into a deathlike slumber. He calls her by her various names, one of which was Herodias. She arises from the bluish vapor with a startled shriek. He reproaches her for having served the Templars, and commands her to try her wiles upon the youth who now approaches. She rebels, but he asserts his power over her, and when she longs for death, admits that the one who shall spurn her brings her release from the evil power. With a cry of passionate protest she disappears.

When Parsifal draws near, Klingsor sounds his horn and calls his warriors to the defense of the castle and its inmates. Parsifal valiantly engages them, and because he is pure and fearless each blow he gives them takes effect, and they fall away before him until he stands alone upon the ramparts. Then Klingsor, murmuring that if Parsifal but once falls from purity he remains forever in the power of evil, sinks slowly into the depths with the whole tower on which he stands, and as he vanishes a magical garden rises, luxuriant of vegetation, while from every side rush beautiful maidens with garments hastily flung about them.

The maidens say that the tumult of the onslaught awakened them, and they execrate Parsifal for the slaughter and wounds of their lovers. He descends into the garden among them, and charmed with their beauty, frankly expresses his admiration. They invite him to play with them, and tell him that by love, not gold, he will win their favor. They go into bowers of the garden and return clad as flowers or garlanded with them, and surround him, each claiming him for herself. As they dance about him and caress him he takes innocent delight in their beauty, but when their advances become bold and seductive he repulses them. Though they taunt him, he withstands them, and half in anger turns away just as Kundry from an arbor calls him by the name of Parsifal. He stands amazed, remembering that his mother once called him that. Kundry then bids him linger, and sends the flower-maidens back to their wounded knights.

Parsifal sees a maiden of surpassing beauty, the transformed Kundry, lying lightly clad upon a bed of flowers. She tells him how his father, Gamuret, had called him Parsifal before his birth, and how she had seen his mother playing with him, her infant and her pride. While he gazes in delight and amazement upon her, she tells him of his mother's effort to bring him up unknowing of mortal strife and the arms of men, that he might be spared her, and how he wandered away and never came home, and his mother waited long, then of anguish and loneliness died.

As she speaks Parsifal forgets her beauty and grows more and more earnest, and at length, deeply affected, sinks at her feet and bemoans his own heartlessness, which brought upon his loving mother such unendurable sorrow. Though Kundry bends over him and tries to comfort him, putting her arms about his neck, he will not heed her, but in deep remorse confesses that he is, indeed, a fool. She invites him to the joys of love as solace for his grief, reminding him of his father's and mother's affection for each other, and, bending, she prints on his lips a long kiss.

A great change comes over him and he starts up in intense terror, pressing his hand upon his heart as if in great pain and thinking of Amfortas and the wound, and that he himself has received the unhealing hurt and bleeds. Then he realizes that it is simply the surging of his blood, the terrible yearning. He remembers the vision of the Grail, and how he heard the words bidding him redeem the shrine of its pollution. Filled anew with keen remorse that he had not obeyed, but had turned and fled, he throws himself upon his knees in despairing prayer.

Kundry timidly approaches him, and bending over, caresses him, but he realizes only that she is the one who tempted Amfortas, and pushes her away, bidding her be gone. With great passion she throws herself on his pity, tells how once she saw the Saviour and mocked him, and that she now searches for him, seeking to expiate her sin, but is doomed by the yearning within her to be the temptation of others. She begs him to redeem her by blessing her with his love if but for an hour. He replies that then they both would be hopelessly lost, but that he brings her salvation if she will no longer cling to the yearning.

First by wiles and then by rage she tries to move him, even threatening him with the Sacred Spear. When he recoils violently from her offered embrace, she calls for help, and Klingsor appears on the ramparts, while the flower-maidens rush in. Klingsor sends the Sacred Spear hurtling through the air to strike Parsifal, but it remains poised above his head, and reaching up, he grasps it, saying that with it he will ward off magic and close the wound that once it made. He makes the sign of the cross with it, and suddenly, as in an earthquake, the castle falls in ruins, the garden withers, and the flower-maidens lie strewn around as if dead. Kundry falls with a cry, but as Parsifal departs he calls out to her that she knows where to find him.

Act III. Within the realm of the Grail Gurnemanz, now extremely old, comes forth from his hermitage, and led by a hollow moaning, finds Kundry in a thicket, senseless and apparently dead. He revives her and she starts up, all wildness gone from her appearance, arranges her penitent's garb, and seeking to do some service, takes from the hut a water jar and goes to fill it at the spring. She tells Gurnemanz that a knight in black armor is approaching.

It is Parsifal, and when he seats himself hesitatingly upon a mound, Gurnemanz accosts him, but receives no answer. He admonishes him that it is Good Friday and bids him lay aside his armor. Parsifal obeys, thrusting the Sacred Spear into the ground and kneeling in prayer before it. Gurnemanz observes him closely, and both he and Kundry recognize the wanderer as the one who long ago killed the swan. With great joy Gurnemanz realizes what the presence of the Spear means. Parsifal rises and extends his hand in greeting, and tells them that he has been seeking, through long wanderings and many conflicts, to guard the Sacred Spear and bring it at last to the castle of the Grail.

Gurnemanz tells the wanderer how Amfortas suffers, praying for death, and nevermore since the day that Parsifal saw the Grail has he been moved to assume the holy office; so

Titurel has died, and all the knights wander weary and faint-hearted, and no more succor the oppressed. Parsifal feels the blame of their sore distress and sinks, fainting with remorse, upon a mound, while Kundry brings water to sprinkle upon his face. They minister to him, Kundry bathing his feet and wiping them with her hair, while Gurnemanz anoints his head unto the sacred service that he shall that day perform. Parsifal takes water of the sacred spring, and sprinkling it upon Kundry's head, baptizes her, while she weeps bitterly.

Parsifal gazes about him in wonder, for forest and meadow look fairer than ever he has seen. Gurnemanz says it is the spell of Good Friday that lends them glory, for they are watered by the tears of penitent sinners. As Kundry slowly raises her head pleadingly, Parsifal kisses her gently upon the brow. Gurnemanz brings the tunic and mantle of a Knight of the Grail and they array Parsifal in it. They all three start out, the landscape changes, the door in the rocks opens to them as once before, and soon they come to the temple.

Into the great hall of the inner sanctuary comes the procession of the Knights of the Grail, now in mourning garb. Titurel's body in its coffin is borne in, and Amfortas is placed upon a canopied throne behind the catafalque, for he is to perform his high office this once only. The coffin is opened, and sorrowfully do the knights lament as they view the body of their lost king. Amfortas, raising himself to look upon it, in utmost repentance begs his father to intercede for him that he may die. The knights ask Amfortas to reveal the Grail, and he, exposing his bleeding wound, bids them bury their swords within it and bring him blessed release. They shrink back, and Amfortas stands alone as Parsifal, who has with his companions entered unnoticed, comes forward. With the Sacred Spear he touches the side of Amfortas, who in a state of rapture is supported by Gurnemanz, while Parsifal proclaims the absolution vouchsafed of Heaven.

Parsifal then holds the Sacred Spear high above him, and while all are gazing upon it, he bids that the shrine be opened. Taking the Holy Grail, he sinks on his knees before it. The Grail shines with glory as of old. Titurel, restored to life for the moment, raises himself up and blesses the knights. A white dove descends from the dome of the temple and hovers over the head of Parsifal, who solemnly swings the Grail to and fro, while the eyes of all the knights are fixed upon it. Kundry, her glance upon Parsifal, sinks to the ground and dies. Amfortas and Gurnemanz kneel in homage before Parsifal, and voices are heard from on high offering adoration to the Redeemer.

LES PÊCHEURS DE PERLES
(*Lā Pā-shur dĕ Pŭrl*)
(THE PEARL FISHERS)

FRENCH tragic grand opera. Music by Georges Bizet. Book by Michel Carré and P. E. Piestre ("Cormon"). First production, Paris, 1863. The scene is Ceylon in barbaric times.

CHARACTERS
NADIR ....*Tenor*
ZURGA ....*Baritone*
NOURABAD ....*Bass*
LEILA ....*Soprano*

Singhalese fishermen, their wives and children.

ACT I. Within their village on the shore of Ceylon the Singhalese pearl fishers are gathered, singing and dancing in their annual festival. Zurga announces that it is time to appoint a chief to rule them, and they choose him by acclamation, and promise to obey him. Nadir comes and is greeted cordially by Zurga as a friend of his youth. Zurga asks him to tarry with them, and all welcome him. When the dance is over the two friends converse, and Zurga asks Nadir if he has kept his word, been friend or traitor. Nadir replies that he has been a friend and has mastered his love. Zurga responds that he, too, has forgotten their day of folly, but Nadir protests that calmness may have come, but not forgetfulness. Then they recall how when on their last voyage together, at a certain port they had gone to a Brahman temple and within its recesses had caught sight of a very beautiful young woman, whom the people were worshiping as a goddess. She had lifted her veil and stretched out her arms toward the two men, then had vanished through the door of a small passage. Within each man's heart love of her had sprung up, and from friends they became jealous rivals. Therefore, they had promised each other never to see her more, and now, having kept their promise through years, they vow to remain friends until death, shunning as in the past the return of the fatal love.

Zurga sees a canoe coming, and tells Nadir that, according to ancient custom, an unknown maiden, as beautiful as wise, is brought veiled from a distance to take up her abode in a ruined temple upon a high cliff, and there during the fishing season pray and sing to the god Brahma, and thereby drive away evil spirits and protect the fishermen. The canoe draws near the shore and the veiled virgin and Nourabad, the Brahman priest, land. The fisherfolk welcome the maiden with friendly acclaim and present gifts. Zurga administers to her the oath of her service,—that she keep lowered the veil that conceals her, that she pray and sing night and day, and that she live without friend or husband or lover. He promises that if she remain faithful, they will give her the most beautiful pearl that they gain, but if she betrays their confidence, she shall die. Nadir exclaims out at the terrible alternative, and the veiled maiden, who is none other than Leila, the goddess of their former encounter, recognizes his voice and trembles. Zurga, noticing her emotion, gives her a chance to withdraw, but she pledges herself to remain. Nourabad, under whose protection she is, echoes with Zurga the words of her vow, and the people unite in a prayer to Brahma for his favor.

When she has gone into the temple and the people have dispersed, Nadir is left alone. He has recognized her and his love is revived. He laments remorsefully his treachery to Zurga, but drawn by his desire to hear Leila's voice again, he approaches stealthily the cliff where stands the temple. Soon Nourabad comes, conducting her to the solitary rock where she is to remain, and she begins to offer a prayer, in which the people join from afar. After a time, Nourabad having left her, Nadir calls gently to her, saying that he is near and will defend her. She rejoices, and softly declares her love for him.

Act II. From the ruined temple Nourabad and Leila watch the fishing boats gain the shore, and he tells her that she may sleep that night. She asks if he is to leave her alone, and he says yes, but that the rocks are inaccessible and that at the camp the guards watch well armed. When she prays to Brahma for protection, Nourabad tells her that if her heart remain pure she need have no fear, and warns her to keep her vow. She tells him how once, when she was a child, a fugitive came seeking refuge, and a fierce band of men pursued him, and threatened her with a dagger when she would not reveal where he was, but she kept silent. That night the fugitive escaped and was saved, and before he went he gave her a necklace to keep in memory of him.

Left alone, Leila cannot sleep, for she feels a presence and surmises that Nadir watches near as on another night. He serenades her and she tells him where the path is. He comes to her, and she, remorseful and fearful, bids him go. He pleads with her and tries to quiet her fears. He tells her of his promise to Zurga and how impossible it is to keep it. They declare their love for each other and joyously embrace, when suddenly she is seized with terror at the great risk they take and bids him go, promising to meet him again on the morrow. Nourabad, who has suspected the lovers, enters, followed by the people, who are frightened by a fierce storm that is beginning to rage, and fear the wrath of their god. Nadir flees, but is seized and brought back. Nourabad tells of the stranger who stole up to the retreat of the priestess, and the two culprits are brought forth. The crowd recognizes Nadir, and terror-stricken by the storm, will have no pity, but condemns the two to death. The lovers are in despair, Leila frantically praying Brahma for protection, while Nadir defies their fury.

Zurga enters and says that it belongs to him to decide the fate of the guilty, and dismisses the people. Because of his friendship for Nadir he would show mercy, and he bids them go away together. Nourabad, however, snatches the veil from the priestess, and Zurga, recognizing her, is very angry and condemns the lovers to death. Leila prays in much terror, but Nadir remains defiant, while the people echo Zurga's words with joy. The storm has become so terrific that all now turn to prayer, the people trying to appease their god by promising to atone for the sacrilege.

ACT III. Zurga is seated alone in his tent at the camp. The storm is now over and the people have dispersed. Zurga mourns because Nadir, the friend of his youth, is to die at sunrise, and because he himself has delivered him to death. He thinks of Leila and her radiant beauty, and remorsefully regrets the blind rage that filled him and the revenge he took upon them. Leila suddenly appears, asking to speak with him. Tremblingly she addresses him, and he reassures her. She begs him to spare the innocent Nadir, and to slay only her. In her eagerness to save Nadir she avows her love for him, and asks Zurga to grant her Nadir's life in order to help her die. Zurga says that he might have pardoned him, for he was his friend, but the fact that she loves the man arouses all his fury, and that in trying to save him she has lost him. Then he avows his own love for her. When he accuses them of a guilty love, she denies it, and he says that Nadir's crime is in being loved when he is not. She taunts him with being barbarous and cruel, and that his remorse will haunt him ever. Nourabad enters, saying that the hour is come. Leila says that the victim is ready, and she gives to Zurga a necklace that he may take it to her mother when she is dead. Startled, he recognizes it, for it was he who, a fugitive, long ago gave it to her.

The people are wildly calling upon Brahma, and gloating over the blood they are about to shed. Nadir wonders what they have done with Leila, for whom he would give his life. At last the sacrificial pile is erected and the people dance about it in ecstasy. Leila comes to Nadir, and they encourage each other, happy if in dying they may be together. As the people watch for day, Zurga enters, announcing that the camp is burning and telling them to hasten to save their children and their property. The people depart to put out the flames and the lovers are left alone with Zurga. He confesses that he lighted the conflagration to save them, and bids them flee. He tells Leila that once she saved his life, and that now he saves hers. When they realize his danger and ask him to come with them, he resignedly says that God alone knows the future, and bids them good-bye. When the people return, Nourabad, who has overheard Zurga's confession, denounces him, and the crowd, clamoring for vengeance, determines that he must die. While the funeral pyre flames, the forest is seen to be afire, and the people prostrate themselves, frightened at this sign of the displeasure of Brahma.

PELLÉAS ET MÉLISANDE
(Pĕl'-lā-ăs ā Mā-lē-sahnd)
(PELLEAS AND MELISANDE)

FRENCH tragic grand opera. Music by Claude Debussy. Book by Maurice Maeterlinck. First production, Paris, 1902. The scene is a medieval castle.

CHARACTERS

ARKEL, King of Allemonde	Bass
PELLEAS } grandsons of Arkel	{ Tenor
GOLAUD }	{ Baritone
LITTLE YNIOLD, a son of Golaud by a former marriage	Soprano
GENEVIEVE, mother of Pelleas and Golaud	Contralto
MELISANDE	Soprano

A physician, a porter, serving women, and beggars.

ACT I. Melisande, a beautiful young woman, sits weeping by a well in a forest when Golaud, who has strayed from the hunt and lost his way, finds her. She is frightened, has wandered far, and has lost her crown in the water. He offers to get it for her, but she will not let him, and only after much persuasion does he succeed in getting her to go away with him as night falls.

In a hall of the castle Genevieve is reading to Arkel a letter from Golaud to Pelleas, telling how he found Melisande. It says that he cannot find out who she is, as she seems to have suffered some great fright and if questioned answers only by tears. She was dressed like a princess and had lost her golden crown. He tells how he married her, and that now, six months after, he is bringing her home. He asks Pelleas to break the news to his old grandfather, whose plans for his marriage he has thus disturbed. If

Arkel consents to receive them Pelleas is to put a light upon the summit of the castle tower. If there is no light Golaud will sail by in his vessel and never return. Arkel says that because Golaud was so sad and lonely after his wife's death and would attend only to little Yniold, he had sent him to ask the hand of a princess, marriage with whom would settle many troubled matters of state; yet as the young man has done differently, one must bow to the inevitable and let character develop as it will. Pelleas enters weeping because his friend Marcellus has written him to come at once, for he is about to die. Arkel reminds him that his brother is coming and that his own father lies in the room above more ill than his friend. As Arkel goes out Genevieve bids Pelleas be sure that the lamp is lighted each evening until his brother arrives.

Genevieve is walking with Melisande in the dark woods of the castle grounds when Pelleas comes upon them. He has been down to the sea, and though it is calm weather now, he predicts a storm for that very night. As they watch they see a great ship set sail, and recognize it as the one in which Melisande and Golaud came. She has a foreboding that the vessel will be wrecked. Genevieve goes to look for little Yniold, and Pelleas escorts Melisande to the castle. He tells her that he goes away that night, and Melisande questions him why he goes.

Act II. Pelleas and Melisande are sitting by a fountain in the park. She is lying upon the marble edge and leans over, trailing her hands in the water and reaching as far as she can. Pelleas asks her of her meeting with Golaud, but she tells him little except that Golaud tried to kiss her and she would not let him. She toys with the ring that Golaud has given her, her marriage ring, tossing it in her hands above the water. Pelleas protests lest she lose it, but she does not heed, and soon, just as the clock strikes twelve, it slips from her hands and falls into the depths, hopelessly gone, for the well is deep. She is much distressed, but Pelleas says that another ring will do as well. She knows better, however, and wonders what she can tell Golaud when he asks about it, and Pelleas says that she must tell the truth.

In their apartment Golaud is lying upon a bed and Melisande sits beside him. Golaud is telling how, while he was hunting, his horse at the very stroke of twelve o'clock suddenly swerved and dashed against a tree, and how when he recovered consciousness he felt a great weight upon him, as if his heart was crushed, but it seems there was no real harm done. Melisande watches and tends him, but when he refuses to let her spend the night caring for him she bursts into tears. She answers his earnest inquiry by saying that she is tired of this place and unhappy, and will die if she has to stay here. He tries to draw from her the cause of her sorrow, but she does not seem to know it clearly. He thinks that Pelleas has been neglectful of her and says that he has always been somewhat peculiar, but that later he will be different. She says it is not Pelleas that troubles her.

As Golaud tries to comfort her he takes her hands, and discovers that her wedding ring is gone. She tells him that when she was gathering shells on the beach that morning with little Yniold the ring slipped off, and that the tide came up and she could not find it. He says that she does not know what that ring is nor whence it came, and he sends her at once to look for it before the next tide shall have swept it away, and tells her that he cannot sleep until it is found. He commands her to ask Pelleas to go with her, and she, very reluctant, finally goes out weeping.

Pelleas and Melisande come to the entrance of a cave

on the seashore, where she told Golaud she lost the ring. Pelleas invites her to enter, saying that she must be able to describe the place, but that they will have to wait for the moon to rise, as it is very dark and dangerous within, yet very beautiful, and they brought no torch. They must not, however, go many steps from the door, but will stay in the light of the entrance. She is frightened, but he takes her hand and leads her in. Soon the moon floods the entrance with light and in the dimness within the grotto they espy three old beggars, who because of the famine have taken refuge there and fallen asleep. Pelleas and Melisande hurry out and away, and he promises to bring her again.

Act III. At the window of her room in one of the towers of the castle Melisande is combing her long beautiful hair. Pelleas comes by the window and hails her. They talk together and he asks her not to stay so far back but to lean out. When she does, he exclaims at her beauty, and wishes her to lean further. He tells her that he is going away on the morrow and asks her to give him her hand to kiss in farewell. She urges him to stay and when he promises to she tries to reach him her hand but cannot. As she leans out her hair falls loose over her head and about him. He is lost in its beauty and seizes it, winding it around his neck, and saying that he will not let her go. He twines it about the willow branches near. Some doves fly from the tower and about them in the darkness. Melisande is much alarmed and begs him to release her. They hear a step and Golaud approaches. Pelleas tries to free her, but Golaud comes upon them and asks them what they are doing there so late. He tells Melisande not to lean so far out or she will fall, and laughing nervously at them as a pair of children he takes Pelleas off with him.

In the vaults of the castle Golaud is showing Pelleas the great underground dungeons, where is a lake of stagnant water, the stench of which sometimes comes up and poisons the air of the whole castle. Golaud leads Pelleas to the very edge of the lake, guiding him by the light of the lantern. Suddenly Golaud makes a misstep, the light disappears, and Pelleas, not seeing clearly, would have at another step been in the gulf had not Golaud seized his arm and drawn him back. Golaud says that the place should be walled up, for the arches of the vaults are decaying and the whole castle might some day be engulfed. As they look down the abyss together, the light of the lantern trembles in Golaud's hand, and Pelleas is alarmed at the appearance of the place and overcome by the stifling odor. They go out together in silence.

On the terrace outside the vaults they recover their breath, catch the fragrance of the garden, and see their mother and Melisande at one of the tower windows. Golaud tells Pelleas that he overheard what passed last night, that though he understands it was only child's play it must not be repeated. He says that Melisande is young and delicate and must be spared any shock, as she is about to become a mother. Significantly he tells Pelleas to avoid her, but not too pointedly.

It is twilight as Golaud with little Yniold comes into an open space before Melisande's window. Golaud questions his little son about what Melisande and Pelleas say and do when they are together. The child says that they are always together when Golaud is not about. Golaud unconsciously tightens his hold on Yniold's arm, and he cries out in pain. The father coaxes him to tell what they say, but Golaud makes little of the artless admissions, except that Melisande and Pelleas seem unhappy and that she is always weeping.

Golaud asks if they never kiss each other, and the child says that they did once. When Golaud asks how it was, the child kisses him on the mouth, laughing, and then notices how gray his hair and beard are. A light shines out from the window and Golaud lifts the child up and asks him what Melisande is doing and whether she is alone. Yniold says that Melisande and Pelleas are both there, that they are standing apart motionless staring at the light. Golaud's grip upon the child makes him whimper with pain, but the father persists that he continue to watch and tell him what he sees until he is thoroughly frightened, then the father releases him, and they go into the castle together.

Act IV. In a hallway Pelleas and Melisande meet. He tells her that his father's illness has taken a turn for the better and now nothing prevents his going away, so he will start the next day. He asks her to meet him that night in the park by the fountain to say farewell. Though mystified by his manner she promises to come.

In a room of the castle Arkel is telling Melisande his regrets that the castle has been so sad ever since she came, with the atmosphere cast over it by his son's illness. He is very tender with her and hopes that now all will be changed and that she will find the happy conditions that her youth and beauty would attract to her. He kisses her forehead and tells how he has pitied her, but she says she has not been unhappy.

Golaud enters with blood upon his forehead. To Arkel's question he says that he was only scratched by thorns. When Melisande asks him to bend down that she may wipe the blood away he repulses her and demands his sword. Melisande hands it to him and trembles at the anger so clearly directed against her. He asks her why she trembles and says he is not going to kill her. He asks Arkel to note the beauty of her eyes, and how they glory in their power, but Arkel sees only their innocence. Golaud seems infuriated by her eyes, and seizes her by her hair and forces her to her knees before him, swinging her back and forth and calling her "Absalom." Arkel attempts to interfere and Golaud suddenly becomes calm, and with a veiled threat goes out. Melisande bursts into tears declaring that he hates her, and the aged and half-blind Arkel pities them both.

Near a wall of the park Yniold is trying to move one of two stones between which his ball has fallen and stuck. His attention is diverted by a flock of sheep passing. He hears them bleating piteously, apparently frightened, then notes their sudden silence, and calls to the shepherd. There is no answer, but he sees that they are not on their way to the stable though it is getting dark. Seized with sudden terror and loneliness he runs off.

That night to the fountain in the park Pelleas comes meditating. He suddenly realizes that he loves Melisande greatly, and that he must now look upon her once more and fill his memory with pictures of her to take away with him. He longs to look once deeply into her eyes and tell her all that is in his heart. She enters and he wants her to come into the shadow, but she prefers the moonlight. She says that Golaud is alseep and Pelleas complains that she came so late that they have but an hour before the castle doors are closed. He tells her that he loves her and that therefore he must go away. As he kisses her she quietly tells him that she loves him also. They find that they have each cared for the other since first they met. He can scarcely believe her, but she says that she always speaks the truth to him, that she lies only to his brother. He takes her hands in his, and would now draw her into the light that he might see her, but she shrinks into the shade. They look into each other's eyes and kiss passionately.

They are startled by hearing the great doors of the castle close and the bolts and bars slip into place. They cling together, torn between love and fear. Melisande starts up and says that Golaud is behind a tree and that he has his sword. They know that he has seen them embracing and at first pretend that they do not see him. Golaud advances toward them and they kiss each other desperately. He rushes forward with drawn sword and cuts down Pelleas, who falls by the fountain, while Melisande flees in terror, pursued by her husband.

Act V. Melisande lies in bed in her chamber and a little apart stand Arkel, Golaud, and the physician. The physician says that as the wound is trivial they may be able to save her yet. Arkel is fearful and thinks her labored breathing and silence ominous. Golaud exclaims in penitent grief that he killed her in a frenzy without cause,—for only a kiss between a brother and a sister. Melisande awakes and asks that the window be opened that she may look upon the setting sun. She seems to have a deep knowledge of something she will not tell. When she asks who is there, Arkel says it is some one who will not harm her,—her husband. She asks why he does not come to her, and Golaud staggering to the bedside calls her name. He begs that they be left alone together, then he asks her to forgive him. She forgives him but he has to tell her what for. He says that he has wronged her from the first day, that his love spurred him on. Telling her that some one is about to die, that he will not live, he begs her therefore as to the dying to tell him the truth, then asks if she loved Pelleas. She says that of course she loved him, and asks where he is. Golaud tries to make her understand, and asks her if she loved him with a guilty love. She says no. He beseeches her to tell him the truth, as both he and she are going to die and there must be truth between them. She is dazed by the thought and as she seems to slip away from him he summons Arkel and the physician.

When Arkel calls her name she responds. He asks her if she would like to see her child, and brings the babe to her, but she is too weak to take it and only pities the small, crying thing. As the maidservants enter mourning, Golaud starts up angrily, but Arkel silences him, saying that Melisande sleeps and in her sleep is weeping. Golaud begs once more to be left alone with her, but Arkel will not let him again disturb her. The servants kneel as Melisande's spirit passes. Golaud bursts into sobs and Arkel leads him away, marveling at the terrible mystery and pitying the poor babe whose turn it now is to live.

THE PIPE OF DESIRE

AMERICAN allegorical grand opera. Music by Frederick S. Converse. Book by George Edward Barton. First production, Boston, 1906. The scene is a mountain glade in springtime.

CHARACTERS

IOLAN, a peasant	*Tenor*
NAOIA, his betrothed	*Mezzo-Soprano*
THE OLD ONE, king of the elves and keeper of the Pipe	*Baritone*
FIRST SYLPH	*Soprano*
FIRST UNDINE	*Alto*
FIRST SALAMANDER	*Tenor*
FIRST GNOME	*Baritone*

The Elves: sylphs (sopranos); undines (altos); salamanders (tenors), and gnomes (basses).

In a woodland glade in the early spring the elves are busily working and singing joyously. They hear the song of a mortal, Iolan, and mischievously plot to tease him, until they remember his hospitality and kindness to them and prefer to give him a gift. They have none worth while for one who has his home, his strength, and his loved one, so they plan to dance and sing about him as he passes. Now no elf should ever allow a mortal to gaze upon him, but to-day they are reckless, intoxicated with the spring. As they call to him, the Old One comes and rebukes them for breaking the elf law. They scatter and hide behind trees, but Iolan espies some of them and they all come forth and dance about him. He invites them to his wedding with Naoia on the morrow.

The Old One recalls them to their allegiance to him, and warns them that they must have nothing to do with an alien.

Iolan demands proof that he is their king, as he has no crown nor scepter nor purse of gold. The Old One declares that the dignity of ten thousand years is his crown, and taking a pipe from about his neck says that that is his purse of gold and his scepter of the world. The elves ask him to play that they may dance upon this first day of spring, and though he wishes to wait until the mortal has gone, they insist and he plays for them. All dance away in their joy, except four who stay with the Old One and Iolan. The First Gnome tells Iolan that the pipe could make even him dance. Iolan still scoffs at its power and asks why he, who has all his desires, should fear it. He puts his strength and his love against its magic spell, yet as the Old One plays he dances perforce. At length he seizes the pipe from the Old One, breaking the cord by which it is hung. The elves cry out in terror and then are silent. Iolan springs upon a rock and taunts the Old One, who compassionately tells him that the elves led him here meaning well by him, and that now they will give him whatever he desires on condition that he shall not play the pipe, which is sacred, being the one God gave to Lilith in the Garden of Eden. The Old One warns him that the penalty for the mortal who shall play the pipe without knowledge of it is

"To pale with terror at its meaning,
And die when he has understood."

Defiantly Iolan plays upon it, but only with harsh, discordant notes. The elves rush to the forest and darkness spreads over the scene. Iolan feels surging through him a desire for Naoia, his betrothed. He sees a vision of the beautiful valley where lie the meadows that he tills, of his flocks, his home, his wife, Naoia. As in a trance he calls out to her to leave all and come to him. The Old One, who has stood by sad and pitying, now takes the pipe as Iolan turns to go, and tells him that the pipe but played his desire, but that his desire helps to rule the world. He bids him listen, and the Old One plays, going away through the forest.

Iolan sees a vision of Naoia's cottage, of her lying within upon the bed while her mother weeps beside her. He sees her, as she seems to hear his voice, rise fevered and ill to come to him. Iolan, when he realizes the inexorable power that draws her, and her great suffering, tries to stop her, but on she rushes, across fields, through the forest, the stones cutting her feet, through the icy stream and clambering over rocks. He sees her approach, and bitterly repentant, for though he called her he did not know what it would mean to her to come, goes to her as she staggers toward him exhausted, bewildered, and trembling. When she recognizes him, she says that across the world she heard him call.

Despairing, he wonders how he, loving her, could have brought such suffering upon her body, and is in an agony of remorse. She, however, with triumphant love says that she fears only that he will cease to love her, and she begs him never to leave her. He promises, and she, delirious, babbles of their little son, of their home, and of the prosperity and the joy of the years that are to come. At length as she sinks fainting Iolan places her upon a mound, supporting her and passionately calling to her. As she dies he bursts into violent weeping over her body.

From the forest come the elves, lamenting the change from power to agony and from life to death in the two lovers. Sadly the Old One approaches, meditating of the laws that must be kept. Iolan grieves over his lost one and in his anguish cries out against God, who has permitted this to happen. He curses him and feels a murderous desire to wreak upon him bodily his vengeance. Then he realizes how futile are his curses, and declares that there is no God. The Old One, wise with a deeper knowledge, then solemnly speaks, saying that there is a God, but that His laws must be obeyed. He tells Iolan that when he blew upon the God-given pipe his one desire, forcing thus his own man's will upon the God-ordained order, he obtained his desire but he also had to pay the penalty. Iolan angrily threatens the Old One, asking if he, who cared so greatly for Naoia, was the one who killed her, and declaring such punishment without reason. He raises his hand to strike the Old One, who asks if Naoia would desire revenge. Iolan, knowing that she would show forgiveness, gives up his own will to hers and throws away his staff. Going to the mound where her body lies he sinks down before it. The elves sing softly around him, regretting that they have brought him only misery.

The Old One bids them sing the song of autumn that the mortal may learn that all things wither. As they sing, the meaning of their song and of life sinks into Iolan's soul, and soon he realizes that the sound of the pipe is soothing him to sleep, and is content to lay down his life there where his love lies. The Old One, comforting, tells the elves that nothing is wasted. Iolan feels that his old desires have passed from him and are as dead, and slowly he struggles up, realizing that it was in himself he failed and not among men. As he stands by Naoia's body he looks to the heavens and, seeing her there, joyously calls her name and dies, while all the elves echo the Old One's words, "Nothing is wasted."

PRINCE IGOR

(LE PRINCE IGOR)

RUSSIAN sentimental grand opera founded on an ancient Russian national epic, "The Epic of the Army of Igor." Both music and book by Alexander Porphyrievitch Borodin, finished by N. A. Rimsky-Korsakoff and A. C. Glazounoff. First production, St. Petersburg, 1890. The scene is central Russia in the twelfth century.

CHARACTERS

IGOR SVIATOSLAVITCH, Prince of Seversk	Baritone
VLADIMIR IGOREVITCH, son of Igor by a first marriage	Tenor
VLADIMIR JAROSLAVITCH, Prince Galitzsky, brother of Princess Jaroslavna	Bass
SCOULA } gamblers	Bass
EROCHKA }	Tenor
KONTCHAK } Khans of the Polovtsi	Bass
GZAK }	Bass
OVLOUR, a Polovtsian convert to Christianity	Tenor
JAROSLAVNA, second wife of Igor	Soprano
KONTCHAKOVNA, daughter of Khan Kontchak	Alto

A nurse (soprano), a young Polovtsian girl (soprano), Russian princes and princesses, nobles and their wives, old men, Russian soldiers, young girls, and the people, Polovtsian khans, companions of Kontchakovna, slaves of Khan Kontchak, Russian prisoners of war, sentinels, and the Polovtsian army.

PROLOGUE. In the public square of Poutivle the people are gathered bidding farewell to the troops. Prince Igor, who is heading an expedition against the Polovtsi, an eastern nomadic tribe of invaders, who have already been defeated by Sviatoslav, Prince of Kiev, comes from the cathedral in great pomp with princes and nobles, while the people acclaim him as hero and victor. The prince declares that it is a holy war he wages and that he will return victor of a distant country. He gives the order for marching, and nobles and people pray for the death of their enemies and the defeat of the khans.

Suddenly the heavens grow dark and the sun is eclipsed. The people regard the omen with dismay and terror, while Prince Galitzsky and Vladimir Igorevitch exclaim out in apprehension that it means a fatal ending to the expedition. The people try to deter Prince Igor from starting forth, but he answers valiantly, urging his men to be not fearful but determined to conquer or die. The nobles also protest, yet the prince will not listen but orders his troops to pass in review before him. Erochka and Scoula, mercenary and treacherous men, try to stir up mutiny among the soldiers, and throwing down their arms, steal furtively away.

Igor sends for the women that the farewells may be said, and when his wife, Jaroslavna, also entreats him to remain, he gently tells her that his duty is to go. His son, Vladimir, is eager to start with his father, and Galitzsky agrees that for honor's sake they must set forth. Prince Igor commends his wife to the care of her brother, and Galitzsky accepts the charge, acknowledging his obligation to the prince, who, when his own father had in great anger cast him out from his domains, had harbored him and offered protection until he should receive his father's pardon. Jaroslavna, the princesses, and the wives of the nobles return to their homes, an old man blesses the troops, and Igor and the princes mount their horses and march forth at the head of the army, while the people cheer in great enthusiasm.

ACT I. In a courtyard of the mansion of Prince Galitzsky a group of men of the people are gathered enjoying his lavish hospitality and offering him their adulation. Scoula enters and asks the cause of the tumult, and is told that a young girl, who had been abducted, has just been brought in. Erochka relates how the girl in tears threw herself at the feet of the prince, begging protection and that she be allowed to go away. He refused and the crowd laughed at the girl's distress. Galitzsky enters and while the fawning rabble seek to know his pleasure, he complacently points out the difference between his tastes and those of Prince Igor,—that the prince prefers the hazards of battle while he desires the joys of peace and love. He promises the people speedy justice in their complaints, wine, and gaiety, and generous expenditure of the princely treasure. Princess Jaroslavna, he tells them, now devotes herself wholly to prayer and will obtain pardon for them all. A band of maidens enters to intercede for the young girl who was seized, but he promises them no mercy and drives them away frightened. When Galitzsky has gone out Scoula and Erochka stir up the people to scorn the rule of their absent prince and his sorrowing wife, saying that Igor has abandoned them and that the army is far distant. They propose that the people give their allegiance to Galitzsky, who will be lenient with them, and that they offer him the crown. So they acclaim Galitzsky Prince of Poutivle.

In her chamber Jaroslavna sits alone, mourning the absence of her husband and the young prince, and apprehensive of disaster. A band of young maidens seeks audience with her and beseeches her to give her protection to them and to the young girl who was abducted. Jaroslavna asks who was the offender, and they name Vladimir Galitzsky. They say that all Poutivle shudders under his oppression and recalls the benevolence of Igor. Suddenly Galitzsky enters and the girls cry out in terror and at his angry dismissal hasten away. Jaroslavna confronts him with his crime and threatens that upon Igor's return she will accuse him. He defies her, saying that Igor is dead, and declaring that he is master. When he insults her, she threatens to send him to his father, but he goes out unabashed and unfearing.

A delegation of the nobles enter and, paying her their homage, remind her of the evil omen of the day when Igor set forth, and they tell her that the hordes of the pagan Polovtsi are approaching the city and have become masters of the country. They tell her also that the army has lost all its battles, and that Igor is wounded and a captive. She falls senseless, but, recovering, asks of the nobles how she shall defend them and the people. They say that the city is well fortified and that they will defend it and conquer in the name of Prince Igor. She is thanking them when great alarm and tumult is heard and they realize that the enemy has surprised them and taken the city. As the flames of a conflagration rise, the nobles prepare for battle.

ACT II. Within the camp of the Polovtsi Prince Igor and his son Vladimir are held prisoners. The young man has fallen in love with Kontchakovna, the chieftain's daughter. A band of young girls are singing and dancing when Kontchakovna enters and joins their song of the joys of love. A group of Russian prisoners, accompanied by guards, passes by and the girls offer them food and drink, which they accept gratefully. The Polovtsian patrol comes and the girls go away. Night falls and at length Ovlour comes on guard. Then Vladimir Igorevitch comes from his tent and serenades Kontchakovna, beseeching her to come to him. She comes, braving the law that makes death the penalty for converse with a prisoner. They declare their love and pledge themselves to each other. They part as Igor enters, unable to sleep and bodeful of further ill. His army has been exterminated, and he is conquered, wounded, and a captive. He mourns over his country and for his loved wife.

Ovlour, who though a pagan Polovtsian has been baptized into the Christian faith of the Russians, approaches and tells him that he has hope for the future of Russia and for him, and says that a fleet courser awaits him. Igor, however, spurns the thought of flight as dishonorable in a prince, but Ovlour urges him and pleads the great need of his people. Still Igor refuses, and Ovlour goes sadly away.

Kontchak, the chieftain, comes at dawn and magnanimously endeavors to lessen the sorrows of Igor's captivity, paying a tribute to his courage and honor. He offers him every hospitality. Igor grasps his hand in gratitude but refuses his hospitality. Then Kontchak offers him his freedom and a return to his people if he will pledge himself to cease from war and become the friend of the khans. Igor firmly refuses to accept freedom at that price. Kontchak admires his spirit and is eager to be his friend. He motions him to a seat by his side as slaves, bearing musical instruments, enter with officers of the khan's suite. Maidens dance and sing, and then a band of men dances, and all join in adulation of their ruler. Kontchak gives Igor his choice of the maidens, but Igor refuses the gift. The entertainment ends with an elaborate dance.

Act III. Khan Kontchak and his officers are gathered to receive Khan Gzak and his army, who has made a raid on the city of Poutivle and now returns with much loot and many prisoners. The Russian prisoners at the camp watch the scene with harried souls and listen with bated breath to the details of the triumph that means the utter destruction of their home and friends. Kontchak dismisses the army and newly taken prisoners, and the khans confer about their further policy. When they have gone out and the Russians only are left, Igor and Vladimir learn that their city has been sacked and the inhabitants either massacred or taken prisoners. Vladimir urges upon his father his duty to escape in order to save his people and his country, and Igor acknowledges that Ovlour was right and that he should have gone.

The trains of booty arrive and the people gloat over the treasure, and show their hatred of the Russian prisoners, for whose blood they cry out. The prisoners are led away to their tents and the soldiers go off, all but the groups of sentinels, who vow a close watch of the prisoners and death to any who attempt to escape. They then pass around the wine which Ovlour brings in generous quantity. Gradually the guards succumb to the influence of the wine, and when all are sleeping Ovlour goes silently to Igor's tent and tells him that the coursers await by the river, and that he and Vladimir must come quickly when he gives the signal. Kontchakovna, however, has overheard the plan, and comes running toward the tent of Vladimir in great agitation. She calls to him and asks if he would flee from her. Vladimir comes to her and tries to quiet her, bidding her good-bye and telling her that honor calls him hence. Igor comes and urges his son not to hesitate, not to become the slave of the pagans. Vladimir is torn with the choice he is forced to make, while Kontchakovna pleads and his father would draw him away. The girl, feeling that in spite of her he will go, gives the alarm, and Igor and Ovlour make off, but Vladimir is seized and remains a prisoner, escaping death only through Kontchakovna's pleas for his life. Kontchak calls off his soldiers from pursuing the valiant Igor, whom he admires.

ACT IV. At early dawn upon a terrace overlooking the public square of Poutivle Jaroslavna comes, weeping for her husband and for her city and people. As she sits absorbed in thought a group of villagers pass. When they have gone she looks out on the far distance and sees two horsemen approaching. One appears to be a Polovtsian warrior, the other a Russian lord. As they enter the city she recognizes her husband, who dismounts and hastens to her and embraces her with great joy. The two go slowly toward the citadel and linger before it. Erochka and Scoula, plotting as ever their treachery, come into the square and stop aghast when they see Igor and Jaroslavna. They wonder how they may save themselves from the penalty of their treason if Igor now returns to power. They decide to sound the alarm bells, and the people rush in from all sides. Erochka and Scoula then announce the return of Prince Igor and point him out as he stands with Jaroslavna near the kremlin. All are rejoiced at the news. Some gather around Ovlour and question him. The nobles and the ancients come and, when all are gathered, the people acclaim their prince with great jubilation. Igor and Jaroslavna come from the kremlin and receive them, and there is universal joy.

QUO VADIS?
(*Kwō Vahd'ēss*)
(WHITHER GOEST THOU?)

FRENCH tragic grand opera, after the Polish romance of the same name by Henry Sienkiewicz. Music by Jean Nouguès. Book by Henri Cain. First production, Nice, France, 1909. The scene is Rome in ancient Latium, and the time is the first century of the Christian era.

CHARACTERS

MARCUS VINICIUS, nephew of Petronius	*Tenor*
PETRONIUS, Arbiter of Fashion	*Baritone*
CHILO CHILONIDES	*Baritone*
PETER THE APOSTLE	*Bass*
NERO, the Emperor	*Tenor*
SPORUS, innkeeper	*Baritone*
DEMAS, quarryman	*Bass*
A YOUNG CHRISTIAN	*Tenor*
LYDON, gladiator	*Tenor*
TIGELLIN ⎫	*Baritone*
VITELLIUS ⎬ Augustans	*Bass*
VATINIUS ⎪	*Bass*
THE YOUNG NERVA ⎭	*Tenor*
NAZAIRE, son of Myriam	*Soprano*
LYGIA	*Soprano*
EUNICE, slave of Petronius	*Soprano*
POPPÆA, wife of Nero	*Contralto*
IRAS, slave of Petronius	*Soprano*
MYRIAM, wife of Demas	*Mezzo-Soprano*
LILITH, Ethiopian waiting-maid of Poppæa	*Soprano*
PSYLLIA, wife of Sporus	*Soprano*

A centurion, a sailor; Ursus, who is servant of Lygia; Croton, a gladiator; Theocles, a doctor; Pythagorus, a favorite of Nero; Augustans, dancers, slaves, musicians, men of the people, sailors, quarrymen, gladiators, attendants of the Circus, soldiers of the Pretorian Guard, children, Vestals, Roman ladies of quality, patricians, plebeians, and senators.

ACT I. In the courtyard of the palace of Petronius amid flowers, fountains, and statuary Eunice and Iras are decorating the statue of Venus and paying their devotions before her altar. Chilo, a lame and deformed Greek, enters, and it is disclosed that Eunice loves her master, Petronius. She says that she has offered Venus all her jewels and many flowers, that she may be propitious to her love.

Petronius enters with his nephew, Marcus Vinicius, whom he loves as a son. Eunice conceals Chilo behind a drapery and the slaves continue their worship of Venus, singing of love, while Petronius watches them and comments on their beauty. When they have gone out Vinicius tells Petronius that he has fallen in love with a very fair and beautiful young girl in the household of Aulus, whom he has espied in her bath. Petronius suggests that he buy her if she is a slave, and finding that she is not, he offers, in order to cure love by love, to give Vinicius his own fair and beautiful slave, Eunice. She is gathering lilies and at his words lets drop her flowers in dismay. Vinicius wishes only the unknown maiden, and even when Petronius commands Eunice to follow her new master, Vinicius still refuses to accept the gift. Eunice is heartbroken and throws herself at the feet of Petronius, beseeching that he will not send her away. Angered that she dare address him so, he orders Tiresias to bring the lash, but Eunice is content if only he will keep her. She acknowledges that she has a lover here, and her love for the unknown is so evident that Petronius consents to keep her. Gratefully she tells them of Chilo, who knows much and can predict the future, and who may help Vinicius in his effort to meet the maiden whom he loves. When they wish to see him, she lifts the drapery and the Greek steps forth.

Chilo introduces himself as one who knows all things that go on in the city, both public and private, and says that the young woman they seek is Lygia, the daughter of a conquered barbarian king, and is held as a hostage by the Romans and confided to the care of Aulus. He says that she is not alone, but has a slave, a terrible giant. Vinicius says that he saw him, and tells how when he spoke to Lygia she made no answer but traced the outline of a fish in the sand. Chilo says that that is a mysterious sign whose meaning he does not know, and goes away charged to find out what he can about the maiden, first accepting greedily a generous purse from Petronius.

The Arbiter tells Vinicius that he will obtain from Nero an invitation for Lygia to the emperor's festival on the Palatine the next night. He speaks in exaggerated appreciation of the emperor's artistic and musical talents, then adds significantly that the day will come when, wearied of life, he will tell Nero the truth and die happy. As Petronius and Vinicius go out, Eunice in an ecstasy of longing embraces the statue of Petronius and with great fervor kisses the impassive marble.

Act II. From the terraced gardens of Nero's golden palace on the Palatine Hill the city of Rome spreads out visible in the twilight of a resplendent evening. Through a broad portal of the palace come sounds of an orgy, feasting and dancing. Behind a statue of Apollo in the garden Poppæa watches what goes on in the palace. Lilith comes furtively and tells her that Petronius is the one who is responsible for the presence of the beautiful stranger. Poppæa sends Lilith to summon Petronius to her, as amorous couples come out on the great staircase of terraces, then return to the dance. Poppæa accuses Petronius, whom she thought was her friend, of having brought the fair barbarian girl to please Nero. Petronius calmly tells her that he did it for the sake of his nephew, who is in love with the girl. With flattering words he restores Poppæa to good humor, and she with her train of admirers enters the festal hall.

Within the garden Vinicius, drunk with wine and with love, seeks to detain Lygia, but she is frightened. She listens, however, while he declares his passion, but, trembling, repulses him. When he would have her yield to the power of love, she declares that she fears God and serves Him only, and because his god is not hers, she would send him away. When she seeks to escape and he, seizing her in his arms, would detain her by force, Ursus, her slave, comes through the bushes, strikes down Vinicius, and, seizing Lygia, bears her away through the gardens.

Entertainers and guests come out of the palace followed by Nero with Poppæa by his side. Loud is their praise and adulation of the emperor. Tigellin approaches and tells Nero that his desires are fulfilled, and points out where flames are suddenly springing up from the city. He begs the emperor to sing now as Homer once sang before a city wrapped in flame. The guests watch the fire in amazement and dismay, and Petronius indignantly demands of Nero if he has permitted this execrable deed. The emperor watches the flames with great exultation, flattered by the demands of his courtiers that he immortalize the scene in song. He calls for his lute, but as he starts to sing his voice is drowned by the cries of the populace, clamoring for the death of Nero, the incendiary. Frightened, he asks where are the soldiers, and Petronius wonders what can stand before the rabble, who, armed with stones and cudgels, wrathfully advance. Hearing their demands for the criminal, Nero in despair names first one and then another of his retinue. The soldiers have given way before the mob and as it draws nearer the royal party and the courtiers turn and flee. Petronius alone is undismayed and, taking from Nero the Roman eagles as insignia of the command of the soldiers, goes down the hill to meet the crowd, while within the palace Nero commands that the singing and dancing continue that they may drown out the cries of the people.

ACT III. On the shore of the Tiber near the Pons Subricius among humble dwellings stand the house of Demas and the inn of Sporus. Within the inn Croton and some gladiators from the Circus are gathered. Chilo is going from group to group of the people, always with keen eye and alert ear. At length he seats himself at a table before the inn and orders wine. He learns from Sporus only that the emperor has gone to Ostium and will return in time for the sports, when the Christians, the incendiaries of Rome, are to appear in the Circus with the gladiators,—all of which he already knows. Chilo tells Sporus that he is seeking for a young woman accompanied by a giant. Sporus says there is a giant there, and calls Croton, but Chilo finds that he is not the one, although he notes that Croton alone could resist Ursus the Lygian.

With his finger dipped in wine he draws a fish upon the table. Demas, seeing it, approaches and, as Sporus goes off, tells Chilo, as a brother Christian,—for he had traced the sign of the Saviour,—that the Christians are gathering at his house, for Peter the Apostle is to meet them there that evening. Chilo receives the news without betraying himself and later asks of Demas if he can tell him anything of a Lygian maiden and her servant, Ursus. Demas replies that they are at his house with his wife Myriam and his son Nazaire. Chilo then pays Sporus well to find Croton, who has gone away.

At twilight Demas comes from his house with Myriam, Lygia, and little Nazaire, and they seat themselves upon the river-bank. Little by little other Christians arrive. At length the Apostle comes by boat, and as he lands the Christians gather respectfully about him. He tells them that when he with others had started out from the city on their exile, a great sadness came over him, for he was leaving his children without defense. Suddenly a light shone from heaven and he saw coming toward him the Christ. He prostrated himself and asked him, "Lord, whither goest thou?" and the Lord replied, "Peter, since you flee from my people, I go to Rome, there again to be crucified."

The Christians exclaim out at the miracle, and Peter counsels them to watch and pray for the hour of danger is near. As the crowd slowly disperse, Lygia kneels before the Apostle, confessing that there is a love in her heart that she cannot forget. He tells her that God does not forbid love, and gives her his blessing.

When the Apostle has gone and all have reëntered the house, Chilo appears and watches while Vinicius and Croton also enter stealthily. Soon loud cries are heard and Chilo is seized with terror. Ursus comes forth bearing upon his shoulder the lifeless body of Croton, whose back has been broken, and throws it into the river. Chilo, jibbering with fright, rushes off.

ACT IV. Within the Coliseum the Christians are gathered to suffer martyrdom for the sport of the Roman emperor and the populace. Myriam and Demas are among them, with Lygia, who lies on a pallet watched over by Ursus. Nazaire is seized by a centurion and taken away, and the Christians fall upon their knees in anguished prayer that God may spare them the horrors they are suffering. Peter the Apostle appears among them and strengthens their hearts with faith and hope, picturing the joys of heaven. As he blesses them Vinicius appears, distressed and fainting, and calls Lygia's name. The Apostle points out Lygia to him and prays that Christ, who has opened the young man's eyes to His light, may preserve her for him. Vinicius, who has been converted to the Christian faith while he lay in the house of Demas recovering from the wound he received in his attempt to abduct Lygia, says that he brings her life perhaps, and tells of a plan for having Lygia taken that night with the dead out of the city gates, where he will deliver her. The Apostle gives him his blessing and goes away.

Vinicius approaches Lygia and kneels beside her. His sobs arouse her and she calls his name joyously. She acknowledges her love for him and pledges herself to him for eternity. He says that he hopes to save her and take her away to Sicily with him. Their dreams of the happiness of a life together are interrupted by the sound of trumpets. Petronius appears with a centurion and tells Vinicius that it is impossible to save Lygia. The Christians raise their voices in a holy hymn, and Petronius in wonder asks the meaning of such calm chants within those somber walls. Peter the Apostle answers him, saying that they rejoice that they are going to die for God. Lygia has an ecstatic vision of the Christ, and calmly bids farewell to Vinicius when the guards come to take her away. Vinicius avows that he is a Christian and begs to be taken also. As Lygia is torn from his arms Petronius leads him away.

Within the Circus the imperial party is entering the royal box to the acclamations and adulation of the multitude. Nero himself announces the great event of the day,—the contest of a northern barbarian with an aurochs from Germany, upon the back of which a maiden has been bound. As Ursus appears within the arena the young Nerva calls the attention of the Augustans to Chilo, the betrayer of the Christians, who trembles and is livid with fear. Men and women rail at the terrified Greek, who, when Petronius taunts him, replies angrily. As Ursus dashes out to meet the aurochs, which bears Lygia upon its back, Petronius throws a toga over Vinicius. In a moment Petronius removes it and tells him to look. Vinicius cries out, "A miracle!" Petronius tells how Ursus seized the monster by the horns, held it immovable, then twisted the neck of the animal until it went down, and Lygia was saved. Ursus appears holding up the body of the young girl in supplication toward the royal box. Vinicius dashes into the arena, addresses the people, tears off his garments and shows them the wounds he has suffered in their defense, and begs that he may be granted the life of Lygia. The multitude take up his plea and beseech the emperor for mercy, and he grants it. Vinicius covers Lygia with his cloak and, taking her in his arms, hastens from the arena amid the applause of the people.

Nero, wild with fury, threatens to make the other Christians pay for the mercy he has shown, and orders them thrown to the beasts. He summons Chilo to his side, to look upon the death of those whom he has delivered over. Chilo stands as if in a trance at the sight of the martyrs, whom slaves drive into the arena where crosses are being prepared. He cries out in horror, and declares that he did not wish this, and turns to flee. Demas, from the arena, calls to him to repent, and when Chilo realizes that the Christian forgives him, suffocating with remorse and made terrible by despair, he stands before the emperor and declares that the Christians are innocent, that the real criminal, the incendiary, is Nero. The emperor, beside himself with rage, orders Chilo thrown into the arena; then though his voice is silenced, the people have heard his words and take up the cry, and turn upon Nero, protesting that they have had enough of blood, and hurling projectiles at him as he, with Poppæa and his retinue, flees.

Act V. At his villa upon the Laurentian shore, near Antium, Petronius with Vinicius and Lygia and guests recline on their couches in the twilight. Music is still sounding as Petronius reads aloud a letter which he is sending to Nero. He is bidding him farewell, for the end of his life approaches. He expresses his disgust at Nero's pretensions in art, and his horror at the emperor's criminal deeds, which he recounts. Lygia and Vinicius rise up astonished as Petronius gives the letter to a slave to be delivered to Nero. Petronius then tells his guests that this is his last banquet, and distributes among them jewels from golden caskets. Vinicius and Lygia beseech him to flee with them to Sicily, but Petronius refuses. Then he bids them a loving farewell and they go away.

Petronius turns to Eunice and asks for wine. He drinks with his guests and then calls for Theocles. Eunice, sobbing, throws herself at his feet. He bids her not to mourn, for she is no longer his slave, as he leaves her all his property. She says that she will always be his slave, and asks but one favor—to die with him. Petronius draws her to him and says that he has not understood her love, but that the gods have now in this last hour given him the supreme delight, that of being loved. As he takes up a cup and drinks from it she desires it too, but he will not let her drink of it. They embrace and as the physician enters Petronius and Eunice both extend their arms. The physician opens an artery in each, and heart to heart, with words of love on their lips, they die just as the Pretorian Guards enter to carry out the vengeance of the emperor.

RIENZI
(Rĭ-ĕnt́-sē)

GERMAN tragic grand opera, based upon the novel, "Rienzi, The Last of the Roman Tribunes," by Edward Bulwer-Lytton. Both music and book by Richard Wagner. First production, Dresden, 1842. The scene is Rome in the middle of the fourteenth century.

CHARACTERS

COLA RIENZI, Roman Tribune and Papal Notary......*Tenor*
STEFFANO COLONNA, head of the House of Colonna......*Bass*
PAOLO ORSINO, head of the House of Orsini............*Bass*
RAYMOND, Papal Legate............................*Bass*
BARONCELLI } Roman citizens............ { *Tenor*
CECCO DEL VECCHIO } { *Bass*
ADRIANO, son of Steffano Colonna...........*Mezzo-Soprano*
IRENE, sister of Cola Rienzi.....................*Soprano*

A messenger of peace (soprano), a herald, foreign ambassadors, Roman nobles, citizens, messengers, priests and monks of various orders, and Roman soldiers.

ACT I. Orsino and an armed party of nobles enter the street before the church of St. John de Lateran in Rome one night for a raid. Placing a ladder under a house window he ascends, seizes a very beautiful young woman in her chamber, and starts to carry her off in spite of her frantic cries and entreaties. Colonna, head of the opposing faction of nobles, comes with a numerous following and engages the Orsini. Adriano rushes in and seeks to protect the young woman, Irene. The people of the city are aroused, and, armed with stones, hammers, and cudgels, try to separate the nobles. Raymond, the papal legate, enters and commands them to keep the peace, but the nobles rail at him.

Suddenly Rienzi appears followed by Cecco and Baroncelli. At his word the people become silent and the nobles stand amazed at his control of the plebeians. He calls upon all factions to withdraw, reminding them of their oath to respect the law and the church. Irene rushes to his arms and he sees the ladder and realizes the cause of the uproar. With great indignation he makes a spirited appeal to them all as Roman citizens to raise their city from the disgrace into which she has been cast by their crimes. The people applaud, but the patricians will not desist from their struggle for supremacy, and appoint a place outside the city gates to meet at dawn and continue the battle. The people gather about Rienzi and he, supported by the papal legate, determines to strike a decisive blow to rid the city of the tyranny of the nobles by shutting upon them the city gates, and letting none reënter until he has taken oath to keep the peace and respect the law. Rienzi tells the people to rally to his support at the sound of the trumpet.

As they depart Irene tells her brother how Adriano protected her and deserves their thanks. Rienzi realizes then that the young man, the son of Colonna, has heard his instructions to the people and can betray his plans to the nobles. He and Irene join their entreaties that the young noble shall assist in saving the city, and, moved by the girl's beauty and his boyhood friendship for her brother as well as by his own patriotic pride, he consents to help. Rienzi goes away, asking the young man to accept his hospitality and committing Irene to his care. Adriano has from his first sight of Irene fallen in love with her, and when they are alone rejoices to find that his affection is returned. The lovers' joy is tinged with premonition as Adriano points out that the people are fickle and that Rienzi has done a very daring thing in defying the powerful and cruel barons.

As they talk morning comes and with it the blast of the

trumpet assembling the people, who fill the square. The church doors open and Rienzi, completely armed but with uncovered head, appears accompanied by Raymond and a crowd of priests and monks of all orders. The people receive them with great enthusiasm and he is borne as chief magistrate at the head of a procession, and addresses the people, promising them a just rule of the city. When at Cecco's suggestion the people would make him king, he repudiates the thought, saying that a senate should govern the new state, and asks only for the ancient title of Tribune of the People.

Act II. Within the great hall of the Capitol the Tribune sits in state with Baroncelli and Cecco as pretors and the new senators, and receives the ministers from foreign courts and the heralds and messengers of peace from all parts of the land. Colonna, Orsino, and the other nobles, who have been obliged to take oath of allegiance in order to return to their homes, come in and salute Rienzi with mixed deference and defiance. The people receive with acclaim every advance in the establishing of law and order. The nobles, however, realize that it is Rienzi whose strength as leader of the people keeps them in check, and draw aside to plot his overthrow.

Adriano, unobserved, joins them and, hearing their conspiracy, protests that they are breaking their solemn oath and threatens to denounce them. Colonna, his own father, dares him to do that which would make him a parricide. Adriano, heartbroken at the dishonor of such betrayal, throws himself on his father's pity and begs him to kill him first but not permit such treason. Colonna repulses him and the nobles leave him with threats. In furtherance of their plan they join Rienzi where he is addressing the people and announcing the beginning of a fête in celebration of the peace. Adriano warns him of danger, but he is incredulous. Orsino plunges his dagger at him. Rienzi's steel corselet prevents injury and the guards seize the conspirators.

The people, much disturbed by the incident, are dismissed, and the senators, at Cecco's instigation, decree that the assassins be killed without mercy. They are conducted into an inner hall and Rienzi is left alone. Adriano and Irene come, beseeching him that he will spare the nobles. When Rienzi hesitates, Adriano threatens him, saying that he will avenge the death of his father. Rienzi hears the monks who are preparing the condemned for death, and himself prays, then to Irene's frantic entreaties relents and calls in the people. At last he wins them over to pardon rather than vengeance. The nobles are again obliged to take the oath of allegiance if they would go to their homes free. As they depart they mutter threats of vengeance.

Act III. In a public square the people are excitedly discussing the flight of the nobles from the city for the purpose of conquering it and reëstablishing their supremacy. All are terrified and beseech Rienzi to deliver them, and blame him for the mercy shown the nobles. As they march off toward the Capitol Adriano enters the square, despairing because he must either bear arms against his own father or slay Rienzi, the brother of the woman he loves. Rienzi enters on horseback with the Roman troops on their way to the city gates to fight the nobles. Adriano in one last effort to save bloodshed stops Rienzi's horse and begs that he be allowed to make another attempt to appease the wrath of the nobles. Rienzi refuses, and the troops march on to the battle.

Adriano turns to Irene, who has come on foot by her brother's side, and bids her a last farewell, saying that he goes to fight for his father. She clings to him, telling him that he should kill her first, that losing him she dies. He is overwhelmed with the torment of his conflicting duties and knows of no escape but death. As the sounds of the fight grow loud the women kneel in prayer. At last the noise is changed to shouts of victory, and Rienzi and the plebeians return triumphant. Irene runs to greet the victor. As the wounded and dead are brought Adriano recognizes the body of his father, and in great grief cries out against the Tribune, and with a vow of vengeance and hate goes away.

Act IV. At night before the church Baroncelli, Cecco, and some of the leaders among the people are meeting. Baroncelli announces that the pope and the emperor are both leagued with the nobles against the people, and have recalled their legates and ambassadors to show their displeasure at the uprising. Baroncelli charges Rienzi with treason, saying that he had mercy upon the nobles because his sister loves the son of Colonna. When the people demand proof, Adriano wrapped in his cloak advances and declares it to be true. As he speaks he sees the shade of his father and promises to avenge him. Then he reveals who he is and declares that he himself will kill the Tribune.

Suddenly Raymond with his attendant priests appears and enters the church. The conspirators are dismayed, doubting the truth of the papal withdrawal. As Rienzi comes with a large following of the people, the conspirators take their stand near the doors of the church as if to bar the way. Adriano presses forward that he may strike the Tribune down, but when he sees Irene accompanying her brother, he cannot perform his vow. Rienzi sees the sad and sullen men and addresses them with patriotic fervor. They slink back and he is about to enter the church when the doors open and Raymond appears and, forbidding him to approach, pronounces the anathema of the church upon the Tribune.

All fall away from him as he stands dazed and horrified and hears the doors of the church close upon him. Adriano approaches Irene and tries to lead her away, but she will not go, and clinging to her brother, says she will not leave him. Rienzi recovers himself and, embracing her, says that all of Rome is here with him.

Act V. Rienzi is kneeling in the Capitol earnestly praying for his people and his city. Irene comes and he begs her to leave him that she may not share the exile and dangers that await him. She declares, however, that she will not, even though by staying with him she sacrifices her love,— how great a sacrifice he cannot know as he has never loved. He then reveals to her his passionate love for his dear city, Rome, even though she has betrayed him. Together they pledge themselves to be true to Rome to their latest breath. He goes out to make one last effort to regain his power over the people. Adriano enters and pleads with her to flee for her life, as the mob is coming to kill Rienzi and burn the Capitol. She calls him traitor and says her love for him is dead and refuses to go. He reminds her of her vow to him and declares his devotion to her, but she will not go. The flames break into the hall, and the crash of falling rocks and stones is heard. He tells her that he will not leave her, but die with her; again she calls him traitor, and then rushes away.

The square before the Capitol is filled with an angry mob, having lighted torches and stones in their hands. Rienzi, in complete armor, but with uncovered head, from a balcony strives to address the infuriated citizens, but Baroncelli and Cecco, among the mob, make his efforts futile and incite the people to violence. They fire the Capitol, that it may be his funeral pyre, and he is seen standing amid the flames with Irene in his embrace. The people are stoning them as Adriano dashes breathlessly in at the head of the nobles returning to Rome, and seeing Irene, cries out for mercy for her. As the façade falls, he dashes toward Rienzi and Irene within the ruins, while the nobles keep back the people.

RIGOLETTO
(*Rē-gō-lĕt'-tō*)

ITALIAN tragic grand opera, after Victor Hugo's drama "Le Roi s'amuse." Music by Giuseppe Verdi. Book by Francesco Maria Piave. First production, Venice, 1851. The scene is laid in Mantua and vicinity in the sixteenth century.

CHARACTERS

DUKE OF MANTUA, a titled profligate..................*Tenor*
RIGOLETTO, a hunchback, jester to the Duke........*Baritone*
COUNT CEPRANO } nobles of the dukedom of { *Bass*
COUNT MONTERONE } Mantua .... { *Baritone*
SPARAFUCILE, a hired assassin........................*Bass*
BORSA, a domestic to the Duke......................*Tenor*
MARULLO ....*Bass*
COUNTESS CEPRANO..............................*Soprano*
GILDA, daughter of Rigoletto......................*Soprano*
GIOVANNA, duenna to Gilda........................*Soprano*
MADDALENA, a Cyprian, sister of Sparafucile.......*Contralto*

Courtiers, cavaliers, pages, and servants.

ACT. I. In a hall of the palace of the dissolute Duke of Mantua nobles and ladies are gathered at a brilliant fête. The duke enters, telling Borsa that he has been much attracted by a beautiful young woman whom he sees every Sunday at church, who lives in a remote part of the city, and who is visited each night by a mysterious man. Countess Ceprano, of whom also the inconstant duke is enamored, approaches, and he pays her flattering attention, in defiance of the ill-concealed jealousy of her husband. As they go out Rigoletto enters, and makes sport of the count. The jester has just left when Marullo comes in with the news that Rigoletto, the ugly and deformed, has a mistress. The laugh thus raised is checked by the entrance of the duke and Rigoletto, who is suggesting to the former that he carry off Countess Ceprano in spite of the count, whom he can imprison, or banish, or behead. Ceprano has advanced and, taunted by Rigoletto, draws his sword. The buffoon gaily declares himself safe within the duke's favor, and the courtiers, each with some wrong to be avenged, conspire with Ceprano to meet him armed on the morrow and vent their wrath upon the jester. Suddenly Count Monterone forces his way in to call the duke to account for the disgrace he has brought upon his daughter. Rigoletto scornfully answers for the duke, who has the intruder arrested. As Monterone is led away he hurls a parent's curse upon them both, and Rigoletto is strangely agitated.

At the end of a street having no thoroughfare Rigoletto comes that night, still thinking of the fearful curse upon him. Sparafucile, with sword under cloak, approaches, and on the suspicion that Rigoletto has a mistress thereabouts, suggests that he can rid him of a rival. Rigoletto is horrified at the man's cold-blooded manner, nevertheless asks him his terms and methods, but declines his services, and the man goes away. Rigoletto thinks remorsefully how like the assassin he himself is, using his tongue instead of sword, and resolves now to become a changed man. Opening a door, he enters a yard, and a young and very beautiful woman, his daughter, comes hastening to him. They greet each other affectionately, and when he seems sad she tries to comfort him. She asks him of their family and of her mother, but the grief and anguish of his memories are so great that he cannot tell her. In his anxiety he questions her whether she ever goes out, and she says that she goes only to church. He tells her never to leave the house; he fears that she may be stolen from him as men would lightly regard dishonoring

© Mishkin

FELICE LYNE
AS GILDA, IN "RIGOLETTO"

the daughter of a buffoon. He questions Giovanna, her duenna, whether any one ever comes, and she says no. Rigoletto hears a noise without the wall and goes to the door and looks out. The duke in disguise steals in unobserved. Rigoletto, returning, asks if any one has ever followed her from church; Giovanna replies in the negative and Rigoletto goes away, after warmly embracing his daughter.

Gilda tells Giovanna that she is sorry that she did not tell her father of the young man whom she sees at church. She confesses that she loves him and longs to tell him of her love. The duke, overhearing all, comes forward and declares his love for her. To her questions he replies that his name is Walter Maldé, and that he is a student. Borsa and Ceprano enter the street, the latter pointing out the house where Gilda lives. Fearing that her father has returned, Gilda tells Giovanna to guide Walter away, and they bid good-bye with vows of eternal affection.

Gilda goes into the house just as Marullo, Ceprano, and Borsa, accompanied by courtiers, armed and in masks, enter. Ceprano points her out, and they exclaim at her beauty and wonder that she can be the mistress of Rigoletto. Just then the jester comes along, absorbed in thought. The courtiers, now avenging themselves upon him, plan not to slay him until the morrow. So they accost him, and to his questions answer that they are taking off Ceprano's wife. He, relieved from his fears for Gilda by handling the keys bearing the crest of Ceprano, offers to aid them. They put on him a mask like the others wear, but in tying it blindfold him, then bid him hold the ladder. Some go up the ladder, enter the house, then open the door to others, and finally bring out Gilda, gagged and helpless. As they bear her off her scarf falls. They are already distant when Rigoletto gets impatient of waiting, realizes that his eyes are bandaged, and freeing them, recognizes Gilda's scarf. He rushes through the open door and drags forth the frightened Giovanna. He is at first stupefied, then tears his hair in agony, and remembering the father's curse upon him, swoons.

ACT II. The duke enters an apartment of his palace much agitated. He found Gilda gone and the house deserted, and fancies that he truly loves her. Marullo, Ceprano, and the courtiers enter and tell him that they stole Rigoletto's mistress and have brought her to the palace. The duke rushes off to seek her. Rigoletto enters, concealing his great distress by an appearance of carelessness, that he may trace her. They watch him, but he sees no sign of her presence, and is about to go away when a page from the duchess inquires for the duke, and from the replies it is evident that he is within the palace, but cannot be seen. Rigoletto, his suspicions now confirmed, charges the courtiers with having taken a maiden from his house. They tell him to seek his mistress elsewhere. He exclaims that she is his daughter, and they fall back amazed. When, however, he rushes to the door of the inner chamber and seeks to open it, they bar his progress. In a fury of anger and despair he assails them, and in the name of a father defending the honor of his child he bids them restore her to him. He struggles with them until exhausted, then falls to pleading. At length she rushes into his arms, and he clasps her joyously until from her tears and broken words he learns her anguish. The courtiers leave the two together, and Gilda confesses how the young man followed her from church and how she came to love him, and then of their taking her from her home here to dishonor. Her father tries to comfort her, saying that they will go away together, then in a fury of rage vows vengeance. Monterone, under guard, passes through the corridor and, seeing the duke's portrait, says that his curse against him is vain, for still he lives in triumph. As the prisoner is led off Rigoletto replies that not in vain has the curse fallen, and that he himself will bring retribution upon the profligate. Gilda, who still loves the man, tries to temper her father's anger with thoughts of pardon as they go away together.

Act III. In a lonely spot by the River Mincio, outside the city of Mantua, stands a dilapidated inn, so nearly in ruins that what goes on within can be seen and heard from the outside. It is the lurking-place of Sparafucile, whose services Rigoletto has engaged, and who has, with the aid of his sister, Maddalena, lured the duke hither. Rigoletto and Gilda come along the road by the river, the girl telling her father that she still loves the man who in the guise of a student won her affection. Rigoletto intends to prove to her the man's faithlessness, and leading her to a place where the interior of the inn is visible, bids her watch. The duke enters the living-room of the inn dressed as a private soldier. Sparafucile gives him wine and calls his sister, a smiling lass in gypsy costume. Sparafucile then comes out, speaks with Rigoletto, and goes off. Within the tavern the duke is making love to Maddalena with flattering words and promises such as Gilda has before heard. When Gilda's faith in the man is quite destroyed, Rigoletto urges her to go home, take what gold is there, dress herself as a youth, and hasten on horseback to Verona, where he will meet her on the morrow. She begs him to go with her, but he will not, and she goes off alone.

Rigoletto confers with Sparafucile, pays him half the money he stipulates, and says that he will return at midnight and pay him the other half upon evidence that the duke is dead. A terrible storm comes up. Sparafucile enters the inn and interrupts the duke's advances to Maddalena. The duke, obliged by the storm to spend the night, retires to a room upstairs and is soon asleep. Sparafucile and his sister discuss the deed that is about to be done. Gilda, attired as a youth and with whip and spurs, comes in the darkness toward the house, and standing just outside, watches and listens, still desiring to save the duke's life, against which she fears her father plots. She hears Maddalena beg Sparafucile not to kill the man, who is so young and handsome and pleasing. Sparafucile commands her to mend the sack into which he plans to put the body. At length she suggests that he spare the man and yet obtain the money by killing the hunchback when he comes. Gilda, in great horror, hears Sparafucile object to such perfidy, saying that he always keeps his word with his employers; and then Maddalena vows that she will warn the duke. Sparafucile relents sufficiently to promise that if another man comes before midnight, he will kill him instead of the duke. They wait and the storm rages louder, while Gilda contemplates the sacrifice of her life for that of her base lover. At length when the hour approaches, she knocks at the door. As she enters Maddalena rushes forth, while Sparafucile, dagger in hand, closes the door behind his victim.

Rigoletto, wrapped in his cloak, comes along the road just as the clock strikes midnight. The storm has abated. Sparafucile comes from the inn dragging a sack, which he gives to Rigoletto in exchange for a purse, then withdraws. Rigoletto rejoices that his enemy is dead, and is dragging the sack toward the river when suddenly he hears the duke's voice singing as he leaves the inn by the rear door. Panic-stricken, Rigoletto tears open the sack, and by a lightning flash recognizes his daughter. He cannot believe his eyes, but frantically calls her name. She recovers consciousness and speaks to him, telling him that she has given her life for the man whom she loved too much. She begs her father's pardon and blessing, and says that by her mother's side in heaven she will pray for him. As she dies Rigoletto, wild with grief, acknowledges that the curse is upon him, and falls in a frenzy upon the body of his daughter.

DER RING DES NIBELUNGEN
(Der Rĭng dăss Nē-bā-lōōng'-ĕn)
(THE RING OF THE NIBELUNG)

"THE RING OF THE NIBELUNG" is "the vastest achievement in the history of opera."* The sources of the plots are to be found in the national epic of Germany, the "Nibelungenleid," derived from that division of the old Norse Sagas known as the Eddas. The work covered a long period of years of the composer's prime.

I. DAS RHEINGOLD
(Dahss Rine'-gold)
(THE RHINE-GOLD)

German heroic music-drama. Both music and book by Richard Wagner. First production, Munich, 1869. The scene is mythological Germany and the Upper and Nether Worlds during antiquity.

CHARACTERS

WOTAN	Gods (Æsir)	Baritone
DONNER		Baritone
FROH		Tenor
LOKI		Tenor
ALBERICH	Nibelungs (Gnomes)	Baritone
MIME		Tenor
FASOLT	Giants	Baritone
FAFNIR		Bass
FRICKA	Goddesses	Mezzo-Soprano
FREYA		Soprano
ERDA		Soprano
WOGLINDA	Nymphs of the Rhine	Soprano
WELLGUNDA		Soprano
FLOSSHILDA		Alto

Nibelungs.

*"The American History and Encyclopedia of Music," page 37, Vol. II of "Operas," W. L. Hubbard, Editor. (New York, 1908.)

© Aimé Dupont

DAVID BISPHAM
AS ALBERICH, IN "DAS RHEINGOLD"

SCENE 1. At the bottom of the River Rhine three nymphs are disporting themselves joyously when they espy Alberich, prince of the Nibelungs, a race of gnomes dwelling in the bowels of the earth, watching them. He accosts them, and charmed with their grace and beauty, makes love to them each in turn, but all spurn him. As they frolic about him the sun slowly rises, and piercing with its rays the waters, lights up the Rhine-gold, a wonderful treasure, which the three naiads are set to guard. Alberich asks about it, and the maidens tell him of its magic might, and that he who secures the golden treasure and makes from it a ring shall thereby secure measureless power, but that only he who forswears the sway and delights of love can fashion the ring. Alberich looks greedily at the glittering treasure. When flouted and rebuffed by each of the maidens, he angrily forswears love, and declaring that the treasure shall be his, springs to the rock on which it rests, climbs to the top, and seizes it. The nymphs dive after him in dismay, lamenting their folly and seeking to detain him. He has torn the gold from the rock and disappeared in the depths of Nibelheim below. Amid their cries of dismay as they swim about now in deep darkness is heard Alberich's mocking laughter.

SCENE 2. The scene gradually changes from the dark rocky depths of the river to the misty mountain heights above, where Wotan and Fricka lie sleeping side by side. The dawning light reveals at the top of a cliff on the other bank a castle with glittering pinnacles. When the gods awaken and see it, Wotan is delighted that the castle, which he has had the giants Fafnir and Fasolt build for him, pledging them that in return they should have the goddess Freya for their own, is now done. Freya is the fair goddess of the spring and of love, the one who tends the garden of the gods wherein grow the apples that, eaten day by day, give eternal youth. So Fricka reproaches Wotan for the bargain he has made, and in defense he says that he has no thought of keeping it.

Even as they speak Freya comes sadly seeking their help, for the giants, who, unslumbering, built the castle that they might win them a woman winsome and sweet, pursue her. Wotan anxiously awaits the coming of Loki, the spirit of cunning, who has pledged Wotan that Freya shall be ransomed when the wage is due. Fricka reproaches Wotan for trusting in one so deceptive, and he tries to parley with the giants; but they, to the terror of the goddesses, approach, well armed and threatening. Freya calls upon her brothers, Donner and Froh, to save her.

Fasolt tells of the toil and wage, and demands the goddess according to the contract. When Wotan asks them to name other recompense, they become very angry and charge him with being false to his word, and tell him that they desired the maiden for the sake of the golden apples of eternal youth that grow in her garden and that she alone knows how to secure. They threaten to take her away by force, and then the gods will lose strength and beauty, too. Wotan, impatient that Loki does not come, temporizes, but the giants press toward Freya to seize her. Donner and Froh come running in and menace the giants, and Wotan acknowledges his pledge.

At last Loki enters. Wotan rebukes him for being slow to mend the bargain he made, but Loki says he only vowed to do all he could, and so has done. All the gods and goddesses are very angry with him, but Wotan suspects him of some scheme and orders patience. Then Loki tells of his wanderings in search of a priceless treasure that would redeem the maid, but that he found nothing so rare as the true love that man bears for woman's worth. Yet he met with one, Alberich, the dwarf, who had forsworn love for gold and had stolen the Rhine-maidens' treasure. He brings to Wotan their prayer that the gold shall be returned to them again; but the father of gods is too burdened with his own trouble to think of theirs.

The giants, however, have been listening eagerly to the tale of the gold and now question Loki about it. He tells them of the magic ring by which he who can fashion it shall rule the world. Fricka desires the gold and coaxes Wotan to seek for it, but when Loki reminds them of the condition that the one who possesses it must swear to love no more, Wotan turns away. When Donner says that if Alberich has the ring they are all in his power, Wotan vows to seize it. Meanwhile the giants have conferred together, and, although Fasolt is reluctant, yet Fafnir makes the proposal to Wotan that he get for them the Nibelung gold and they will give up their claim upon Freya. Wotan at first says it is not possible for him to get the gold, so the giants seize Freya as hostage, giving Wotan until nightfall to decide.

As Freya is borne away a pale mist comes over the scene and the gods become aged and withered. Alarmed at the change, they stand around looking expectantly at Wotan, who meditates with his eyes upon the ground. All feel the aging, weakening process, and Loki tells them that it is because Freya is no more there to give them the apples from her garden, and that the giants knew that with Freya gone the gods could not long withstand them. Wotan starts up and calls to Loki to go with him to Nibelheim to obtain the gold as a ransom. Bidding the gods await his return, he and Loki disappear down a cleft in the rocks, from which sulphurous vapors rise. Soon ruddy gleams break forth and there is a sound of anvils. As the hammering ceases they enter a deep cave, into which open narrow clefts or shafts, leading to other parts of Nibelheim.

SCENE 3. Alberich, who since he came into possession of the Rhine-gold and fashioned the ring, has been a hard taskmaster over the Nibelungs, enters, dragging the shrieking Mime with him. In answer to his threats Mime, amid wails, tells him that he has forged for him the helmet he wished. Alberich charges Mime with desiring to keep the Tarnhelm for himself, as it has the power to make its wearer invisible. Alberich puts it on his head to test it, and immediately becomes invisible, disappearing in a column of vapor. Mime still feels the unseen blows showered upon him, and Alberich calls to the gnomes that he is now their master and they must all work his will. Alberich's voice is heard in the distance and the column of vapor disappears just as Wotan and Loki enter through a shaft and find Mime still crouching in a corner and groaning. They raise him up and he tells them of his brother's hard-heartedness, and how all the Nibelungs have fallen into his clutches and been made the slaves of his will since he forged the magic ring. Mime tells how he himself forged the Tarnhelm, but before he had learned its magic power Alberich took it from him.

Mime runs about in terror as Alberich's voice is heard, and he enters. He has removed the Tarnhelm and hung it at his girdle, and now drives before him a crowd of Nibelungs laden with the golden treasure, which he bids them pile in one place. He is lashing them mercilessly when he sees Wotan and Loki. He drives Mime and the whole crowd off into the shafts to the tasks he has set them, then gazing at the gods suspiciously, accosts them. Wotan replies that they have heard strange tidings of the wonders worked by him and have come to be his guests. Alberich says that envy brought them, but Loki reminds him how much he is indebted to him, the god of fire. Alberich, mistrustful though flattered, displays his wealth, saying that it grows daily and that soon he will rule the whole world. Wotan becomes angry at his defiance, but Loki restrains the father of the gods, and telling Alberich that they saw the power he exercises over the Nibelungs by means of the ring, asks what would happen if it were stolen.

Alberich then boasts of the Tarnhelm, which can change him at will into any form he pleases or make him invisible to all eyes, so that he need fear the power of no one, even the crafty Loki. The fire-god is doubting, but Alberich proves the Tarnhelm's power by putting it on and immediately becoming a huge serpent, rearing himself up and opening his jaws at Wotan and Loki. The latter feigns great fear and Alberich resumes his own shape, laughing at his terror. Loki is very deferential to such power, but still incredulous, asks if he can assume a small as well as a large form. Alberich again dons the Tarnhelm and vanishes from sight, but a tiny toad is crawling over the rocks. Loki orders Wotan to put his foot on the toad as he seizes the Tarnhelm. Alberich in his own shape becomes visible, writhing under Wotan's foot. They bind him firmly and drag him to the shaft down which they came, and pulling him along with them, begin to ascend, hearing as they pass the sounds of the anvils and the forges.

SCENE 4. Wotan and Loki drag Alberich up a mountain height shrouded in mist. Loki taunts the captive, who bitterly complains and threatens. Wotan tells him that he must pay a price for his freedom. When they demand his hoard of gold, he is content if he may keep the ring. He asks to be freed, but Wotan will not permit it until the ransom is wholly paid, so he stands by ignominiously captive while his slaves bring the gold up the shaft and pile it high. When the Nibelungs, having finished their task, disappear, Alberich asks the gods to let him depart with the Tarnhelm. Loki claims it, however, and throws it upon the pile of gold. When Wotan demands the ring, Alberich pleads abjectly that he may keep it and tells of the terrible oath by which he won the power to make it. Then, seeing Wotan proudly putting the ring upon his own finger, the Nibelung utters a curse upon the ring, saying that no more shall wealth come at its call, but that care and fear and death shall be the portion of every one who holds it until he himself again possess it. Then, laughing, he vanishes into the cleft.

As the mist over the scene rises the gods Froh and Donner appear, and Fricka also, while Loki announces that Fasolt and Fafnir approach, followed by Freya. When the latter comes a gentle breeze begins to blow, lifting the veil of mist, and the gods are restored to their former aspect of youth and strength. Fasolt forbids Freya to join the gods, and declares that they have kept her free from harm and will according to their word accept a ransom for her. Wotan replies that the hoard of gold awaits them. Fasolt is reluctant to part with her, but bids them pile the gold high enough to hide the goddess from their sight.

So Loki and Froh hastily pile the gold, and Fafnir greedily bids them fill in all the chinks. When the pile is high, he says that he still sees Freya's hair, and orders them to put the Tarnhelm upon the heap. Reluctantly they have obeyed, when Fasolt, pining that he must lose one so beautiful, says that he can still see the gleam of her eyes and that he cannot part with her while so beholding her. The gods tell them that all the gold has been piled up, but Fafnir demands the ring that is upon Wotan's finger.

Angrily Wotan protests that he will part with it to no one. Then Fasolt exultantly starts to carry off the maid, and all the gods beseech Wotan, who is still obdurate. As he turns away in wrath darkness comes over the scene, and from a rocky cleft breaks a bluish light, in which the goddess Erda suddenly appears rising to half her height. She stretches out her hand toward Wotan, and in warning tones tells him that the ring and the gold bring only hopeless woe. Wotan demands her name, and she says that she is Erda, the world's wise one, who knows all that is and that shall be, and who now predicts that a gloomy day dawns for the gods. Wotan, anxious to know more, would follow Erda as she disappears, but Froh and Fricka hold him back. He meditates within himself for a time. Donner stays the giants, telling them that Wotan will give them the ring, and Freya wonders if she is worth the price. At last Wotan arouses himself from deep thought, orders Freya to return to her place among them, for she is now free, and gives up the ring to the giants.

Each of the gods in turn embrace Freya with great delight. Fafnir spreads a huge sack in which to pack the gold, but Fasolt interferes, claiming that he is taking the larger half. They quarrel and Fasolt seizes the ring, but Fafnir strikes him dead with his staff and wrests the ring from his hand, while the gods stand appalled at this speedy fulfillment of Alberich's curse. Wotan, weighed down with sorrow and foreboding, determines to seek wisdom of Erda, but Fricka reminds him of his new-bought castle. Donner with thunder and lightning clears the mists away and the castle walls spring into view. As the clouds disperse he and Froh together build a rainbow bridge over the river to the castle, now bright with the gleams of the setting sun. Wotan and the other gods are astonished at the glorious sight, and he turns to Fricka and bids her come with him to Valhalla. She asks the meaning of the name, but he tells her only that if the castle fulfill his desire, then shall the meaning be clear. The gods go over the rainbow bridge, Loki last of all and brooding over his future and theirs. As the gods pass, from below in the waters of the Rhine are heard the laments of the Rhine-maidens, who still mourn the loss of their treasure and pray Wotan to restore it to them.

II. DIE WALKÜRE

(*Dēē Vahl-kuer'-rĕ*)

(THE VALKYRIE)

German heroic music-drama. Both music and book by Richard Wagner. First production, Munich, 1870. The scene is laid in the forests of Germany during antiquity.

CHARACTERS

SIEGMUND	*Tenor*
HUNDING	*Bass*
WOTAN	*Baritone*
SIEGLINDA	*Soprano*
BRÜNNHILDE	*Soprano*
FRICKA	*Soprano*

The Valkyries—Gerhilda, Ortlinda, Valtrauta, Sverleita, Helmviga, Siegruna, Grimgerda, Rossvisa.

The ring of the Nibelungs is now in the possession of the giant Fafnir, who in the form of a dragon guards it and the hoard of gold within his cave. Wotan, troubled by the dark prophecy of Erda, woos her, and she bears him nine strong and beautiful daughters, the Valkyries. Theirs it is to brood over battlefields when Wotan stirs up strife among mortals, theirs to bear the noblest and mightiest of the fallen heroes to Valhalla, where, revived, they live in fellowship

© Aimé Dupont

LILLIAN NORDICA
AS BRÜNNHILDE, IN "DIE WALKÜRE"

with the gods, that they may fight valiantly in their defense in the day of doom. Lest, however, Alberich and his unloved breed should again obtain the ring, Wotan, wandering on earth as Volsung, has begotten of a mortal a twin son and daughter, Siegmund and Sieglinda, from whom shall rise a mighty hero, who shall restore to the Rhine-maidens the fateful ring.

Act I. Into a woodland lodge built around an ash-tree comes Siegmund, hunted and exhausted, and finding the room empty, sinks down upon the hearth. Sieglinda, the wife of the owner, Hunding the Neiding, comes from an inner room and, though at first alarmed, bends over the prostrate man anxiously. She gives him drink, which he eagerly accepts, looking searchingly at her. She bids him welcome, and when he tells her that he is wounded and weaponless, she is very compassionate and would serve him. His wound heals at the sight of her and, refreshed, he starts to go, reluctant to bring upon her the misfortune ever present with him. She bids him stay, saying that where ill luck so long has been he can bring no worse, and she tells him that she was stolen from her home by Hunding and later forced to marry him. Thus prevailed upon, he awaits Hunding's return, and the two, conversing, gaze at each other with increasing emotion.

Soon Hunding comes and gives grudging welcome, saying that his hearth is holy and the stranger will there find a haven. As they eat together Hunding notices the resemblance between his wife's features and those of the stranger, and questions him. Siegmund replies that his name is Woeful, that his father was Wolfing, the Volsung, and that one day when they two returned from the hunt they found their home in ashes, his mother slain, and his twin sister gone,—

all the lawless work of the Neidings. Thereafter he and his father dwelt in the forest, until one day his father vanished, and since then he has wandered alone, pursued by disaster and strife. Sieglinda hangs eagerly upon the words of Woeful and further questions him, while at the word "Neidings" Hunding's brow grows dark. Siegmund tells how but now he has come from a fray in defense of a maiden whom heartless brothers were forcing to marry a man she did not love, and whom he left only when she was dead and he wounded and weaponless. Hunding rises in wrath, declaring that he is a Neiding, mortal enemy to Woeful, who for the night shall be safe, but in the morning must fight him and die. Sieglinda is alarmed at his words, but mixes for him his evening drink and retires, while Hunding, repeating his dire threat, follows her.

As Siegmund broods over his plight he remembers that his father promised that when in great need, he should find a sword. He thinks, too, of Sieglinda, held here in bondage, to whom his heart has already gone out in love and longing. Soon Sieglinda comes and bids him hasten away while Hunding, whose drink she drugged, sleeps. She tells him how, at her wedding, a mighty man in tattered garments, with hat worn low over a missing eye, came and stuck a sword into the ash-tree's trunk, saying that it should be only his who could draw it forth; that many tried, but none succeeded; and that now her hero and deliverer, whose name she long has known, has come and will take the sword. Enraptured with the deep love they feel each for the other, they trace the likeness of their features and realize that they are twin brother and sister, destined to be, in the fashion of primitive races, bridegroom and bride. He says that the stranger was Volsung, their father, and she declares that his name is, then, Siegmund. Exultant, he springs up, and with great exertion draws the sword, "Needful," from the ash-tree, and claims her as his wife.

Act II. In a wild and rocky pass stand Wotan and Brünnhilde, the Valkyrie, both in full armor. He bids her aid Siegmund in his fight with Hunding. Promptly she goes, springing from rock to rock up the height, and disappears, calling back that Fricka, his goddess-wife, approaches in wrath. Wildly speeding, Fricka comes in her ram-driven car. She, as the preserver of the home, has heard Hunding's prayer, and bids Wotan punish the guilty wife and her lover. Wotan would defend them, but Fricka reminds him of his own unfaithfulness to her, and demands that he take back the sword he gave Siegmund. Neither arguments nor warnings of the disaster that awaits the gods can move her, and Wotan, sore distressed, finally promises to withdraw his aid from his hero-son. When Fricka goes, calling to Brünnhilde to return, he countermands his decree. Long they talk together, she trying to comfort him in his great sorrow, and he revealing to her the plight of the gods should no mortal restore the ring to its owners. She sees how simply thwarted is his long-cherished hope, and is eager to do his heart's will; but at the thought of her rebelling against his spoken command he threatens her, and wrathfully declaring that Siegmund shall fall, departs. She turns sadly away as Siegmund and Sieglinda approach.

Sieglinda, joyful in being the loved bride of one whom she loves, is yet remorseful over her broken vows, and when she hears Hunding's horncall, she starts from Siegmund's embrace and, delirious with fear, foresees the fight and its disastrous outcome, and falls fainting in her lover's arms. He is bending anxiously over her when Brünnhilde appears before him. She tells him that he is to die. Calmly he questions her, fearless and unbelieving, and defiantly boasting the prowess of his father's sword. Pitying, she tells him its magic is fled, and promises to care for his wife for the sake of the child that will be born. Then Siegmund, convinced and despairing, would in love despatch the mother, but Brünnhilde, mastered by compassion, stays his hand, and declaring her defiance of Wotan's decree, pledges Siegmund her protection in battle, and goes away.

While Sieglinda still sleeps Siegmund, hearing again Hunding's horn, tenderly kisses her farewell and goes to the mountain top, and mid thunder and lightning meets his foe. Sieglinda, awakened, rushes forward to separate the combatants, but blinded by the lightning, staggers back helpless. Brünnhilde soars over Siegmund and protects him with her sword. Suddenly Wotan appears and holds his spear defensively before Hunding. Brünnhilde draws back in despair, and Siegmund's sword breaks on Wotan's spear. Hunding thrusts Siegmund through the breast and he dies. Brünnhilde hastens to Sieglinda, lifts her on her horse, and disappears with her. Wotan bids Hunding tell Fricka that her husband has avenged her slight, but at his contemptuous gesture Hunding falls dead. Wotan starts up in wrath against Brünnhilde, who has dared to have other will than his, and disappears in the forest.

ACT III. On a rocky mountain peak assemble the Valkyries, each with a slain warrior upon the pommel of her saddle. Brünnhilde comes last of all, and bearing Sieglinda. She tells them that Wotan pursues her in great anger, and asks that they hide her in their midst. Sieglinda, aroused from her daze, reproaches Brünnhilde for saving her, but Brünnhilde bids her live that she may bear a son, the world's greatest hero. Enraptured, the woman prays the maidens to save her child, and as Wotan draws near in thundering clouds Brünnhilde commands her to flee to the forest at the east, where Fafnir guards his gold and where only will she be safe from Wotan's wrath. She gives Sieglinda the fragments of Siegmund's sword, which the child, Siegfried, shall forge anew, and Sieglinda hastens away.

In terrible tempest Wotan arrives and demands Brünnhilde, threatening the Valkyries when they seek to protect and justify her. With firm step, but humbly, Brünnhilde comes forward and faces him, asking her sentence. Great is Wotan's grief, for she, his favorite daughter, knew his heart; but he tells her that her doom is fixed by her deed, that no more a Valkyrie will she ride in battle, no more serve in Valhalla's hall. On this mountain top in unbroken sleep shall she lie, and she shall be given to the man who shall awaken her. The Valkyries raise loud laments and on their knees pray that their sister may be spared the shame of bending to the will of man. Their prayers avail naught, and the All-father dismisses them wrathfully.

Brünnhilde, prostrated at Wotan's feet, asks if her deed was so shameful that shame should henceforth be her lot, and for him to make clear the guilt she cannot own. Long they talk together, she appealing to his own heart's love for Siegmund and he reminding her of his vow to Fricka and of the obedience that was her one duty as a wish-maiden. Sadly he tells her that their companionship is now ended forever, that henceforth they are strangers. At length one last prayer she makes—that while she sleeps hindering terrors may be cast about her, so that only a man of the bravest heart will dare approach and awaken her. Wotan, deeply moved and sorely grieving, raises her to her feet, grants her request, then gazes long into her eyes, and embracing her tenderly, kisses her, with the kiss taking away her godhood.

Her powers gently leave her, and she sinks in his arms. He lays her upon a mossy mound beneath a wide-spreading tree, and after a long look upon her, closes her helmet, lays upon her her shield, which completely covers her body, and slowly turns away. Waving his spear, he commands Loki, the fire-god, to encircle the rock with his flames. Fire springs up and surrounds the peak. Wotan, again stretching forth his spear, weaves a spell that whoso fears the spear of Wotan shall never enter the circle of flame, and passing through the fire, slowly departs.

III. SIEGFRIED
(Zēkh'-frēt)

German heroic music-drama. Both music and book by Richard Wagner. First production, Bayreuth, 1876. The scene is laid in the forests of Germany during antiquity.

CHARACTERS

SIEGFRIED	Tenor
MIME	Tenor
THE WANDERER (Wotan)	Bass
ALBERICH	Bass
FAFNIR	Bass
ERDA	Contralto
BRÜNNHILDE	Soprano

Sieglinda wandered far within the forest, and there Mime, the Nibelung, half-brother to Alberich, came upon her, sick and wearied, and took her to his cavern. She gave birth to a son, the promised Siegfried, and died. Mime has reared the lad, keeping him ignorant of his parentage, and purposes that when he is grown he shall kill the dragon, Fafnir, and thus obtain for him the hoard of gold, the Tarnhelm, and the ring,—the triple treasure that gives world-power.

Act I. Within his sooty cavern, with its large hearth, its anvil, and its tools, Mime hammers upon a sword for Siegfried, discouraged because every sword he fashions the stalwart youth breaks. Siegfried enters, clad in a wild beast's skin and with a silver horn hanging from his shoulder. He is leading a bear, which he mischievously drives toward Mime, who takes refuge behind the forge. After releasing the bear into the woods he takes the sword on which Mime has been working, and with one blow shatters it upon the anvil. Angrily he berates the cowering smith for his lack of skill, and flings himself upon a stone seat. Mime whines of his ingratitude for all the years of shelter and labor, for toys and teaching, and when Siegfried spurns the food he brings him, bursts into sobbing. The youth looks at the cringing dwarf and acknowledges that from him he has learned much, but that he feels only loathing of his presence, and wonders why he ever returns to the smith, when he finds so much more agreeable companions in the forest. With evil cunning Mime tries to make Siegfried believe that it is true affection for him, his father, that bids him return, but Siegfried indignantly repudiates the possibility of Mime's being his father. The beasts and the birds resemble their parents, he argues, and his own face and form as he sees himself in the brook are very different from those of the dwarf. The youth asks Mime for knowledge of his parents, seizing him by the throat and threatening him until he is willing to speak. Then Mime acknowledges that he is none of his kin, that Siegfried's father was slain, and that Sieglinda, his mother, died in giving him birth. When Siegfried demands proof of his words, Mime brings the fragments of his father's sword, "Needful," whereupon Siegfried commands him to weld them together speedily. Siegfried goes off into the forest and Mime sits down on a bench in despair, well knowing that no dwarf can weld the hero's sword.

The Wanderer enters, wrapped in a dark mantle and with broad-brimmed hat down over his missing eye. Mime, frightened, gives grudging welcome, but the Wanderer pledges his head as pawn in a war of wit and tells the smith to ask any three questions and they will be answered. Mime asks first about the Nibelungs, then about the giants, and finally about the gods and their king, Wotan. The Wanderer answers each with explicit knowledge, then in turn asks three, Mime's head now as pawn. First Mime tells him of the Volsungs, then of the sword of Siegmund, which Siegfried must wield if he would kill Fafnir. Rebukingly the Wanderer reveals to the dwarf his evil plan for seizing the gold when Siegfried shall have conquered the dragon, then asks the final question,—By whom shall the victorious sword be welded? Mime, terror-stricken at the hopeless task and Siegfried's certain anger, acknowledges that he has no skill of his own to do it, nor knows who has. The Wanderer says that only he who fear never felt will be able to fashion "Needful" anew, and goes away prophesying that Mime's head, now forfeit, shall fall to the same fearless one.

Mime sinks down behind the anvil trembling. Soon Siegfried enters, and the dwarf, believing that his one hope is in making the young man know fear, describes to him what fear is and how it affects one. Siegfried is interested in the novel experience, and Mime promises to lead him to Fafnir, who will teach him fear. When Siegfried demands his father's sword, Mime says that he could by no means weld it, that only could one who knew not fear; so Siegfried prepares to weld the blade himself. Meanwhile Mime, realizing that whatever the outcome of Siegfried's encounter with Fafnir, he himself will lose either the hoard or his head, brews a drink to offer Siegfried when the dragon is disposed of, that will put him to sleep so that the dwarf may kill him. Skilfully Siegfried works upon the fragments and at length hammers the metal into shape. While the crafty dwarf pictures the triumph which the possession of the ring will give him, Siegfried puts the finished blade into its socket, swings it triumphantly, and smites the anvil, which is split from top to bottom and falls asunder with a great clatter. Mime falls to the ground helpless from terror.

ACT II. In the depths of the forest near the cave of Fafnir Alberich is watching when he sees the Wanderer near, and recoils in dread. Recovering his courage, he taunts the god with his former treachery and threatens him with the curse of the ring. The Wanderer, however, disclaims all desire for the ring, and in proof calls, arousing Fafnir. Alberich tells the dragon of the approaching danger, hoping thereby to gain the ring as reward for his warning; but the dragon cares not, and Wotan, leaving, tells Alberich that he need fear only Mime, for Siegfried knows not of the treasure.

Alberich hides as Siegfried and Mime come, the latter trying to frighten the young man with descriptions of the dragon's terrors. Mime hides for safety and Siegfried seats himself under a tree until the dragon shall come forth. He is meditating upon his mother, and listening to the songs of the birds, which he wishes he understood. He blows his horn and the dragon rushes out. Undaunted by the creature's terrifying roar and fierceness, Siegfried cleverly evades his coils, and after a fierce fight buries his sword in the dragon's heart. A few drops of the dragon's blood spurt stingingly upon his hand and he carries it to his mouth. Suddenly he finds that he understands the songs of the birds. Listening, he hears one telling him of the treasure within the cave, of the Tarnhelm and the ring. He enters, and while within Alberich and Mime come from their hiding-places, each seeking the treasure. Greedily they quarrel for the possession of it, but both again hide as Siegfried reappears with Tarnhelm and ring. He hears again the bird's song, and it tells him of the treachery Mime plans against him. The dwarf comes with his brew, which he offers Siegfried, exulting that the hoard is so nearly gained. Siegfried, when the dwarf has persistently urged the drink upon him, realizes the plot, and with one blow strikes him dead, then throws his body into the cave and closes the entrance with the body of the dragon. He lingers under the linden-tree, listening again to the bird. Now the song is one of triumph and promised reward. He learns that a bride awaits him, Brünnhilde, the Valkyrie, sleeping on a fire-encircled mountain peak, and may be won by him who knows no fear. Siegfried springs up and follows the bird's flight.

Act III. To a wild and rocky region at the foot of the mountain the Wanderer comes, and there calls upon Erda to tell him of the future. Wearily she rises out of her long sleep, and to his eager questions has little of prophecy, but refers him to the Norns. The Wanderer, knowing of the day of doom for the gods that she has already foretold, would learn how to delay its dawn. She tells him to ask Brünnhilde. With a final word of startling revelation Erda sinks back into the ground, and Wotan, having learned that the heroic Volsung has won the Nibelung's ring and is now on his way to the circle of flame, awaits his coming. Siegfried approaches, following the bird, which has but now escaped his vision. Wotan challenges him and Siegfried, defiant, will brook no delay. He catches sight of the fire-encircled peak above him and starts forward, determined. The Wanderer bars the way, presenting his spear and saying in warning that once before has "Needful" been broken upon it. Siegfried then knows that his father's slayer stands before him, and, undaunted, eagerly strikes with his sword. The spear falls shattered. Wotan, thus made aware that his power is ended, calmly picks up the fragments and goes away, back to Valhalla, where he tells the gods that their day is over, and bids the heroes hew down the world-ash.

Siegfried springs up the sheer and dangerous cliff, blowing his horn gaily, and, unterrified, passes through the flames into the circle. There under a tree lies a figure in armor. He removes the helmet and shield, and entranced at the sight of the beautiful maiden before him, kisses her fervently upon the lips. She awakens and beholds him with delight. Long and gently he woos her, for the first time experiencing through his awe and tender reverence the emotion of fear. He overcomes her maidenly alarm, and at last makes her willing for love of him forever to leave the deathless state and the bliss of Valhalla and share with him a mortal's lot, facing a mortal's death.

IV. GÖTTERDÄMMERUNG

(*Goet-ter-daem'-mer-ungk*)
(THE TWILIGHT OF THE GODS)

German heroic music-drama. Both music and book by Richard Wagner. First production, Bayreuth, 1876. The scene is laid in the forests of Germany during antiquity.

CHARACTERS

SIEGFRIED	Tenor
GUNTHER	Baritone
ALBERICH	Baritone
HAGEN	Bass
BRÜNNHILDE	Soprano
GUTRUNE	Soprano
VALTRAUTA	Mezzo-Soprano
WOGLINDA ⎫	Soprano
WELLGUNDA ⎬ Nymphs of the Rhine	Mezzo-Soprano
FLOSSHILDA ⎭	Contralto
FIRST NORN	Alto
SECOND NORN	Mezzo-Soprano
THIRD NORN	Soprano

Vassals (tenors and basses) and women (sopranos).

PRELUDE. Upon the rocky mountain top near the Valkyrie's rock through the night the three Norns sit twisting their rope of fate and singing of the past, the present, and the future. They tell how once they sat beneath the great world-ash, near the limpid well of wisdom, for a daily draft of which Wotan sacrificed an eye; how Wotan had fashioned his unconquerable spear from a limb of the ash, which thereafter died; and also how the All-father came home bringing the spear in fragments and bade the gods cut down the ash-tree and pile it like fuel about Valhalla, within whose hall he now sits upon his throne in silence, with all the gods about him, waiting the end of his rule. Suddenly their rope breaks, and as dawn dims the light of the flames the Norns slowly disappear in the ground, seeking Erda, their mother.

With daybreak Siegfried and Brünnhilde come out of the cave where they have made their home. He, clad in armor and with sword and shield, starts out upon the quest of fresh exploits. Brünnhilde leads to him her horse for his journey, and courageously sends him forth to his hero's task, yearningly bidding him not to forget her, as she waits his return within the circle of flame. With great love Siegfried pledges

© Aimé Dupont

EDOUARD de RESZKE
AS HAGEN, IN "GÖTTERDÄMMERUNG"

her his devotion, giving her the Nibelung's ring as seal of their troth, and bids her farewell. She watches him out of sight, listening to the notes of his hunting-horn as he goes down the mountain.

Act I. Within the hall of Gunther the Gibichung's ancestral castle on the Rhine, Gunther and his sister Gutrune sit talking with Hagen, their half-brother. Hagen is the son of their mother, Grimhilde, and Alberich, the Nibelung, and from his father knows the story of the ring, which is in Brünnhilde's possession, and that Siegfried is now approaching the castle. Filled with treacherous designs to restore the ring to his father, Hagen plots to obtain it, and to that end suggests to Gunther that it is his duty to his house to marry. He tells him of the peerless Brünnhilde, but Gunther is daunted by the wall of flame that surrounds her. Hagen tells them that Siegfried, the hero who alone can pass the barrier, is coming, and they plot to win his assistance. At Hagen's suggestion Gutrune agrees to win Siegfried by giving him a potion that will blot out all memory of Brünnhilde and center his love in herself.

Siegfried's horn is heard and he approaches by boat with Brünnhilde's horse, Grane. Gunther and Hagen go to the landing to welcome him. They greet him as a friend and conduct him to the hall. Siegfried wonders that they call him by name, and Hagen says that the Tarnhelm, which hangs at his belt, is sign enough. He tells Siegfried that the magical helmet bestows a change of form or invisibility upon its wearer, and asks him about the hoard and the ring. Siegfried replies frankly that the hoard remains within the cave, guarded by the dragon's body, and that a woman wears the ring.

Gutrune offers the guest a horn of wine, and Siegfried,

in his heart drinking to Brünnhilde, drains a draft that deprives him of all memory of her. Looking upon Gutrune, he finds her very beautiful and desires her for wife. He asks Gunther if he has a wife, and at Hagen's suggestion Gunther tells Siegfried that there is one whom he would marry, but that she is surrounded by flames which he dare not attempt to pass. His words much impress Siegfried, but why he cannot remember. He offers to pass the circle of flame and win the maiden as Gunther by the aid of the Tarnhelm, if he may himself have Gutrune to wed. The two men then solemnly swear blood-brotherhood, and set out together for the rock of the Valkyrie. Hagen is left in charge of the castle, and gloatingly plans how to obtain possession of the ring and avenge its theft from his father.

Upon the mountain summit Brünnhilde longingly awaits her husband's return. Her sister, Valtrauta, appears before her and tells her how Wotan that day, as he sat on his throne among the gods, who now no more eat of the apples of youth, remembered Brünnhilde, and murmured that if she but gave back the ring to the Rhine-maidens, gods and the world would be made free of its curse. Brünnhilde cries out in alarm, and tells Valtrauta that the ring is the pledge of Siegfried's love and that with it she will never part, though Valhalla fall. Valtrauta has gone away with Brünnhilde's message of defiance, when suddenly a horn is heard and Brünnhilde starts up in great joy, thinking that Siegfried has returned. She sees, however, a stranger, a dark man, far different from Siegfried, who, nevertheless, steps through the flames and approaches her. With the voice of Gunther he claims Brünnhilde as his bride, for he has made way through the fire. Brünnhilde, horrified, resists him and holds up the ring as guard. Then Siegfried, in the form of another, wrests from his own loved wife the ring and commands her to enter the cave. Drawing his sword to lay between them as symbol of his loyalty to Gunther, he follows her.

Act II. Hagen as he guards the hall of the Gibichungs is in his sleep visited by Alberich, who urges him to desperate endeavor to seize the ring, whose power Siegfried does not know. Hagen promises to accomplish it and awakens just as Siegfried returns, the ring upon his finger, and announces the success of his quest and that Gunther, with Brünnhilde, follows him. Gutrune comes to meet Siegfried, who claims her as his bride, and they repair to the hall. The vassals are summoned and soon Gunther and Brünnhilde arrive by boat and are given a royal welcome. Siegfried and Gutrune come to meet them. Brünnhilde, pale and downcast, looks not up until Siegfried's name is mentioned, then with a joyous cry she recognizes him and rushes toward him, but he looks upon her as upon a stranger. To her questions he replies that he is to marry Gutrune, as she Gunther, and when she almost swoons with dismay he places her in the care of her promised husband. She sees her ring upon his finger, and turning to Gunther, asks what he did with the ring he took from her. He is confused and then she realizes what has been done, and declares that Siegfried is her husband.

Gunther, alarmed, thinks that Siegfried has not respected his oath to protect Brünnhilde as a brother's bride, but Siegfried takes his oath, swearing upon the point of Hagen's spear that the accusation is false. Brünnhilde also takes her oath in the same manner, upon the same spear, that Siegfried alone is her husband. However, the preparations for the double wedding continue, and Siegfried, Gutrune, and the vassals return to the hall, while Gunther and Hagen are left alone with Brünnhilde, who is beside herself with grief.

Hagen offers to avenge her wrong by slaying Siegfried, but Brünnhilde contemptuously declares that to be impossible, for she herself has made him invulnerable, all but his back, which would never be exposed to the foe. Gunther, convinced that Siegfried has betrayed his trust, plots with Hagen and the despairing Brünnhilde to slay the hero on the morrow, making the deed appear like a hunting accident to the then-widowed Gutrune.

Act III. To a wild valley on the banks of the Rhine Siegfried has wandered in his search for the quarry. The three Rhine-maidens rise to the surface of the water and beg him to restore to them their ring. He refuses and they seek by wiles and warnings to make him give it up, at last telling him that he is to die that very day. He who knows no fear laughs to scorn their prophecy, though not blind to their beauty. When they have disappeared Gunther, Hagen, and the hunting party come and find a place in the valley to take their refreshment. Hagen asks Siegfried the story of his life and the fearless hero relates it. When he has told of the songs of the birds and the finding of the Tarnhelm and the ring, he drinks from a horn into which Hagen has put an antidote for the draft of forgetfulness that Gutrune had given him. Then, unsuspecting, he relates how first he passed through the fire and found and awoke Brünnhilde, wooing and winning her. All are amazed, and Hagen, who has stolen up behind him, plunges a spear into his heart. Siegfried, thinking only of Brünnhilde, sees a vision of her beckoning to him, and with her name on his lips, dies, while Gunther remorsefully bends over him. The hunters place his body upon a shield and bear it back to the hall.

Into the hall of the Gibichungs comes Gutrune from her chamber at nightfall, eagerly awaiting the return of the hunters. Hagen enters and tells her that her husband has been slain by a wild boar. The vassals follow him and lay the body upon a bier in the center of the hall. Hagen claims Siegfried's ring as his right, but Gunther declares that it should belong to Gutrune. They draw their swords and in the fight Gunther is killed. When Hagen approaches the corpse to take the ring, the hand of the lifeless body is raised threateningly, and all start back in horror.

Brünnhilde enters and approaches the bier, bending over the body of her husband in grief and tenderness, her anger gone. She takes unhindered the ring from his finger and puts it once again upon her own hand. Then she bids the vassals build a huge funeral pyre upon the river-bank. She declares her purpose of perishing in the flames with him, and bids the Rhine-maidens come and from the ashes take the ring, thus purged evermore of its curse. With her own hand she applies the torch to the pyre, and springing upon her horse, Grane, she dashes into the midst of the flames, which rise high about her. They die out at length, and the river rises up and overflows its banks, dashing its waves where glowed the fire. The Rhine-maidens swim up and get the ring, and Hagen, rushing in to seize it first, is drawn by them under the flood to his death. The black ravens of Wotan fly from encircling the pyre to carry the news to Valhalla, which, now aflame, glows in the sky, while the gods are seen sitting calmly within, awaiting their long-predicted doom.

ROMEO AND JULIET

(ROMÉO ET JULIETTE)

FRENCH tragic grand opera, founded on Shakespeare's drama of the same name. Music by Charles François Gounod. Book by Jules Barbier and Michel Carré. First production, Paris, 1867. The scene is Verona, Italy, in the fourteenth century.

CHARACTERS

THE DUKE OF VERONA	Bass
CAPULET, a Veronese noble	Bass
TYBALT, nephew to Capulet	Tenor
GREGORIO } kinsmen to Capulet	Baritone
PARIS	Baritone
ROMEO, son and heir of Montague, a Veronese noble	Tenor
MERCUTIO } friends of Romeo	Baritone
BENVOLIO	Tenor
FRIAR LAURENCE	Bass
STEPHANO, page to Romeo	Soprano
JULIET, daughter of Capulet	Soprano
GERTRUDE, nurse to Juliet	Mezzo-Soprano

Ladies and nobles of Verona, citizens, soldiers, monks, and pages.

A bitter enmity has long existed between the Veronese houses of Capulet and Montague, which has given rise to so much strife that the Duke of Verona has decreed that the next person who shall break the peace in defense of either side shall be banished.

ACT I. Within the ballroom of Capulet's house a gay masked ball is going on, at which Juliet, the young daughter and heiress of the host, is being introduced into society. As the guests go to the banquet hall Juliet lingers behind a moment and, still moving in the steps of the waltz, sings

© Aimé Dupont

EMMA EAMES
AS JULIET, IN "ROMEO AND JULIET"

in girlish enthusiasm of her delight in the evening's enjoyment. Romeo, who has ventured masked into the house of his hereditary enemy, enters, and watching her, is much attracted by her gracefulness and beauty. He approaches and would detain her. She is nothing loath, and as they talk each feels a strong attraction to the other. Sudden and fervent love springs up between them, and Romeo, taking her hand, begs of her a kiss, which, after slight protests from her, he takes. As they linger Tybalt, a hot-headed and impetuous supporter of his kinsman, Capulet, comes in and recognizes Romeo. He denounces him as an enemy and would kill him for thus treacherously intruding where he knew he was not welcome. Juliet stands by, dismayed that the man whose aspect and manners she found so pleasing is separated from her by a mortal enmity. Only Capulet's entrance with his guests, and his adherence to the laws of hospitality, prevent Tybalt from carrying out his threat. Capulet orders the dancing to go on, and Romeo reluctantly takes his departure.

Act II. Over a high wall and into the garden of Capulet that night steals Romeo, unable to tear himself from his love's presence. He hides where he can watch the windows of her apartments, and at length she comes out upon the balcony, and there alone in the silence meditates upon the young man who has enchained her fancy. She loves him—all but his name, which she would have him refuse, denying his father, or else, if he but plight his troth to her, she will no longer be a Capulet. Romeo speaks to her, and she is at first alarmed, then recognizes his voice, and lingers to speak with him, although anxious over his grave peril. Having already learned how her heart holds him, he pours forth to her his love, pledging her his devotion, and asking her to meet him on the morrow at Friar Laurence's cell and marry him. He will not be put off, and eager with longing and in great trepidation they plight their troth to each other. Suddenly Grègorio, suspicious that the masked intruder is still lurking near, comes with retainers and searches the garden. He does not, however, succeed in finding Romeo, who, when they have gone, again comes forth to speak with his love. At length they bid each other a lingering goodnight, mindful of their promise to meet on the morrow.

Act III. Within the cell of Friar Laurence the lovers meet and lovingly greet each other. They avow their love to the friar and beseech him to marry them speedily. He prudently protests that their love is sudden and their risk grave, because of the enmity of their families; but at length, in the hope that this marriage may bridge in friendship the long-standing breach, he consents. The ceremony is performed and soon Juliet hastens back to her home with her nurse.

Into the street before the house of Capulet comes Stephano searching for his master. Thinking that he might be lingering near for a glimpse of Juliet, he sings a song, which arouses Gregorio, who appears and recognizes the youth as the companion of Romeo at the ball. They draw their swords and fight. Mercutio and Tybalt both happen along and take part in the quarrel, when suddenly Romeo comes. He is very anxious to have no fray, but when Tybalt kills Mercutio, he, too, is forced to fight, and in turn kills Tybalt. Benvolio, Romeo's friend, and Paris, a Capulet and suitor of Juliet, also arrive and engage each other, and the uproar brings Capulet himself. The Duke of Verona, who happens to be passing, enters with his retinue, and hearing the account of the tumult, judges that Romeo is responsible for this fatal breach of the peace and condemns him to banishment. As they disperse Romeo vows that he will see Juliet before he leaves the city.

Act IV. Within Juliet's apartments in the early dawn she is saying farewell to Romeo, who at imminent risk of death if discovered has gained the chamber of his bride. With great sorrow at their separation they part lovingly, though she begs him not to go. He has but just gone when her father enters, accompanied by Friar Laurence. Their errand is to tell her that it has been arranged that she shall marry Paris, and that preparations for the ceremony are now being made. Astounded, she raises objections and pleads for delay, but her father will not listen. He leaves abruptly to attend to guests, and when alone with the friar she appeals to him, who knows of her vows to Romeo and of her great love for him, to help her. The friar gives her a vial containing a potion which, though harmless, will induce deep and prolonged sleep. He tells her that if she will drink the potion when her marriage to Paris is about to take place, she will be thought dead and he will send word to Romeo of the plot and arrange for him to meet her at the tomb and take her away with him. She consents to the scheme, rejoicing at any hope of being restored to her husband. The wedding preparations progress and the guests are gathered within the great hall. Juliet keeps courageously to her purpose, and as her father and Paris approach her, she falls unconscious, having drunk the potion. All believe her to be dead and great is their grief.

Act V. To the tomb of the Capulets, where Juliet lies upon a bier, apparently still in death, Romeo comes, having heard the news of her decease, but not having received the message of Friar Laurence as to her restoration. He is beside himself with sorrow and frantically decides that life holds naught else for him. He, therefore, drinks of a deadly poison which he carries, and happily resigns himself to die by her side. As he calls her loved name, suddenly she stirs and awakens and speaks to him. He is enraptured at the thought that she lives, and forgetting his doom, he bids her hasten away with him. Suddenly he cries out in great horror, for he remembers that the poison is doing its deadly work. He shows Juliet the vial and tells her of the draft. She makes sure that no drop of it is left, then seizes her dagger, and as Romeo sinks down overcome, she plunges it into her heart, although her lover, in agony of soul, tries to prevent her. Thus they die together.

DER ROSENCAVALIER
(*Der Rōz'-ĕn-kahv-ah-lēēr'*)
(THE CAVALIER OF THE ROSE)

GERMAN comic grand opera. Music by Richard Strauss. Book by Hugo von Hofmannsthal. First production, Dresden, 1911. The scene is Vienna, Austria, in the eighteenth century, during the reign of Maria Theresa.

CHARACTERS
BARON OCHS OF LERCHENAU	Bass
HERR VON FANINAL	Baritone
VALZACCHI, an intriguer	Tenor
OCTAVIAN, Count Rofrano	Mezzo-Soprano
PRINCESS VON WERDENBERG	Soprano
SOPHIA, daughter of Herr von Faninal	Soprano
MARIANNE LEITMETZER, duenna of Sophia	Soprano
ANNINA, a companion of Valzacchi	Alto

A singer (tenor), a flute player, a notary, commissary of police, four lackeys of Faninal, a master of ceremonies, an innkeeper, a milliner, a noble widow and three noble orphans, a hair-dresser and his assistants, four waiters, musicians, guests, two watchmen, kitchen servants, and several suspicious apparitions.

ACT I. Within the luxurious apartments of Princess von Werdenberg, whose husband, the Field Marshal, is in Arabia on a hunting trip, she is entertaining a young cavalier, Octavian, Count Rofrano. He is complimenting her on her beauty and charm and paying her loverlike attentions, while she, taking delight in the handsome youth, conceals her misgivings about her own fading attractions. Suddenly a loud and persistent ringing of the bell is heard, and the princess fears that by some chance her husband has returned. The resourceful Octavian, however, puts on woman's clothes, that he may appear as the waiting-maid. The visitor proves to be a provincial cousin of the princess's, Baron Ochs of Lerchenau. He comes to confide in her a plan by which he may obtain money, of which his estate stands greatly in need. He purposes to marry Sophia, daughter of Herr von Faninal, the rich army contractor. The baron, pompous and of great self-conceit, frankly avows that money alone is the motive for this alliance, though he is not loath to boast of his many social conquests. He plans to follow the established custom of sending to the young lady by an ambassador a silver rose, symbolic of his love and fidelity. He asks the princess to advise him whom to send.

She invites him to lunch with her and they are served by Octavian in his new rôle. The baron pays considerable attention to the supposed maid, and even goes so far as to make an appointment to meet her. The princess is angered by the nobleman's fickleness, and thinking to complicate matters, suggests Octavian as cavalier of the rose. The baron, well-pleased with the idea, departs. Tradespeople come for orders, a hair-dresser serves the princess, a noble widow with three noble orphans seeks assistance, and various matters of business are transacted. The princess, facing her looking-glass, sees that she is growing old, and thinks pensively that Octavian will soon no longer care for her. She fears that she has made a mistake in suggesting him as rose-cavalier, if she would continue to hold her sway over him.

Act II. Into the ornate salon of the rich and socially ambitious Faninal comes Octavian with dignified and solemn attendants, bearing the silver rose, which as ambassador of the elderly and boorish Baron Ochs he presents to Sophia. Faninal is greatly elated at having so close a connection with nobility. Octavian, when he first sees Sophia, falls in love with her and thinks only of winning her for himself. Sophia is equally taken with him, and when the baron comes with his retinue to talk with Faninal about the marriage settlements, she feels as strong aversion to him as she felt attraction to his ambassador.

The baron makes clumsy and vulgar overtures to her, but when he and her father withdraw, Octavian's advances are much more satisfactory. Two of the baron's men, whom he has left to observe the young people, report to him the situation, and enraged and jealous, he returns to the salon. An excited discussion occurs, in which Octavian tells him of Sophia's antipathy, which the baron resents, as her father has already promised him her hand. Octavian is so incensed at the baron's unmannerly wooing that he makes game of him in every way, and at length the two men draw their swords. The baron is as deficient in valor as in refinement, and at a slight cut on the arm he shouts that he is murdered. Servants enter, and taking sides with the contestants, create a great fracas. Faninal commands his daughter to accept the baron on pain of spending her life in a cloister. The baron is given wine and left alone to recover, which he speedily does when he remembers his appointment with the maid of the princess.

Act III. To a private room of a hotel in the suburbs of Vienna Octavian, with a maid's dress over his own costume, comes with some of the baron's servants, whom he has bribed to help carry out his plan. A table is set, music provided, and everything made gay and festive, according to the baron's orders. When he comes landlord, waiters, and attendants beset him to know if everything fulfills his wishes. So persistent are they that the baron's efforts to carry on a flirtation with Octavian are frustrated. He orders food brought, but the coy maid refuses everything. At length so intractable is she, with her moralizings and her emotions over the music, so persistently cold to his ardors, that he is greatly irritated.

Faces appear and vanish unaccountably, strange apparitions enter, and the baron thinks that the room is haunted. Frightened and furious at the upsetting of his plans, he is already in a terrible state when the Guardian of Public Morals enters and asks to know the maid's name. The baron vouches for her as his betrothed, Sophia. Herr von Faninal comes in, with Sophia, the princess, and others, and indignantly exposes the fraud. Octavian slips from his disguise, and the baron is the butt of the laughter and the wit of all. When Octavian insists that Sophia is his betrothed and not the baron's, and Faninal gives his consent to the transfer, the baron rushes away in mortification. The princess, at first greatly exasperated, decides to be magnanimous, and when the young couple become oblivious to her presence, she silently leaves them.

THE SACRIFICE

AMERICAN tragic grand opera. Both music and book by Frederick S. Converse. First production, Boston, 1911. The scene is southern California in 1846.

CHARACTERS

CAPTAIN BURTON, an American officer	Baritone
BERNAL, a Mexican officer	Tenor
PABLO, Bernal's servant and son of Tomasa	Baritone
PADRE GABRIEL, a Mexican priest	Bass
CORPORAL TOM FLYNN, an American soldier	Bass
LITTLE JOCK, an American soldier	Baritone
CHONITA, a young Mexican lady	Soprano
TOMASA, an old Indian servant	Contralto
MARIANNA, a young Indian servant	Soprano
MAGDELENA, an Indian girl	Soprano
A GYPSY GIRL	Mezzo-Soprano

Señora Anaya, who is aunt of Chonita, American and Mexican soldiers, and Spanish and Indian girls.

ACT I. In the garden of Señora Anaya's hacienda one afternoon Chonita lies on a divan while Tomasa is combing her long, black hair. The girl is playing upon a guitar and singing. A message is brought her that Bernal, whom she loves, has succeeded in evading the American soldiers and will be with her shortly. Meanwhile Captain Burton comes to call on her. He urges his suit upon her, and she, although she does not love him, cannot dismiss him summarily, because upon his favor depends the safety of her aunt and all their family. While she is talking with him she sees Bernal hiding behind an olive-tree in the grove close by, and dismisses the captain, still evading the giving of a definite answer. Bernal comes to her and is very jealous of the attention that the captain has shown her.

ACT II. The next day within a mission church, which the American soldiers have made their headquarters after the night attack, the soldiers are lying around as in their barracks. Some are polishing their weapons, others are playing cards, and some are wounded. All are telling of the attack and its outcome. A band of Spanish and Indian girls comes in, and the soldiers go out into the garden to dance with them. Chonita and Tomasa, her servant, come to ask of the fight, and are received by Captain Burton, who tells them that the Mexican officer, Bernal, was killed. Chonita's emotion at the news betrays her love for him. Burton is called out and while Chonita is alone Bernal, who has only been wounded, enters disguised as a priest. He reveals himself to Chonita, and she joyfully greets him. When the officer returns Chonita hides Bernal in the confessional. The captain renews his attentions to Chonita, pledging her his devotion even though he knows he cannot win her love. When she hesitates to tell him the great favor she would ask of him, Bernal rushes out to kill the captain. The two men begin to fight, and Chonita, dashing between them, is slightly wounded by Burton's weapon, as she tries to save Bernal, who is seized and led away to be shot as a spy.

ACT III. The next morning, within a bedchamber in Señora Anaya's house, Chonita is lying delirious. Her fears for Bernal keep her constantly listening for the shot which means his death. Padre Gabriel, secretly attended by a band of Mexicans, comes to offer her consolation, and sends Tomasa to the American officer with the request that he let the dying girl see her lover. Burton personally comes with Bernal, and Chonita is overjoyed to see her lover again. Burton, watching them, realizes that the girl's happiness lies in his hands, and determines to sacrifice himself to insure it.

She calls him also to her bedside and pleads with him to save Bernal's life. He replies that he cannot save a spy, and she tells him that Bernal came not as a spy, but as her deliverer, to take her away to peace and safety. Burton believes her, but sees no honorable way of rescuing the prisoner. As the band of Mexicans surround the house and surprise him, he rushes upon the first Mexican weapon that presents itself. He dies, and Chonita and Bernal, as they pray by his body, realize that he has sacrificed himself to restore them to each other.

SALOME

GERMAN tragic grand opera, founded upon a highly imaginative interpretation of the Biblical account of the death of John the Baptist. Music by Richard Strauss. Book by Oscar Wilde. First production, Dresden, 1905. The scene is Tiberias, Galilee, the capital of Herod's kingdom, in 30 A. D.

CHARACTERS

HEROD ANTIPAS, Tetrarch of Judea..................*Tenor*
JOCHANAAN, John the Baptist, prophet of the Lord..*Baritone*
NARRABOTH, a young Syrian, captain of the guard....*Tenor*
HERODIAS, wife of Herod....................*Mezzo-Soprano*
SALOME, daughter of Herodias.....................*Soprano*

A page of Herodias, a young Roman, the executioner, five Jews, two Nazarenes, two soldiers, a Cappadocian, and a slave.

It is night on the great terrace in the palace of Herod. In the foreground some soldiers stand on guard about an old cistern in the shrubbery. Before a large door from which the lights and sounds of feasting and revelry come, stands Narraboth. He is gazing within to where sits the woman whom he loves,—Salome, the daughter of Herodias. The sound of a man's voice in calm, prophetic proclamation of the near coming of a Messiah, rises from the cistern. Salome, entrancingly lovely but now angry at the insistent attentions of Herod, comes through the door. Everywhere she moves within the hall the little, restless eyes of Herod, her stepfather, follow her, and she would escape them out under the moon and the night. The young Syrian watches her movements tenderly. The voice of the prophet still rises, and Salome asks who it is and what his words mean. She goes to the dark pit and peers in. In answer to her curiosity

© Mishkin

MARY GARDEN
AS "SALOME"

Narraboth commands the prophet, and he rises and stands impassive by the opening. In the pale moonlight she sees him, and the flaming passion of her desire, of the lust that all eyes show toward her, springs in her heart for the passionless, spirit-worn, ascetic man. In long-drawn rapture she dwells on his physical perfections and offers him every enticement, begging him that she may kiss his lips. The prophet tells her of the Messiah and commends her to Him, but when she still persists in her frenzy of desire, he tells her that she is accursed, and withdraws into the darkness of his pit, while she crouches in the shadow of the wall.

Meanwhile the young Syrian, whose eyes have led his heart too far, hot with desire of her and shudderingly horrified at her fevered desire for the prophet, has killed himself, and lies prone on the stone pavement. Herod and his train come seeking Salome, and the tetrarch slips on the blood of the Syrian. Herodias is with him, and he, weak, passion-ridden, and desirous of Salome, is impatient to her. From the depths of the cistern again comes the voice of the prophet, saying that the time which he foretold has come. Herod hears and is frightened, but Herodias becomes defiant and angry. The Jews in the company denounce the prophet, but two Nazarenes declare that the Messiah has already come, and tell of great wonders wrought by a man of Galilee.

Herod spies Salome and bids her dance, persuading her with a promise to give her whatever she shall ask. She dances the Oriental dance of the seven veils. It is over, and Herod asks her desire. Wild with frenzy of revenge for her scorned passion, she cries, "The head of Jochanaan." Herod, fear-stricken, begs her to name anything else,—opals, emeralds, even the holy veil of the Temple sanctuary. But nothing else suffices, and supported by Herodias, with redoubled fury she demands her price. The executioner descends into the cistern, while she crouches above. Soon out of it rises a black arm, lifting high a silver charger on which lies the ashen head of the prophet. Salome seizes it, exults over it,—kisses it. Herod, surfeited with disgust, hides his face. Herodias, not displeased, watches. Salome cries in her bloody revenge, "I have kissed thy mouth, Jochanaan." Herod withdraws in horror along the terrace and orders the guards to kill her. They close upon her and crush her with their shields.

SAMSON AND DELILAH

(SAMSON ET DALILA)

FRENCH tragic grand opera, founded on the Biblical story of Samson. Music by Camille Saint-Saëns. Book by Ferdinand Lemaire. First production, Weimar, 1877. The scene is laid in Palestine at Gaza and its vicinity, about 1140 B. C.

CHARACTERS

SAMSON	*Tenor*
ABIMELECH, Satrap of Gaza	*Bass*
HIGH PRIEST OF DAGON	*Baritone*
AN OLD HEBREW	*Bass*
FIRST PHILISTINE	*Tenor*
SECOND PHILISTINE	*Bass*
DELILAH, daughter of the High Priest of Dagon	*Mezzo-Soprano*

A messenger (tenor), Hebrews, and Philistines.

ACT I. In a public square of Gaza near the temple of Dagon Hebrews are assembled in attitudes of grief and prayer, Samson among them, weeping over the destruction of their cities and the profanation of the temple. Samson tells them of a hope within his heart that their bondage is broken and that once more they may raise their altars to Israel's God. He reminds them of what the Lord has done for them in the past, and they are encouraged and rally about him. Abimelech, Satrap of Gaza, enters with Philistine warriors and asks the cause of the disturbance. With blasphemous words he defies the God of Israel and extols Dagon. Samson as if inspired sees a vision of the hosts of Israel triumphant, and rallies the Hebrews about him. When Abimelech attacks him with sword in hand, Samson wrests it from him and stabs him. At Abimelech's call the Philistines rush to his aid, and Samson, brandishing the sword, keeps them off while the Hebrews retire unmolested.

Through the open gates of the temple of Dagon comes the high priest with guards and attendants. At the sight of Abimelech's dead body he stops and the Philistines draw back. He urges them to vengeance, but the soldiers tell how their blood froze in their veins and how they stood as if bound. He taunts them with fearing the God of Israel, and when they counsel flight, he curses the Israelites and especially their leader, Samson, praying that the woman who wins his heart may destroy him. The high priest and the Philistines depart, bearing the body of Abimelech, and hasten to the mountains, leaving their houses, their women, and their gods. The Hebrews come and take possession of the city.

While the Hebrews are gathered rejoicing, Delilah comes from the temple of Dagon followed by Philistine priestesses bearing garlands of flowers with which to wreathe the conquerors. With words of devotion and love Delilah approaches Samson and invites him to come away with her to her home in the valley of Soreck and receive her comfort. Samson prays that he may be strong against so dear a voice, so enticing a temptation, and an old Hebrew warns him of the treachery planned and pronounces a curse upon him if he heeds the voice of the Philistine woman. The priestesses of Dagon accompanying Delilah dance and try to entice the Hebrew warriors with Samson, who against his better judgment cannot but follow with his eyes the movements of Delilah and notice her ardent glances at him. As she vanishes within the temple he hesitates and betrays his trouble and emotion, while the old Hebrew sternly watches him.

ACT II. Night is falling on the valley of Soreck where stands Delilah's dwelling. She, richly attired, is seated near the door plotting the vengeance that the Philistines will take, for to-night Samson is coming to her and to-morrow he will be captive. The high priest of Dagon comes, weary from his flight over lofty mountains, and tells her how the Philistines flee before this Samson, who has the force and will to conquer because he believes himself called to free his people. The high priest tells her also how it is said that the love that Samson showed for her for a day is vanished, but she boasts that yet he loves her and that he still trembles beneath her glance. Then he beseeches her to aid her people and betray Samson, and she may have whatever she desires. She spurns the thought of reward, and says that ever has she hated Samson and now will betray him for her own hate's sake. To his questions she replies that three times she has sought from Samson the secret of his power, but that with his present coming she is sure to learn it. Together they vow his death and the high priest goes away.

Delilah waits long, wondering if her love has lost its power. At length as the night grows dark and lightning flashes, Samson enters hesitating. He is lamenting his own weakness and the unholy force of the passion that chains him. Delilah greets him with tender love, but he reproaches her for her transports and feels anew the shame of his surrender. He tries to say farewell to her and tells her that he has vowed his God to do His will only, that he is called to deliver his people from bondage. Delilah reminds him of his promises to her and defies his God to strike her down. At her desperate and passionate words his love flames, and he relents and accepts her caresses. She feigns to doubt his love and when he says that he is false to his God and faithful only to her, she would have him prove his devotion by telling her the secret of his power. He refuses and she accuses him of thinking her a traitor. He protests in anguish of spirit, calling upon God in his pain, but she repeats her demand. The crashing storm is now upon them and she rushes into her house. Samson raises his arms as if to call on God, then lets them fall and hastens toward Delilah's dwelling, and finally within. Philistine soldiers approach the house. Delilah signals them from a terrace and they rush in and seize Samson.

Act III. In a prison of Gaza Samson, shorn of his hair, blind, and in chains, is grinding at a mill. He prays in anguish of soul and deep penitence, while Hebrew captives in their laments rebuke him for his broken vows and for the sorrowful plight of his people. Patiently he takes their accusations and prays that God will spare His chosen nation. Philistines come and take him away.

Within the temple of Dagon before the altar, whereon is a statue of the idol, the high priest stands surrounded by the chief Philistines. Delilah comes followed by young women with wine cups in their hands. A great throng of Philistines is present and as day dawns a hymn of rejoicing is raised. Samson is led in by a little child. The high priest greets him derisively as judge of Israel and taunts him with succumbing to the charms of Delilah. They offer him drink and would toast with him the fair Delilah, while Samson, truly repentant, prays for death. Delilah approaches and offers him her hand, saying that she will lead him as when they two went away to be alone together, and shamelessly relating how she tore the secret from him and sold him to his enemies. Samson repents him for bestowing upon one so false a love thereby profaned. The high priest orders the captive to rehearse his love and chant the praises of Delilah, or call upon his God to heal his blindness.

At the priest's blasphemous words Samson in horror cries

out to God that He should permit such challenging of His power to go unanswered, and begs as one last boon that he may avenge the Glorious One thus dishonored, that for one moment sight and strength may be restored. The Philistines only laugh at him. The high priest and Delilah pour the libations and raise the invocation. As the flames break out on the altar the high priest commands Samson to kneel before Dagon and present his offering. Samson, grief-stricken and devoutly praying, bids the child guide him to the two marble pillars that support the structure. While the sacred dance goes on Samson, still praying, bends his strength to move the pillars, and suddenly they give way and the temple falls amid the cries and shrieks of the people.

IL SEGRETO DI SUSANNA

(*Ēl-Sā-grā'-tō dē Sōō-zan'-nah*)

(SUSANNA'S SECRET)

ITALIAN comic grand opera, founded on a French play. Music by Ermanno Wolf-Ferrari. Book by Enrico Golisciani. First production, Munich, 1909. The scene is a drawing-room of a castle in Piedmont at the present day.

CHARACTERS

COUNT GIL (aged thirty) .... *Baritone*
COUNTESS SUSANNA, his wife (aged twenty) .... *Soprano*
SANTE, a servant (aged fifty) .... *Acting Part*

Count Gil returns home unexpectedly and discovers in the handsome living-room of his palace the indisputable odor of Turkish tobacco. He himself does not smoke, so he decides to investigate the matter. He interviews Sante, who denies that either he himself or his mistress smokes. The young countess, dressed for out-of-doors, has, unobserved, followed her husband in and manages to slip into her room. Through the open door Sante vainly tries by signs to warn her of her husband's suspicions. The count is tormented with jealousy, for he thinks she must have had a man caller, yet he cannot doubt his modest little wife of a month. As she enters he greets her lovingly and tells her that he fancied he saw her on the street, but knows that he must have been mistaken as he has forbidden her to go out without him.

Sante brings in the tea service, trying again to make Susanna understand. When he withdraws the young couple joyously remind each other of their first days of love. As he starts to embrace her he again smells the tobacco even in her hair and clothes. She trembles, fearing that he knows her fault, and he accuses her of hiding something from him. She begs him to tolerate her folly and not to watch her too closely, saying that other women do as she does, that her mother knew———. He is furiously angry, thinking that her admissions are far more serious than she means, believing that she is lost to a sense of shame, and he will not for a moment listen to the idea of toleration. She bursts into tears and calls him a brute, and he denounces her.

He rushes about in his wrath demolishing everything that he can lay hands on. Susanna goes into her room and locks the door. Count Gil flings himself into an easychair, his head in his hands, while Sante tries to restore order to the room. Gil decides that he must catch her in the very act of wrongdoing, and when Susanna comes from her room and meekly hands him his gloves, hat, and umbrella, saying that his friends will be expecting him at the club, he thinks she wants him to go. She detains him, however, to ask him for one friendly look, a little kindness, and humbly begs his pardon. Gil is touched, and when she promises to reform and asks him for one kiss, he goes so far as to kiss her on the forehead, and departs.

Susanna sits musing on her husband's temper when Sante enters and gives her the package that she handed him when she came in. Taking from it a cigarette, she lights it and daintily smokes, regretting that her husband hates it and vowing that she will be more careful. Sante takes a pinch of snuff, and the two laugh merrily. A knock is suddenly heard and Susanna jumps up in dismay. She hides the cigarette, directs Sante to conceal himself behind the window drapery, and opens the door. Her husband rushes in, looking around and sniffing. He is much stirred up because of the delay in opening the door, the hurried footsteps, and the smoke. He looks around to find a man hiding somewhere. As he does not succeed he calls Sante and orders a thorough search of the palace, and as Sante goes out he himself searches all over the apartment, rushing wildly about.

When Count Gil again goes away Susanna gets the hidden cigarette, relights it, and settles herself to the enjoyment of it, although very anxious over her husband's actions. After a time a tapping is heard at the window and she starts suddenly from her revery. Gil enters through the window, thinking that he has caught her this time. He seizes her hand and gets burned with the cigarette. At his exclamation she, kneeling, asks him to forgive her. He, aware now of the facts, kneels and asks her forgiveness, confessing that he was jealous. They decide to forgive each other and when she promises never to smoke again because she loves him, he says that they will smoke together. She gives him a cigarette and he lights it from hers. They are so very happy over being reconciled that they neglect their cigarettes, which go out. Sante enters with a candle, takes in the situation, and grinning, offers them a light.

THE TALES OF HOFFMANN

(LES CONTES D'HOFFMANN)

FRENCH sentimental grand opera, after three tales by E. T. A. Hoffmann. Music by Jacques Offenbach. Book by Jules Barbier. First public production, Paris, 1881. The scenes are laid in various parts of Europe in the nineteenth century.

CHARACTERS

THE POET HOFFMANN	*Tenor*
COUNCILOR LINDORF }	
COPPELIUS } his opponents. (Usually one artist.)	
DAPERTUTTO } *Bass or Baritone*	
DOCTOR MIRACLE }	
SPALANZANI, an apothecary	*Tenor*
COUNCILOR CRESPEL, father of Antonia	*Bass*
ANDRES }	
COCHENILLE } (Usually one artist.)	*Tenor*
PITTICHINACCIO }	
FRANZ }	
LUTHER, an innkeeper	*Bass*
NATHANIEL	*Tenor*
SCHLEMIHL, admirer of Giulietta	*Bass*
HERMANN	*Bass*
NICKLAUSSE, friend of Hoffmann	*Mezzo-Soprano*
OLYMPIA }	
GIULIETTA } The ladies with whom Hoffmann falls in love.	
ANTONIA } (Usually one artist.)	*Soprano*
STELLA }	
THE MUSE	*Mezzo-Soprano*
A SPIRIT	*Mezzo-Soprano*

Prologue. Within a tavern at Nuremburg a gay crowd of students is gathered, drinking, singing, and making merry. Nathaniel proposes the name of Stella, a beautiful singer at a near-by theater, as a toast, and all drink. They wonder where Hoffmann, the poet, known to be her admirer, is and call for him just as he enters with his friend, Nicklausse.

Hoffmann is grave and sad, and silently sits down at a table, holding his head in his hands. The students question him, and at length he sadly starts to tell them of something that happened but now at the theater, but breaks off and bids them laugh and drink with him. All are his friends but Councilor Lindorf, who in various guises appears always as his evil genius. They demand of Hoffmann the song of Klein-Zach, the dwarf, and he is singing it when suddenly he describes, instead of the dwarf's features, those of the beautiful singer for whom he left his father's house. They rally him, saying that he is in love. He, however, orders the punch lighted and speaks scornfully of love and of all women; then confesses that he is in love with three women, and asks if his friends would care to hear the story of his foolish loves. Eagerly they reply that they would, and settle down to smoke and to listen. Hoffmann begins his tale by saying that the name of the first was Olympia.

Act I. Hoffmann enters a physician's room, richly furnished, in the house of the noted scientist, Spalanzani, with whose beautiful daughter he has become enamored by glimpses of her through the window. He lifts the portière to an inner room and sees her lying asleep, and meditates on her beauty and the love he feels for her. Nicklausse enters and his words show that he has no delusions about Olympia. Spalanzani comes with his guests and, summoning Cochenille to bring Olympia, he presents her to them. With much emotion Hoffmann watches the young woman, whose beautiful eyes, shapely figure, and fine apparel win flattering comments from the guests. Spalanzani says that his daughter will sing for them, so the harp is brought and he accompanies her. The performance is very creditable and soon supper is announced. As Hoffmann steps forward eager to escort her,

Spalanzani tells him that she is a bit tired and asks him to remain with her. When her father has conducted her to a seat and gone out, the delighted lover approaches her deferentially. He avows his love for her and as he happens to touch her shoulder she answers him "Yes." He is exultant and taking her hand, gently presses it, whereupon she rises, walks up and down, and then goes off into her room. He is about to follow when Nicklausse comes in, and Hoffmann excitedly tells him of his avowal and that she loves him. Nicklausse, still skeptical of her charm, takes him away to the feasting.

Coppelius comes in great fury, declaring that he has been robbed by Spalanzani and that he will have his revenge. He rushes into Olympia's room as the guests reënter and the dancing begins. Hoffmann desires to dance with Olympia and they waltz out of the room together, while the guests comment on her marvelous dancing and the speed with which she moves. After a time there are excited cries and Hoffmann and Olympia reappear dancing madly. Nicklausse tries to stop them but receives a violent blow. It is only when Spalanzani touches Olympia on the shoulder that she ceases her motion, and Hoffmann disengages himself and falls on a sofa exhausted. Cochenille conducts her to her room and Nicklausse asks if Hoffmann is dead. Spalanzani says he is not, but that his eyeglass is broken. Cochenille enters in great excitement and a sound of breaking springs comes from Olympia's room. Spalanzani exclaims that she must be broken, and Hoffmann rushes toward the room as Coppelius issues, laughing and saying that she is smashed! Spalanzani is denouncing Coppelius when Hoffmann returns exclaiming that Olympia is an automaton. The guests burst into loud laughter at his expense, while Spalanzani in despair laments his ruined masterpiece.

Act II. In the gallery of a palace overlooking the Grand Canal in Venice the guests of Giulietta, a courtesan, are seated. Giulietta and Nicklausse are heard singing a barcarole celebrating the beautiful night of love, and soon enter. Hoffmann, who is among the guests, sings a bacchic song celebrating pleasure. Schlemihl enters and is introduced to Hoffmann, whom he greets with surly humor, which Hoffmann meets with irony. Giulietta invites her guests to the gaming tables, and as Hoffmann offers his hand to conduct her Schlemihl jealously comes between them. Hoffmann and Nicklausse linger behind and his friend tells the poet that he has two horses saddled and will carry him off at the first symptom of infatuation. Hoffmann denies the possibility of his falling in love with a courtesan, and as Nicklausse warns him, saying that the devil is clever, Dapertutto appears at the back. Hoffmann laughingly wagers his soul that the devil cannot make him love her, and they go out.

Dapertutto accepts the challenge given the devil and plots Hoffmann's conquest. As Giulietta appears he places a ring containing a fine diamond upon her finger and orders her to use her fascinations to obtain for him the image of Hoffmann, saying that he heard him deny her power. Quite willingly she promises to do it. Hoffmann comes as Dapertutto leaves, and when he also starts to go Giulietta wilily causes him to declare his love for her. She tells him that it may cost him his life, for Schlemihl may strike him dead, but she offers to follow him wherever he goes. Quite deceived by her apparent love and devotion he is in an ecstasy of joy. She asks him for a reflection of himself to keep in her heart and holds a polished glass before him; then her tone suddenly changes and she calls Schlemihl. He enters followed by Nicklausse, Dapertutto, Pittichinaccio, and others. Giulietta in a low voice tells Hoffmann that Schlemihl has the key to her house.

Pittichinaccio and Schlemihl advance threateningly toward Hoffmann, and Dapertutto, telling him that he is pale, holds the glass before him, from which Hoffmann starts back in amazement. Giulietta announces that the gondolas have arrived and that it is the hour for barcaroles and farewells. Schlemihl conducts the guests away; Giulietta goes out, but Dapertutto remains. Nicklausse tries to get Hoffmann to go, and when he refuses, determines to watch over his friend. Schlemihl returns and Hoffmann demands of him a certain key. He refuses to give it and they fight, Dapertutto having proffered Hoffmann his sword. Schemihl falls mortally wounded and Hoffmann takes the key from around his neck. He rushes toward Giulietta's room, but in a moment returns and sees her going off in a gondola with Pittichinaccio. Nicklausse rushes in, saying that the police are coming, and drags away Hoffmann, while Giulietta and Pittichinaccio laugh derisively.

ACT III. In a humble German home in Munich, Antonia is seated at the clavichord singing and thinking of her lover, Hoffmann, from whom she has been suddenly separated. Her father enters and gently reproaches her for singing against his wishes. She again promises that she will not and goes out, and Crespel muses sadly on her frailty. She has inherited from her mother a wonderful voice, but now she is ill of consumption and her father is in an agony of fear that some day while singing she will bring on fatal symptoms. Franz, the old and deaf servant, comes in, and after giving him orders to admit nobody, Crespel goes out. Franz is capering around, under the impression that he can dance, when Hoffmann and Nicklausse enter.

Hoffmann sends Franz for Antonia, who soon enters in great delight at seeing him. Nicklausse goes out and the lovers are left together to talk over their sudden separation, the reason for which neither knows. Hoffmann promises to make her his wife on the morrow, and joyously they plan the future. Longing to sing to him as she used to, she breaks her promise to her father and they sing. She grows faint and after vainly trying to go on stops. She hears her father coming and goes out. Hoffmann hides, thinking to learn the reason for Crespel's command about the singing. Crespel thinks that Hoffmann is there, and when he does not see him he consigns him to the devil.

Scarcely is the word spoken before Franz announces that Doctor Miracle has come. Although Crespel refuses to admit the weird doctor, whom he believes to be an assassin, Miracle appears, saying that he can cure Antonia and asking to see her. Crespel refuses and threatens him, but the doctor simply extends his hand toward Antonia's room and the door opens. Crespel and Hoffmann, from his hiding-place, watch in strange horror as the doctor acts as if Antonia had entered, taken the chair he placed for her, extended her hand and let him count her pulse. He commands her to sing and the two observers chill with fright when Antonia's voice is heard singing. Doctor Miracle seems to dismiss her and the door to her room closes quickly. The doctor takes vials from his pocket and leaves them for her with directions. Crespel pushes the doctor through the door but in a moment he appears walking through the wall. Crespel at last drives him away, himself going out with him.

Antonia reënters the room and Hoffmann adds his entreaties that she should not sing. They part happily, looking forward to their marriage on the morrow. She falls in a chair and Doctor Miracle appears suddenly behind her. He argues with her not to bury her voice, her great talent, in a home when the applause of multitudes could be hers. Her love for Hoffmann helps her to withstand the temptation, and her heart longs to confide in her dead mother. Doctor Miracle tells her that her mother speaks through him. Thereupon her mother's portrait upon the wall lights up and her mother's voice calls her. Miracle seizes a violin and bids Antonia join with her mother in singing. Antonia's voice soon fails her, but Miracle urges her on until she stops breathless. She falls on a sofa dying, and Doctor Miracle, laughing, sinks through the ground. Her father rushes in and she expires in his arms. Hoffmann comes, and Crespel thinks it is he who has killed her by bidding her sing, and makes at him with a knife, but Nicklausse stops him. Hoffmann calls out for a doctor, and Miracle appears and, feeling Antonia's pulse, pronounces her dead, while her father and lover bend over her in grief and despair.

Epilogue. In the tavern at Nuremburg Hoffmann is bringing the story of his three loves to a close. The students heartily applaud him and he tells them that there is left after love only the intoxication and oblivion of alcohol, for the doll-woman is smashed, the true woman is dead, and as for the false woman—her fate accords with her nature, and he jovially sings the last stanza of his interrupted song of Klein-Zach. They all go into another room to continue their carousing, but Hoffmann remains as if in a stupor, meditating deeply.

In an aureole of light the Muse appears to him, telling him that she is left to him, that her love is his, and that when the man of passion is no more, the poet survives. She says that love makes great, but tears make still greater, and vanishes. Hoffmann voices the solemn ecstasy with which his soul is filled, and gives himself up fully to the fire that the Muse has inspired within him. He falls face forward on the table. As he lies thus Stella enters and approaches him, but Nicklausse, ever his good genius, tells her that Hoffmann is dead drunk and she is too late. So she goes out, led away by Councilor Lindorf, yet she pauses long enough to look lingeringly at the poet and throw a flower from her bouquet at his feet.

THE TAMING OF THE SHREW

(DER WIEDERSPAENSTIGEN ZAEHMUNG)

GERMAN comic grand opera, founded on Shakespeare's drama of the same name. Music by Hermann Goetz. Book by Joseph Victor Widmann. First production, Mannheim, Germany, 1874. The scene is Padua, Italy, and its vicinity in the Middle Ages.

CHARACTERS

BAPTISTA, a rich gentleman of Padua	Bass
HORTENSIO } suitors of Bianca	Bass
LUCENTIO	Tenor
PETRUCHIO, a gentleman of Verona	Baritone
GRUMIO, servant to Petruchio	Bass
A TAILOR	Tenor
KATHARINE } daughters of Baptista	Soprano
BIANCA	Soprano

Baptista's and Petruchio's servants, wedding guests, neighbors, and friends.

ACT I. Into a street of Padua, before Baptista's house in the late evening Lucentio is serenading Bianca, when with great commotion the servants rush from the house, saying that a fiend lives there and railing against Mistress Katharine. Baptista appears and tries to mollify them, and at last, when the whole neighborhood has been aroused, makes such generous offers of pay and wine that the servants reënter the house. Soon all is quiet and Lucentio again begins his serenade, to which Bianca responds.

Hortensio also comes to serenade her. She bids good-night to the young Lucentio and laughs at the old suitor's attentions. The latter espies Lucentio, who orders him off; but Hortensio defies him and soon they draw their swords. Baptista again appears at the door, very irate at this second commotion, and especially at Hortensio, whom he has before ordered from his house. Lucentio presents himself, declares his love for Bianca, and asks for her hand in marriage, telling of his father's wealth and saying that he himself is studying in Padua. Baptista tells both the suitors that until he has married off his elder daughter, he will not listen to offers for his second. He leaves them, and each suitor commends to the other a marriage with Katharine. Both also conceive of the idea of applying for the position of teacher to Bianca, who is to be kept at her studies.

As they separate Hortensio runs into Petruchio with his servant, Grumio. Petruchio greets him cordially as an old friend, and to his questions answers that he is traveling because, as he is so very wealthy, life offers him little variety. Hortensio says that the women must all be eager to please him, and Petruchio declares that he would bestow his best affection on one who would oppose his will. Hortensio, remembering that Petruchio is noted for his impoliteness, tells him of the violent-tempered Katharine, who drives all suitors away. The description pleases Petruchio, who recalls her as a child when once he visited her father. He tells Hortensio that he has fought with many weapons and loves nothing so much as a conflict, therefore Katharine is the mate for him.

ACT II. Within their chamber Katharine is rebuking Bianca for her womanish softness toward the young serenader. She sings a song of independence, declaring that she will live free from all suitors, which is overheard and warmly applauded by Lucentio, Petruchio, and Hortensio, who are with Baptista. Katharine indignantly takes Bianca off with her to the garden.

Baptista receives the three men, Hortensio and Lucentio

go, and bids him depart. He warns her not to drive him too far, but she defies him. Hand on sword he commands the guests not to interfere and when Katharine in shame wishes she were a thousand miles away, he determines to go at once. Though she begs him to let her stay with her father, he motions to Grumio, who leads in two horses. Petruchio springs upon the table, snatches Katharine to him, leaps into the saddle, placing her before him, and rides away, followed by Grumio.

Act IV. In Petruchio's country house the servants are grumbling as they set the table that they cannot endure the contentions of the newly married couple, and Grumio is saying that Petruchio is only taming his wife, for she was far more headstrong than he. Petruchio and Katharine enter. She is pale and suffering and Petruchio is flourishing a riding whip. He drives out the servants and objects to everything that is set before him. When Katharine begs him to be gentle, he says that is but a lady's part. He throws the food off the table in disgust and goes out. When the servants have cleared up, Katharine, left alone, acknowledges to herself that she is tired of fighting, and though she does not abhor her husband, yet she would see him placable. She determines to show such resignation as to move his heart to mercy and win his love. Grumio ushers in a tailor, who lays his stock before her. Petruchio comes and objects to everything that Katharine would buy. When she refuses to take them because her husband does not wish to pay for them, he berates the tailor well, but aside pays him liberally, while Grumio enjoys the trick and Katharine longs to make her husband somewhat mild and meek.

Petruchio would then have her come to walk with him in the moonlight, and though at first she says that the sun is shining, for it is midday, she changes it to the moon to please him. At length she breaks down and in tears tells him that she sees what he has meant by his joking, and that her shrewish disposition is tamed, that she now desires a wife's honor. She declares her love for him and sinks to the ground at his feet. He raises her, embracing her tenderly, and says that the test is happily ended. She rejoices, and though she wishes that she could hate him, yet only sorrowfully repents that she vexed him. As they rejoice together Baptista, with Bianca and Lucentio, now betrothed, and Hortensio and his newly married wife, come in. Petruchio and Katharine greet them graciously, and to her sister's questions Katharine answers that she is perfectly happy. They all wonder at the change in her, and when they congratulate her she gives all the credit to Petruchio.

TANNHÄUSER

(*Tann'-hoy-zer*)

(OR, THE SINGERS' CONTEST AT THE WARTBURG)

GERMAN tragic grand opera, founded upon Hoffmann's novel, "Sängerkrieg," and a poem by Ludwig Tieck. Both music and book by Richard Wagner. First production, Dresden, 1845. The scene is the vicinity of Eisenach at the beginning of the thirteenth century.

CHARACTERS

HERMANN, Landgrave of Thuringia		Bass
TANNHÄUSER		Tenor
WOLFRAM VON ESCHENBACH		Baritone
WALTHER VON DER VOGELWEIDE	Minstrel	Tenor
BITEROLF	Knights	Bass
HEINRICH DER SCHREIBER		Tenor
REINMAR VON ZWETER		Bass
ELIZABETH, niece of the Landgrave		Soprano
VENUS		Soprano
A YOUNG SHEPHERD		Soprano
FOUR NOBLE PAGES		Soprano and Alto

Thuringian nobles and knights, ladies, elder and younger pilgrims, sirens, naiads, nymphs, and bacchantes.

According to Teutonic mythology Holda, the northern Venus, dwelt in a hollow mountain known as the Hörselberg, where all the delights of love were enjoyed by her devotees.

ACT I. Within the Hörselberg amid flowery dells and by a limpid lake nymphs and sirens, naiads and bacchantes, and many loving couples are dancing or resting on mossy banks, and taking their pleasure in a roseate atmosphere far different from that of earth. Venus reclines upon her couch. Tannhäuser, a minstrel knight, the many-times winner of the Singers' Contest at the Wartburg, has voluntarily sought this abode of the goddess of love and beauty and for a whole year has been fascinated by her charms and under the spell of her power. Now, however, he is satiated with pleasure and longs for the mingled sadness and joy of the earth life. He is kneeling by the couch of the goddess, but dejected and abstracted. To her questions he confesses that he would breathe the air of earth once more. She tries to renew his thralldom and bids him play upon his harp and sing of the joys of love. He rises and stands before her and with somewhat of his former fervor he sings her praise, pledging himself always to sing only of love; but soon he falters and passionately yearns to be free, as a mortal to go forth to struggle, whatever may come of it. Venus is deeply grieved and exerts her softest enchantments to hold him. As she rises before him in her beauty she is angered to see that his gaze is into the past and not upon her. She spurns him, bidding him go, but, warning him that human intolerance will refuse him welcome, she tells him to return to her without fear.

Suddenly Venus and all her nymphs vanish, the roseate light changes to the clear air of day, and Tannhäuser is lying upon a hill slope near the Wartburg. Sheep are feeding near and a shepherd boy on a near-by height is singing a ballad of Venus and the fabled joys of her realm. Beside the highroad at the crossways is a shrine to the Virgin. A band of venerable pilgrims in penitential garb passes chanting their prayers for the forgiveness of their sins. The shepherd boy calls out for them to pray for him at Rome, and they wend their way past the shrine and down the valley filling the air with prayer. Tannhäuser, conscience-stricken for the year he has wasted in pleasure, falls on his knees before the shrine and prays for mercy.

© Aimé Dupont

OLIVE FREMSTAD
AS VENUS, IN "TANNHÄUSER"

The Landgrave's hunting party of minstrel knights comes, and observing the knight, accosts him. Surprised, they recognize him as their long-absent fellow minstrel, Henry. Some are still jealous of his former triumphs, but Wolfram von Eschenbach joyfully greets him and the others follow his example. When they question Tannhäuser of his absence, he says that he has wandered in a land where there was for him no peace. The Landgrave urges him to return with them to the Wartburg, but he says that henceforth he is a wanderer. Wolfram reminds him of Elizabeth, the Landgrave's beautiful niece, whom he once loved. He trembles at her name, but is determined to depart. Then Wolfram, himself long a devoted lover of Elizabeth and nobly desiring only her happiness, begs the Landgrave's permission to disclose the fact that since Tannhäuser went away Elizabeth appears no more at the song contests and has become wan and sorrowful. Tannhäuser, greatly heartened, for long since he loved her, now consents to return and take part in the tournament of song upon the morrow. The knights raise a joyful chorus of welcome and all repair to the hall.

Act II. Within the great Hall of Song of the Wartburg Elizabeth stands radiant with love and hope, awaiting the coming of Tannhäuser. She addresses the dear walls that have witnessed her happy dream of love and that of late she had shunned for their too painful memories. Through a secret door comes Wolfram conducting Tannhäuser, who flings himself, adoring and penitent, at the feet of his loved lady, while Wolfram in quiet self-effacement withdraws. Elizabeth, in maidenly confusion at the homage offered her, bids Tannhäuser arise, but he confesses with contrition that he has wandered far and that only the memory of her remains from the oblivion of the past. Generously she forgives him for she knows not what, and rejoicing together in their love, they vow never to part again.

As the Landgrave approaches Tannhäuser leaves, and Hermann greets her with great tenderness, glad that again she honors with her presence the minstrels' meeting. From the balcony where they stand apart they watch the knights and nobles with their ladies come into the hall and take their places, followed by the minstrel knights, all greeting the Landgrave and Elizabeth and uniting in a chorus of praise of the noble Hermann for his patronage of the art of song. When all are seated the Landgrave makes announcement of the contest, welcomes Tannhäuser again to the ranks he has honored, gives the theme of the contest as love and the signs by which it is known, and proclaims the prize to be bestowed by Elizabeth as whatever is the dearest desire of the winner.

Four pages then mingle the lots in a golden cup from which Elizabeth draws, and Wolfram von Eschenbach is announced as the first singer. He rises and unassumingly sings a lofty strain of a love that is prayerful and void of wild desire,—a song filled with a noble tribute to one unnamed but not unknown to the hearers. Tannhäuser, aroused by the singer's restraint, which he takes for coldness, starts up in his place and protests that love is not such. Walther von der Vogelweide resents such criticism and himself expatiates upon a scarcely less noble love. Tannhäuser more and more hotly continues his protest and Wolfram defends his ideal, abating not a whit from the worshipful attitude of heart. Whereupon Tannhäuser, all too impatient, and mindful of the goddess in whose praise alone he has vowed to sing, bursts out in scorn, saying that one might thus love a star; then ardently he pictures the sensual pleasures of love. Biterolf hotly springs to his feet and, voicing the general indignation, challenges Tannhäuser for the insult he has given to womanhood and to the ideals of chivalry. His words win great applause, and Tannhäuser in anger taunts him for his grim, wolflike visage, and avows it impossible for him ever to know the delights of love; then, wildly exultant, he extols Venus and bids the knights go enjoy her pleasures if they would know love.

The knights now rush upon him with drawn swords, ready to slay him for his blasphemous words and for the confession that he has been at the Hörselberg. Only Elizabeth's impassioned intercession for him, as she springs from the dais and stands to shield him, prevents his death. She pleads for his life, condoning not in the least his sin, but begging the knights that as upon her he has struck the deepest blow, they may listen to her prayers and spare him, nor forbid him hope of Heaven's forgiveness. As they fall away from him, who is now conscious of his defilement and deeply penitent, the Landgrave tells him that a band of pilgrims, of which the elders started that very day, leave on the morrow for Rome, there to pray for absolution from their sins. He bids him join them, and by prayers and penitence seek pardon, if pardon may be found, for this his so great sin. From afar comes the chant of the pilgrims as they wend their way, and Tannhäuser, desiring only forgiveness, rushes out to join them.

Act III. Along the path by the crossways Wolfram von Eschenbach comes one afternoon and beholds Elizabeth kneeling before the shrine of the Virgin. There often has Wolfram seen her as daily in all the year since Tannhäuser's departure she has knelt there in prayer for him. The pilgrims have long since been expected home and Elizabeth, pale and worn with suspense, is ever hoping that he may return with them, pardoned and nevermore to leave her. Wolfram, still unselfishly devoted, joins his prayers with hers that her lover may be restored to her. They are both aroused by the sound of the pilgrims' chorus. They approach, wearily but happily returning from the long and painful journey on foot. Wolfram and Elizabeth stand at one side and watch them pass, eagerly scanning each face to see if Tannhäuser is among them.

As the last one passes and he has not come, Elizabeth in utter despair sinks before the shrine and in agony prays for death, vowing that while life shall last she will remain consecrate to the Virgin, and interceding for the loved sinner, who still wanders afar. At length slowly and weakly she goes toward the castle, with a gesture thanking Wolfram for his faithful sympathy and bidding him farewell. He watches her out of sight and sorrowfully meditates on her impending fate; then as the twilight falls and the evening stars come out he takes up his harp and sings a strain filled with a holy melancholy, commending the soul of his loved one to the tender care of the heavenly hosts.

As the song dies away a lone pilgrim, more weary and footsore, more bowed and tattered than the rest, comes leaning heavily upon his staff. Wolfram with difficulty recognizes Tannhäuser, and when he sees the worn and hopeless face he asks eagerly if he has not been absolved, bidding him not go to the Wartburg unless he brings news of forgiveness. Tannhäuser, however, is not seeking the Wartburg, but the Hörselberg, the path to which he finds not so readily as of old. Wolfram, horrified, begs an account of his journey and its outcome, and will not let him pass. Tannhäuser then tells of a sorely painful pilgrimage, on which by every method he sought hardship and suffering, that he might mortify the flesh and make himself worthy of pardon. At length he came to the holy city and knelt with thousands of other pilgrims, who rejoiced in pardon. When he confessed to the Pope himself his grievous sin and that he had spent a year at the unhallowed hill of Venus, the holy father rose up in horror, declaring that for him there was no hope of salvation, no more than hope of flowering for the barren staff within the pontiff's hand.

As Tannhäuser turns away, well knowing that neither in this world nor the next shall he see Elizabeth, Wolfram urges him to a yet deeper penitence; but he would deaden his suffering in the pleasures of Venus and desperately calls upon the goddess to guide him to her abode. Along the hill slope she appears with the nymphs of her train, holding out her arms in the long-promised welcome. He starts toward her, but Wolfram seizes him by the arm, and suddenly is heard from the Wartburg the sound of a funeral chant. The minstrel knights come, bearing the body of Elizabeth. Tannhäuser stands spellbound while Wolfram tells him of Elizabeth's devotion, and of her last prayer for him, and encourages him that through her intercession on high he may yet obtain pardon. As hope springs up Tannhäuser turns from Venus, who vanishes with her attendants. The funeral procession approaches, and Wolfram bids them halt and uncover the bier. Tannhäuser sinks on his knees before it, and praying for forgiveness dies, just as the band of pilgrims enters with the Pope's absolution for him and bearing the withered staff, which has miraculously burst into bloom.

THAÏS
(Tah-ēs)

FRENCH tragic grand opera, after a romance of the same name by Anatole France. Music by Jules Massenet. Book by Louis Gallet. First production, Paris, 1894. The scene is Alexandria and the Egyptian desert in the early Christian era.

CHARACTERS

ATHANAËL, a Cenobite monk	Baritone
NICIAS, a wealthy Alexandrian	Tenor
PALEMON, an aged Cenobite monk	Bass
THE SERVITOR	Baritone
THAÏS, actress and courtesan	Soprano
CROBYLE } slave girls	Soprano
MYRTALE }	Mezzo-Soprano
ALBINE, an abbess	Mezzo-Soprano

Cenobite monks, the White Nuns, citizens, servants, dancers, actors, comedians, philosophers, friends of Nicias, and the people.

ACT I. On the banks of the Nile the Cenobite monks are seated at their frugal evening meal. Athanaël is absent but at length comes, slowly and burdened with thought of the scandals that center about the beautiful courtesan, Thaïs, a priestess of Venus, whom once he saw and on whose threshold once he stood. God had saved him and given him peace in the desert. Now her sin and shame weigh heavily upon him and he would fain win her soul back to God. That night in sleep he sees a vision of the stage of the theater at Alexandria and of Thaïs, lightly clad, dancing and posing as Aphrodite. He starts up in fear and anger, then believes that he is called to save her. A holy enthusiasm seizes him, and telling his brethren of his mission, he receives Palemon's and their blessing and starts upon his journey out into the solitude of the Theban desert.

To Alexandria, to the house of Nicias, a former friend, he comes, and waiting on the terrace looks out with strong yearning over the godless city. Nicias enters from the banqueting hall, leaning on the shoulders of Corbyle and Myrtale, two beautiful slave girls, who are laughing heartily. Nicias greets Athanaël cordially. The monk tells him that he has left the desert but for a day, and asks Nicias if he knows Thaïs. Nicias replies that she is his mistress for a single day more, won at the price of all his vineyards and other domains. When the monk says that he purposes to lead her back to God, Nicias bursts into loud laughter. Athanaël repeats his conviction that he will snatch her from her present life and that she will enter a convent that day. Nicias tells him she is to come to his house after the theater to sup with him for the last time. When Athanaël would appear at the feast, Nicias orders Corbyle and Myrtale to attire him in a festal robe.

When Thaïs arrives amid the acclamations of a company of actors, philosophers, and friends, Nicias invites them into the banqueting hall, but detains Thaïs and sadly reminds her that this is their last evening together, to which she replies coldly. Athanaël comes toward them, looking at her sternly. When Nicias tells her that Athanaël is a saint and has come for her, to convert her to his holy religion, she looks at him incredulously and tells him to go his way, that love only can move her. Athanaël is angered at her defiance and, oblivious of the guests, bids her not to blaspheme. She smiles at him and asks him whence such folly in a man so made to love, who has not yet tasted life or passion. She bids him stay with them, and all, even Nicias, join in the invitation. He spurns them with loathing, and turning away, says that he awaits her at her house. Thaïs, daring him to defy great Venus, starts to pose as he beheld her in his vision, and he flees in horror.

Act II. The evening over, Thaïs returns to her house, wearied, restless, and fearful of growing old. Athanaël enters and watching her from the threshold, prays fervently that he may not be seduced from his purpose by her beauty. He tells her that he comes to win her from the love of earth to the far holier love of heaven. She laughs at him, but with such confidence does he speak of her conversion that she begins to fear his words. Suddenly he tears off the festal robe and appears in his monk's garb, and tells her that he is Athanaël, monk of Antinous, and that he curses the things of the flesh and the death that possesses her. She casts herself at his feet, saying that she has great fear of death and that she is not responsible for her life or her nature. He replies that she shall live for the life eternal. She begins to desire forgiveness and when Nicias's voice is heard fondly calling her, she shudders in repulsion. Athanaël says that he will wait at her door till day for her coming, but she vows she will remain and be Thaïs the courtesan still, then bursts into tears.

Shortly before dawn Thaïs comes from her house and arouses Athanaël, who sleeps at the foot of the steps. She says that God has spoken to her by his voice and that she will come with him. He tells her that he will take her to the monastery where Albine is the abbess, and there she shall live her life, devoted to holy things. Thaïs catches his fervor and is eager to go, but he tells her that first she must destroy all that belonged to her life of shame. She would keep a little statue of Eros, the beautiful figure of a child, but when Athanaël learns that Nicias gave it to her, he smashes it upon the pavement. She trembles at his harshness but submits, and they enter the house to carry on the work of destruction.

Nicias, slightly intoxicated and accompanied by gay companions, comes from his house. He is jubilant, for in gambling he has won thirty-fold the price he paid Thaïs. Corbyle and Myrtale sit beside him and dancers enter. While the dance is going on Athanaël appears on the threshold of Thaïs's house with a lighted torch in his hand. Nicias and the slave girls call to him, thinking that he has succumbed to the courtesan's charms. He severely interrupts their laughter, announcing that Thaïs is no longer theirs but, new-born, is the bride of the Lord. Thaïs comes, clad in a woolen tunic and followed sadly by her slaves, as flames burst from the building. When Athanaël bids her come with him, Nicias interposes and all her former companions protest, saying that he shall never take her from them. She declares that he is right, and he starts to lead her away. The crowd gathers about him and, seeing that the house is doomed, they are aroused to fury by the thought of the jewels and robes it contains, and wildly threaten him as the cause of the disaster. Some one throws a stone and wounds him in the face, but he and Thaïs stand side by side, firm and determined. As others take up stones Nicias, trying to defend Thaïs from the violence of the crowd that shouts for Athanaël's death, throws out handfuls of gold from his purse. As the crowd rushes to gather it, sorrowfully Nicias bids Thaïs good-bye and Athanaël draws her away, while Nicias with more gold stops the crowd from following.

ACT III. To an oasis in the desert Athanaël has brought Thaïs. Not far distant are the white tents of Albine's retreat. Thaïs is overcome with fatigue and begs Athanaël to let her rest; but he urges her on, commanding her to spare not her flesh but purify herself by repentance. When she staggers and cannot continue, he helps her to a seat in the shade and repents his harshness when he sees that her feet are bleeding. Prostrating himself before her, he calls her holy, and weeps and kisses her feet. Comforted by his approbation, she suggests that they continue their journey, but he brings food and water from a traveler's shelter near by. As he ministers to her they each realize with joy that her life has been confided to him by Heaven. Albine, the Abbess, and the nuns approach and he gives Thaïs over into her care. As Albine greets her tenderly Athanaël realizes that he must part from Thaïs. He charges her to live a life of holiness and to pray for him. Thaïs, overcome with emotion, kisses his hand in great gratitude and weeps to part from the one who has restored her to God. Deeply touched, he gazes upon her face, which seems to him beautiful with a divine radiance. They say good-bye until they shall meet in the celestial city, and when left alone he stands gazing after her, he cries out in anguish of spirit.

At sunset a terrible storm threatens the huts of the Cenobites on the banks of the Nile. The oppressive air is whipped by gusts of the simoon, and thunder and lightning rend the sky. Athanaël is missed, and Palemon says that since his return he has tasted neither food nor drink, that soul and body seem utterly crushed by his battle with the forces of evil. He comes, and passes among them unseeing. Alone with Palemon he confesses to him that since he won the soul of her who was the impure Thaïs his peace is dead, that vainly he has chastised his body but still the beauty of the woman haunts his dreams. The old monk laments that he ever went away, and, praying for him, leaves him. Alone Athanaël is again troubled by visions of Thaïs, and at length one in which he hears women's voices chanting that a saint is soon to leave this earth, that Thaïs of Alexandria is to die. He starts up and cries out against the divine justice, and wildly raves that he must behold her once again, for she is his. Desperate he rushes out into the night and the terrible storm.

In the garden of the monastery of Albine under a fig tree Thaïs lies as if dead, surrounded by the praying abbess and nuns. Albine recalls how in the three months since Thaïs came among them she has watched and prayed and wept, and that now her body has sunk under the weight of her penitence. Athanaël, pale and troubled, appears at the gate, and Albine welcomes him, knowing that he has come to pronounce a blessing on the dying woman. He strives to master his emotion, and advances toward Thaïs, calling her name. The nuns withdraw and, overwhelmed with grief, he falls prostrate, then drags himself to her couch and holds out his arms to her. She opens her eyes and gazes wistfully at him, but already earth is receding and she does not hear or understand what he says. In her delirium she recalls with delight their journey together; he remembers only her beauty. She speaks of the hours of repose in the oasis; he thinks only of the thirst that she alone can quench. She recalls the holy counsel he gave her when he taught her the only love; he passionately tells her that then he lied. In rapture she greets a dawning vision of heaven, while he denies heaven and says that nothing is true but life and passion, and avows his love for her. She raises herself up, seeing the outstretched arms of angels and ignoring the open arms of him at her side. In ecstasy she cries out that she sees God; and he in heart-rending anguish cries out that she is dead.

TOSCA
(*Tŏss'-kah*)

ITALIAN tragic grand opera, founded on a drama by Victorien Sardou. Music by Giacomo Puccini. Book by Luigi Illica and Giuseppe Giacosa. First production, Rome, 1900. The scene is laid in Rome in June, 1800.

CHARACTERS

Mario Cavaradossi, a painter	Tenor
Baron Scarpia, chief of the police	Baritone
Cesare Angelotti	Bass
A Sacristan	Baritone
Spoletta, a police agent	Tenor
Sciarrone, a gendarme	Bass
A Jailer	Bass
Floria Tosca, a celebrated singer	Soprano
A Shepherd Boy	Contralto

A judge, Cardinal, officer, sergeant, soldiers, police agents, a scribe, a hangman, artisans, ladies, nobles, and citizens.

Act I. Into the church of St. Andrea in Rome steals a man in convict's garb. From the base of a statue near the altar he draws forth a key, with which he unlocks the door of a chapel, and enters. The sacristan comes into the church bringing a pail of newly cleaned paint brushes and a basket of lunch. As he approaches a scaffolding near the altar Mario Cavaradossi enters and draws back the curtain from a partly finished picture of the Magdalen kneeling at the feet of Christ on the cross, and prepares to paint. The sacristan notices that the features of the Magdalen are those of a beautiful woman whom he has often of late seen worshiping. To his comments Mario replies that he copied the features of the unknown while she was praying. The

© Mishkin

GERALDINE FARRAR
AS "TOSCA"

sacristan deposits the brushes and the basket of food and wine, surprised when the painter says that he does not expect to eat to-day, and goes off. Mario looks at the features of the Magdalen, then takes from his pocket a picture of Tosca, his betrothed, and contrasts the two portraits, his heart turning fondly from the fair loveliness of the Magdalen to the dark vivacious beauty of the singer.

Startled by a sound, he looks about him and sees a convict coming toward him from the door of a chapel. The man calls him by name and he recognizes Cesare Angelotti, a friend who was imprisoned for political reasons. Angelotti throws himself on Mario's mercy and begs him to help him escape. He finds concealed near the altar a bundle of woman's clothes, which he says his sister secreted there for him. He is worn and famishing, and as Tosca's voice is heard calling to Mario, the painter urges upon him the basket of lunch and bids him again lock himself in the chapel. Tosca suspects from the delay that there was some one with Mario, and being of a jealous nature she accuses him of an intrigue, but he, though anxious and distracted by the peril of Angelotti, succeeds in reassuring her without telling her the cause of his anxiety. Tosca, who truly loves him, plans for them to slip away that evening, when she is through with her singing, and go to her villa, and joyously they repledge each other their love. She happens, however, to catch sight of the Magdalen and recognizes the features as those of Lady Attavanti, the sister of Angelotti. Although he says he does not know the lady's name but was impressed by her beauty, her jealousy again flames. Tenderly he assures her that no beauty attracts him like hers, and they are happy again and bid good-bye until evening.

When she is gone Mario tells Angelotti of a hidden path to the villa and of an old well on the way, where he could hide if followed. A cannon shot is heard, showing that Angelotti's escape is known. The two men have scarcely gone out when the choir boys enter with the sacristan, and soon Scarpia and his police come, having traced Angelotti to the church. In the empty chapel are found a fan with a crest upon it that Scarpia recognizes as that of the Attavanti, and the now empty lunch basket. Scarpia questions the frightened sacristan closely but finds out only that the lunch basket was Mario's, who had however declared that he did not care for food that day. While Scarpia sends his officers to trace the fugitive and Mario, whom he believes is assisting him to escape, he remains at the church, and soon Tosca returns, troubled by Mario's manner. She is disturbed at not finding him, and Scarpia, who has long been an admirer of the beautiful singer, now determines to turn her against her lover and win her for himself. He greets her with flattering comments upon her devotion in coming to the church to pray and not to meet a lover, as some do. Tosca, doubly suspicious, asks his meaning and he shows her the fan with the crest, which she also recognizes. She now thinks that Mario is in love with Lady Attavanti, and in tears leaves the church, followed by Scarpia's spies. The chief of police, his mind filled with evil plots, with great show of devotion joins in the service celebrating the victory of his forces over those of Buonaparte, and hypocritically kneeling, offers his homage as the Cardinal enters.

Act II. Scarpia is dining that evening in his apartments on an upper floor of the Farnese Palace. Knowing that Tosca is to sing there at the palace at the queen's celebration of the victory, he sends her a note of invitation representing that he has news of her lover. Cruel and conscienceless, he delights in the thought that he has her within his power and he gloats over his triumph. Mario is brought in, a prisoner, but the officers say that no trace of Angelotti has been found. Scarpia is wildly angry and demands of Mario information as to where the fugitive is hidden. Mario firmly refuses to tell. Scarpia, finding threats unavailing, orders Mario taken into the next room and tortured. Tosca comes and runs to embrace her lover, and he bids her be silent about what she has seen lest he be killed. He is then led away.

Scarpia asks where Angelotti is. She hears Mario's long-suppressed moans, then sudden shrieks, and her own heart is tortured beyond endurance. For some time she obeys his injunction not to tell, then in utmost horror she declares that Angelotti is hidden in the well in the garden. Scarpia commands that the torture cease and that Mario be brought in. Tosca hovers fondly over him, grieving, soothing, restoring, but he reproves her for divulging the secret. When Sciarrone comes with the news that Buonaparte was victorious, Mario predicts the early downfall of Scarpia and his tyranny. Scarpia, furious, orders him executed, and he is led away to prison to await death. When Tosca would go with him, she is commanded to stay.

Alone with Scarpia she asks at what price she may purchase Mario's freedom. Scarpia tells her that he has long loved her and that she has scorned him; now only at the price of her honor can Mario be freed. Long she refuses to submit to him. Spoletta reports that Angelotti committed suicide when they were about to take him. When Scarpia says that Mario has but an hour to live, Tosca, weeping with shame and passionately praying for deliverance, consents. Scarpia tells her that it will be necessary for Mario to go through a mock execution, and she demands also that safe conduct be given them both from the city that night. While Scarpia is writing the order she contrives to possess herself of a dagger that lies upon the table. He advances toward her with open arms and she stabs him to the heart. He falls and as he lies prone she takes the paper from him, washes her hands at a bowl on the table, and is about to leave the room when, realizing the solemnity of death, she takes two candles and places them either side of his head, and the cross upon his bosom, then steals away.

Act III. That same night on the terrace of San Angelo, where the lights of Rome are visible, Mario is listening to his death warrant, which the guard reads him, saying that he has but an hour to live. The doomed man requests paper and ink that he may write to Tosca. Memories of their happiness come to his mind and the bitterness of death overwhelms him, and he sobs in grief. He is startled by some one's approach and, looking up, sees Tosca herself. She tells him of his reprieve, that the execution is to be but a sham one, and that she has safe conduct for them both. He asks her how she obtained such favors, and she confesses the desperate bargain she made. He listens with shuddering horror until she tells him of securing the dagger and of plunging it into Scarpia's heart, then he seizes the hands she would withhold from him as defiled with blood, and kisses them, exulting in her high courage. She bids him fall when the soldiers shoot, but to lie still until she gives him word to get up, so that none may interfere with their departure. He promises and bravely they await the appointed time, rejoicing together in the happy future that awaits them.

At length the squad of soldiers appears, and Mario is led to his place against the wall. With Tosca standing at one side, where none may see the happy smile with which she encourages her lover, the squad line up and fire. Mario falls. The soldiers go down the staircase, and at length when all is quiet, Tosca goes to him and bids him rise. He does not stir and in horror she realizes that he is killed. In agony she flings herself upon his body. Soon she hears footsteps on the stairs. In sudden terror she rises and faces Spoletta, who, followed by Sciarrone and guards, approaches her. With a gesture she indicates that Mario is dead. Spoletta accuses her of having killed Scarpia and advances to arrest her. She dashes to the parapet and leaps from it off into space, while Spoletta and the soldiers gaze over it in horror.

LA TRAVIATA
(*Lah Trah-vē-ah'-tah*)

ITALIAN tragic grand opera, based upon the story of Camille in "La Dame aux Camélias" by Alexander Dumas, the Younger. Music by Giuseppe Verdi. Book by Francesco Maria Piave. First production, Venice, 1853. The scene is laid in Paris and its vicinity in the reign of Louis XIV, about 1700.

CHARACTERS

ALFRED GERMONT, lover of Violetta	*Tenor*
GIORGIO GERMONT, father of Alfred	*Baritone*
GASTONE DE LETORIERES	*Tenor*
BARON DOUPHOL, a rival of Alfred	*Bass*
MARQUIS D'OBIGNY	*Bass*
DOCTOR GRENVIL, a physician	*Bass*
GIUSEPPE, servant to Violetta	*Tenor*
VIOLETTA VALERY, a courtesan	*Soprano*
FLORA BERVOIX, friend of Violetta	*Mezzo-Soprano*
ANNINA, confidante of Violetta	*Soprano*

Ladies and gentlemen, who are friends and guests of Violetta and Flora; matadors, picadors, gypsies, servants, and masks.

ACT I. In the drawing-room of Violetta's house in Paris is gathered a gay party drinking and making merry. Among the guests is Alfred Germont, a young man from Provence, who almost against his will has been strongly attracted to Violetta. He sings a jolly drinking song, to which she responds, and the guests join in on the chorus. As the guests go into the ballroom Alfred and Violetta remain behind, and he asks her about her life. She tells him that early she was left alone in the world and drifted into a life of gaiety and folly. He pours out to her the love that she has stirred within him. They recall their first meeting and she finds herself strangely responding to the deep and noble feeling that he expresses. He would have her leave her present companions and come away with him, to be his alone far from the dazzling whirl of these false pleasures. She listens with longing, and when he bids her farewell and goes away she meditates on her dream of love, of which this seems the fulfillment,—of a love such as she has never known, a gentleness and tenderness that would shield and cherish her through all her life, which she feels will not be long. She hears, however, the sound of the dance music and reminds herself that for her there is no returning, that only the life of pleasure with its unsatisfactory and ever fresh delights is possible, and with reckless gaiety she rejoins her guests.

Act II. Within a country house near Paris Alfred and Violetta have been living quietly and happily for three months. Alfred, sitting alone, rejoices in the happiness they find in each other, and at Violetta's contentment and her devotion to him. He laments his wild life and feels remade by the peace that Violetta's love has brought him. He happens to learn from Annina that her frequent journeys to Paris are to dispose of some of Violetta's jewels or property in order to keep up their establishment. Sorely ashamed at his thoughtless acceptance of Violetta's support and this further proof of her great love for him, he leaves hastily for Paris that he too may obtain some money. Violetta returns and is surprised and troubled by his departure. Soon Giorgio Germont, his father, comes. He has been searching for Alfred and at length has found him. He upbraids Violetta for influencing his son to lead a spendthrift and dissolute life, but she only smiles at the charge. He begs her to release Alfred from his promises to her and permit him to go home to Provence. She is willing to do anything but give

Alfred up, and his father cannot but recognize her devotion and sincerity.

She will persuade Alfred to go back home; but Germont points out that it is impossible for her to go with him there, for he has a daughter whose engagement to a young man of estimable family would be broken if Alfred's alliance with Violetta were known. So the father pleads with her that she renounce Alfred once for all. At first she will not consider it, but when the father pleads for his daughter, whose love and happiness will otherwise be sacrificed, she consents to leave him. Greatly touched by her nobility Germont embraces her as though she were his daughter, and in tears she pledges her word. He leaves and she writes a note of farewell to Alfred, which leads him to think that she has wearied of him. She has gone when he returns and reads her note. Incredulous at first, then torn with grief and doubt and despair, he prepares to go to Paris and seek her. His father comes and pleads with him to return home. Alfred, wild with outraged affection, will not listen, but is deaf to his father's appeals to filial piety and honor, and departs to seek Violetta.

In a richly furnished salon at the house of Flora Bervoix her friends and Violetta's are gathered. They speak of the separation of the lovers and her recent return to the city and acceptance of the attentions of Baron Douphol. Alfred comes in, and when questioned about Violetta, disclaims all knowledge of her movements. He sits down at the gaming table and, gambling for heavy stakes, wins large sums of money. Violetta comes accompanied by Baron Douphol. She is greatly disturbed at the sight of Alfred, but he does not seem to see her. He challenges Baron Douphol to a game and continues to win. The guests go out to supper, but Violetta and Alfred both linger behind. He harshly upbraids her for leaving him, and begs her to return. She, although she longs to grant his wish, remembers her pledge to his father and gives him to understand that she cares for Baron Douphol. Outraged by her words, he throws open the doors to the dining-hall and bids the guests return. Then he points out Violetta to them, and scornfully accuses her of having made him greatly indebted to her, and having then disdained him. He flings at her feet the bag of money he has just won and declares that he pays his debt. The guests rebuke him for so wounding one who has loved him. His father enters and, shocked at the insult to Violetta, would disown him. Alfred, aroused from his jealousy and anger, realizes how shameful a thing he has done. The baron challenges him to a duel, and Violetta, fainting from shame and weakness, pities Alfred for the remorse he will feel when he knows the truth, while his father leads him away.

ACT III. Within Violetta's apartment she lies on the couch while her maid watches near by. Dr. Grenvil comes and attends her and tells Annina that her mistress has not long to live. When he has gone Violetta, who longs for Alfred but will not break her word and send for him, receives a letter from his father saying that the baron was wounded in the duel but is improving, that Alfred is leaving for a foreign country, but not until he comes to ask her pardon, for her sacrifice has been told him. Violetta is happy, though she knows that she is very ill and that Alfred comes too late for them to be happy together. Cherishing the memory of his love and praying for forgiveness of her sins, she calmly faces death. Alfred comes and flings himself at her feet in remorse for his distrust of her. Violetta, happy again in his love and forgetting her impending fate, vows that they shall be separated no more, and plans to go away with him. Exhausted by her joy she collapses, and he realizes how wasted and pale she is. Dr. Grenvil comes, and also Germont, who bitterly regrets the suffering he has brought upon her. Violetta, blissfully content in the warm affection thus shown her, smiles on them, but she has suffered too long, and quickly expires.

TRISTAN UND ISOLDE

(*Trĭs'-tahn ōōndt Ees-ŏl'-deh*)

(TRISTAN AND ISOLDA)

GERMAN tragic grand opera, the plot of which was derived from an old Celtic poem by Gottfried of Strasburg, who lived in the thirteenth century. Both music and book by Richard Wagner. First production, Munich, 1865. The scene is Cornwall, Brittany, and the sea, in antiquity.

CHARACTERS

TRISTAN, a Cornish knight, nephew of King Mark	Tenor
KING MARK OF CORNWALL	Bass
KURVENAL, servant to Tristan	Baritone
MELOT	Tenor
A SHEPHERD	Tenor
A STEERSMAN	Baritone
A SAILOR LAD	Tenor
ISOLDA, Princess of Ireland	Soprano
BRANGÆNE, Isolda's friend and attendant	Soprano

Sailors, knights, esquires, men-at-arms, and attendants.

Tristan, the nephew of King Mark of Cornwall, had slain in single combat Morold, brother of the King of Ireland, who had come to Cornwall exacting tribute. The head of Morold was, according to the custom then, sent back to Ireland to his betrothed, Isolda, daughter of his brother, the king. Tristan, however, sustained a severe wound, which no skill in his own country could cure. Therefore, having heard of the wonderful healing art of Isolda, in which she had been trained by her mother, a woman famous for her skill with drugs, he had set sail in a small boat, and under the name of "Tantris" and the guise of a minstrel arrived at the Irish court. There he was hospitably received and Isolda herself attended to his wound. One day, observing his sword, she discovered a notch in it. Aroused, she compared the sword's notch with the sword splinter she had found buried in the skull of Morold. No doubt remained, and sword in hand she stood over Tristan, whose life she vowed to have in revenge for his deed. Unflinchingly he looked into her eyes, and the sword dropped from her hand. To her compassion he owed his life, and love sprang up between them.

When, restored, he set sail for Cornwall, he spoke solemn vows of gratitude to Isolda. In his own land he so sang her praise that the nobles proposed to King Mark that he take the Irish princess for his queen and thereby cement the friendship of the two kingdoms and provide an heir for his throne. Tristan alone was silent at the suggestion, and the jealous nobles turned upon him and accused him of considering only his personal advantage as his uncle's prospective heir. The young knight, quick to resent a slur upon his honor, proposed that he himself go to Ireland and bring back the bride. In regal state he came to the Irish court, was welcomed, and his mission favorably regarded. Isolda alone knew his betrayal of her peace, and felt herself unpardonably wronged. She knew whom she loved, and felt that by him she was beloved, —yet he came seeking her for another. Resignedly she bowed to his will and with her faithful servant, Brangæne, went aboard his ship to be carried as bride to King Mark. For a night and a day she has spoken no word.

ACT I. On Tristan's ship a large section of the deck has been curtained off as Isolda's private cabin. Here she lies upon a couch, her face buried in a pillow. Long she has thought over her plight, and her grief is now turned to a dark rage which finds in every circumstance fuel for its flame. Aroused by the song of a young sailor, she asks Brangæne

© Aimé Dupont

LILLI LEHMANN
AS ISOLDE, IN "TRISTAN UND ISOLDE"

where the vessel is, and learns that already the land of Cornwall is in sight. Desperate, she pours forth her wrath and invokes the winds and the waves to engulf the ship. Brangæne, frightened, begs her mistress to take her into her confidence. Isolda in the stress of her emotions gasps for air and the servant draws aside the curtain so that the whole deck is exposed to view. Isolda sees the sailors at the mainmast, the groups of knights and attendants seated in the stern, and apart from the others Tristan standing, gazing over the waters, while Kurvenal, his faithful body-servant, lies at his feet.

Isolda, watching Tristan, murmurs of her love for him, now past, for she has doomed him. She scornfully points him out to Brangæne as a craven who dares not meet the look of her eyes. She haughtily tells her to go and command him to come to her. Brangæne goes and at first as a request then as a command delivers the message. Tristan inquires considerately after Isolda, but excuses himself, saying that honor keeps him from her. Kurvenal, resenting the command, gives answer that his master but conveys the princess as bride to King Mark, and that he is in honor bound not to choose her for his own. As Brangæne, offended, returns to her mistress Kurvenal sings of Tristan's victory over Morold, and the knights take up the refrain, and Isolda, hearing, is thrice angered. She has also heard Kurvenal's reply, and wildly she tells Brangæne that this Tristan is the very man whom as "Tantris" Brangæne helped to nurse back to life.

When Isolda curses Tristan and her own compassion that spared him, Brangæne throws herself upon her mistress and, drawing her to the couch, endeavors to soothe her, telling her that Tristan gives her the kingdom of Cornwall, otherwise his own heritage, and would make her the wife of the noble

King Mark, whose praise all men sound and who is served by such noble knights as Tristan. Brangæne also reminds Isolda that the king must perforce love her, and lest by any chance he should not, the queen, her mother, has sent with her the magic love potion to be given by her to King Mark on their wedding night. This reminds Isolda, and she calmly asks for the casket of drugs that her mother prepared for her use. Searching therein she finds the draft of death. Brangæne is horrified, but they are interrupted by the cries of the sailors, and Kurvenal brings message from his master that land is near and he would have Isolda prepare to meet the king.

Isolda replies that if Tristan would lead her to the king he must first ask her pardon for his trespass. She bids Brangæne prepare the cup of peace, and hands her from the casket a philter to be poured into a golden cup, saying that Tristan will drink truce with her. Brangæne, alarmed by her mistress's exultation, perceives her purpose and in fear and trembling takes the flask and flings herself at Isolda's feet, beseeching; but the princess will not change her purpose and commands her to obey.

Tristan enters and Isolda reproaches him for not coming to her. He says that honor forbade it. She tells him that, though the old feud was abandoned by the people, yet there is blood-guilt between him and her, for she was Morold's betrothed. Tristan, very sorrowful at her words, offers her his sword and bids her now not fail to take his life, if she so loved Morold. She will not have the sword, but says that they will drink together an end of strife. She motions to Brangæne, who, trembling, prepares the cup. Tristan is silent; then, at her taunt, says that he knows what she conceals, and himself conceals more than she knows. She proffers him the cup, saying that ere long they must stand by

King Mark together. Tristan takes it, declaring that he now drinks the cup of complete recovery, and toasting his own honor, fearlessly drinks. Isolda wrests the cup from his hand, demanding half the draft, and drinks to him, then flings the cup aside. They stand gazing at each other, shuddering at, yet defiant of, the impending death. Gradually their gaze changes to gentleness, then to passion. They tremble and cannot understand, then drawn to each other with increasing longing, in an ecstasy of love they embrace, oblivious to the shouts of the people acclaiming King Mark. Brangæne, aroused to a sense of what she has done, rushes between them, and Kurvenal, coming to Tristan, explains to him that the king comes to receive his bride. Brangæne, despairing, confesses to Isolda that she gave them the love potion, and Isolda, turning to Tristan in horror, asks of him if she must live. All is confusion as the king and his retinue draw near.

Act II. On a bright summer night in the palace garden, before the tower within which is Isolda's chamber, sounds of hunting are heard coming from the near-by forest. In the open door of the tower a flaming torch is fixed, and Brangæne is watching on the tower steps. Isolda comes from her chamber, impatient to have cease the sounds of the king's hunting party that she may signal her lover. Brangæne is exceedingly anxious and delays extinguishing the torch, because she believes that treachery is afoot. When the impatient Isolda, hearing no further sound, herself quenches the light, Brangæne, again confessing her crime in mixing the love potion, warns her that Melot, Tristan's trusted friend, seeks to betray him and her; but Isolda is incredulous. She waves her handkerchief and soon Tristan approaches.

With deep emotion the lovers meet and give themselves up to the enjoyment of a companionship denied to them by day. Tristan draws her to a flowery bank and they recline there. Brangæne remains on watch, and as day breaks she calls again and again to her mistress, but the lovers do not heed. Suddenly Kurvenal comes, seeking his master and urging him to instant flight. Already it is too late, for Melot comes, followed by King Mark and his retinue. Isolda, leaning still upon the bank, turns her face away in shame, and Tristan stretches out his mantle to conceal her, then remains motionless, facing the men before him.

The silence is broken by the traitor Melot, who asks if his words were not true. King Mark, deeply moved and with trembling voice, stands looking at Tristan like an aggrieved father who cannot believe his son's crime. Tristan slowly lowers his eyes before the gaze of the king, torn with ever-increasing grief and shame. King Mark reminds Tristan of his affection, of their long companionship, of Tristan's valiant deeds, and this his last great favor,—the bringing of a beautiful and lovable bride to him, who yet has not taken her to wife,—and asks the explanation of this, his present treachery. Tristan has none to give, but turns tenderly to Isolda and solemnly asks her if she will follow him where he goes. She as tenderly replies, knowing well his meaning. He kisses her on the forehead, at which Melot indignantly starts forward, drawing his sword. Tristan also draws, and not denying his own treachery, sets upon Melot as former friend and present traitor. When Melot presents his blade Tristan drops his guard and receives a deadly wound. He sinks in Kurvenal's arms, while Isolda throws herself upon him and the king holds back Melot.

Act III. In the garden of an old and almost ruined castle

upon high cliffs above the coast of Brittany, beneath a lime-tree, lies Tristan, apparently lifeless, watched over by Kurvenal. The pipe of a shepherd, who has been set to watch for the vessel that brings Isolda, is heard at intervals. Kurvenal has with great sacrifice and devotion brought his master back to his ancestral home and there tended him. Despairing of the wound, he has sent for Isolda, and now, weary and spent with watching, he anxiously awaits her coming. At length Tristan stirs and becomes conscious, to Kurvenal's great joy. To his questions the servant tells him where he is and that Isolda comes. Tristan, who has fallen back exhausted, is aroused by the name, and affectionately embraces his faithful servant for all his devotion and this last, best hope. In his fevered imagination he seems to see the ship coming, but when Kurvenal says there is no ship in sight, he grows melancholy and at length falls back senseless. Kurvenal sobs in terror, thinking him dead, but he revives and asks if the ship has come. Suddenly the shepherd pipes joyfully and from the watch tower Kurvenal sights the vessel and goes to meet Isolda.

Tristan, delirious with joy, raises himself up, then stands erect, and exulting in Isolda's healing skill, tears the bandage from his wound, which bleeds anew. He hears her voice and staggers forward, to be clasped in her arms, then sink slowly to the ground. With only one word, one look of recognition, he dies. She bends over him, praying him to speak to her, then as she realizes the truth, sinks senseless on his body.

Kurvenal stands motionless, gazing at his master, but suddenly hears sounds of combat, and the shepherd cries out that another ship has come. He springs up, and with but a handful of retainers seeks to barricade the gate of the castle and keep out King Mark and Melot. Brangæne's voice is heard calling her mistress. As Melot approaches the gate

Kurvenal, exulting, cuts him down. As he dies Brangæne cries out to Kurvenal that he mistakes, but still he and his men fight valiantly. Brangæne succeeds in getting in and flies to her mistress, while King Mark and his followers drive Kurvenal back and force their way in. Kurvenal, wounded, points out his master and dies at his feet. The king, seeing that Tristan is dead, kneels, sobbing, by his body. Brangæne has revived Isolda and tells her that she confessed to the king her giving of the love potion. Then King Mark tells Isolda how, learning that Tristan had been as ever true, he hastened to come to them in order that he might bestow her upon her lover as bride. Isolda, however, unconscious of those about her, hears not his words, but looking upon Tristan, pours out her soul in love and longing, then sinks in Brangæne's arms by Tristan's body and dies.

IL TROVATORE
(*El Trō-vah-tō'-rā*)
(THE TROUBADOUR)

ITALIAN tragic grand opera, after a Spanish drama of the same name by Antonio Garcia Gatteerez. Music by Giuseppe Verdi. Book by Salvatore Cammarano. First production, Rome, 1853. The scene is Biscay and Aragon in the fifteenth century.

CHARACTERS

COUNT DI LUNA, a powerful young noble of the Prince of Aragon .... *Baritone*
FERRANDO, a captain of the guard of Count di Luna.... *Bass*
MANRICO, a young chieftain under the Prince of Biscay, and reputed son of Azucena................. *Tenor*
RUIZ, a soldier in Manrico's service................. *Tenor*
AN OLD GYPSY..................................... *Baritone*
DUCHESS LEONORA, lady in waiting to an Aragon Princess .... *Soprano*
INEZ, confidant of Leonora....................... *Soprano*
AZUCENA, a wandering Biscayan gypsy...... *Mezzo-Soprano*

Followers of the Count di Luna, a messenger, a jailer, soldiers, nuns, gypsies, and attendants.

ACT I. In a vestibule of the Aliaferia Palace the soldiers and retainers of Count di Luna are awaiting his coming, and Ferrando is telling them the story of the count's younger brother. While yet a babe in his cradle his nurse one day surprised an old gypsy woman sitting by his side and looking at him malevolently. Gypsies were then regarded with superstitious terror, and when the child began to be sickly the present count's father searched for the gypsy and she was burned at the stake for witchcraft. She had a daughter, who sought revenge. That night the ailing child disappeared and among the embers of the fire were found the bones of a babe. Ferrando's story is received with horror, and the soldiers denounce and curse the gypsy, while the captain of the guard prays that he may yet come across her. He tells how the old count died, unbelieving that it was his child that was burned, and making his son promise to search for his lost brother.

In the garden of the royal palace Duchess Leonora, lady attendant of the princess, is walking with her friend, Inez. She speaks of the love she feels for the valiant knight, Manrico, whom she first saw when she herself crowned him as winner of all honors at a tournament, and who has since nightly serenaded her below her window. The ladies have reëntered the palace when Count di Luna, who also harbors a deep passion for the duchess, comes into the garden. The song of the troubadour is heard, pleading and beautiful, and the count is filled with rage and jealousy. He watches and soon Leonora comes eagerly from the palace. In the dimness she sees only where he stands and goes up to him, but instead of the troubadour, faces the count. At her surprised exclamation Manrico comes forward and unmasks himself, and the count recognizes him as one whose life is forfeit because he has taken up arms against the government. Manrico accepts the count's challenge, in spite of Leonora's protests and her efforts to calm their jealous passion. They withdraw to fight, leaving her swooning.

Act II. Within a gypsy camp in the Biscay Mountains in the early morning the gypsies are beginning their day's tasks, hammering upon the anvils shoes for their horses, and joyously singing. Azucena, whose mother had perished at the stake by the Count di Luna's command, is among them, and when all go off on their forays she is left at the camp

© Aimé Dupont

ENRICO CARUSO
AS MANRICO, IN "IL TROVATORE"

with her son Manrico, who, though still weak, is recovering from an almost mortal wound received on the field of battle. Azucena, who seems obsessed by a horrible memory, relates to Manrico her mother's death, begging him to help her avenge it. She tells how she herself stole the count's youngest child and with her own babe in her arms, distraught and heedless, threw a babe into the fire, and when the flames had died looked about her and beheld—not her own, but the count's son.

Manrico starts up in amazement, and asks if he, then, is not her son. Trying to convince him that he is, in spite of her admission, she recalls all her fondness and care, and how but recently she sought him among the dead at Petilla, where after his duel with the count he had fought against the government's forces, and finding him yet alive, had nursed him back to health. Azucena asks him why he failed to kill the count, and he tells her that, though he soon worsted his rival, yet as he stood above him he heard a voice as if from heaven bidding him spare him, and he obeyed. Azucena commands him never again to fail, but to avenge her mother's wrong. A messenger comes from Ruiz with orders from the Prince of Biscay for Manrico to take command of Castellor and defend it; also, with the news that Duchess Leonora, believing him dead, is that evening to enter a convent. Manrico starts up and hastily departs, although Azucena would detain him.

To the cloister of a convent near Castellor the Count di Luna, with Ferrando and other followers, has come to seize Duchess Leonora before she takes the veil. They hide in the garden and the count watches and rejoices that she is soon to be his. The chant of the nuns is heard and they come out of the convent to receive Leonora, who, with Inez, enters. The two women bid each other farewell, Inez passionately weeping, and her friend sad and calm. The count intercepts Leonora as she would enter the convent. The nuns surround her, seeking to protect her as he attempts to seize her, when suddenly Manrico appears like a phantom and places himself between the count and Leonora. She with great joy recognizes her lover and turns to him gladly, eager for him to take her away with him. The count furiously tries to prevent it, but Manrico's soldiers, under Ruiz, enter, and engage the count's forces and drive them back.

Act III. In the camp of the Count di Luna's troops before Castellor, where Manrico has conducted Leonora, the soldiers seize a gypsy, who they think is a spy, and are bringing her to the count. It is Azucena, who, in her effort to reach Manrico, had wandered within the enemy's lines. To their questions she replies that she is from Biscalia, and the count and Ferrando both start at the word. Ferrando scrutinizes her features and recognizes her, and the count questions her until she makes incriminating admissions regarding the crime of more than twenty years before. Realizing that she is in the hands of her archenemy, she involuntarily calls on Manrico for aid. The count, doubly exultant that he has in his power the mother of his rival, condemns her to be, like her mother, burned at the stake.

In a hall near the chapel in Castellor Manrico and Leonora are joyfully anticipating their immediate marriage when they hear the clamor of arms. Manrico says that they are besieged and that on the morrow he must engage the foe. He tries to quiet her fears, and his triumphant love gives him rare courage and hope. They are about to enter the chapel to solemnize their marriage when Ruiz intercepts them with the news that Azucena is bound to a stake in the enemy's camp and is about to be burned. Horrified, Manrico summons his soldiers at once and rushes off to her aid, telling Leonora that the gypsy is his mother.

Act IV. Manrico's forces were repulsed and he himself taken prisoner. Count di Luna stormed Castellor, but did not find Duchess Leonora, so went with his troops and prisoners back to his Aliaferia Palace. Hither outside a wing of the castle, near the prison tower, come Leonora and Ruiz by night, enveloped in dark cloaks. Leonora dismisses Ruiz, saying that even yet perhaps she may save Manrico. As she watches she hears within the mournful chant of priests who pray for the souls of the doomed prisoners, and her heart is overwhelmed with terror. Then suddenly there comes to her the voice of her troubadour, singing a passionate farewell to his loved one. Torn with grief and almost despairing, she conceals herself as the count and his followers enter, and hears him give orders for the death of Manrico and Azucena at daybreak. When he is left alone he laments that he cannot find Leonora, and she comes and stands before him. She prays him to have mercy on the prisoner, but he simply exults the more in his triumph. In despair, she then says that she will consent to become his wife if he will spare Manrico's life. The count rejoices in obtaining his greatest desire and accepts her proviso, while she, purposing to suck poison from a ring she wears as soon as she is assured of Manrico's freedom, forgets her own fate in her joy that Manrico will live.

Within the prison cell Azucena lies upon a pallet of straw, while Manrico watches over her or looks longingly from the grated window and thinks of the love now lost to him. Delirious with fear and grief, the gypsy now relives her mother's death and now sings dreamily of the home mountains, then at last, soothed by Manrico's tenderness, falls asleep. Leonora enters and the lovers joyfully embrace. She tells him that he has his liberty and urges him to flee at once. He is incredulous, and when she says she cannot go with him, he demands how his pardon was obtained. He reads in her gaze the price, and in horror and anger spurns her. Still forgetting herself, she urges him to flee, and at last, as he will not, she begins to feel the stupor of the poison which she took before entering the cell, and sinks down at his feet. Then he realizes what she has done, and prays her to forgive him for his dark suspicions. In passionate grief he bends over her as she dies.

Count di Luna enters, and realizing the strategy, in his wrath orders the soldiers to take Manrico at once and behead him. As he is led away Azucena wakes, and the count leads her to the window to behold the death of her son. Wildly she cries out that the count has killed his brother, and falls dead, while the count swoons with horror and remorse.

VERSIEGELT

(*Fer-sēē'-ghelt*)

(SEALED)

GERMAN comic light opera, adapted from the story "Der Versiegelte Bürgermeister," by Ernest Raupach. Music by Leo Blech. Book by Richard Batka and Pordes-Milo. First production, Hamburg, 1908. The scene is a small German village about 1830.

CHARACTERS

BRAUN, the Burgomaster........................*Baritone*
BERTEL, son of Mrs. Willmers, clerk of the council....*Tenor*
LAMPE, messenger of the council, the Burgomaster's bailiff ....*Bass*
NEIGHBOR KNOTE ....*Bass*
ELSE, daughter of Braun........................*Soprano*
MRS. GERTRUDE SCHRAMM, a young widow....*Mezzo-Soprano*
MRS. WILLMERS, a widow..........................*Alto*
THE CHAMPION SHOT (a speaking part).

Mrs. Gertrude is sewing in her sitting-room when Mrs. Willmers rushes in to say that the Burgomaster, having let her taxes run on without notifying her, is now demanding them, and that everything she has, including her wardrobe, an heirloom, must be sold at auction. Mrs. Gertrude consents to have the wardrobe brought to her house. Mrs. Willmers thereupon goes out to get Neighbor Knote to bring it over at once. The young widow sits musing upon her loneliness, and decides that she will marry the Burgomaster. After the wardrobe is placed Mrs. Willmers tells Mrs. Gertrude of the love of her son, Bertel, for the Burgomaster's daughter, Else. The young pair enter with the news that the Burgomaster will not listen to their marrying.

Gertrude offers to help them, but reproves them for their criticism of the Burgomaster, saying that he is quite right—marriage is not a matter to be entered upon in haste. The lovers assure each other that their love will endure, and Else tells Mrs. Gertrude how much her father admires her, and she begs her to plead their cause with him. Left alone, Mrs. Gertrude rehearses her part in doubly subduing the stern father.

Lampe, the bailiff, comes in, bringing greetings from the Burgomaster. Suddenly his eye falls upon the wardrobe. He leaves hurriedly to go to Mrs. Willmers. Shortly the Burgomaster himself comes, and Mrs. Gertrude treats him very hospitably. During their talk he tells her how perplexed he is to know what to do with his daughter now that she is in love. Gertrude counsels gentleness and is tenderly sympathetic. Under her skillful leading the Burgomaster avows his love and starts to kiss her when the voices of the bailiff and Mrs. Willmers are heard without. The Burgomaster does not wish them to find him there, so he takes refuge in the wardrobe, which the widow then locks. She admits the bailiff and her neighbor. Lampe asks Mrs. Willmers if the wardrobe is hers, and she has to confess it is. The key is missing, so he seals it very elaborately. Trying to find out what it contains, he pokes through the carvings with his umbrella, and declares that there is something alive in it. Gertrude suggests that it may be a cat or a mouse, but Lampe grows suspicious and thinks it may be a lover, so he goes off to tell the Burgomaster. Else and Bertel enter, and again the lovers and the two widows consult how they may best win over Else's obdurate parent.

When the widows go out, the lovers woo each other openly and complain of the Burgomaster's hard-heartedness. Else finally tells Bertel that she will give him a hundred kisses and then bid him farewell. Her father thereupon furiously calls out to her. They search for the voice. He begs them to let him out of the wardrobe, and they say they cannot because of the official seals. He continues to beseech them and they make his consent to their marriage the condition on which they will let him out. Almost suffocated, he consents, but Else adds another proviso—a rich dowry, including a house and garden. Bertel draws up the agreement and when it is ready for the Burgomaster's signature, they release him. At that moment the three, hearing footsteps approaching, hide, the Burgomaster first locking the wardrobe, into which the lovers have hastened.

Mrs. Gertrude enters, accompanied by an admirer, the champion shot of a contest that had that evening been held, and followed by many villagers. The people dance around the wardrobe and joke about the Burgomaster's being hidden therein. At last Gertrude produces the key and opens it. Instead of the Burgomaster, out come the two lovers. Lampe hurries in with the alarming news that the Burgomaster has disappeared; but his Honor himself, stepping forward from his hiding-place, announces that the Burgomaster is dead. He orders that the wardrobe be restored to its owner, gives his blessing to his daughter and her lover, and asks Gertrude to be his wife. She readily consents, and the sport ends with merrymaking, in which all join.

WERTHER

(*Vehr'-tĕr*)

FRENCH tragic grand opera, founded upon Goethe's "The Sorrows of Werther." Music by Jules Massenet. Book by Edouard Blau, Paul Milliet, and Georges Hartmann. First production, Vienna, 1892. The scene is Frankfort, Germany, from July to December, 178—.

CHARACTERS

WERTHER (aged twenty-three) .... *Tenor*
ALBERT (aged twenty-five) .... *Baritone*
THE BAILIFF (aged fifty) .... *Bass*
SCHMIDT } friends of the bailiff .... { *Tenor*
JOHANN }   { *Baritone*
BRUHLMANN, a young man .... *Baritone*
CHARLOTTE, daughter of the bailiff (aged twenty) .. *Soprano*
SOPHIA, sister of Charlotte (aged fifteen) .... *Soprano*
KATCHEN, a young girl .... *Mezzo-Soprano*

Six younger children of the bailiff: Fritz, Max, Hans, Karl, Gretel, Clara (all sopranos).

ACT I. Within his garden the bailiff is seated with his six younger children about him one July midday, and he is directing their rehearsal of some Christmas carols. His friends, Johann and Schmidt, come along and applaud the music. The children run to them and greet them cordially. Johann tells them that they rush the season with their carols, and the bailiff complains that they do not sing as well for him as for their sister Charlotte. Sophia comes, and there is talk of the ball to be held that night at Weltzlar, to which Charlotte is going with young Werther. They speak of Werther as an educated and distinguished young man, rather melancholy, yet gay at times, and say that they hear the prince has promised him an ambassadorship. They think

LLOYD d'AUBIGNÉ
AS "WERTHER"

he is much attracted to Charlotte, and express their opinion that he would not be as thrifty and provident a husband as will Albert, to whom Charlotte is betrothed. They speak of the accounts of Albert's success, and having made the bailiff promise to come to the tavern that evening, they go away.

That same evening at supper time the bailiff is sitting in his armchair in the living-room, with his children about him. The curtains are undrawn and through the bay window Werther, who has come into the garden, sees the happy family as he lingers by the fountain. He is touched by the simplicity and joy of the scene, and as the children again practice the Christmas carol he envies them their innocent faith. Charlotte enters the room dressed for the ball, and the children leave their father and crowd around her. The bailiff kisses her and admires her gown, telling her that she is beautiful. She brings bread and cuts it and dispenses it to the children. As Werther comes up the steps the bailiff catches sight of him and goes to meet him. Charlotte greets him with a quiet smile, and soon Bruhlmann and Katchen, who are also going to the ball, come. The bailiff watches smilingly the young couple, who are very much in love with each other. Charlotte bids her father and the children good-bye, and admonishes Sophia to look out for them well, and the young people set forth.

When the children have retired and the bailiff gone to the tavern, Sophia steps out into the garden in the moonlight, and is there surprised by Albert, who has come back unexpectedly. He asks after Charlotte, and Sophia tells him where she is and how disappointed she will be not to have been home to welcome him; she tells him all the news, and how every one is talking of his approaching marriage with Charlotte. He goes off, saying that he will be around in the morning to see them all, and rejoicing in his heart at the evident love for him of the faithful and beautiful Charlotte.

Into the garden some hours later come Charlotte and Werther on their return from the ball. He is telling her how much he admires her for her tender care of her younger brothers and sisters, and she tells him of her vow to her dying mother that she would try to take her place in the home. Werther, more and more touched by her unaffected goodness, avows to her the love that has sprung up in his heart. Just then the bailiff, within the house, calls out to her that Albert has returned, and she hastens to tell Werther that she is betrothed to Albert, having promised to marry him in order to relieve her dying mother's anxiety about her daughter's future. Werther is in despair, for he knows that he sincerely loves her and that she is strongly attracted to him.

Act II. In September of the same year at Weltzlar, in the square before the tavern and the Protestant chapel, the people are gathered to celebrate with their pastor and his wife their golden wedding. All are entering the church, where a service is to be held. Johann and Schmidt sit at a table before the tavern, philosophically commenting upon married life. Charlotte and Albert, now married for about three months, approach the church, and the two friends agree that there is an example of a happy and fitting marriage, and go into the tavern. Werther comes along the highway. From the distance he has recognized the couple and watched their happy intimacy, and is greatly agitated. He starts to go away, but cannot bear the thought of not seeing Charlotte, and flings himself upon a sheltered seat, his head in his hands. Johann and Schmidt appear at the tavern door with Bruhlmann, who seems distressed and speechless. Schmidt is just saying to him that Katchen cannot go back on a seven years' engagement and forget it in that fashion. Bruhlmann turns back into the tavern, and the two friends go gaily off to the dance.

The people come from the church and go to the parish house, where the dance is to be held. When Albert appears he sees Werther, and approaching him, lays his hand upon his shoulder. Werther would turn from him, but Albert with brotherly sympathy acknowledges that he sometimes feels remorse for Werther's suffering. He reminds Werther that "to understand is to forgive," and Werther cannot but shake hands with him and promise to go away to some distant land. As they talk Sophia comes running out with flowers in her hands, seeking Albert for the dance. She rallies Werther on his gloomy face, when all others are happy. Albert sends her off, saying that he is coming, then suggests to Werther that happiness may not be so far away, but may stand before one with flowers in her hands. He goes to join Sophia, and Werther wonders how he can go away, as he promised, and never see Charlotte more. He feels his burden intolerable.

Charlotte comes from the church and he approaches her. Again he declares his love, and she is kindly and tender, acknowledging that she cares for him, yet not leaving in question her loyalty to her husband. When Werther says that he must go away forever, she thinks to soften his pain and tells him to go away, but not to stay always,—to come back occasionally, say, at Christmas time. As she leaves him he looks after her with great longing. Sophia comes again, and in heartbroken words he bids her farewell forever. She is frightened and saddened as he goes away down the road, and when Albert finds her weeping, he thinks that Werther and Sophia are in love with each other.

ACT III. It is the twenty-fourth of December of the same year. Charlotte is seated that late afternoon in the drawing-room of Albert's house. Above an old-fashioned secretary is a brace of pistols. She is sewing near a table and her thoughts are with Werther. She takes from the secretary some of his letters and reads them over again. It seems to her as if she had never thought of him so much as since he went away. Sophia comes in and she hastily conceals the letters. Sophia is gay and tries to cheer her sister, and brings word from their father that he wants Charlotte to come and see him. When Charlotte seems serious, Sophia complains that there is no laughter here since Werther went away. At last Charlotte promises to go to her father the next day, and Sophia goes out.

Charlotte resumes her sewing and suddenly the door opens and Werther enters and, closing it, stands leaning against the wall. He seems ill, almost fainting, and Charlotte greets him with joy and gentle anxiety. He talks to her of the happy hours they spent together when first they met, and then tells her of his present sorrow and despair. She is much affected, and her emotion is so great as to show that she loves him. He gazes at her in surprise, then with great joy; despite her protests, he takes her in his arms and kisses her again and again. In a moment she, deeply hurt, struggles from him, and he realizes how he has distressed her and begs her pardon. She tells him that she cannot pardon him, that he must see her no more, that her very soul is fleeing from him. She goes into her chamber and shuts the door. In utter misery he stumbles from the house, believing that nothing remains for him but death now that Charlotte has condemned him.

Albert returns with the news that Werther has been seen, and he finds the street door open. He calls to Charlotte, who comes from her room distressed and seems frightened at the sight of her husband. He tells her of Werther, and her silence and fear confirm his wildest suspicions. He is exceedingly angry and knows not what to think. The servant enters with a note from Werther, which says that he is going away and asks Albert to lend him his pistols. Albert coldly and significantly bids Charlotte give them to the servant, and she, chill with horror, is obliged to reach them down. The servant goes out, Albert angrily goes off into his chamber, and Charlotte, sick with terror and praying that she may not reach Werther too late, goes out into the night.

Act IV. Through the windows of Werther's study the clear, cold moonlight lies upon the table, the books, and the floor. Near the table lies Werther, mortally wounded. Charlotte's voice is heard calling to him. Receiving no answer, she comes into the room in an agony of suspense. She kneels by him and takes him in her arms. He wakes from the stupor and again avows his great love for her. She declares her love for him, and they pledge each other their vows for eternity. The sound of children's voices, singing their Christmas carols at the church, comes to them through the night air. Charlotte weeps in unrestrained sorrow and the dying man tries to comfort her. At length his voice is hushed and he dies, and nothing is heard but Charlotte's sobs and the joyful music of the carols.

GUGLIELMO TELL

(*Gu-yel'-moh Tell*)

(WILLIAM TELL)

ITALIAN heroic grand opera, founded on Schiller's drama of the same name. Music by Gioacchino Antonio Rossini. Book by V. J. Etienne ("Jouy") and Hypolite Bis. First production, Paris, 1829. The scene is laid in Switzerland in the thirteenth century.

CHARACTERS

WILLIAM TELL ⎫ ⎧ Bass
ARNOLD, suitor of Matilda ⎬ Swiss patriots....... ⎨ Tenor
WALTER FÜRST ⎭ ⎩ Bass
MELCTHAL, father of Arnold..........................*Bass*
GESSLER, Governor of Schwitz and Uri..............*Bass*
RUDOLPH, captain of Gessler's body-guard............*Tenor*
RUODI, a fisherman.................................*Tenor*
LEUTHOLD, a shepherd...............................*Bass*
JEMMY, Tell's son..................................*Soprano*
HEDWIGA, Tell's wife...............................*Soprano*
MATILDA, daughter of Gessler and a princess of the
    House of Hapsburg..............................*Soprano*

Peasants of the Three Cantons, knights, pages, ladies of the train of Matilda, three brides and their bridegrooms, hunters, soldiers, and guards of Gessler.

Matilda, the beautiful and kindly daughter of the tyrant Gessler, has been saved from drowning by Arnold, son of Melcthal, a venerable leader among the Swiss and an opponent of Gessler. The young people have fallen in love with each other, although political strife permits little hope of their union.

ACT I. In a village of the Canton of Uri, near the house of William Tell and by the lakeside, the people are happily preparing for the Shepherds' Festival to be held that day.

Fishermen sing as they make ready their boats, and all is peace and contentment. At the signal of a horn the shepherds enter and the people gather. Three marriages are to be celebrated by the patriarch Melcthal. Arnold, his son, withdraws to one side, saddened by the thought of the weddings and the difficulties that beset his marriage with Matilda. William Tell seeks him out and speaks with him about the wrongs of the Swiss under Gessler's rule, and calls upon him to help in the tyrant's overthrow. Arnold, grieving that by being faithful to his country and his people he must betray his love, seems reluctant, and Tell fears that he has already betrayed the cause of the Swiss. Arnold, however, reassures him, and valiantly pledges his support to his nation. Then Arnold goes away to tell Matilda of his decision and bid her farewell.

As the festival progresses the horns of Gessler's hunting party are heard in the mountains near. The three young couples are married by Melcthal, and all is gaiety until suddenly Leuthold, an aged shepherd, rushes in, crying out to his friends to save him from the tyrant. One of Gessler's officers attempted to abduct Leuthold's daughter and the father killed him, whereupon Gessler and his soldiers started in pursuit. Leuthold begs Ruodi, the fisherman, to row him across the lake, for upon the other shore he will be safe; but he, fearing the vengeance of the tyrant and the storm that has arisen, refuses, and no other fisherman will make the attempt. The soldiers are approaching and Leuthold is almost lost when William Tell steps to the front, seizes a boat, and puts off with Leuthold just in time to escape. Gessler and his soldiers rush in, and furious over being baffled, raze the village, burning it and devastating the fields. Not content with that, they seize and cruelly kill the loved patriarch Melcthal.

Act II. In a valley on the shore of the Lake of the Four Cantons at twilight that day Matilda sits thinking of Arnold and their love for each other. He comes, and with deep emotion they declare their love, deploring the evil chance that would separate them. William Tell and Walter Fürst come seeking Arnold, and Matilda leaves him. Tell, recognizing the young woman as Gessler's daughter, again fears that Arnold has not been true to his oath of loyalty to the Swiss, but Arnold declares that, though he loves Matilda, he will not let his love for her make him untrue to his people. They then tell him of his father's death at Gessler's order, and Arnold, horrified that he should have been away from his father in his time of need, seeking the daughter of the man by whom he was so foully slain, vows vengeance and singlehearted defense of his country, forgetting in grief for his father to grieve for his love. Then the three patriots, aroused by this fresh atrocity of murder and devastation, swear valiantly to free their country, inspired by the spirit of the martyred Melcthal. At their summons representative men from all the cantons gather in the open country and swear allegiance to Switzerland, and vow to arouse the people to arms against the tyrant.

Act III. In the grand square at Altorf before his house Gessler and his barons are gathered, enjoying the amusements of a fête given for their entertainment. At one side a pole, bearing a cap, has been set up as the symbol of Gessler's authority, and the populace have been ordered to bow to it in token of their loyalty. Gessler from his seat of honor observes the crowd and notices that among all the bystanders only one man and the boy with him fail to bow before the cap. He orders them arrested and brought before him. The man is William Tell and the boy his small son, Jemmy.

When he charges them with disloyalty, Tell is defiant, and as Gessler notices the father's fondness for this his only son, and remembers the patriot's great reputation for marksmanship, he determines upon a unique punishment. He decrees that Tell shall shoot an apple placed on the head of his son at a hundred paces, or that both shall die.

Tell will not at first take the chance, but the boy reminds his father of his well-known skill as a marksman, and is so confident of success that at length Tell consents. From the arrows offered him he carefully chooses one, at the same time concealing another within his coat. The space is measured off, and the bystanders watch breathlessly as father and son take their stand. At length Tell, with a look of hatred at the smiling tyrant, shoots. In a moment his son comes running joyously to him, saying that he knew he would do it and that the arrow struck straight at the center of the apple. Tell faints with relief from the terrible suspense, and the arrow falls from his coat. Gessler asks who the second arrow was for and Tell fearlessly replies that it was for Gessler, had Jemmy been killed. The governor, infuriated, orders both put to death. There is general consternation, and Matilda, who now comes upon the scene, pityingly demands the boy's life and takes him away with her, while Tell is led off to prison, and the Swiss wildly vow vengeance on the tyrant.

Act IV. Arnold, not knowing of Tell's arrest and imprisonment, has gone off to the ruined village, where he and his father and Tell lived, for one last look at his boyhood home and to nerve himself for the work of vengeance and deliverance before him. A band of patriots, aroused to decisive action by Tell's imprisonment, come seeking him to lead them. They tell him of Tell's wonderful feat and his present danger, and fired by the hero's spirit and valor, he goes off with them to lead them to victory.

Beside the Lake of the Four Cantons Hedwiga sits resting. She is on her way to Altorf to demand of Gessler her husband and her son. Suddenly she hears Jemmy's voice and is overjoyed to see him running toward her. She clasps him in her arms with deep emotion, and as Matilda, who was bringing him to her, approaches, she anxiously asks about her husband. Matilda tells her that he has been removed from the Altorf prison and taken across the lake. The wife looks with anxious eyes upon the stormy sky, but her fears are at once allayed, for Tell himself appears before her. He relates how he escaped from the boat, and also how he has slain Gessler with an arrow. Arnold and the band of patriots come and rejoice to see the hero free. Arnold tenderly tries to comfort Matilda for her sorrow at her father's death. Suddenly amidst the storm there is calm, and the sun bursts forth, lighting up the mountain peaks. All rejoice, taking it as a good omen for their country, the loved Switzerland, now freed from the tyrant's yoke.

ADDITIONAL OPERAS

ANDREA CHÉNIER

(*Ahn-drĕ́-ah Shā-nyā́*)

ITALIAN tragic grand opera, based upon the events of the French Revolution and the personality of the French poet, André Chénier. Music by Umberto Giordano. Book by Luigi Illica. First production, Milan, Italy, 1896. The scene is Paris, France, and the time, during the French Revolution, about 1794.

CHARACTERS*

ANDREA CHÉNIER	*Tenor*
CHARLES GÉRARD	*Baritone*
ROUCHER PIETRO FLÉVILLE, the romancer, pensioned by the king FOUQUIER-TINVILLE, public accuser	*Bass or Baritone*
MATHIEU, the sans-culotte, called "Populus"	*Baritone*
A SPY THE ABBÉ	*Tenor*
SCHMIDT, jailer at St. Lazare THE MAJOR-DOMO DUMAS, President of the Tribunal of Public Safety	*Bass*
COUNTESS DE COIGNY MADELON	*Mezzo-Soprano*
MADELEINE, daughter of the Countess de Coigny	*Soprano*
BERSI, a mulatto woman, maid to Madeleine	*Mezzo-Soprano*

Mute personages: A music teacher, Albert Roger, Filandro Fiorinelli, Horatius Coclès, a boy, a chancellor, the father of Gérard, Robespierre, Couthon, Barras, a serving monk, etc.

Chorus of lords, ladies, abbés, lackeys, grooms, postilions, musicians, domestics, pages, valets, shepherdesses, and beggars. The following tableaux: bourgeois, sans-culottes, carmagnoles, national guards, soldiers of the Republic, armed police, shopkeepers, fish-wives, strolling merchants, marketwomen, knitting-women, spies, girls and beaux, Representatives of the Nation, judges, jurors, prisoners, the condemned, and newsboys.

*The rôles in braces are held by a single artist.

SCENE I. In the conservatory-salon of the chateau of the counts of Coigny, servants prepare for a party. Charles Gérard, in livery, is assisting other lackeys. He is alone when an old gardener comes, walking with difficulty under the weight of a piece of furniture. It is his father, and he springs to assist him, then watches him go away, and thinks of the sixty years of service the old man has given to his arrogant protectors, who have taken his strength, his spirit, and even the service of his children. Gérard strikes his breast with his hand, murmuring amid his tears that he, like his father, is a slave. He notes his hated livery, and cries out to the gilded walls that the death hour of such a vain and frivolous world is already striking. Madeleine enters, accompanied by Bersi, and Gérard looks upon the beautiful daughter of the house with the greatest admiration and devotion. The countess, having given orders to the major-domo, learns from Gérard that all is ready, but is surprised to see that Madeleine has not dressed for the evening. She bids her hasten, and turns away. Bersi reveals her delight in her mistress's beauty, but does not succeed in coaxing her into a mood of vanity, for Madeleine decides to dress very simply in white with a rose in her hair. They vanish as guests arrive, whom the countess greets with elaborate courtesy.

Together come three personages, one of advanced years, Fléville, the romancer, who introduces his companions, the young and beardless poet, Andrea Chénier, and the old Italian knight and musician, Filandro Fiorinelli. The Abbé, lately come from Paris, arouses general apprehension by his news of the state of the government, but Fléville treats it lightly, urging the guests to enjoyment. Shepherdesses sing and dance. Chénier sits apart, and Madeleine promises a group of her girl friends that she will make him poetize.

Refusing her request, he says that his Muse is capricious, even as is Love, whereat Madeleine and her friends laugh. As the guests crowd around, Madeleine says that the Muse, when implored, said by the poet's mouth the word that all,—and she nods to indicate several of the guests, even some of the oldest and least likely ones,—have said to her that evening. Chénier resents her words and the general laugh, and offers to make Madeleine a poem on the subject of Love. In impassioned verse he tells how the ideal of his country grew in his soul and became the object of his love, his sweetheart, and then to his sorrow he saw everywhere throughout the land, even in the churches, the poor exploited to add to the treasures of the rich.

The Abbé and the nobility present become infuriated while Chénier is speaking, but at the end of the salon Gérard listens approvingly though in great agitation. Chénier tells Madeleine that from the pity in her face he thought her an angel until she spoke so scornfully of love, which is the soul and life of the world; then, strongly moved, he walks away and disappears. The countess and her guests are arranging for the dance as Gérard enters at the head of a crowd of wretched beggars, whom he announces as "His Highness, Misery." The countess orders them put out, and Gérard the first, although his aged father on his knees begs for him. Gérard bids his father come with him, and casting off his livery, leads the crowd out. The dance is resumed, and all is pleasure among the guests.

Scene 2. In the Place de la Revolution in Paris, near an altar upon which is a bust of Marat, stand the Sansculotte Mathieu and Coclès. The bridge of Perronet leads into the square in the background, and on the left is the Café Hottot. Under the trees on the banks of the Seine

Chénier is sitting alone. Newsboys bring papers, and Mathieu and Coclès seat themselves upon the altar steps to read. Bersi comes, and conscious that she is watched, addresses the spy. The spy recognizes her as the companion of the woman whom he is seeking, and notes that she makes a sign to Chénier but goes off without speaking to him. Soon Roucher enters the square, greets Chénier joyfully, and hands him his passport, saying that the city is dangerous for him and begging him to leave. Chénier at first refuses to hide or go, declaring that he believes in destiny. Then he tells Roucher that he must remain, as he is in love with a lady who has sent him several charming letters of counsel or reproach, and a recent one asking for a rendezvous. He knows nothing of the writer, who signs herself "Hope." Roucher believes it to be some trick of the revolutionists, and pleads with him to go away at once. Chénier is convinced and about to depart when there comes through the square a procession of revolutionists, Robespierre, Gérard, and others of note among them.

The spy draws Gérard aside and questions him about the appearance of the young woman he seeks, and Gérard describes enthusiastically the blonde beauty of Madeleine, whom he loves. The spy promises that he shall see her this very night, then draws near where Chénier and Roucher stand. After the procession, among a crowd of women of the town, Bersi comes. She whispers to Chénier to wait there, then as the spy accosts her, goes with him into the café, but soon returns. Chénier recognizes Bersi, but is surprised that she addresses him. When she says that a woman in great peril, whose name is "Hope," wishes to speak with him, all of Roucher's warnings do not deter him from awaiting her coming, though he goes to procure arms.

Night falls, the lanterns under the trees and along the

streets are lighted, the patrols pass, and the spy returns. A woman comes cautiously across the bridge, looks about, and seeing Chénier, approaches and calls him by name. At his reply she cannot speak for emotion, but leans trembling against the altar, while the spy draws near unobserved. She asks Chénier if he remembers her, and repeats the poem he recited at the chateau of Coigny. He begs to see her face. She drops her mantle, and in the light of the lantern before the bust of Marat he sees the wonderful beauty of Madeleine. Her name springs to his lips, and the spy, hearing it, hastens away to inform his employer. Chénier realizes that she is the hidden friend whom he loves. Madeleine tells him that she is alone, that Bersi is her only helper, and that, in her distress, she has thought of him as a brother, as one who was powerful and might protect her now that she is a fugitive. Chénier is deeply moved and in great exultation declares his love for her and that he will defend her. Responding to his tenderness, she goes to his arms, and he bids her fear no more, for until death they will be together.

Gérard comes and calls her by name. She recognizes him, and with a cry of dismay turns to Chénier, who bids Gérard be gone. When Gérard lays his hand upon Madeleine to lead her away, Chénier draws his sword and strikes him. They fight as Roucher, at Chénier's command, takes Madeleine away, intimidating the spy, who runs to call Gérard's friends. Gérard, wounded, falls upon the altar steps, but tells Chénier to save himself, as the public accuser already has his name, and bids him protect Madeleine. When the spy comes with a band of police and they ask Gérard who struck him, he murmurs, "Unknown."

SCENE 3. In the hall where the Revolutionary Tribunal meets, Mathieu is futilely haranguing the people to give men and money to the cause, when Gérard, recovered from his wound, comes and addresses them. By his plea all are stirred. Women cast their jewels into the great urn which stands on the president's table. An old blind grandmother, Madelon, presents her last grandson, whose father and brother have already perished, and offers him to the cause. At length the people go out, and can be heard singing and dancing the Carmagnole in the street. The spy comes and tells Gérard that Chénier has been arrested that morning, and now the lady will doubtless come forward voluntarily. Gérard, though glad, fears that Madeleine will hate him for bringing danger upon her lover. The spy urges him to draw up the accusation against Chénier and places the pen in Gérard's hand; and the latter, though he knows only too well that if Chénier is accused he will be condemned, begins to write. He struggles with his conscience and the memory of his former ideals of justice, but at length, inspired by the hate of his rival that grows out of his deep love for Madeleine, he charges him with being an enemy of the people, a foreigner, because born in Constantinople, a soldier and an accomplice of Dumouriez, and, as a poet, a corrupter of the morals of the people. At last he puts his name to the accusation and hands the paper to the clerk.

He is alone when Madeleine comes to intercede for Chénier. He tells her that the spy was in his employ, and that he has had her lover seized. He pours out the story of his own love for her since as a child she ran in the meadows with him, of his despair when he found that she loved another and turned with a cry of horror from him. But he still hopes, for he believes that the flame of his love will inspire hers. Madeleine, terrified, and at first not understanding, seems overcome with weakness, then becomes desperate to escape him. She determines to go into the street and shout her name, knowing that then death will deliver her, but he prevents her. Suddenly she becomes calm, and offers herself in exchange for Chénier's life. Moved by the sublimity of her sacrifice and power to love, Gérard bursts into sobs. She tells him that her mother is dead, her home burned, and Bersi has aided her at great personal sacrifice,—that she brings disaster upon every one who helps her; that there was nothing before her but misery and danger when love came and made earth heaven; and that now, without that love, she will be as if dead.

The clerk hands Gérard a list of the accused, on which is Chénier's name. Gérard knows that all is already lost, though now he would give his life to save the man whom Madeleine loves. He promises her to do his utmost to defend Chénier. The people come back into the hall, the members of the Revolutionary Tribunal take their places, and the prisoners are brought in. Chénier is the last. The names are called and judgment is given. Chénier denies the charges against him and makes an eloquent appeal, begging that they take his life but leave him his honor. Fouquier-Tinville presses the charges, and Gérard makes a fervent plea in defense, finally running to Chénier and embracing him,—an act which brings tears to the prisoner's eyes. The jurors retire, and when they return, the president announces as their verdict—death.

SCENE 4. In the court of the prison of St. Lazare that night Chénier sits under a lantern, writing with great ardor. Roucher is near, and to him Chénier reads these his last verses, which celebrate the joy of his life, the inspiration of his poetry, and his love. Schmidt, the jailer, comes, and the two friends embrace and part with emotion. A knocking is heard and the jailer admits Gérard and Madeleine, whose permit to see Chénier is shown. Gérard is overcome with unavailing sorrow as Madeleine asks the jailer if there is not a woman among the condemned. He answers that there is, one Legray. Madeleine tells him that she wishes to die in the place of that woman, that she will answer to the name of Legray when summoned, and she gives him a purse and jewels. The jailer goes to call Chénier, and she bids farewell to Gérard, who is heartbroken at his deed, but hastens off to Robespierre in a final effort to save the lovers. With solemn joy Chénier greets Madeleine. She tells him that she comes not to say farewell but to die with him at dawn. In ecstasy they embrace, their love triumphing even in death. At length the condemned are summoned. Chénier answers to his name, and at the name of Ida Legray Madeleine steps forth, and they take their places in the tumbril side by side.

THE CANTERBURY PILGRIMS

AMERICAN comic grand opera. Music by Reginald De Koven. Book by Percy Mackaye. First production, New York, 1917. The scene is Southwark and Canterbury, England, and the time is April 16, 1387.

CHARACTERS

GEOFFREY CHAUCER, First Poet Laureate of England..*Baritone*
RICHARD II, King of England.........................*Tenor*
KNIGHT ....*Baritone*
SQUIRE, son of the Knight...........................*Tenor*
FRIAR ....*Tenor*
MILLER ....*Bass*
PARDONER ⎫ ....*Tenor*
SUMMONER ⎬ Alisoun's Swains.........................*Baritone*
SHIPMAN ⎬ ....*Baritone*
COOK   ⎭ ....*Bass*
JOANNES, Servitor to the Prioress..................*Tenor*
MAN OF LAW..*Baritone*
HOST ....*Bass*
HERALD ....*Bass*
THE PRIORESS, Madame Eglantine..................*Soprano*
THE WIFE OF BATH, Alisoun....................*Contralto*
JOHANNA ....*Soprano*

Pilgrims, nobles, choir-boys, priests, acolytes, nuns, Canterbury brooch-girls, tap-girls, heralds, citizens, etc.

ACT I. In the court of the Tabard Inn at Southwark, near London, Pilgrims are thronging. Some are seated at the tables drinking, others are standing by the ale-barrels flirting with the tap-maids. One starts a song, in which all join. The poet enters, reading. When questioned by the Friar, he answers that "to live a king with kings, a clod with clods," to be "the equal of each, brother of every man," is his psalm; then, lifting a tankard, he sings and drinks with the company. A Knight and a Squire enter, and greet Chaucer courteously. The Knight has just returned from the Holy Land and is on his way to Canterbury. The Squire, his son, is in love. The poet quotes some love verses, which the Squire recognizes as those of Chaucer, the Poet Laureate, and he rebukes his new acquaintance for claiming them.

A Prioress, with Joannes and a retinue of nuns, enters. Joannes, who carries the lady's small pet hound, happens to get in the way of the Miller as he recoils from his rush against an oaken door, which he has broken with his head on a bet, and the hound bites him. The Miller is about to wring its neck when Chaucer seizes the Miller by the throat and makes him beg the pardon of the Prioress, whose gratitude the poet thus wins.

Soon with loud song and merrymaking, Alisoun, the Wife of Bath, enters. She espies Chaucer, likes his appearance, and asks his name. He tells her it is Geoffrey, and gives a fanciful account of himself. The Squire recognizes him as the Poet Laureate, but Chaucer requests him to be silent, as he is traveling incognito. Alisoun insists that Geoffrey help her alight from her mount, a small white ass, although her swains and the Miller and the Friar are much vexed by the attention she gives him. She says that she has vowed to take to herself another husband, although already five times married, and if she likes this fellow, can she not still like them all? They rush to get ale for her, and she taunts Geoffrey into kissing her just as the Prioress enters unobserved. When Chaucer sees Lady Eglantine, abashed he seeks to restore himself in her favor. He learns that she goes to Canterbury to meet her brother, a Knight just returned from the Holy Land, whom she has not seen since childhood and whom she is to recognize by the ring he wears, upon which is the same inscription as upon the brooch which dangles from her wrist,—"*Amor vincit omnia,*" "Love conquers all things." The Prioress asks Chaucer's protection upon the road, which he gladly grants, thinking it not necessary to disclose the brother's identity until he and the Prioress have had a morning's ride together.

When she leaves the room, the Friar, who has listened to the conversation, intrusively examines the Knight's ring, and, thinking to win Alisoun's favor, hastens to report his information to her. She, having dismissed her swains, comes to Geoffrey as he sits reading, and coquets with him, finally acknowledging that she is jealous of the Lady Prioress. Chaucer rebukes her for coupling that lady's name with his, but she dares to insinuate that the Prioress goes to meet a lover, not a brother. Chaucer thinks Alisoun daft, but is eventually cajoled into making a bet with her to the effect that, if the Prioress gives the brooch she wears to other than her brother, Chaucer will marry Alisoun at Canterbury. He is confident of the integrity of the Prioress, and Alisoun is determined to win the wager and so Geoffrey for her husband. By an ambiguous promise of reward she enlists her swains to help her. Pilgrims, dressed for riding, come into the court, the Lady Prioress appears, and all start off for Canterbury.

ACT II. The Pilgrims have come to the One Nine-Pin Inn at the hamlet of Bob-up-and-down, near Canterbury. Chaucer and the Squire are walking in the garden, talking of the unpoetical name of Johanna, the Squire's lady love. Chaucer suggests that the Squire use instead the name of Eglantine in his verses, and offers to write the poem for him. The Squire agrees and leaves him alone in the arbor to write. The Friar, having heard the conversation from behind the garden wall, goes to report it to Alisoun. The Prioress enters the garden, then takes refuge in the summerhouse as the shouts of Alisoun and her swains are heard.

She sees Chaucer and is about to retire, when he picks a spray of honeysuckle and hands it to her, and begs her pardon for intruding in her bower. They withdraw into the recesses of the arbor as Alisoun and her swains enter, singing and dancing to the Miller's playing. As the dance grows merrier, the Prioress clicks her beads rhythmically, and Chaucer invites her to dance with him. They become absorbed and step within sight of Alisoun, who stops the dance and gaily taunts them. The Prioress is abashed, but Chaucer, with a dignified rebuke to the Wife of Bath, escorts the lady into the inn.

The Pilgrims also retire, and Alisoun is left alone in rage. She plans revenge, tells the Friar of her bet with Geoffrey, sends the Miller for a gag and a rope, and tells the swains to seize the Knight and keep him prisoner in the cellar of the inn while she, clad in his clothes and with his ring upon her finger, pretends to the Prioress to be the long-absent brother and so obtains the golden brooch upon which hangs her bet with Geoffrey. They go away as Chaucer comes, reading some verses, for which the Friar represents himself to have been sent by the Squire, and which he receives. Chaucer has gone when the swains come along and the Knight enters from the inn. Alisoun engages the Knight in conversation, and at a sign from her, he is seized and borne away.

The Squire and Johanna, who has unexpectedly returned from Italy, enter the garden. Johanna asks for the verses he promised her, and he is explaining when the Prioress, reading a paper, comes from the inn with the Friar. She is amazed at the verses, which the Friar assures her are a love poem that Chaucer bade him deliver to her. Chaucer enters, and the Prioress in confusion hands him the paper, questioning him. He is acknowledging the verses when the

Squire and Johanna appear. The Prioress is grieved that she can no longer trust Chaucer, and he is hurt that she is offended, while Johanna is jealous because the verses are addressed to Eglantine. Only the Friar and Alisoun are pleased at the discord they have caused.

Act III. From the hall of the inn that evening the Pilgrims start for the chapel service. The Prioress comes last, and Chaucer asks her to walk with him in the garden, as he has news of her brother. When all have gone out, the Miller, the swains, and the Friar enter, followed by the Wife of Bath. The Friar is disguised as a chimney-sweep, for protection against the wrath of the Squire, and Alisoun wears the Knight's garb. All withdraw to the cellar but the Friar and Alisoun, who hide. Chaucer and the Prioress come and stand at the casement in the moonlight, acknowledging their love for each other, and dreaming of a life on some other star where they may be together. The Prioress withdraws, and Chaucer goes to find the Knight as the Squire and Johanna come in, making up their quarrel over the verses. The Friar sings out mockingly, and falls into the fireplace. The Squire does not recognize him, but goes with him to search for the Friar. Johanna also goes out, and Alisoun comes from her hiding-place when Chaucer and the Man of Law enter, searching for the Knight. The Man of Law points out Alisoun, but it is not until Chaucer hears this strange knight asking for the Prioress that he mistrusts this may be her brother. To his questions the supposed knight admits that he but passes for the Prioress's brother, and Chaucer is about to strike him when he notices the ring upon his finger. The man tells of the brooch his sister wears, the Prioress comes, exclaiming, "Welcome, brother!" and Chaucer, appalled, hastens off.

The Miller summons the swains, and they listen to the conversation between Alisoun and the Prioress. The latter is at first incredulous, but when the new-found brother remarks that Geoffrey said he was betrothed to the Wife of Bath, the Prioress, deeply wounded, flings herself into his arms, seeking a brother's protection, much to the enjoyment of the swains, at whose loud laughter she starts up in dismay. Alisoun coaxes her till she gives up the brooch, and then flatters her so grossly that the gentle lady turns from the supposed brother in dismay, calling for help. Chaucer enters, draws his sword, and forces Alisoun to fight with him. There is uproar and commotion until Alisoun, hard-beset, holds up the locket of the Prioress, tears off the beard and wig of her disguise, and announces that she has won her bet and Geoffrey is hers by law. The real Knight, disheveled and with cut ropes dangling, enters and calls the Prioress by name. She turns from him, aghast. Chaucer, realizing the game that has been played, bursts into laughter and drinks to Alisoun and woman's wit, while the Miller sulkily withdraws.

ACT IV. The next day in front of Canterbury Cathedral crowds of Pilgrims are assembled, talking, praying, and sight-seeing. Chaucer comes along, richly and gaily dressed, and talking with the Man of Law in spite of the solicitations of a bevy of brooch-girls. The Man of Law accepts Chaucer's money, and tells him that the law reads that no woman may be wedded but five times. Chaucer feigns distress at the fact, especially when Alisoun, dressed as a bride, comes and claims him for her husband. She is much taken aback when she finds out how the law stands and that the penalty for a sixth marriage is hanging. Chaucer protests to the Man of Law with mock severity, and they find that they will have to appeal to the king for a special dispensation. Chaucer purposes to make the appeal, and Alisoun is almost convinced that he does care for her. The Miller and the swains come, the former so jealous that he is about to fight Chaucer when Alisoun interferes, saying that she has the man she wishes and will herself fight to keep him.

Chaucer takes opportunity to beg the Prioress to think charitably of him but a little while. She disdains him, however, saying that she seeks another hero, for she holds in high respect the Poet Laureate, who it is rumored will attend the king. Heralds announce the king, and the Pilgrims make way as a procession comes from the cathedral to meet him. Choir boys and priests, bearing pictured banners of St. Thomas and his shrine, appear, and lastly the Archbishop in his regalia. King Richard Second, a lad of foppish appearance, enters the square with his retinue, among whom are the Duke of Gloucester, John of Gaunt, followers of the nobility and gentry, and with them, Johanna. Pilgrims, Archduke, and nobles salute the king. He, noting the frowning countenance of his uncle, John of Gaunt, fixed upon the royal apparel, seizes a looking-glass from a courtier's sleeve, and with gay gibes turns it toward those about him, then flings it into the crowd. It falls and breaks at Chaucer's feet, and he picks it up and addresses the king, who joyfully greets him as Laureate and embraces him.

The Prioress is overcome with amazement; but Alisoun, nothing daunted, tells the king that the man is hers. Chaucer whispers to the Man of Law, who gains the king's ear while Chaucer acknowledges his betrothal to Alisoun. The Miller can scarcely be restrained, so great is his rage, as Chaucer asks the king's dispensation for the marriage. Richard, who pays good attention to the Man of Law, says that the laws are sacred, but that he will make an exception and permit this woman to wed the sixth husband *if he be a miller*. The herald sounds the verdict, and Alisoun, outwitted, shakes her fist at Chaucer, who eyes her slyly, then both burst into laughter. The Miller rushes forward, eager to claim his bride.

The Pilgrims crowd joyfully about Chaucer, who, having passed among them as only the son of a vintner, promises to brew them such a vintage that they who drink of it, although after a thousand years, shall see a vision of Merry England and their pilgrimage. The king announces that St. Thomas will receive his Pilgrims, and the procession forms to enter the cathedral. Chaucer asks the Prioress to walk with him, and she consents, bidding him offer her brooch at the shrine, and shyly reminding him of their star, which he declares he can never forget,—

"Not while the memory of beauty pains
And *Amor Vincit Omnia.*"

THE CHILDREN OF DON

ENGLISH heroic grand opera, "founded chiefly on the Cymric legend of Math Mathonwy." Music by Josef Charles Holbrooke. Book by Lord Howard de Walden ("T. E. Ellis"). First production, London, 1912. The scene is the Cymric underworld and the Northern isles in the mythological period.

CHARACTERS

GODS

NODENS, God of the Abyss	Bass
LYD, the Sea King	Bass
DON, the Nature Goddess	Soprano

MORTALS

MATH, king of Arvon	Bass
GWYDION ⎫	Baritone
GOVANNION ⎬ the children of Don	Bass
ELAN ⎭	Contralto
GWION, a Druid	Tenor
GOEWIN, a priestess	Soprano
ARAWN, king of Annwn, the northern underworld	Tenor
FIRST PRIEST OF ANNWN	Tenor
SECOND PRIEST OF ANNWN	Baritone

Ghosts of the priests, chorus of Druids.

PROLOGUE: SCENE I. In a cave in Annwn, beyond which lies a lake choked with ice and obscured by mists, upon an altar stone bubbles the cauldron of Caridwen. Two priests are preparing their rite, and bind to the altar the sacrifice, a living maid. Arawn comes, takes the sacrificial knife, and is approaching the altar to dispatch the victim when Gwydion enters the cavern slowly and grimly. He announces that he is the son of Don, and comes as venger of Arvon to take the cauldron of Caridwen. He demands that the king "yield it in peace or stand for it in war." Arawn, defiant, orders the priests to seize the intruder that they may torture him. Gwydion grapples with them, killing both, then slays Arawn himself. Fearless before man, he stands hesitant before the mystery of the great cauldron, whose wreathing steam was meant to grace the brows of the old gods. For the cauldron contains disastrous exciting principles, and Gwydion realizes that he holds in his hands the "future and the torment of his race."

SCENE 2. To a wild and ice-bound ravine near the sea comes the Nature Goddess, Don, robed in red and with a red jewel upon her forehead. She calls upon the winds, the rocks, the waters, frost, and fire, and upbraids them for permitting Gwydion to bear away the mysterious cauldron from its stronghold in the world of the dead. She summons Lyd, the Sea King, and tells him that his rule is menaced now that the "hoard of the Gods, the bowl of dreams," is stolen. Lyd, in blue armor and mantle, rouses from sleep to hear her plaint. She says that the same phantasies that caused the downfall of the old gods, the exciting dreams of revolt and desire, all the vast ambitions breeding conflict, symbolized in the cauldron, are in Gwydion's keeping, and he is now crossing the seas. She begs Lyd to overwhelm him with disaster, that the name and rule of Don may continue and that this menace to the world may be destroyed. The Sea King calls upon Nodens, God of the Abyss, and through the clouds beyond the rocks appears the reclining figure of an old but powerful man. Nodens rouses himself from the sleep the gods have set upon him, and laments that he must lie thus changeless amid all change, thus dreaming and denied of achievement. Yet he sends forth his dreams to lodge in the souls of men and thus have fruition while he dreams on. As the clouds close upon Nodens, Lyd acquiesces, and refuses to stay Gwydion.

ACT I. In a forest in Arvon Druids come, bearing the cauldron of Caridwen, and followed by Math and Gwion. As they pass out by an avenue of monoliths, Gwydion enters and stands by a great oak, watching them and listening to their prayer, wherein Gwion abjectly beseeches the gods to deliver them from the dread power of the shrine of inspiration which they now possess. Gwydion angrily thinks of the perils he dared in obtaining it, and contemns the craven spirit of the worshippers of a sacred vessel which is his by right of daring. As Gwion curses any one who scorns or menaces the cauldron, Gwydion curses him who will not boldly dare the aspirations and the deeds that the cauldron brews.

As the Druids pass out, Math asks Gwydion the cause of his anger, and reminds him that his mother was Math's own sister, given as pledge of peace to his sire, with whom the Gael had long waged war; that Math had taught Gwydion all his learning and had treated him as a son, sending him forth in quest of the fateful bowl, of which he warns him. Gwion says that three drops only of the contents of the cauldron are "wisdom's wine"; the rest is poison, bringing passions and wild desires that end in oblivion. Math decrees that it shall stand in the sacred grove, guarded by virgins, in order that no disaster may come to his people because of it, and he appoints Gwydion as ward of the sacred vessel. Math and Gwion go, and soon Gwydion follows.

Govannion enters cautiously, shuddering at the forest shade and the spot, now the seat of magic rites, but late the home of nature worship. He comes seeking Goewin, and when she enters, greets her tenderly. She is afraid of the arts of Math, but Govannion reassures her, urging her to come away with him to the uplands. She says that she has been made priestess of the deadly cauldron. He protests that that should not stand against their love for each other. Elan comes quietly, surprising the lovers, and bidding them away from the somber forest. As they talk, Gwydion enters, aghast that they linger there in danger of the wrath of Math. Govannion resents his reproaches, calling him traitor to his own kin, since he is servant of the Gael. Gwydion, realizing that he cannot let his brother and the priestess go except he break faith with Math, yet, pitying, bids them depart, and as they go out together, he turns to Elan. She recalls to him the ancient custom of early peoples, and declares that it was foreordained of the Fates that she should be his bride. To her eager words he turns a deaf ear, saying that he has the spirit hunger and will not be lured from the conflict of his life, and bids her go. Sadly she goes away, and Gwydion valiantly faces his unknown destiny.

Act II. In the forest temple of trilithons, upon the altar, burns the cauldron with a low red glare. Goewin stands near the altar, tending for the last time the wavering fires. There Govannion finds her, having hunted other trysting places, and is amazed now that she has taken refuge from him here. He pleads with her, but she says that he is changing love to fear, and that she longs only to forget awhile. Govannion tells her that he came here unafraid, daring the Gael and the ban upon invasion of that place, through love of her. Goewin, still distrait, turns from him. Gwydion enters, angered that they should linger with Math so near. He reminds them that once again he gives them leave to depart. Govannion, sorrowing that love has perished, pleads no more, but curses the forces that have driven them on, and lays them to the charge of the cauldron that Gwydion brought. He goes away, and Gwydion tells

Goewin to make her choice, whether to go with Govannion or face Math's anger. She chooses the latter and bids Gwydion defend her.

Math and Gwion enter. Math looks sternly at Gwydion and questions him as to what he and Goewin do there in that sacred place. Goewin confesses that she is no longer a maid. Math demands the name of the man, and she acknowledges that it was Govannion and pleads for mercy. Math sends her forth to sorrow alone in a distant vale. He turns to Gwydion in great grief, to pass judgment upon him whom he regards as a son. Gwion declares that Gwydion is "too great for mercy" and that he should be cast from manhood. Such is the decree, and the Druids bind him to the pointed altar stone in spite of his savage resistance. Math laments Gwydion's faithlessness, and decrees that he shall pass one last hour alone in the presence of the cauldron, and shall then be changed in flesh and spirit from the mold of man to that of beast. The king of Arvon then passes out, followed by Gwion and the Druids, and Gwydion is left alone in darkness which is lighted only by the flames of the cauldron.

He is bemoaning the dread magic which sets on him a yoke beyond all bearing, when Elan comes in and asks if she shall unbind him. He tells her that she cannot, and she asks that she may continue with him. He tells her how he is to be thrust from form of man to that of beast, and asks her if she will dare to fill a horn with the contents of the cauldron. Though she fears that it means death, she attempts it, and brings the horn to Gwydion. He drinks, and she after him, then crouches beside him. Far away rises the chorus of wild fowl, and then is heard the voice of the Sea King in a song of yearning love. At his words, Elan becomes more and more agitated, then, as the voice ceases, she starts up, mad with the poison of the gods, and saying that she is torn by a strange sea-song, goes away.

Gwydion, left alone, sees springing up about him fantastic figures whom he recognizes as Arawn of Annwn, and the ghosts of others whom he has slain. Arawn taunts him with his fate yet to come, and demons also make their threats, till Gwydion cries in consternation that "the gods alone are fools," but determines that neither death nor change shall find him craven. He calls upon Nodens, and Arawn and the demons disappear as a vision appears of Nodens lying bound on his high rocks. He prophesies that "the gods in agony must waste, to be by nascent man replaced" and that finally "the vaster gods" shall replace all else. The vision of Nodens fades, and Gwydion feels the spell of change coming over him, and knows that he is lost, though he came so near to the understanding of his fate. Darkness settles down, and the bonds that held Gwydion are empty. A wolf comes from behind the stone to which Gwydion was bound, and slinks across the stage, while all around gleam the red eyes of wolves.

Act III, Scene 1. Three years later, in the forest of Arvon, now stripped by autumn winds, at close of day a pack of wolves slink restlessly about. Voices of Druids are heard, and the wolves leave as Gwion enters. He hears their howling and feels the subtle power of magic around its old resort. Goewin enters breathlessly, terrified by the wolves and burdened by her sorrow, seeking in her old haunt, where once lurked love and deadly anger, a mercy that will let her die among her kind. Gwion refuses her prayer, and terrifies her yet more by saying that the wolf whose cry they hear is Govannion. Pitilessly he drives her forth, saying that the kiss of wolves shall sear out her offense.

Horrified and in deadly fear, Goewin revolts against a doom of hate wrought out by one she loved, saying that "never fault should earn so foul a forfeit." Gwion relents not, and as Math enters, her last wailing cry is heard in the distance.

To his question Gwion replies that he has thrust Goewin forth and that her wolfish kin have devoured her. Math laments her fate, and reproaches Gwion for overreaching his mild anger with bitter hate. Gwion regrets the softness of Math's spirit, and warns him that perils threaten should he be lenient toward the evil forces. Math in his wisdom knows that where Gwydion strove, others will strive, and grieves over the loss of that one and the weakening of his regal power that it presaged. Gwion anxiously reminds Math that none return from the beast form the same in spirit, and futilely warns Math against releasing his doomed son. Math addresses himself to the magic rites, and calling to Govannion and Gwydion, bids them come, freed from their spell, back to him. The wolf pack approaches, and soon Gwydion appears in man form, worn and emaciated, a wolf's head for helmet and a wolf's pelt for clothing. Govannion also appears, similarly clad, but slips away among the trees. Math tells Gwydion that he is free if he will restore a maid to their services in place of the maiden whom they lost. Gwydion tells of his sister Elan, who may perchance perform the sacred rites, and they go, seeking her.

ACT III, SCENE 2. On the seashore sits Elan, lamenting the downfall of her race. She believes Gwydion and Govannion dead, and knows that she herself but adds shame to the name of Don. She thinks of the spirit of the sea, and of that night of mysterious ecstasy. She thinks of her son, offspring of the wave, and wonders how he shall fare. Govannion appears, and she greets him with surprise. To his questions she replies that she mourns for his lost love, for good Gwydion's aim, and the shame to be endured. Govannion says that Goewin is dead, that he himself killed her, and that he seeks revenge on the powers that so doomed them. He tells Elan that Gwydion seeks her in order to make his peace with Math, and as Gwydion and the king approach he goes away.

Elan, long accustomed to sorrow, begins to hope, and thinks that here her sacred grief will not be probed. She greets her brother joyously. He tells her his request, and at Math's question she gives her consent. But Math asks if she is a maiden, and drawing upon the ground with his staff a magic line that can discern the heart's secrets, bids her overstep it. She hesitates, then attempts to cross, but recoils, and beside her springs up a small boy. She takes him in her arms and sinks down ashamed. At Gwydion's question she reminds him of the night they drank from the cauldron together.

Math in terrible anger tells Gwydion that he shall endure a hundred lives as beast to pay for this deception, and breaks all bonds between them. Holding his staff aloft and calling from the mist impalpable figures to support him, he declares that the fate of the children of Don is disaster "till the seas have these plains and the sons of the sea this rule." Gwydion, strongly defiant, calls upon Nodens, and against the magic of Math he pits his spear. As Math waves his staff and his guard of spirits surround him, Gwydion hurls himself against them. They give way, and when Math raises the staff in a final spell, Gwydion drives his spear at him. Math falls. Elan becomes unconscious with terror, and Govannion steals in, seizes the boy from her arms, throws him into the sea, then draws her away.

As Gwydion stands watching Math, he revives and Gwydion supports him. Math, dying, tells Gwydion that it was by worth that magic could not break that death comes to him, and prophesies that to Gwydion shall come such an hour of black defeat; then, bidding him a tender farewell, he dies. Gwydion, standing by the body, lays down his spear and, determined to hold his realm without magic power, takes up the staff and breaks it, thus destroying all spells save the doom already set. Dylan, Elan's child, climbs out of the sea onto the rocks. Gwydion looks at him in astonishment, then realizes what his appearance means, and says, "Sons of the sea shall rule. So be it!" Dylan turns to Gwydion, who tells him that he will make him king and teach him all his art. Govannion comes to them, and when Gwydion tells his purpose to make this child his heir, Govannion protests that he himself should be thus set aside. Gwydion will brook no opposition, and they fight, Govannion being worsted.

Gwion and the Druids enter and discover the body of Math. Gwion accuses Gwydion, and calls upon the Druids to weave their magic spells in bitter vengeance. Gwydion bids them cease, and shows them the broken staff. In answer to Gwion's threats, Gwydion gives the priest into the power of Govannion, bidding him take vengeance on the one who without pity sent to her death Goewin. Govannion kills Gwion, and the Druids shrink away as if paralyzed. Gwydion, with Dylan, takes his leave of Math Mathonwy, greatest of the Gael. Then they go away, and the Druids keen over the body of Math.

DIE ENTFÜHRUNG AUS DEM SERAIL
(*Dē Ent-fü'-rōōng ows dĕm Sĕ-rä'*)
(IL SERRAGLIO) (THE ABDUCTION FROM THE SERAGLIO)

GERMAN sentimental comic opera, adapted from "Belmont and Constance," a drama by Christopher Frederick Bretzner. Music by Johann Wolfgang Amadeus Mozart. Book by Gottlob Stephani. First production, Vienna, 1782. The scene is laid in Turkey, and the time is the sixteenth century.

CHARACTERS

BELMONT, a young Spanish gentleman............Tenor
PEDRILLO, servant of Belmont, for the time in the service of the Pasha.......................Baritone
OSMIN, major-domo of the country-house of the Pasha..Bass
CONSTANCE, beloved of Belmont, and now in the seraglio of the Pasha......................Soprano
BLONDA, the English servant of Constance, beloved of Pedrillo................................Soprano

Selim Pasha, a black mute, guards, etc.

ACT I. Belmont stands before the palace of the Pasha, eager to catch sight of Constance, who with Blonda has been spirited away to the seraglio of Selim. Osmin, the Turkish major-domo, refuses the Spaniard's request that he may speak with Pedrillo, for he has a grudge against the new servant and says he is a rascal, which Belmont denies. Osmin is irascible, and tries to drive Belmont away with threats. Pedrillo enters the garden, and Osmin shows his resentment that he has made such swift advance in the Pasha's favor. He accuses him of following the women about, says he is up to some trick, threatens to expose him, and hopes eventually to see him hanged. As Osmin goes away, Belmont calls to Pedrillo, who joyfully recognizes him. To the lover's eager questions Pedrillo replies that Constance is alive and that he may still hope to rescue her from the Pasha. Pedrillo says that his skill in gardening has given him favor with the Pasha and greater freedom than others have, and that the only difficulty is in their all getting away from the palace. Belmont has provided everything, including a ship outside the harbor which at a signal will take them on board. Pedrillo plans to arrange an audience with the Pasha for Belmont as a skilled architect, and says that the Pasha is now returning from a water excursion upon which Constance has accompanied him. Belmont is distracted between hope and fear, and hides as the Pasha's retinue of janissaries approaches.

As Selim and Constance pass, the former is trying to win her from her melancholy. He offers her his love, and she tells him that she loves another to whom she is promised, and that she sorrows at her parting and absence from him. She goes into the palace, and while the Pasha is walking in the garden, Pedrillo presents the new architect. The Pasha, much interested, promises him an audience on the morrow, and orders that he be well entertained. When Pedrillo would conduct Belmont into the palace, he meets Osmin, who stoutly protests, being very suspicious of both of them and warning Pedrillo that whatever plot he has afoot, he will not find Osmin sleeping.

Act II. In the garden, upon which opens his house, Osmin meets Blonda and arrogantly seeks to force his attentions upon her, telling her that the Pasha has given her to him. She defies him, saying that she is a free-born Englishwoman, and that love is won by tenderness and not by surliness. He suspects that she loves Pedrillo, and she fosters his jealousy. Yet when he orders her into his house and she refuses to go, he dare not compel her for fear she will tear his eyes out. Constance comes, and immediately, the Pasha, who, when he learns that she is still firm against his suit, tells her that she must decide to love him by the morrow, or suffer torture for her obstinacy. She goes away and he seeks some method of winning her love, for he admires her fidelity and courage. Blonda and Pedrillo come when he has gone, and Pedrillo tells of Belmont's presence, and the plan to carry off herself and Constance that very night.

Later Constance is alone, lamenting her bitter fate and dreading the torture that awaits her, when Blonda tells her of the hope of deliverance. They have gone away together when Pedrillo comes, meditating on the hazards of their enterprise. As Osmin comes on him there, he plies the Turk with wine and at last brings him to a state of apparent drunkenness, then leads him to Osmin's house that he may go to bed. Pedrillo returns and calls Belmont from his hiding-place. Soon Constance and Blonda come to the rendezvous, and Pedrillo tells them to be ready at midnight for a summons. Both the lovers tremble at the duress in which their sweethearts are held, and make them renew their promises of faithfulness, until the women are so offended that Pedrillo says it is sure proof of their fidelity, and the lovers seek forgiveness.

ACT III. At midnight Belmont and Pedrillo meet in the garden, see that everything is quiet, and place a ladder at the window of the palace. At Pedrillo's signal Constance opens the window, Belmont goes up the ladder and enters, and in a moment the two come out at the door. Pedrillo seizes the ladder and places it against the side of Osmin's house by Blonda's window. Osmin suddenly appears in the garden, espies the ladder, and still much the worse for drink, reels toward it and seats himself upon a lower rung. Pedrillo, coming down, is almost upon him before he sees him, and re-ascends with alacrity. Osmin calls up to Blonda, then raises the cry of robbers. Pedrillo and Blonda come out at the house door, pass under the ladder, and try to hasten off, but Osmin, having sighted them, starts in pursuit. The guards seize them, as they do Belmont and Constance also, and in spite of Pedrillo's twitting Osmin about his drunken state and Belmont's offer to buy his silence, the major-domo cannot be prevailed upon, and the prisoners are led away, while Osmin openly exults at the death that surely awaits them.

In the apartments of Selim Pasha, who has been aroused by the noise, Osmin relates the effort at elopement and calls attention to his efficiency in balking it. Belmont and Constance are summoned, and Constance tells the Pasha that Belmont is the man whom she loves, and prays that she be allowed to die in his stead. Belmont will not listen to that, but kneels to the Pasha, for the first time to any man, and acknowledges that he is Latades, the son of a great Spanish family, who will give up all to ransom him. Selim starts up, astonished and exultant, exclaiming that Belmont is then the son of the Commander of Kau, and so the Pasha's bitterest enemy, the man who was the cause of Selim's exile from his home, his country, and his happiness.

The Pasha withdraws to give directions to Osmin for the torture of the prisoners, who, despairing yet happy if they may but die together, embrace almost joyously. Pedrillo and Blonda are also brought in as Selim returns to give judgment. He asks Belmont what punishment he expects, and the latter declares himself expectant of atoning for the injustice his father committed against the Pasha. Selim, however, declares that he despises that father's example too much to follow it, and gives Belmont his freedom and also his sweetheart, with the proviso that he tell his father that he was in Selim's power and that Selim set him free. Belmont is overwhelmed with gratitude. Pedrillo asks for mercy for himself and Blonda, and in spite of Osmin's passionate remonstrance, the Pasha gives them all their freedom, together with passports, and orders that they be accompanied aboard ship. The four erstwhile captives voice their lasting gratitude to the Pasha and extol his greatness of soul, while Osmin, consumed with rage and hate, pictures in imagination the torture to which, rather, he would put them.

GOYESCAS, O, LOS MAJOS ENAMORADOS

(*Gō-yās'-kahs, ŏ, Lŏs Mah'-hŏs Ay-nah-mō-rah'-dōs*)

(GOYESCAS, OR, THE LOVE-SICK GALLANTS)

SPANISH tragic grand opera, based upon paintings by the great eighteenth-century painter, Francisco de Goya y Lucientes. Music by Enrique Granados y Campina. Book by Fernando Periquet. First production, New York, 1916. The scene is the Hermitage of San Antonio de la Florida, near Madrid, Spain, about 1800.

CHARACTERS

FERNANDO, a young captain of the Royal Spanish
 Guards, lover of Rosario......................*Tenor*
PAQUIRO, a toreador............................*Baritone*
ROSARIO, a high-born lady......................*Soprano*
PEPA, a young girl of the people, Paquiro's sweetheart ....*Soprano*
Majos and majas.

PICTURE I. In the Campo de la Florida, in Madrid, with the church of San Antonio and the Manzanares River in the distance, a group of *majos* and *majas* are gathered celebrating a holiday. The *majas*[1] are tossing a *pelele*[2] in a blanket and singing gaily. They philosophize about love and the way to keep a sweetheart. The gallants accuse them of cruel coquetry, but they claim that as their right and the secret

---

[1] "For the Spanish *maja* (mah'hah) there is no exact English equivalent. Flitch, in a study of Goya and his times, describes her as follows: 'She was a native of Madrid and flourished at the close of the eighteenth century. She was an explosive, flashy young person, with a vivid taste for finery in dress and jewels ... The *majo*, her masculine companion, who did a little tinkering or huckstering in his more strenuous moments, shared her passion for extravagance in attire, her indolence, arrogance, audacity, and fire.'" (See Introduction to the score of the opera.)

[2] Tossing the *pelele* (pay-lay'-leh), or stuffed figure of a man, is an ancient popular sport in Spain.

of their fascination. All the *majas* acknowledge the desirability of having a lover, and that life in Madrid is made up of "wit and a dagger, flowers and women." As the gallants declare their devotion and their willingness each to be a *pelele* for the women daily, the women toss the *pelele* about with frantic gaiety.

Paquiro, a daring toreador, pays florid compliments to the *majas,* and they, though pleased with his flattery, say that love is his toy and that he likes to sip every flower. The gallants are jealous of his popularity, and declare that some other woman calls him her own. The *majas* say that they know he loves Pepa, who is even now coming. They stop their game as a dogcart appears, and sing out to Pepa that Paquiro is there. Pepa alights and is greeted as their queen. She smilingly acknowledges their homage. Paquiro advances to meet her, and she shows her affection for him, though he jealously declares that her favors are not for him alone. Pepa tells him that she loves him only, while her friends remark how worthy they are of their bliss, and that never has such love been seen.

A sedan-chair is seen approaching, borne by richly dressed lackeys. Silence falls on the group as Rosario descends from the chair and looks about her for Fernando, her lover, with whom she has a rendezvous. Unseen he watches her as she shows embarrassment at the presence of the curious crowd. Paquiro approaches her gallantly, while Pepa and the others look on in surprise. He recognizes Rosario and insinuatingly reminds her of a *baile de candil** at which he once met her, and invites her to attend another to be held that night. Fernando, overhearing the invitation, is seized with doubt and jealousy. Rosario espies him, and turns to him for protection against the advances of Paquiro; but Fernando, when she

* A low ball given in a lantern-lighted hall.

asks where he was, replies that he was wondering what was the meaning of her blushes when Paquiro addressed her. Rosario passionately resents his suspicion, says that he will see her dead rather than untrue to him, and affectionately protests that he should so needlessly doubt her love. Fernando reveals his own affection for her, but admits his jealousy, and says that she must give proof of her love for him. Pepa, who has witnessed the whole scene with flashing eye, scornfully expresses her contempt for the lady of rank, and her determination to outshine her in Paquiro's eyes. The gallants and the *majas* comment on the uncertainty of love as they see Pepa and Paquiro at odds with each other.

At length Rosario declares with utter abandon her love for Fernando, but still Fernando is unconvinced, and says that if she once went to the ball, then she must go again and prove her fidelity to him. Pepa defiantly says that attendance upon the ball would be daring; and the crowd comments upon the hard test to which Fernando, little knowing where he takes her, would put Rosario. Both Rosario and Fernando are disquieted by fears, and Pepa warns Rosario to beware of her. She also whispers to Fernando that the ball is at nine that evening, while Paquiro asks the young officer if they really do mean to come. Fernando replies that he intends to; Rosario exclaims in dismay, and Pepa acknowledges that the captain is no coward. Fernando turns haughtily to Rosario and demands that she attend with him. Fernando and Rosario go away, and the crowd goes back to its former entertainment. Pepa and Paquiro mount the dog-cart and go off together amid great cheering and huzzas.

PICTURE 2. It is night, and the ball in a long hall lighted by a single lantern is in progress. Two imperative knocks resound, and Paquiro himself opens the door to Fernando and Rosario. The latter pleads with the captain not to bring her there, but he haughtily insists, and she enters. Pepa taunts her with ever having come to such a ball, and Fernando tries to console her by saying that soon he will make them all hush up. The men are defiant and scornful at his pride, but the women admire his bravery. Paquiro suggests that Fernando and Rosario might wish to dance, and Pepa impudently asks Fernando why he brought the high-born lady to this poor ball. He replies provokingly. Rosario is already greatly frightened and eager to go, but Fernando whispers to her to be calm, for now it is not so easy to get away. Pepa leads the women in taunting remarks.

Paquiro tells Fernando that if he and his lady were not guests of the ball, every man there would resent Fernando's offensive bearing. Fernando smilingly replies that he regrets the circumstance. Paquiro can hardly restrain his animosity, and urged on by Pepa, continues to anger Fernando. The quarrel progresses, Fernando haughtily declaring that he sees no man of valor there. Paquiro says that he does not here accept Fernando's challenge, but that he will give proof of his valor in some better place. The crowd comments on the angry men, saying that they are both brave, that each is in love with Rosario, and each hopes to win her, but they have now quarreled so that life is the hazard. Rosario makes a futile attempt to make them cease quarreling, and at length she and the captain are permitted to leave.

Picture 3. Rosario is sitting in the moonlight in the garden of her palace, meditating sadly. Two mysterious figures are seen passing along behind the garden. They are Paquiro and Pepa. Fernando comes, and Rosario greets him sadly, but as always affectionately. He tells her of his persistent foreboding of the loss of her love, and she reassures him, earnestly declaring that he is the only one whom she has ever loved. The hour strikes, and Fernando must leave her in order to keep his appointment with Paquiro. Rosario pleads with him not to go, but neither her love nor her sorrow prevents him. Silence reigns through long moments of suspense, then the voice of Fernando, wounded to the death, is heard. The stealthy figures of Paquiro and Pepa creep back beyond the garden gate in the opposite direction from that in which they came. Through the gate staggers Fernando, supported by Rosario. He dies in her arms, convinced at last of her great love and hopeless grief.

GRISÉLIDIS
(*Grē-zā-lĭ-dĭs*)

FRENCH sentimental operatic miracle play. Music by Jules Massenet. Book by Armand Silvestre and Eugene Morand. First production, Paris, 1901. The scene is Provence, and the time is the fourteenth century.

CHARACTERS

THE MARQUIS DE SALUCES	Baritone
ALAIN, a shepherd	Tenor
THE PRIOR	Baritone
GONDEBAUD	Baritone
THE DEVIL	Baritone
GRISÉLIDIS	Soprano
BERTRADE	Soprano
FIAMINA, the Devil's wife	Soprano

Loys, son of the Marquis; men-at-arms, spirits, the Voice of the Night, servants, celestial voices, etc.

PROLOGUE. In Provence near a forest Alain stands at sunset, thinking that, because soon he will again see Grisélidis, the gates of Paradise are opening to him. The Prior and Gondebaud come along, seeking the Marquis, who is out hunting. They accost Alain, and as they pass, the Prior is saying that doubtless the reason why the Marquis has never married is, he has never seen a woman who charmed his soul. Alain says that then the Marquis has never seen Grisélidis, and tells of her beauty and grace. They see the Marquis standing among the trees, and looking toward the depths of the forest in a sort of ecstasy. As they approach, he points out a figure whom he takes to be an angel. Grisélidis is slowly coming toward them in the sunset glow. The Marquis, strongly moved, falls to his knees, and believing her an apparition from God, as she passes him, gently and simply asks her if he may be her husband. Equally simply Grisélidis says that, as his will is doubtless that of Heaven, she has no other wish than to obey him. Celestial voices chant Alleluia as the Marquis kisses her hand. He tells Grisélidis that on the morrow the Prior will conduct her to the castle. She and the others go away, all except Alain, who has watched the scene in agony of heart, and now, alone and despairing, sees the gates of Paradise close before him, for he has lost Grisélidis.

ACT I. In the oratory of Grisélidis at the castle, Bertrade sits spinning when Gondebaud comes to announce that the Marquis is about starting for the wars with the Saracens. She summons her mistress as the Marquis and the Prior enter. The Marquis is greatly grieved that he must leave his wife and son. He and the Prior kneel in prayer before a triptych within which is a statue of St. Agnes with a lamb in her arms, and at her feet the stone figure of the devil. As they rise from their knees, the Prior promises that Grisélidis and her son shall never leave the castle, whereat the Marquis is displeased, and takes oath that two things he will never doubt,—his wife's fidelity and her obedience. The Prior protests, reminding him that the devil is very sly. The Marquis impatiently asserts that he would still swear that oath though the devil were here; whereupon the devil springs from the triptych and greets them. In proof of his identity he tells them that he and his wife,—for the Lord, he says, avenged himself by marrying the devil to a coquette and evil woman, thus consoling the shade of Menelaus,—spend their nights in stirring up trouble between married couples, that he has heard the Marquis's defiance of his power, and he accepts the challenge. The Marquis, as pledge that he does not doubt his wife, gives the devil his marriage ring, which the latter accepts as closing the wager, and goes out of the window, laughing. Grisélidis comes, and with great tenderness husband and wife say farewell, she renewing her vows of love and obedience. Bertrade brings Loÿs, and at length the Marquis departs, while Grisélidis, weeping, watches from the window his going, then bids Bertrade read again to her the account of the parting of Ulysses and Penelope.

Act II. To the terrace before the castle comes the devil, rejoicing that he is far from his wife. Suddenly she appears, jealous and suspicious. They quarrel fiercely until Fiamina discovers that he is planning to destroy the soul of Grisélidis, whereupon she offers to help him, and they are fully reconciled. Grisélidis comes and stands looking sadly over the sea, thinking of her husband, now six months gone. Bertrade comes with Loÿs, and as the Angelus sounds, mother and son pray for the absent father. Bertrade says that a man and a woman seek audience with Grisélidis. As the nurse and child go away, the devil and Fiamina enter, disguised as a Levantine slave-dealer and his Moorish slave. The devil shows the ring of the Marquis and says that the latter has acquired Fiamina as his chattel, and has ordered that upon reaching the castle she be installed as its mistress. Grisélidis, though revolted, is yet obedient, and decides to leave her home. As she goes into the castle, the devil, baffled by such obedience, determines upon another test.

Night has fallen, and, Fiamina having gone away, the devil conjures up the spirits of woods and mountains. To them he gives the task of calling Alain, who still loves Grisélidis, and of blowing kisses upon her lips, and of bathing her head in perfumes heavy with ardent dreams. Soon Alain comes into the moonlit garden. Grisélidis, almost unconscious and, like Alain, as if led by an unknown power, also comes. They greet each other eagerly, and she reads in his eyes his love for her. He recalls their former companionship, his hope, and, though she protests that she is no longer her own mistress, he forgets all but his longing for her and clasps her in his arms. She, almost swooning, wonders at the strong emotion that tears her heart and whether it is indeed love. He begs her to flee with him, and she, remembering that she is already obliged to leave her home, is almost consenting when little Loÿs comes running from the castle. She breaks away from Alain and seizes the child in her arms, and Alain, despairing, goes away distractedly. The devil, his spell broken, suddenly appears, and bethinks him of one last test for Grisélidis. As she fondly calls after Alain, dropping the boy's hand for a moment, the devil seizes the child and makes off, laughing mockingly. Grisélidis hears the child's cries, but cannot find him, and, conscience-stricken, prays that her son may be restored to her or that she may die.

Act III. The castle has been aroused, and all night the retainers have been searching far and near but fruitlessly for the child, while Grisélidis weeps and prays, and watches by the window of the oratory. The triptych has been closed, and as she opens it, she is greatly agitated to see that the statue of the saint has disappeared. Bertrade comes, saying that an old man wishes to talk with her. The devil enters in disguise and tells Grisélidis that a lover of hers, the leader of a band of the pirates that infest that coast, holds the child for ransom, demanding as the price a kiss from her. She cannot believe that she must lose her honor for the child's life until the devil says that her refusal may mean slavery or death for little Loÿs; then, horror-stricken, she consents. The devil is beside himself with joy as Grisélidis seizes a knife, in order to guard herself better, and hastens away.

The Marquis appears at the door of the oratory, without helmet or arms. No one meets him but the devil, still disguised as an old man. To the Marquis's question the devil replies that Grisélidis, whom he points out from the window, is hastening to a young lord whom she loves and who awaits her on board his ship. He hands the Marquis a poignard, urging him to overtake and kill her. The Marquis espies his own ring on the old man's hand and knows with whom he has to deal. Watching Grisélidis, he sees her suddenly turn back, and with great joy he awaits her. She comes, but stops upon the threshold, asking, "Am I still your wife?" The Marquis, his jealousy aroused by her question, asks, "Can I still believe in you?" At last Grisélidis tells him of the woman sent by him, who has usurped her place. He swears that he sent none such, and Grisélidis assures him of her fidelity to him. The Marquis asks her pardon for his doubt, telling her of the wager the devil forced on him. Reassured, they embrace with great joy.

The devil, however, appears and taunts the wife with the loss of the child she vowed to guard, then goes away, laughing in triumph. Their sorrow is great, and the Marquis calls for weapons, vowing that he will snatch the child from the ruffians. Suddenly his weapons vanish from the wall on which they hung. Undaunted, he still declares he will go, and husband and wife are kneeling together before the triptych in prayer for the success of his quest, when suddenly the cross upon the altar becomes transformed into a shining sword. He seizes it, swearing that he goes never to return unless he brings his son. Thunder and lightning shake the castle as the triptych flies open, disclosing the saint's image upon its pedestal and Loÿs in her arms. Retainers stand amazed on the threshold, and an invisible celestial choir sings praise to the Lord. The Marquis takes the child and places it in the mother's arms, and they are assured that the Holy Spirit has driven the devil from that region forever.

LIST OF COMPOSERS

Auber, Daniel François Esprit. Fra Diavolo, 155.
Aubert, Louis François Marie. La Forêt Bleue, 151.
Balfe, Michael William. The Bohemian Girl, 34.
Beethoven, Ludwig van. Fidelio, 141.
Bellini, Vincenzo. Norma, 349.
Bizet, Georges. Carmen, 41. Djamileh, 84. Les Pêcheurs de Perles, 390.
Blech, Leo. Versiegelt, 539.
Boito, Arrigo. Mefistofele, 309.
Borodin, Alexander Porphyrievitch. Prince Igor, 408.
Chabrier, Emmanuel. Gwendoline, 176.
Charpentier, Gustave. Julien, 206. Louise, 237.
Converse, Frederick S. The Pipe of Desire, 404. The Sacrifice, 473.
Damrosch, Walter. Cyrano, 71.
Debussy, Claude. Pelléas et Mélisande, 395.
De Koven, Reginald. The Canterbury Pilgrims, 561.
Delibes, Clément Philibert Léo. Lakmé, 220.
Donizetti, Gaetano. Don Pasquale, 90. La Favorita, 137. Lucia di Lammermoor, 247.
Dukas, Paul. Ariane et Barbe-Bleue, 19.
Erlanger, Camille. Aphrodite, 12.
Erlanger, Frédéric d'. Noël, 346.
Février, Henry. Monna Vanna, 335.
Flotow, Friedrich von. Martha, 297.
Giordano, Umberto. Andrea Chénier, 553. Madame Sans-Gêne, 258.
Gluck, Christopher Wilibald. Armide, 22. Orfeo ed Euridice, 361.

LIST OF COMPOSERS

Goetz, Hermann. The Taming of the Shrew, 495.
Goldmark, Carl. The Cricket on the Hearth, 66.
Gounod, Charles. Faust, 131. Romeo and Juliet, 464.
Granados, Enrique. Goyescas, 583.
Herbert, Victor. Madeleine, 266. Natoma, 339.
Holbrooke, Josef Charles. The Children of Don, 569.
Humperdinck, Engelbert. Hänsel und Gretel, 186. Königskinder, 212.
Kienzl, William. Der Evangelimann, 116. Der Kuhreigen, 217.
Laparra, Raoul. La Habanera, 180.
Leoncavallo, Ruggiero. Pagliacci, 374.
Leoni, Franco. L'Oracolo, 355.
Mascagni, Pietro. Cavalleria Rusticana, 45. Iris, 198.
Massenet, Jules. Cendrillon, 48. Le Cid, 55. Don Quichotte, 94. Hérodiade, 189. The Juggler of Notre-Dame, 204. Manon, 275. Thaïs, 508. Werther, 542. Grisélidis, 588.
Meyerbeer, Giacomo. Les Huguenots, 193.
Montemezzi, Italo. L'Amore dei Tre Re, 5.
Moussorgsky, Modeste Petrovich. Boris Godounov, 38.
Mozart, Johann Wolfgang Amadeus. Don Giovanni, 86. The Magic Flute, 270. The Marriage of Figaro, 289. Die Entführung aus dem Serail, 578.
Nouguès, Jean. Quo Vadis?, 415.
Offenbach, Jacques. The Tales of Hoffmann, 487.
Parelli, Attilio. A Lovers' Quarrel, 243.
Parker, Horatio. Fairyland, 120. Mona, 331.
Planquette, Robert. The Chimes of Normandy, 52.
Ponchielli, Amilcare. La Gioconda, 168.
Puccini, Giacomo. La Bohême, 31. The Girl of the Golden West, 172. Madame Butterfly, 252. Manon Lescaut, 283. Tosca, 514.
Ricci, Luigi and Frederico. Crispino e la Comare, 68.

LIST OF COMPOSERS

Rossini, Gioacchino Antonio. The Barber of Seville, 25. William Tell, 548.

Saint-Saëns, Charles Camille. Déjanire, 78. Samson and Delilah, 479.

Smetana, Friedrich. The Bartered Bride, 28.

Strauss, Richard. Elektra, 103. Der Rosencavalier, 469. Salome, 476.

Thomas, Charles Louis Ambroise. Hamlet, 183. Mignon, 325.

Thuille, Ludwig. Lobetanz, 225.

Verdi, Giuseppe. Aïda, 1. Ernani, 106. Falstaff, 128. The Masked Ball, 303. Otello, 366. Rigoletto, 431. La Traviata, 520. Il Trovatore, 533.

Wagner, Richard. The Flying Dutchman, 147. Lohengrin, 229. Die Meistersinger von Nürnberg, 316. Parsifal, 379. Rienzi, 424. Der Ring des Nibelungen: Das Rheingold, 438; Die Walküre, 466; Siegfried, 452; Götterdämmerung, 457. Tannhäuser, 501. Tristan und Isolde, 525.

Weber, Carl Maria von. Euryanthe, 110. Der Freischütz, 165.

Wolf-Ferrari, Ermanno. L'Amore Medico, 8. Le Donne Curiose, 98. The Jewels of the Madonna, 202. Il Segreto di Susanna, 484.

Zandonai, Riccardo. Conchita, 61. Francesca da Rimini, 158.

KEY TO PRONUNCIATION

A grave accent in an English word denotes that an otherwise silent syllable or vowel is to be pronounced.

In French words, because the stress is so evenly distributed over all the syllables, the accent mark has been omitted.

An occasional secondary accent is marked (″).

1. A macron (ō) over a vowel denotes the name sound in English.

2. A breve (ĕ) over a vowel denotes a short sound, as:

    ă in am   ĭ in pin
    ĕ " end   ŏ " odd
            ŭ in up

3. H following a vowel denotes a very open sound, as:

    ah like a in father   oh like o in or, for
    eh " e " her   uh " u " turn

4. Special vowel sounds are as follows:

    ȯ as in wonder   ōō as in fool
    ü " " rune   ŏŏ " " look

5. Special consonant sounds, other than the name sounds of the letters, are denoted as follows:

    g like g in get   dh like th in these
    ĵ " g " gem   zh " z " azure
         kh like ch in Scottish, loch, or German, ich

INDEX

N.B.—This Index is additional to, and not inclusive of, the titles and pronunciations given in the Contents, the headings of the operas, and the List of Composers.

Abimelech (ă-bĭm'-ĕ-lĕk), 479
Adalgisa (ah-dahl-gē'-zah), 349
Adolar (ah'-dō-lar), 110
Adriano (ah-drĭ-ah'-nō), 424
Ægisthus (ē-jĭs'-thŭs), 103
Agatha (ăg'-a-thah), 165
Alberich (ahl'-bĕ-rĭkh), 438, 452, 458
Alcindoro (ăl-sĭn-doh'-rō), 31
Alfio (al'-fĭ-o), 45
Alladine (ăl-lah-dēn), 19
Almaviva (ahl-mah-vē'-vah), 25, 289
Alvarado (ahl-vah-rah'-dō), 339
Alvise Badoero (ahl-vē'-zĕ bah-dō-ā'-rō), 168
Amelia (ah-mā'-lē-ah), 303
Amfortas (ahm-fŏr'-tahs), 379
Amneris (ahm-nā'-rēs), 1
Amonasro (ah-mō-nahs'-rō), 1
Amor (ah'-mōr), 361
Angelotti (an-jā-lŏt'-tē), 514
Annunzio, Gabriele d', 158
Arlecchino (ahr-lĕk-kē'-nō), 98
Arline (ahr'-lēn), 34
Arnheim (arn'-hīm), 34
Arontes (ah-rohn'tēz), 22
Artemidor (ar-tĕm'-ĭ-dōr), 22
Asdrudale (ahz-drū-dah'-lā), 68
Astrifiammante (ahs"-trē-fē-ahm-mahn'-tā), 270
Athanaël (ah-tăn'-ā-ĕl), 508
Auber, Daniel F. E. (ō-ber), 155
Aubert, Louis F. M. (ō-ber'), 151
Auburn (ŏh-bŭrn), 120
Azucena (ahd-zū-chā'-nah), 533

Baculard-Darnaud, 137.
Balfe, M. W. (bălf), 34
Ballo in Maschera, Un (băl'-lo in mahs-kā'rah, ōōn), 303
Balthazar (bahl-thah'-zar), 137
Baptista (băp-tēs'-tah), 495
Barbara de la Guerra (bahr'-bahr-ah dĕ lah gwer'-rah), 339
Barbier, Jules, librettist, 131, 183, 325, 464, 487
Barbiere di Siviglia, Il (bahr-bĭ-ā'-rā dĕ sē-vēl'-yah, ĕl), 25
Barnaba (bar'-nah-bah), 168
Baroncelli (bah-rohn-chĕl'-lē), 424
Bartolo (bar-tō'lō), 25, 289
Barton, George Edward, librettist, 404
Bartsch, Rudolf Hans, 217
Basilio (bah-sēl'-yō), 25, 289
Batka, Richard, librettist, 217, 539
Beaumarchais, 25, 289
Beckmesser, Sixtus (bĕk'-mĕs-sĕr, zĕx'-tōōs), 316

Beethoven, Ludwig van (bā'-tō-vĕn, lōōd-vĭkh vahn), 141
Belasco, David, 172, 252
Bellangère (bĕl-lahn-zhair), 19
Bellini, Vincenzo (bĕl-lē'nĕ, vĕn-chĕnt'-sō), 349
Bells of Corneville, The, 52
Benelli, Sem, librettist, 5
Bernal (bĕr-nahl'), 473
Bernstein, Elsa, librettist, 212
Bey, Mariette (bā), 1
Bianca (bē-ahn'-kah), 495
Biancofiore (bē-ahn"-kō-fē-ō'-rā), 158
Biaso (bē-ah'-zō), 202
Bierbaum, Otto Julius, librettist, 225
Bis, Hypolite, librettist, 548
Biterolf (bē'-ter-ŏlf), 501
Bizet, Georges (bē-zā', zhŏrzh), 41, 84, 390
Blanchefleure (blahnsh-flŭr), 217
Blau, Edouard, librettist, 55, 542
Blech, Leo (blĕk, lā'-ō), 539
Boccaccio, 110
Boito, Arrigo (bō'-ē-tō, ahr-rē'gō); composer, 309; librettist, 128, 168, 366
Borodin, A. P. (bŏr'-ō-dēn), 408
Bortolo (bohr-tō'-lō), 68
Bouilly, 141
Brangæne (brahng-ā'-nĕ), 525
Brétigny, De (brā-tēn-yē, dŭ), 275
Brigode, De (brē-gŏd, dŭ), 258
Brünnhilde (brün-hĭl'-dĕ), 446, 452, 458
Bulwer-Lytton, Edward, 424
Bunn, Alfred, librettist, 34
Cain, Henri, librettist, 48, 94, 415
Caius (kā'-yŭs), 128
Callidès (kahl-lē'-dās), 12
Calzabigi, Raniero di, librettist, 361
Cammarano, Salvatore, librettist, 90, 247, 533
Canio (kah'-nĭ-ō), 374
Capulet (kăp'-yŭ-lĕt), 464
Carmela (kahr-mā'-lah), 202
Carmen (kahr-mān), 41
Carré, Michel, librettist, 131, 183, 325, 390, 464
Caspar (kăs'-par), 165
Cassio (kăsh'-ĭ-ō), 366
Castro, Guillen de, 55
Catherine Hübscher, Duchess of Danzig (kăth'-a-rĭn hüb'-sher, dahnt'-sēk), 258
Cavalier of the Rose, The, 469
Cecco del Vecchio (chăk'-kō dal vĕk'-kĭ-oh), 424
Ceprano (chĕ-prah'-nō), 431

597

INDEX

Cervantes, 94
Chabrier, Emmanuel (*shau-brē-ā*), 176
Charpentier, Gustave (*shar-pen-tē-ā*), 206, 237
Chenevière, Jacques, librettist, 151
Cherubino (*kā-roo-bē'-nō*), 289
Chezy, Helmine von, librettist, 110
Chézy, Marquis de (*shā-zǐ, dǔ*), 217
Chilonides, Chilo (*kǐ-lon'-ǐ-dēz, kǐ'-lō*), 415
Chimairis (*kē-mā-rēs*), 12
Chimène (*shē-mān*), 55
Cho-Cho-San, 252
Chonita (*kō-nē'-tah*), 473
Chrysis (*krǐ'-sǐs*), 12
Chrysothemis (*krǐs-oth'-e-mǐs*), 103
Ciccillo (*chē'-chǐl-lo*), 202
Cieca, La (*chē-ā'-kah, lah*), 168
Civinini, Guelfo, librettist, 172
Cloches de Corneville, Les (*klohch dǔ korn-vēl, lā*), 52
Clytemnestra (*klē-těm-něs'-trah*), 103
Cobbler and the Fairy, The, 68
Cochenille (*kō-chěn-ēl*), 487
Colonna, Guido (*kō-lohn'-nah, gwē'-dō*), 335; Steffano (*stěf'fah-nō*), 424
Comitti, Enrico, librettist, 243
Concetta (*kohn-chět'-tah*), 202
Conchita Perez (*kōn-kēēt'-ah pā'-reth*), 61
Contes d'Hoffmann, les (*kohnt dohf-mahn, lā*), 487
Contino del Fiore (*kon-tǐ'-nō dāl fē-ō'-rā*), 68
Converse, Frederick S., 404, 473
Coppelius (*kōp-pā'-lǐ-ǔs*), 487
Corneille, 55
Corvain (*kohr'vane*), 120
Crispino Tacchetto (*krǐs-pē'-nō tahk-kět'-lō*), 68
Cuno (*kōō'nō*), 165
Cyrano de Bergerac (*seer'-ah-nō dǔ běr-zhěr-ǎk*), 71
Daland (*dah'-lahnt*), 147
Damrosch, Walter (*dǎm'-rŏsh*), 71
Dancairo (*dahn-kī'-rō*), 41
Dapertutto (*dah-pěr-tǔt'-tō*), 487
Debussy, Claude (*de-bü-sǐ*), 395
Decourcelles, 266
DeGuiche (*dǔgěsh*), 71
Dejanira (*děj-ah-nǐ'-rah*), 78
Delibes, C. P. L. (*deh-lēb'*), 220
Delilah (*dě-lī'-lah*), 479
Demetrius (*dě-mē'-trǐ-ǔs*), 12
Deschamps, Emile, librettist, 193
Desdemona (*děs-dě-mō'nah*), 366
Despreaux (*dā-sprō*), 258
Devilshoof, 34
Dickens, Charles, 66
Didier (*de-de-ā*), 266
Diego, Don (*dē-ā'-gō, dohn*), 55
Dispettosi Amanti, I (*des-pāt'-tō-sē ah-mahn'-tē, ē*), 243

Dmitri (*dmē-trē*), 38
D'Obigny, Marquis (*dō-bēn'-yē*), 520
Doctor Cupid, 8
Donizetti, Gaetano (*doh-nē-dzět'-tē, gah-ā-tah'-nō*), 90, 137, 247
Douphol, Baron (*dōō-fohl*), 520
Dukas, Paul (*dǔ'-kahs*), 19
Dulcinea (*dǔl-sin'ē-ah*), 94
Dumas, Alexander, the Younger, 520

Eglantine (*ěg-lahn-tēn*), 110
Elizabeth (*ā-lě'-zah-bāt*), 501
Elsa, (*ěl'-zah*), 229
Elvira (*el-vē'-rah*), 86
Emilia (*ē-měl'-ǐ-ah*), 366
Ennery, Adolphe d', librettist, 55
Enzo Grimaldo (*ent'-sō grē-mahl'-dō*), 168
Erda (*ěrt'-ah*), 438, 452, 458
Eric (*ā'-rēk*), 147
Erlanger, Camille (*er'-lahng-ehr, kah-měl*), 12
Erlanger, Frédéric d', 346
Erochka (*ā-rok-kah*), 408
Escamillo (*ās-kah-měl'-yō*), 41
Eschenbach, Wolfram von (*esh'-ěn-bahkh, vŏlf'-rahm fōn*), 379, 501
Etienne, V. J. ("*Jouy*"), librettist, 548
Eunice (*ǔ'-nǐs*), 415
Eurydice (*ū-rǐd'-ǐs-ē*), 361
Eva, 316
Fabrizio (*fah-brit'-sǐ-ō*), 68
Fafnir (*fahf'-nēr*), 438, 452
Falstaff (*fŏl'-stǎf*), 128
Fanciulla del West, La (*fahn-chōōl'-lah*), 172
Faninal (*fah-nē-nahl*), 469
Fasolt (*fah'-zolt*), 438
Faust (*fowst*), 131, 309
Feodor (*fā'-ō-dōr*), 38
Fernald, Chester B., 355
Fernando de Zelva (*fǔr-nǎn'-do dǔ tsěl'-vah*), 141
Ferrando (*fer-rahn'-dō*), 533
Ferrier, Jeanne and Paul, librettists, 346
Février, Henry (*fā'-vrē-ā*), 335
Figaro (*fē'-gah-rō*), 25, 289
Flaubert, Gustave, 189
Flauto Magico, Il (*flah'-ōō-tō mah-jē'-kō, ěl*), 270
Fliegende Holländer, Der (*flē'-gěn-dě hohl'-lent-ěr*), 147
Flora Bervoix (*flō'-rah běr-vwah*), 520
Florestan (*floh'-rěs-tahn*), 141
Florestein (*floh'-rē-stīn*), 34
Florindo (*flō-rin'-dō*), 98, 243
Flosshilda (*flŏs-hǐl'-dě*), 438, 458
Flotow, Friedrich von (*flō'tō*), 297
Fouché (*fōō-shā*), 258
France, Anatole, 508
Francisco de la Guerra (*frahn-thes'-kō dē lah gwer'rah*), 339

INDEX 599

François, Duke D'Esterre (*frahn-swah*), 266
Frasquita (*frah-skē'-tah*), 41
Freudhofer, Johannes (*froit'-hohf-ehr*), 116; Matthias, 116
Freya (*frī'ah*), 438
Fricka (*frĭk'-ah*), 438, 446
Friedrich Engel (*frēēt'-rĭkh eng'-ĕl*), 116
Fulgenzio (*fŭl-jent'-sĭ-ō*), 243
Fürst, Walter, 548

Galitzsky, Vladimir Jaroslavitch, Prince (*gah-lĭts'-skĭ, vlah-dē'-mĭr*), 408
Gallet, Louis, librettist, 55, 78, 84, 508
Gaspard (*gahs-pahr*), 52
Gatteerez, Antonio Garcia, 533
Gelsomino (*jal-sō-mē'-nō*), 258
Genevieve (*zhŭn-vyĕv*), 395
Gennaro (*jĕn-nah'-rō*), 202
Gerhilda (*gĕr-hĭl'-dē*), 446
Germaine (*zhair-mān*), 52; Germain, 266
Germont, Giorgio (*jĕr'-mont, jōr'-jō*), 520
Geronte de Ravoir (*zhĕr-ont dŭ rah-vwah*), 283
Gessler (*gĕss'-ler*), 548
Ghislanzoni, Antonio, librettist, 1
Giacomo (*jah'-kō-mō*), 155
Giacosa, Giuseppe, librettist, 31, 252, 514
Gianciotto (*jahn-choht'-tō*), 159
Giarno (*jahr'-nō*), 325
Gilda (*jĕl'-dah*), 431
Gille, Philippe, librettist, 220, 275
Giojelli della Madonna, I (*jō-yĕl'lē, ē*), 202
Giordano, Umberto (*johr-dah'-nō*), 258
Giovanna (*jō-vahn'-nah*), 106, 431
Giovanni (*jō-vahn'-nē*), 86, 158
Giulietta (*jŭ-lē-ĕt'tah*), 487
Glazounoff, A. C., 408
Gluck, Christopher W., 22, 361
Goethe, Johann Wolfgang, 131, 309, 325, 542
Goetz, Hermann (*guhts*), 495
Golaud (*gō-lō*), 395
Goldmark, Carl (*gold'-mark*), 66
Goldoni, Carlo, 98
Golisciano, Enrico, librettist, 8, 202, 484
Gondinet, Edmond, librettist, 220
Gormas (*gohr'-mahs*), 55
Gottfried of Strasburg, 525
Gounod, Charles (*gū-nō'*), 131, 464
Gramont, Louis de, librettist, 12
Grémont, Henri, librettist, 189
Grieux, Chevalier des (*grē-ū*), 275, 283
Grimgerda (*grēm'-gĕrt-ah*), 446
Grimm, Jacob and William, 186
Guglielmo Tell (*gu-yel'-moh tĕll*), 548

Guillot de Morfontaine (*gēl-yō dŭ mohr-fohn-tān*), 275
Gunther the Gibichung (*gŏŏn'-tĕr, gē'-bĕg-ōōng*), 458
Gurnemanz (*gŭr'-ne-mahnss*), 379
Gutrune (*goo-trōō'-nē*), 458
Gwendoline (*gwen'-dō-lēn*), 176
Gzak (*zahk*), 408

Hadji (*ahd-zhē*), 220
Hagen (*hahg'-en*), 458
Halévy, Ludovic, librettist, 41
Harriet Durham, Lady, 297
Hartmann, Georges, librettist, 542
Hedwiga (*hĕlm'-vēg-ah*), 548
Heimchen am Herd, Das (*hĭm'-khen ahm hehert, dahss*),
Heinrich der Schriber (*hĭn'-rĭkh dĕr shrī'-bĕr*), 501
Helmviga (*hĕlm'-vēg-ah*), 446
Henderson, W. J., librettist, 71
Herbert, Victor, 266, 339
Herblet, Jacques (*hehr-blā*), 346
Hercules (*hehr'-kū-lēz*), 78
Hernani (*hehr-nah'-nē*), 106
Herod Antipas, 189, 476
Herodias, 189, 476
Hidraot (*hēd-rah-ō*), 22
Hoffmann, 316, 501; E. T. A., 487
Hofmannsthal, Hugo von, librettist, 103, 469
Hooker, Brian, librettist, 120, 331
Hugo, Victor, 106, 168, 431
Humperdinck, Engelbert (*hum'-pehr-dĭnk*), 186, 212
Hunding (*hŏŏn'-ding*), 446

Iago (*ē-ah'-gō*), 106, 366
Igor Sviatoslavitch (*ē'-gohr*), 408
Illica, Luigi, librettist, 31, 198, 252, 514
Inez (*ē'-nĕz, or ī'-nĕz*), 137
Iolan (*ī'-ō-lahn*), 404
Iole (*ī'-ō-lē*), 78
Irene (*ī-rēn', or ī-rē'-nē*), 424

Jaquino (*yahk-we'-nō*), 141
Jaroslavana (*jah"-rō-slahv'-nah*), 408
Jean (*zhahn*), 204; Jean Grenicheux (*grĕn-ĭ-shuh*), 52
Jochanaan (*yoh-kahn'-ahn*), 476
Jongleur de Nôtre Dame, Le zhohn-glĕr dŭ nōt-rŭ dăm lŭ), 204
José (*zhoh-zā'*; Spanish, *hō-zā'*), 41
José Castro, 172, 339
Juan (*hoo-ahn'*), 94
Julien (*zhü-lyĕn*), 206, 237
Juliette (*zhü-lyĕt'*), 464

Kalbeck, Max, 28
Karamzin, 38
Katharine (*käth'-a-rĭn*), 495
Kezal (*kā'-tsahl*), 28
Kienzl, William (*kĕnzl*), 116, 217
Kind, Johann Friedrich, librettist, 165
Klingsor (*kling'-sohr*), **379**

INDEX

Kontchak (*kohnt'-shahk*), 408
Kontchakovna, 408
Kruschina (*krōō-shē'-nah*), 28
Kundry (*kūn'-drĭ*), 379
Kurvenal (*kōōr'-fĕ-nahl*), 525
Kyoto (*kē-ō'-tō*), 198

Laertes (*lah-ĕr'-tēz*), 183, 325
Laparra, Raoul (*lah-pahr'-rah*), 180
Lefebvre, Duke of Danzig (*leh-fāvr, dahnt'-sēk*), 258
Leila (*lē'-lah*), 390
Lemaire, Ferdinand, librettist, 479
Léna, Maurice, librettist, 204
Leoncavallo, Ruggiero (*la-ōn-kah-vahl'-lo*), 374
Leoni, Franco (*la-ō'-nē*), 255
Leonora di Gusmann (*lā-ō-nō'-rah dē gŭs'-mahn*), 137
Leonora, 141; Duchess, 533
Leporello (*lĕ-pŏ-rĕl'-lō*), 86
Lescaut (*lĕs-kō*), 275, 283
Letorières, Gastone de (*lĕ-tō-rĭ-air*), 520
Leuthold (*loit'-hohlt*), 548
Lionel (*lī'-ŭn-el*), 297
Liszt, Franz, 229
Locle, Camille du, 1
Lodovico (*lō-dō-vē'-kō*), 366
Loki (*lō'-kē*), 438
Long, John Luther, 252
Lorenzo (*lō-rĕnt'-sō*), 155
Lorrain, Jacques Le, 94
Lothario (*lō-thah'-rē-ō*), 325
Louise, 206, 237
Louys, Pierre, 12, 61
Love of Three Kings, The, 5
Lucentio (*lū-chĕn'-tē-ō*), 495
Lucia (*loo-chē'-ah*), 45, 247
Lygia (*lĭ-dgī-ah*), 415
Lysiart (*lĭs-ĭ-ahr*), 110

Madeline, 346
Maeterlinck, Maurice, librettist, 19, 335, 395
Magdalena (*mahg-dah-lā'-nah*), 116, 316; Maddalena (*mahd-dah-lā'-nah*), 431; Magdelena, 473
Malatesta (*mah-lah-tās'-tah*), 90
Malatestino, 158
Maliella (*mahl-yĕl'-lah*), 202
Mallika, 220
Manon Lescaut (*mă-nohn lĕs-kō*), 275, 283
Manrico (*mahn-rē'-kō*), 533
Marcel (*mahr-sĕl*), 193
Marcellina (*mahr-chĕl-lē'-nah*), 25, 141, 289
Margaret of Valois (*văl-wah*), 193; Margaret, 309; Marguerite (*mahr-gā-rēt'*), 131
Marina Mnichek (*mah-rē'-nah mnē'-shĕk*), 38
Mario Cavaradossi (*mah'rē-ō kah-vah-rah-dôs'-sĭ*), 514
Martha Schwerlein (*mahr'-tah shvehr'-lĭn*), 131; Martha, 309

Mascagni, Pietro (*mahs-kah'-nyē*), 45, 198
Masetto (*mah-sĕt'-to*), 86
Massenet, Jules (*mahs-se-nā', zhül*), 48, 55, 94, 189, 204, 275, 508, 542
Massimelle, Reole de Courtroy, Marquis (*mahs-sĭ-mĕl*), 217
Mateo de Diaz (*mah-tā'-ō dā dē-ath'*), 61
Matteo (*maht'-tē-ō*), 155
Mauprat, Chevalier de (*mō-prah*), 266
Mazzilier, 34
Meilhac, Henri, librettist, 41, 275
Meissner, Dr. Leopold Florian, 116
Meister, Wilhelm (*mī'-stĕr, vĭl'-hĕlm*), 325
Melcthal (*mĕlk'-tahl*), 548
Melisande, 395
Menasci, G., librettist, 45
Mendès, Catulle, librettist, 176
Mephistopheles (*mĕf-ĭs-tŏf'-ē-lēz*), 113, 309
Mercédès (*mĕr-thā'-dĕs*), 41
Mérimée, Prosper, 41
Meyerbeer, Giacomo (*mī'-ehr-bār*), 193
Micaëla (*mē-kah-ā-lah*), 41
Micha (*mē'-khah*), 28
Milliet, Paul, librettist, 189, 542
Mime (*mē'-mā*), 438, 452
Mimi (*mē-mē*), 31
Mirabolano (*mē-rah-bō-lah'-nō*), 68
Molière, 8
Molina, Tirso, de, 86
Monostatos, 270
Montano (*mohn-tah'-nō*), 366
Montemezzi, Italo (*môn-tā-māď'-zē, ē-tah'-lō*), 5
Monterone (*mon-tā-rō'-nē*), 431
Moralès (*moh-rah'-lĕs*), 41
Moreau, E., 258
Moussorgsky, M. P. (*mūs-sohrg'-skĭ*), 38
Mozart, Johann W. A. (*mōt'-sahrt*), 86, 270, 289
Murger, Henry, 31
Musetta (*mŭ-zĕt'-tah*), 31
Myriel (*mĭr'-ĭ-el*), 120

Nadir (*nā'-dehr*), 390
Naoia (*nā-oi'-ah*), 404
Narraboth (*nahr'-rā-bôth*), 476
Neipperg (*nĭp-perk*), 258
Nevers (*nŭ-vĕr*), 193
Nibelungs (*nē'-bĕ-lōōng*), 438
Nichette (*nē-shĕt*), 266
Nicias (*nĭsh'-ĭ-ăs*), 508
Nicklausse (*nĭk-lows'sĕ*), 487
Nilakantha (*nē-lah-kahn'-tah*), 220
Norina (*noh-rē'-nah*), 90
Nouguès, Jean (*nōō-gwā*), 415
Nourabad (*nŭ'-rah-bahd*), 390
Nozze di Figaro, Le (*nōt'-sĕ dē fē'-gah-rō, lā*), 289

INDEX

Ochs of Lercheneau (*ohks, lerkh'-a-now*), 469
Octavio (*ŏk-tä'-vĭ-ō*), 98
Offenbach, Jacques (*ŏf-ĕn-bahk*), 487
Ophelia (*ō-fēl'-ya*), 183
Orestes (*oh-rĕs'-tēz*), 103
Oroveso (*ohr-ō-vā'-sō*), 349
Orpheus (*ohr'-fē-ŭs*, or *ohr-fūs*), 361
Orsino, Paolo (*ōr-sē'-nō*), 424
Ortlinda (*ohrt'-lĭn'-dē*), 446
Osaka (*ō-sah'-kah*), 198
Ostasio (*ō-stah'-sē-ō*), 158
Otrud (*ohr'-trōōt*), 229
Ottokar (*oht'-tō-kar*), 165
Ovlour (*ōv-lōōr*), 408

Palemon (*păl'-ā-mŏn*), 508
Pamela, Lady (*pa-mē'-lah*), 155
Pamina (*pah-mē'-nah*), 270
Pandolfe (*pahn-dŏlf*), 48
Pantalone (*pahn-tah-lō'-nĕ*), 98
Paolo (*pah'-ō-lō*), 158
Papageno (*pah-pah-gā'-nō*), 270
Parelli, Attilio (*pah-rāl'le, at-tĭ'-lĭ-ō*), 243
Parker, Horatio, 120, 331
Parpignol (*pär-pēn-yŭl*), 31
Peralta, Father (*pär-ahl'-tah*), 339
Perrault, Charles, 19, 48, 151
Petronius (*pa-trōn'-ĭ-ŭs*), 415
Petruchio (*pā-trōō'-kē-ō*), 495
Phanuel (*fă-nū'-ĕl*, or *făn'-ū-ĕl*), 189
Phenice (*fē-nĭs*), 78
Philoctetes (*fĭl-ŏk-tē'-tēz*), 78
Philodemus (*fĭl-oh-dē'-mŭs*), 12
Piave, Francesco Maria, librettist, 68, 106, 431, 520
Piestre, P. E. ("Cormon"), librettist, 390
Pilar (*pē-lahr'*), 180
Pimen (*pē'mĕn*), 38
Pittichinaccio (*pĭt-tĭ-kĭ-nah'-chĭ-ō*), 487
Pizarro (*pē-tsahr'-ro*), 141
Planquette, Robert (*plahn-ket'*), 52
Plunkett (*plŭn'-kĕt*), 297
Pogner, Veit (*pohk'nĕr, fīt*), 316
Pollione (*pŏl-lē-ō'-na*), 349
Polonius (*pō-lō'-nĭ-ŭs*), 183
Ponchielli, Amilcare (*pōn-kē-āl'-lē*), 168
Ponte, Lorenzo da, librettist, 86, 289
Poppæa (*pŏp-pē'-ah*), 415
Pordes-Milo, librettist, 539
Poushkin, 38
Prévost, Abbé Marcel, 275, 283
Prinzivalle (*prent-sē-vahl'-lä*), 335
Prodana Nevesta (*prō'-rah-nah nĕv-yĕs'-tah*), 28
Puccini, Giacomo (*pōō-chē'-nē*), 31, 172, 252, 283, 514

Quinault, Philippe, librettist, 22

Radamès (*rah'-dah-mās*), 1
Rafaele (*rah-fah-ā'-lē*), 202
Ragueneau (*rahg-nō*), 71
Ramerrez (*rah-mär-rĕth'*), 172
Ramfis (*rahm'-fēs*), 1
Ramon (*rah'-mŏn*), 180
Ranz des Vaches, Le (*rahn dā vahsh, lŭ*), 217
Raoul de Nangis (*rah-ōōl dŭ nahn-zhē*), 193
Raupach, Ernest, 539
Redding, Joseph D., librettist, 339
Reinhart (*rīn'-hart*), 303
Reinmar von Zweter (*rīn'-mahr fōn tsvā'-tĕr*), 501
Remendado (*rā-mĕn-dah'-dō*), 41
Ricci, Luigi and Frederico (*rēt'-chē*), 68
Riccordi, Tito, librettist, 158
Riese, Wilhelm Friedrich, librettist, 297
Rimsky-Korsakoff, N. A., 408
Rodrigo (*rō-drēē'-gō*), 55; Roderigo (*rō-dē-rē'-gō*), 366
Rodrigues (*rō-drēē-gwāth'*), 94
Romani, Felice, librettist, 349
Romeo (*rohm-ā-ō*), 464
Rosamund (*rŏz'-ah-mŭnd*), 120
Rosaura (*rō-zah-ōō'-rah*), 98, 243
Rosina (*rō-zē'-nah*), 25, 289
Rosmer, Ernst, librettist, 212
Rossini, G. A. (*rōs-sē'-nē*), 25, 548; 289
Rossvisa (*rohs'-vē-sĕ*), 446
Rostand, Edmond, 71
Roustan (*rōōs'-tän*), 258
Roxane (*rōks-ahn*), 71
Royer, Alphonse, librettist, 137
Rudolph (*rü'-dŏlf*), 31
Ruiz (*rōō'-ēts*), 533
Ruodi (*rŭ-ō'-dē*), 548
Rustic Chivalry, 45
Ruy Gomez de Silva (*rü-ē' gō-meth' da sēl'-vah*), 106

Sabina, Karla, librettist, 28
Sachs, Hans (*zahks, hahns*), 316
St. Bris (*săn-brē*), 193
St. Georges, Jules H. Vernoy, Marquis, 34; librettist, 297
Saint-Saëns, Charles Camille (*săn-sahn*), 78, 479
Salome (*să-lō'-mē*), 189, 476
Samaritana (*sah-mah-rē-tah'-nah*); 158
Sancho (*săn'-kō*), 94
Santuzza (*sahn-tood'-zah*), 45
Sarastro (*sah-rahs'-trō*), 270
Sardou, Victorien, 258, 514
Scarpia (*skahr'-pē-ah*), 514
Schaunard (*shō-när*), 31
Schikaneder, Emanuel Johann, librettist, 270
Schiller, 548
Schlemihl (*shlā'-mĕl*), 487

Sciarrone (shĭ-ahr-rō'-ne), 514
Scott, Sir Walter, 247
Scoula (skōō'-lah), 408
Scribe, Augustin Eugène, librettist, 155, 193
Sealed, 539
Sélysette (sā-lē-zĕt), 19
Senta (zän'-tah), 147
Shakespeare, 110, 128, 183, 366, 464, 495
Siebel (zē'-bāl), 131
Siegfried, 452, 458
Sieglinda (zĕkh'-lĭn-dĕ), 446
Siegmund (zĕkh-mōōnt), 446
Siegruna (zē-grōō'-nē), 446
Sienkiewicz, Henry, 415
Simoni, Renato, librettist, 258
Singers' Contest at the Wartburg, The, 501
Smaragdi (smeh-rahg'-dē), 158
Smetana, Friedrich (smĕ'-tah-nah), 28
Somma, M., librettist, 303
Sonnleithner, Joseph, librettist, 141
Spalanzani (spah"-lahnd-zah'-nē), 487
Sparafucile (spah-rah-fōō'-chĭ-lĕ), 431
Stephano (stĕf'-ah-nō), 464
Sterbini, Cesare, librettist, 25
Stewart, Grant, librettist, 266
Stolzing, Sir Walter von (shtohl'-tsĭng), 316
Strauss, Richard (strows), 103, 469, 476
Sugana, Luigi, librettist, 98
Susanna (sōō-zahn'-nah), 289, 484
Suzuki (sōō-zū'-kĭ), 252
Sverleita (shvĕrt'-lī-tĕ), 446

Tamino (tah-mē'-nō), 270
Targioni-Tozzetti, Giovanni, librettist, 45
Tasso, 22
Telramund, Frederick of (tĕl'-rah-mōōnt), 229
Thaddeus (thăd'-dē-us), 34
Thaller, Primus (tahl'-lehr), 217
Thibaut, 266
Thomas, C. L. A., 183, 325
Thuille, Ludwig (twē'-lĕ), 225
Tieck, Ludwig, 501
Titurel (tē-tōō-rĕl'), 379
Toinetta (tō-ē-nat'-tah), 258
Trivulzio (trē-vult'-sē-ō), 335
Turiddu (tōō-rĭd'-dōō), 45
Twilight of the Gods, The, 457
Tybalt (tĭb'-ält), 464

Ulrica (ōōl-rē'-kah), 303

Valentine (văl'-ĕn-tēn, or văl'-ĕn-tĭn), 131, 193

Valkyrie, The (văl-kĭr'-ĭ), 446
Valtrauta (vahl'-trow-tĕ), 446, 458
Valzacchi (vahl-tsah'-kĭ), 469
Vaucaire, Maurizio, librettist, 61
Verdi, Giuseppe (vair'-dē), 1, 106, 128, 303, 366, 431, 520, 533
Verga, Giovanni, 45
Verkaufte Braut, Die (fĕr-kowf'-tĕ browt, dē), 28
Villeroi, Henry de (vĕl-rwah), 52
Vinaigre (ven-āgr), 258
Vinicius, Marcus (vĭ-nĭsh'-ĭ-ŭs), 415
Violetta Valéry (vē-ō-lĕt'-tah vah-lā'-rē), 520
Vladimir Igorevitch (vlah-dē'-mĭr ē-gōr'-ĕ-vitch), 408
Vogelweide, Walther von der (fō"gĕl-vī'-dē), 501

Waëz, Jean Gustave, librettist, 137
Wagner, Richard (vahg'-nĕr), 147 229, 316, 379, 424, 438, 446, 452, 457, 501, 525
Weber, Carl M. von (vā'-bĕr), 119, 165
Wellgunda (vĕl'-gōōn-dē), 438, 458
Wette, Adelheid, librettist, 186
Widmann, Joseph Victor, librettist, 495
Wiederspänstigen Zähmung, Der (vēd"-ehr-spaen'-stĕg-ĕn tsae'-mŭng, dehr), 495
Wieland, 270
Wilde, Oscar, librettist, 476
Willner, A. M., librettist, 66
Woglinda (vōkh'-lĭn-dĕ), 438, 458
Wolf-Ferrari, Ermanno (vohlf-fĕr-rah'-rē), 8, 98, 202, 484
Wotan (vō'-tahn), 438, 446, 452, 460, 463

Xenia (zē'-nĭ-ă), 38

Yamadori (yah-mah-dō'-rē), 252
Ygraine (ē-grān), 19
Yniold (ēn-yohl'), 395

Zamiel (zahm-ĭ-ĕl), 165
Zandonai, Riccardo (tsahn-dôn'-ah-ē), 61, 158
Zangarini, Carlo, librettist, 61, 172, 202
Zanoni, Camillo, librettist, 355
Zauberflöte, Die (tsow'-bĕr-flā"-tĕ, dē), 270
Zerlina (tsĕr-lē'-nah), 86, 155
Zuane (tsū-ah'-nā), 168
Zuniga (tsū'-nē-gah), 41
Zurga (tsōōr'-gah), 390

INDEX FOR ADDITIONAL OPERAS

Alain (ă-lăn), 588
Alisoun, The Wife of Bath (al'-ĭ-sōōn), 561
Andrea Chénier (ahn-drĕ'-ah shā-nyā'), 553
Annwn (ăn'-nōōn), 569
Arawn (ăr'-aun), 569
Belmont, 578
Bersi (bĕr'-sē), 553
Bretzner, Christopher Frederick, 578
Canterbury Pilgrims, The, 561
Chaucer, Geoffrey (chŏ'-sehr, jĕf'-rĭ), 561
Constance, 578
De Coigny, Countess (dŭ kwah-nyē), 553
De Koven, Reginald, 561
Devil, The, 588
De Walden, Lord Howard ("T. E. Ellis"), librettist, 569
Don (dŏn), 569
Eglantine, The Prioress, 561. See page 558.
Elan (ĕl'-ăn), 569
"Ellis, T. E.," librettist, 569
Entführung aus dem Serail, Die (ĕnt-fü'-roong ows dĕm sĕ-rā', dē), 578
Fernando (fĕr-nahn'-dō), 583
Fiamina (fe-ah-mē-nah), 588
Fouquier - Tinville (fōō-kyā-tăn-vēl), 553
Gerard (zhā-rar), 553
Giordano, Umberto, 553. See page 559
Goewin (goy'-win), 569
Gondebaud (gŏn-dĕ-bō), 588
Govannion (gŏ-văn'-nĭ-ŏn), 569
Goya y Lucientes, Francisco de (gō'-yah ē lōō'-thĕ-ĕn'-tās, dĕ), 583
Goyescas, o, Los Majos Enamorados (gō-yās'-kahs, ŏ, lŏs mah'-hŏs ay-nah-mō-rah'-dōs), 583
Granados y Campina, Enrique (grah-nah'-dōs ē kam-pē'-nah, en-ree'-kay), 583
Grisélidis (grē-zā-lĭ-dĭs), 588
Gwion (gōō'ĭ'-ŏn), 569
Gwydion (gōōĭd'-ĭ-ŏn), 569
Holbrooke, Josef Charles, 569
Illica, Luigi, librettist, 553. See page 559
Lyd (lĭd), 569
Mackaye, Percy, librettist, 561
Madeleine (mah-d'lān), 553
Massenet, Jules, 588. See page 560
Math Mathonwy, 569
Mathieu (mă-tyuh), 553
Morand, Eugene, librettist, 588
Mozart, Johann Wolfgang Amadeus, 578. See page 560
Nodens (nŏd'-ĕns), 569
Osmin (ŏz'-mĭn), 578
Paquiro (pah-kē'-rō), 583
Pedrillo (pā-drĕ'-llyō), 578
Pepa (pā'-pah), 583
Periquet, Fernando, librettist, 583
Pietro Fleville (pyā'-trō flā-vēl'), 553
Rosario (rō-sah'-rē-ō), 583
Roucher (rōō-shā), 553
Saluces, Marquis de (sahl-yüse, dŭ), 588
Serraglio, Il (sĕ-rrah'-lyŏ, ēl), 578
Silvestre, Armand, librettist, 588
Stephani, Gottlob, librettist, 578
Wife of Bath, The, 561

Caruso — Enrico